MW01252040

Inland Lakes of Michigan

GULL LAKE, KALAMAZOO COUNTY

Courtesy Gage Printing Co
Battle Creek

MICHIGAN GEOLOGICAL AND BIOLOGICAL SURVEY

Publication 30
Geological Series 25

INLAND LAKES OF MICHIGAN

By

I. D. SCOTT

PUBLISHED AS A PART OF THE ANNUAL REPORT OF THE BOARD OF
GEOLOGICAL SURVEY FOR 1920

LANSING, MICHIGAN
WYNKOOP HALLENBECK CRAWFORD CO., STATE PRINTERS
1921

B

LETTER OF TRANSMITTAL

To the Honorable, the Board of Geological and Biological Survey of the State of Michigan

Governor Albert E. Sleeper
Hon Fred Jeffers
Hon Thomas E. Johnson

Gentlemen· I have the honor to submit herewith a monographic report on the Inland Lakes of Michigan, by Dr I. D. Scott with the recommendation that it be published and bound as Publication 30, Geological Series 25

This monograph is the result of several years of field study and its object is to describe and explain the large lakes whose history is a part of the history of the Great Lakes, as well as those smaller lakes having an economic or aesthetic value The book should be of value to students and teachers of physiography, to tourists and those desiring to attract tourists to the State, to State, city and town officials seeking park sites and municipal water supplies, as well as to the fisherman and those who seek recreation.

The field work upon which the greater part of the report is based was made during the summer months of 1913 and 1914 Progress on the writing of the report was interrupted by the War and further field studies and a reconnaisance of a greater number of the smaller lakes were made in the spring and summer of 1920. Earlier publication was· desired but compensation for the delay is afforded in the more comprehensive report of a greater number of small but locally important lakes

Very respectfully yours,

R A. SMITH,
Director

Lansing, Michigan, Dec. 11, 1920.

PREFACE

The number of inland lakes in the State of Michigan is not definitely known but has been placed by some at greater than five thousand. They range in area from thirty-one square miles down to small, unnamed ponds and, in the Southern Peninsula alone, more than seventy have an area of one square mile or more. This number is considerably increased when the lakes of the Northern Peninsula are added It has been estimated that lakes constitute about one-fiftieth of the total area of the State, a percentage so large that one may, with justice, entertain doubt as to their value to the commonwealth.

This doubt becomes almost a conviction if one considers the well-known fact that most lakes cover land of very high fertility A classic example of the value of such land is the bed of former Lake Agassiz upon which is grown a large part of the enormous wheat crops of the Dakotas and Minnesota. Assuming that all of the inland lakes of the State could be drained, more than twelve hundred square miles of land of exceptional value would be opened to cultivation. In addition, it is probable that many nearby swampy areas would likewise be made available for use, and sanitary conditions be greatly improved by the extinction of the breeding places for disease-spreading insects. Also lake deposits, such as marl and peat, are frequently of considerable value and their exploitation, which is usually destructive to the lake, may be a legitimate enterprise. But our initial assumption that all of these lakes can be drained is impossible and, inasmuch as the data at hand is not sufficient for a fair estimate of the areas that can be reclaimed in this way, no attempt is made to state definitely their value It is obvious, however, that it would be enormous.

Yet, on the other hand, lakes in themselves are a very useful resource and function in such varied ways that, although a statement as to their monetary value is impossible, there are many who consider their presence, within limits, a valuable asset Among the functions performed by lakes may be mentioned their service as natural reservoirs. They accommodate the waters of spring freshets and melting snows with comparatively small rise in water level and thus lessen the flooded condition of streams and hinder the stripping of the land. Also, by throwing dams across the outlets the outflow of the lakes may be controlled for a number of purposes, for example,—power, irrigation, logging operations, city water supply, etc. The consideration of lakes as a source of food supply, as highways of commerce and as a tempering effect on climate applies more particularly to the larger lakes and inland seas and is, therefore, mentioned only in passing

But the most important function of lakes is, however, not commercial but lies rather in their unique advantages for the recreation of man. Here one may rest

> "Escaped awhile,
> From cares that wear the life away,
> To eat the lotus of the Nile,
> And drink the poppies of Cathay,
> To fling the loads of custom down,
> Like driftweed, on the sand slopes brown,
> And in the sea waves drown the restless pack
> Of duties, claims and needs that barked upon their track"
>   *Whittier*

The pure air, cool temperatures and simple conditions of life stimulate renewed physical and mental vigor Yet, lakes would fail in their service as recreational centers were opportunities for expression of the revived faculties lacking This, however, appears contrary to fact, as shown by the ever-increasing numbers which migrate to them each summer

The mere mention of the familiar water-sports should be sufficient to emphasize the appeal of lakes to our physical natures. But the appeal is deeper. Lakes are attractive not alone for their beauty but to a large extent because they portray so faithfully our own emotions and intensify the condition of our physical environment During periods of calm, winter's solitude is accentuated by the ice-bound expanse and, in summer, tranquility is reflected from the unbroken surface At times its leaden waters appear sullen, foretelling impending storms, at others boisterous and jubilant, and again, whipped to a state of fury

Nor, is the intellectual side wanting. Of the various phases of the study of nature none is more easily observed and readily interpreted than Earth Science from the physiographic viewpoint and that part devoted to the study of lakes is one of the most interesting. From this viewpoint undrained areas are considered as one of the early phases in the wearing away of a land surface by streams. As the streams deepen their valleys and stretch out tributaries, all parts of the basin become completely drained and lakes are, therefore, considered as transient features of the landscape   From a physiographic standpoint one may study the entire life history of such bodies of water   In this work the principle events to be deciphered are the origin of the basin, its development by the various agencies active upon it and finally its extinction or death   In addition, the study has a much wider application, for lakes are but oceans in miniature, except for tides, and present similar problems on a more convenient scale.

From a practical standpoint the physiographic study of a lake gives a more intimate knowledge of and a closer acquaintance with the conditions not only of the shores but the surrounding country   This knowledge and familiarity cannot fail to be of service to the resorter both in the selection of the lake and the site on it   To illustrate, the larger lakes, although they may often be treacherous in times of storm, have advantages over smaller ones   The summer temperatures are apt to be lower and the very factors which make the lake dangerous, inasmuch as they work on a large scale, are beneficial in various ways   Thus, better and cleaner beaches are built and the submerged terrace is broader and drops into deep water from depths usually greater than a man's height, lessening the danger of accidents due to walking off the "drop off" or "channel bank". The situation of the lake is important and proximity to other large bodies of water is favorable   The ideal location is to the east of a large lake because the winds, prevailingly from the west, are cooled in their passage over the large expanse of water which has a lower temperature than the air in summer.

It would seem axiomatic that the shores and surrounding country should be well drained, if the lake is to be useful for summer homes, in order to secure healthful living conditions and to insure a minimum of pests. However, the writer has seen far too many resorts planned on a magnificent scale which exist only on plats executed for the use of distant real estate dealers and has helped in locating some of the properties only to find them situated on an insignificant lake in the midst of a swamp). Physiographic study would eliminate this   An ideal site, according to the writer, is to be found on lakes which have stood for a considerable time at an appreciably higher level—of which Michigan has many—for under these conditions a sandy terrace is now exposed high and dry above the level, surmounted by a cliff of varying height from the base of which springs of cool, pure water often flow.

As stated above, lakes have served a useful purpose in the storing of water for various projects which, in most cases, necessitates the building of a dam, thereby interfering with the natural level of the lake in question   This may involve a raising or lowering of the

level, or both at different times of the year, and results in serious
inconvenience and often damage to property along the shores. A
lowering of the level means stranded docks and boat houses; a
strip of the bottom exposed that often becomes foul from swampy
conditions and decaying vegetation unless the lowering is permanent   A raising of the level is more serious and results in flooded
shores and an increased activity of the waves   The latter is very
noticeable on many lakes of the State and various means are employed to stop shore destruction by wave action   These, however,
afford only temporary relief and are a source of expense and constant attention   In this case the physiographic principles seem to
be ignored.

From the educational standpoint the study is also of importance.
Physical Geography, in whole or in part, is quite generally taught
in the schools of the State and it is truly educational in scope
Furthermore, the process of reasoning is complete   It puts new
meaning in familiar things and only moderate teaching ability is
demanded to arouse a lively interest on the part of the pupils   But
it is not primarily a text book subject   Illustrative material is a
necessity   Pictures may partially supply the need but by far the
best illustrations are those obtained by direct observation. Exceptional indeed are the localities that do not furnish abundant accessible material for field study.   Our lakes illustrate one phase of
the subject of physiography and, on account of their number and
distribution, should be a most valuable asset to the teachers of the
State   Even the smallest pond is of some value in this respect and
it is urged that advantage be taken of the opportunities

It is hoped that from the brief statements concerning the points
of view from which lakes may be considered it will be clear that
both are well supported   As a matter of fact there are many lakes
in our State that might well be exploited commercially but there
are others which appear to be of greater value in their natural condition   Each lake, then, becomes a problem in itself and a physiographic study of the lake seems a prerequisite to its solution   The
technicalities of such a study need not be overwhelming   No
branch of earth science is more interesting that the study of lakes,
and no special equipment other than an active brain and a reasonably vigorous physique is necessary   It provides both physical and
mental recreation of the best type and is profitable as well as interesting   Familiar features take on new meaning and the changes
taking place are a source of continued interest   The writer is con-
vinced that the report of the studies of Michigan's inland lakes,
undertaken during the summers of 1913, 1914 and 1920, will be of

greatest service if the needs of the increasing number of summer visitors and of those engaged in educational work are kept in mind. Therefore, the attempt has been made to present the essentials of the subject in as untechnical a way as possible in the introductory chapters Following the introductory work are detailed descriptions and discussions of the physiography of some of the more important lakes.

It is obvious that all of the lakes of the State could not be included in this study and therefore a selection was made based on the importance, accessibility, distribution and promise of scientific results Mistakes, both of omission and commission, appear in this selection as the work progressed, the principal difficulty being in the matter of distribution In order to improve this, it was decided to include a large number of lakes in a reconnaisance study during the summer of 1920 and the results of this work are given in the final chapters. In these brief reports an attempt has been made to classify the lake basins and to state the type of the adjustments that have taken place on the shores Also some information as to the accessibility of the lake, localities where the adjustments may be easily recognized, and the desirability of the lake as a summer resort may be included.

It is recognized that there will be some disappointment in the selection of the lakes described in detail but this need not be serious if one of the objects of this report is attained, namely, to present the underlying principles in such a way that they may be applied by those who may study these pages Often the difficulty is in getting a start and it is felt that the final chapters may be of service in this respect.

The first essential in undertaking a study of this kind is to have a reasonably accurate map of the lake and its surroundings Preferably this should show relief features; and the best to be obtained are the topographic maps made by the United States Geological Survey in co-operation with the State These maps are about thirteen by seventeen inches in size and are made on a scale of approximately one inch to one mile for most districts, thus including and area of nearly 220 square miles. They are sold by the Director of the United States Geological Survey, and by the Michigan Geological Survey, at a nominal cost of ten cents and by all means should be procured, if they are available. Unfortunately much of the State is as yet unmapped, but encouraging progress has been made recently and we look forward to a more rapid production of these most useful maps as the demand increases.

Other maps that are useful are those issued by the United States Lake Survey, Detroit, Mich. They are very accurate, both as to shores and depth of water, but only a limited amount of the surroundings is included in the map. These maps are made for navigation purposes and represent navigable waters directly connected with the Great Lakes with one exception, the map of the Inland Route including Crooked, Burt and Mullet Lakes.

In most cases the only maps available are the United States Land Survey plats which give only the outline of the lake, and this is not accurate. Those used in this report were corrected in a rough way and, although far from satisfactory, are sufficiently reliable for the purpose Most county maps and atlases are compiled from these plats and may be relied upon to the same extent

The three main problems to be studied are, as indicated above, the origin of the basin, its subsequent development, and its extinction The first of these involves a knowledge of the topographic features of the region and necessitates an examination of the surrounding country. It is often the most difficult to decide, and valuable information will be found in a publication of the Michigan Geological and Biological Survey by Frank Leverett: Publication 25, Geological Series 21, Surface Geology of Michigan * The inserted maps are especially valuable and should be mounted on cloth to save wear and tear.

The development of the basin and causes working towards extinction are best discovered by making a detailed study of the shores and the off-shore lake bottom. The use of a boat is necessary for the latter and may be serviceable for a traverse of the shores if the lake is large In general, however, a traverse on foot does away with the inconvenience of landing and gives more satisfactory results for the beginner. The sounding of the shallow water requires some apparatus. The writer found an exhausted dry cell a convenient weight but does not recommend any weight under twenty pounds for deep water. Accurate soundings involve both depths and locations. The process is tedious, and expensive instruments are necessary, therefore this is not recommended For our purposes the depths of the water over the terrace and the width of the terrace are desirable The width is the more difficult to obtain but an estimation will answer the purpose unless a detailed and serious study is to be undertaken

If this report is successful, the physiographic study of lakes will

---

*Publication 25 is a revision of two earlier publications, viz Pub 7, Surface Geology of the Northern Peninsula and Pub 9, Surface Geology of the Southern Peninsula of Michigan Both these publications are now out of print

be the result. Workers may benefit themselves and others as well
if their results are known, and the writer will be glad to receive
suggestions, criticisms, and new developments concerning any lakes
of the State whether included in this report or not The use of
the camera is strongly recommended also.

The illustrations in the report are from drawings and photo-
gaphs by the author unless otherwise accredited Acknowledgments
are due to the many individuals who by information and services
made much of the field work possible Mr Frank Leverett, United
States Geologist, has aided the writer in glacial problems both by
personal communication and by placing at his disposal valuable
data, at the time unpublished. The advice and assistnce of Mr R.
C. Allen, former Director of the Michigan Geological Survey and
Mr. R. A. Smith, present Director, have been of especial service in
the prosecution of the field work and the preparation of this report

TABLE OF CONTENTS

TABLE OF CONTENTS

LIST OF ILLUSTRATIONS

PLATES

FIGURES

THE INLAND LAKES OF MICHIGAN

I. D SCOTT

CHAPTER I

THE ORIGIN AND CLASSIFICATION OF LAKE BASINS

Lakes are numerous and the types of basins are many. If the basins are classified according to their manner of formation, complications may arise on account of several factors entering into the formation of a single basin. As the study is extended all of the agencies which are shaping the land surfaces of the earth are involved and it is, therefore, necessary to become familiar with the broader phases of the work and results of these agents.

To the beginner, one of the striking facts derived from the study of earth science is that the surface of the earth is slowly but constantly changing. Uplift and subsidence of the land are fundamental conceptions and no longer is the expression "terra firma" strictly applicable. Elevation has lifted the continents higher above the seas, while depression has served to deepen the ocean basins. On the first land waves, currents, and the atmosphere began their work, and with further elevation other agents—running water, ground water, winds, glaciers—became active. In general, the work of these agents is to wear down the land and transport the material elsewhere, eventually to the oceans. The continents occupy only one-fourth of the surface of the earth and are low in average elevation compared to the depth of the oceans, therefore, if elevation were inefficient or not active, they would soon be worn down nearly to sea level. But the continents have stood for ages far beyond the scope of human experience and, with the land assured, our interest centers on the agents which are fashioning its surface. The agents which are of most importance for our purposes are the atmosphere, running water, wind, ground water, and glaciers.

THE ATMOSPHERE One class of work done by the atmosphere has been given the descriptive term *weathering*. Under weathering is included the action of such agencies as frost, temperature changes, plants, animals, abrasion by the wind, and the chemical action of the gases of the atmosphere, all of which tend to break up the solid rock into smaller and smaller fragments. The comminution continues until the particles are small enough to be removed by the various agents of transportation and, hence, may be considered a process preparatory to transportation.

The lateral movement of the air, or wind, serves as a transporting agent in addition to its action in the process of weathering. In regions where the earthy material is loosely consolidated and whose surface is unprotected by vegetation, e. g., deserts, sand plains, and the shores of bodies of water, the wind is especially active. The finest particles are picked up and often carried great distances while the coarser sand grains are rolled along the surface, collecting here and there in hills which are called *dunes*. The material of the dunes is clean sand, irregularly stratified, and the slopes are gentle on the windward side but steep on the lee. Wherever the sand is widely distributed, as on the sand plains in our State, the dunes tend to assume a crescentic form, but along the shores of lakes the supply is local and the dunes are heaped in wild confusion, with little regularity except that the slopes are characteristic. The latter are well illustrated along the western cost of the Southern Peninsula from Michigan City to the Straits, and the crescentic type may be seen relieving the monotony of the swampy plains of the eastern portion of the Northern Peninsula.

RUNNING WATER. Running water is one of the most important agents at work on the surface of the land. Wherever rainfall is sufficient the water collects in channels and flows onward, joining other streams, until it reaches a trunk stream which carries it to the sea. On account of their flow streams are able to pick up and to transport the solid material supplied them by weathering. The more swiftly flowing streams are able to carry larger particles and greater amounts of all sizes. It is usually the case that active streams are not supplied with enough disintegrated material to tax their energy to the limit and some of this unexpended energy is used by the suspended particles in filing, or abrading, the beds of the streams. In addition, the solvent action of the water removes material and the two processes working together deepen the stream beds. Early in the formation of valleys the process of weathering attacks the sides and reduces the slopes until tributaries develop along them, repeating the process. Also both the main streams and the tributaries tend to work headward and increase their length, pushing their tentacles farther and farther into the land and tapping the undrained areas. Eventually the headward extension is halted by encountering streams flowing in the opposite direction, forming divides and limiting the size of the basin. In this manner streams expand into great river systems which occupy definite basins, and the basins are dissected and lowered by the constant removal of material.

Probably the most important factor in determining the velocity of a stream is the slope of its bed, and it is obvious that the slope, and consequently the velocity, must gradually decrease as the downward cutting proceeds, since the mouth of the stream is fixed at sea level Eventually the transporting power is taxed to its limit and the stream can no longer cut downward because all of its energy is used in transporting suspended material and in friction   This condition is reached first near its mouth and develops upstream, although there may be local exceptions due to more easily eroded rocks

After the limit of downward cutting has been reached any further reduction in velocity is accompanied by a deposition of some of the load. The largest particles are dropped first and, if the decrease in velocity continues, layers of increasingly fine material are added, forming a deposit composed of layers whose constituent particles are assorted in size and graded from coarse at the bottom to fine at the top The ideal condition is where a stream enters a body of standing water, in which case the velocity begins to decrease at the mouth and becomes zero at some point out in the lake But the velocity of streams varies at different times of the year, being great- , est at the spring floods, and enables the stream to transport coarser material at this time   Thus, instead of a single layer becoming finer in size of particles off shore, there is formed a verticle series of strata showing the assortment and gradation mentioned above This assortment and regular stratification are characteristic of deposits by running water.

It must not be assumed that the degrading work of a stream is finished when the downward cutting ceases, for, at about this time, the stream begins to swing laterally, or meander, and develops a flat on both sides which is flooded during high water and is called a flood plain, or better, a *valley flat*. Also the valley sides are being flattened by rain wash and other agencies until finally, after long periods of time, the areas between the water courses have slopes so flat that the material is not removed. At this time there is the broad valley flat adjacent to the stream and on either side low gently rolling plains stretch outward with almost imperceptible slope toward the sea. Such a region is called a *peneplain* (almost a plain) and represents the cessation of erosion by running water

Complete peneplanation is an ideal condition never realized as far as we know because of interruptions of the process by uplift and by the varying resistence of the rocks, some of which stand in relief above the peneplain and are called *monadnocks*. In case of uplift of the land the power of the streams is revived and they renew their attack on the land It is interesting to note in this connection that the peneplains that have been recognized up to the present time have all been elevated above their normal position, but erosion has not as yet obliterated their features.

GROUND WATER. In some regions underground water is a powerful eroding force, although generally not so effective as surface streams It is always present in the rocks and its source is rain. Much of the rainfall sinks into the earth and percolates through the interstices and fissures in the rocks until its downward passage is interrupted, when it flows or seeps laterally, finally reaching the surface again. It is interesting and important to note that water is the greatest solvent known and its action is greatly increased when it contains other substances in solution. Thus, limestone is quite readily soluble in water containing carbon dioxide, one of the atmospheric gases, in solution, and in this way funnels are formed in the surface of the earth through which the water passes underground. The water sooner or later assumes a lateral flow, which is usually localized along the fissures and the beds of the limestone, and dissolves definite channels for itself which are called *caves* or *caverns* As the process continues the interlacing channels enlarge and the roofs become weaker until finally they fall, blocking the cave with rubble.

The surface effects are at first a number of depressions, known as *sink holes,* which increase in number and extent, forming extremely rough ravines with occasional remnants of the roof standing as *natural bridges* The sinks are often clogged with fine material and become lakes

GLACIERS Under this heading we wish to include only the work of the great ice masses which spread over the land and replace the variegated landscape with a cold, white, monotonous solitude,— an absolute desert These continental glaciers advance and retreat over thousands of square miles of the land, grinding and plucking the solid rock, incorporating and carrying forward the disintegrated material, and depositing it near their borders as they melt The movement is outward from centers and is to some extent independent of the slope of the land However, large depressions like those occupied by the Great Lakes serve as channels along which the ice movement is accelerated, forming great projections, or lobes, in the ice front. See Fig 1. Such an ice mass covered northeastern North America in recent geological times and advanced and retreated over the area of the State of Michigan at least five times. The form and distribution of the material deposited by the ice during its last retreat have determined the present land surface to a very great extent and, since the basins of the inland lakes almost without exception occur in glacial formations, some further consideration of the work of glaciers seems necessary.

Fig. 1. A stage of the Wisconsin glacier showing lobate character of the ice front, (after Taylor and Leverett)

It is essential to remember that the ice moves forward constantly. The forward movement continues until temperatures are encountered which are warm enough to melt the ice effectively and this determines the position of the margin of the ice. Thus, at the border there are two factors active, the forward movement of the ice tending to advance the ice edge, and the melting which has the opposite effect. Whenever the forward movement exceeds the melting, the ice front advances and a continuance of this process causes an extension of the glacier. On the other hand, excessive melting causes a retreat of the ice front and when both factors are equal it remains stationary. The movement of the ice particles and the shifting of the ice front should not be confused.

Glaciers of this type profoundly affect the land which they override, in places wearing away the rock and in others depositing great quantities of material which is so characteristic in constitution and form as to be readily recognized   Ice itself has little or no power to wear away the rock over which it passes but, by sinking into the fissures which are universally present in rocks, it grasps the separated blocks and plucks them away in its forward movement. Such blocks of rock when firmly frozen in the base of the glacier become powerful abrading tools which grind away the solid rock leaving smoothed, polished, striated, and grooved surfaces

The various glacial deposits to which the general term *drift* has been given, although differing greatly in form and material, have one predominating characteristic, that of heterogeneity. By this is meant that the material is composed of many different kinds of rock   It is the direct result of the immense size of the glacier which traverses great distances, encountering many different rock formations all of which contributed to its load. Some of the deposits are laid down by the ice alone and these, although varying in form and relief, are readily recognized by the character and disposition of the material. In addition to its heterogeneous constitution, this material, known as *boulder clay* or *till,* is of all sizes from the finest "flour" to immense boulders, with no indication of assortment or stratification as described for stream deposits   However, stratified and assorted glacial deposits are common and these indicate that the glacial material was worked over by running water   Such deposits offer no difficulty of explanation when it is realized that the melting of the ice furnished a great volume of water which flowed away from the ice or was ponded in front of it

The characteristics and manner of formation of the glacial deposits may be best understood by imagining the existence of a glacier   Whenever the ice front remains stationary for a period of time, the constantly forward moving ice with its load of earthy material may be likened to a belt conveyor except that, instead of returning empty, it melts   The earthy material, unevenly distributed in the ice, is carried forward and deposited in hummocks at the margin   The resulting land form, known as a *moraine,* is a long, curved ridge of till whose surface is composed of irregularly distributed knobs and basins. Its width is relatively narrow but its length may be hundreds of miles

At the same time the waters from the melting ice flow forward carrying great quantities of material which is deposited either among the moraine knobs in rounded hills of irregularly stratified sand and gravel, called *kames,* or just in front of the moraine. In the latter case the streams are often heavily clogged with drift and tend to braid rather than keep to definite channels Under these conditions broad plains are formed which slope gently away from the ice and are composed of assorted and often stratified material They are known as *outwash plains*

If the ice advances, the forms discussed above will be overridden by the ice and obliterated or covered, but if the margin of the ice retreats these forms will remain and, in addition, others which were covered by the ice are revealed. Of these the *ground moraine,* or *till plain,* is the most common. As the names signify, it is composed of *boulder clay* and has some of the characteristics of the moraines. Its surface has a knob and basin topography but the slopes are much more gentle and the relief lower. The expression swell and sag is commonly used in describing these features.

Another topographic form bared by the ice is the *drumlin.* These elliptical hills, composed of compact boulder clay, have a smooth, rounded surface and, when viewed from the side, resemble very closely a plano-convex lens which is resting on the flat side Their length varies but is usually a mile or less and the relation of the dimensions to each other will be clear from the statement that the height may be measured in feet, the breadth in yards, and the length in rods An interesting relationship is that of their longer axes which are apparently parallel for local areas but show a radial distribution over larger tracts, indicating an alignment along the direction of ice movement The theories advanced for the manner of their formation are diverse and need not be considered here.

The last of the forms uncovered by the ice to be considered is the *esker,* a low serpentine ridge rising above the till plain It is composed of imperfectly stratified sand and gravel and is usually a few feet high, yards in width, but may extend for miles. It is thought to have been formed by deposition by streams running in definite channels underneath the ice

The forms discussed above may all, with the exception of drumlins, be referred to a definite position of the ice front. When the ice border is stationary a moraine is piled up, the strength depending on the length of the halt and the amount of material in the ice. At the same time the forms deposited by the water from melting—outwash plains, kames, eskers—are developed locally in their respective positions in front, near-by, and back of the ice margin, and may or may not be present in a given locality. Underneath is the till plain on which drumlins may be formed. The relative position of these forms is shown in Fig 2

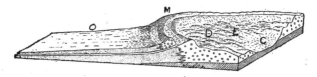

Fig. 2. Relative positions of glacial deposits, (after Tarr and Martin).

As stated above, most of the surface of the State is composed of glacial deposits left by the great ice sheet during its final retreat in recent geological time, and some idea of the nature of this retreat may be gained by a consideration of the distribution of the deposits. The accompanying outline map, Fig. 3, shows the posi-

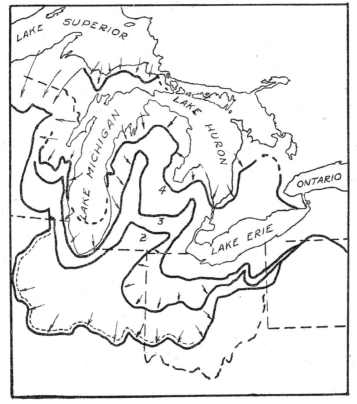

Fig. 3. Map of the principal moranic systems of Michigan. On this map are shown the southern limits of the Wisconsin stage of glaciation; 2, the Kalamazoo-Mississinawa moranic system; 3, the Valpariso-Charlotte moranic system; 4, Port Huron moranic system.

tions of some of the stronger moraines of the Michigan and Huron-Erie lobes, numbered in the order of their formation. Two things are plainly evident, the lobation of the ice and the duplication of the moraines in roughly parallel sequence. The lobation became more pronounced as the ice retreated and the narrow interlobate areas, areas which lie in the angle made by the junction of two lobes, were regions of excessive accumulation due to the presence of two ice margins in close proximity.

The duplication of the moraines, a few of which are shown on the map, indicates a gigantic and thoroughly contested struggle between the forward movement and the warmer temperatures which caused the melting of the ice, with the latter victorious. Thus, the ice advanced overwhelming everything in its path until checked by melting, when it entrenched by building a moraine. This position was held until the margin was forced back to another stand where the process of entrenching was repeated. Again and again this occurred with occasional minor advances which served only to prolong the struggle, and the ice retreated haltingly before the onslaught of the weather.

Another effect of the recession of the ice was the ponding of great bodies of water between the ice front and the divides. It is readily seen that, once the divide had been uncovered, a flat trough-like depression stood in front of the ice edge whose margins were the divide on one side and the ice on the other. The filling of such depressions with water gave rise to a series of lakes adjacent to or filling the present basins of the Great Lakes. As the ice receded, larger and larger depressions were uncovered and lower outlets were found, forming a succession of lakes each of which, with some exceptions, was larger but stood at a lower level than its predecessor. The history of these lakes is complicated and has been fully described in the publications of the Michigan Geological Survey and elsewhere. Yet the history of many of the inland lakes is closely connected with the two stages preceding the present Great Lakes, and a brief description of these is added.

The earlier of these lakes is known as Lake Algonquin and included all of the Great Lakes except Ontario, which was covered by the waters of a lake called Iroquois. The relation of its outline to those of the present lakes is shown in Fig. 4. Its shores now stand at elevations varying from 596 feet above sea level along the southern borders of Lake Huron to 720 feet at the Garden Peninsula, Big Bay de Noc, Lake Michigan, and 940 feet in the vicinity of Marquette, that is, above and at varying distances back from the

12   INLAND LAKES OF MICHIGAN

shores of the present lakes. The map shows that a relatively narrow strip along the Superior shore of the western part of the Northern Peninsula was covered by these waters and that only a small portion of the eastern part was uncovered at this time, the land areas being islands. In the Southern Peninsula a considerable area in the northern part was covered by Lake Algonquin and the shore was very irregular consisting of many bays, promontories, and islands. Farther south the areas covered were narrow strips of land adjacent to the present shores of Lakes Huron and Michigan.

The stage immediately preceding the present is known as Lake Nipissing which occupied the same basins as Lake Algonquin but stood at a lower level and was somewhat smaller, in fact was but little larger than the present lakes. Its outlines are shown in Fig 5.

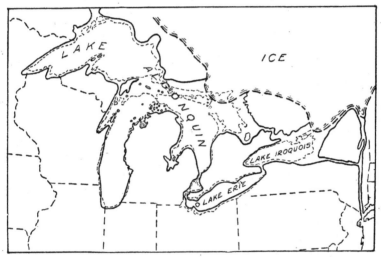

Fig. 4. Map of Lake Algonquin showing relation to present Great Lakes, (after Taylor and Leverett).

On the borders of the Northern Peninsula the Nipissing beaches stand at elevations from 10 to 60 feet above Lake Superior and are usually found a short distance inland. In the Southern Peninsula the beaches drop in level and the areas covered by this lake become smaller to the south. As in the case of Algonquin time, the northwestern part of this peninsula was an archipelago, and many of the inland lakes in this region have the shore lines and terraces of Lake Nipissing standing above their present shores.

It is hoped that the brief statement of the work of these agents given above will enable the reader to comprehend more easily the forces at work on the land, and also aid in understanding the technical terms that are necessary in a report of this nature.

PHYSIOGRAPHY OF THE STATE OF MICHIGAN

The State of Michigan is divided naturally into two distinct parts which have been named the Southern and Northern Peninsulas on account of their positions with reference to Lakes Michigan,

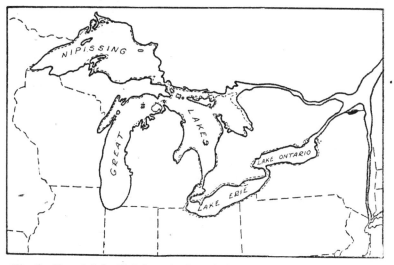

Fig. 5. Map of Lake Nipissing, showing relation to present Great Lakes, (after Taylor and Leverett)

Superior, Huron, and Erie. Thus, the Northern Peninsula is bounded to a large extent by Lake Superior, St. Mary's River, and Lake Michigan, and the eastern part is truly a peninsula. See Fig. 6. Construing the term peninsula rather loosely, the Menominee and Montreal rivers may be included with the lakes, making the land connection less than 70 miles in width for the entire peninsula.

The Southern Peninsula, surrounded on all sides except the southern by the waters of Lakes Michigan, Huron, Erie and their connections, is a broad peninsula which bears a resemblance to a great hand with the thumb just east of Saginaw Bay. See Fig. 7.

NORTHERN PENINSULA. The Northern Peninsula, Fig. 6, is a rather narrow strip of land about 330 miles in length and has an average width that is estimated at less than 50 miles. Its outline

Fig. 6. Map showing physiographic provinces of the Northern Peninsula.

is irregular, having two prominent projections—Keweenaw peninsula on the north and the Menominee district on the south—and numerous smaller points and bays as well.

The altitude ranges from 580 feet above tide at the shores of Lake Michigan to more than 2,000 feet at the Porcupine Mountains in the northwestern part of the Peninsula. On the basis of elevation and underlying rocks, the area may be divided into two definite provinces: One, the Highlands, which is underlain by rocks largely of Pre-Paleozoic* age, lies west of a north-south line passing through Marquette, and the other, the Lowlands, extends eastward from this line and is underlain by Paleozoic* rocks. Glacial drift has been deposited over almost all of the Peninsula, the exceptions being more numerous in the Highland province.

HIGHLAND PROVINCE This province extends from the meridian of Marquette westward and southward beyond the boundaries of the State, and stands at an average elevation of 1600-1800 feet above sea level, or 1000-1200 feet above Lake Superior The region is a table-land which rises rapidly from the Lowlands on the east and north and its surface is covered with a variable thickness of glacial drift through which a relatively small number of hard rock knobs projects. The relief is moderate with differences in elevation which probably do not exceed 500 feet locally and are 100-300 feet on the average. The greatest elevations are rock hills which reach a maximum height of 2023 feet in the Porcupine Mountains

The Highlands are a part of a great uplifted peneplain which was formed in ancient times. The underlying rocks are mainly of Pre-Paleozoic age and consist of crystalline masses and banded rocks the distribution of which greatly influenced the action of streams, causing, thereby, characteristic topographic forms. The erosion was profound and interrupted by several uplifts but, throughout the vast interval of time during which peneplanation was accomplished, the crystalline masses resisted erosion and stood in relief above the peneplain as monadnocks The banded rocks were tipped on edge and presented alternately weak and resistant layers to the action of the streams. The hard layers resisted erosion and stood as monadnock ridges whose longer axes are roughly parallel to Lake Superior, while the softer layers were bevelled by the surface of the peneplain. The ridges were not continuous but

---

*Cenozoic   includes Present
             and Glacial times
Mesozoic
Paleozoic
Proterozoic } Pre-Paleozoic
Archeozoic

The geological time scale, the main divisions of which are given, is tabulated to give the effect of a great column of superposed rocks, the oldest at the bottom and the youngest above in the order of formation The position in the scale gives the relative age It will be seen that the rocks under discussion and of all of Michigan as well, except the glacial deposits, stand low in the scale and are, therefore, ancient

were crossed by streams, forming gaps which served as channels for the advancing ice of glacial times   Upon the peneplain and about the monadnocks were deposited paleozoic sediments which were largely removed by erosion before the advent of the ice.

The effect of the ice action was to scour out the gaps, round off the hills, and fill the valleys with heavy deposits of drift obscuring most of the former surface. Thus, we find today an area covered for the most part with glacial material through which rock knobs, either rounded or linear in form, project. The more important regions where such knobs are found are the Porcupine Mountains, Gogebic Range, Keweenaw Range, Huron Mountains, Marquette Range, Iron River district, and the Menominee district   Of these, Sheridan Hill in the Iron River district and some limestone capped hills in the Menominee district, are composed of Paleozoic rocks.

The glacial deposits of this province were laid down for the most part during the last recession of the ice by the lobes that extended into Lake Superior and Michigan with their subsidiary lobes, Keweenaw and Green Bay. The part first uncovered by the ice is in southern Iron County, an area of till deposits with drumlins or drumlin-like hills. A great moraine swings around this area, formed on the north by the ice of the Superior lobe and on the east by that of the Michigan lobe. The succeeding moraines show the same directions. Thus, the moraines, the inter-moranic till plains, and outwash run roughly parallel to Lake Superior in the western part of this province, except where influenced by the Keweenaw lobe   They have a nearly north-south trend in the eastern part which was covered by the Michigan lobe ʹ

The Highlands are drained to Lakes Superior and Michigan with the exception of a small area in southern Gogebic County which is tapped by the Wisconsin river   The drainage is controlled both by the glacial formations and the pre-glacial topography. In the western part a strong moraine forms the divide, and in the vicinity of Watersmeet are situated the headwaters of the Wisconsin, Ontonagon, and Menominee rivers   To the east the divide shifts northward to a watershed north of Michigamme composed of thinly drift-covered crystalline rocks from which streams flow in all directions   The drainage is incomplete and small lakes and swamps are abundant, especially in the moraine districts and the thinly drift covered area north of Michigamme   There are several lakes of considerable size in this province whose basins are of exceptional interest and will be discussed later

LOWLAND PROVINCE. The Lowlands extend from the meridian of Marquette eastward to the Sault Ste. Marie and swing to the southwest into Wisconsin and Minnesota in a broad semi-circle. The greatest extension of the Lowlands along the northern edge of the Highland region is found in the continuation of Keweenaw Bay to the southwest and this is connected to the main Lowland area to the east by a narrow coastal strip

This region is on the average more than 1000 feet lower than the Highlands and its general elevation does not exceed 250 feet above the Great Lakes, although in places it rises considerably above this It is underlain by Paleozoic rocks which slope gently in a southerly direction. The bevelling of these rocks by stream action in pre-glacial times gave rise to a plain arranged in belts which mark the surface exposures of the various layers of dipping rocks. These belts run roughly parallel to the curve of the north shores of Lakes Huron and Michigan

The hardness of the different layers varies, and the softer were worn into broad valleys whereas the harder stood in relief in forms peculiar to this type of structure. They consist of low, linear ridges which slope gently on the side formed by the surface of the rock layers but are more abrupt on the side which cuts across the layers Such forms are known as *cuestas* In this region they have almost imperceptible southerly slopes but stand usually about 100 feet above the plain to the north, although in places bluff-like escarpments with altitudes of 200-300 feet are found, for example, Burnt Bluff, Big Bay de Noc Two cuestas are present in this province, one near the south shore of Lake Superior in the vicinity of Munising which swings to the south in its eastward extension, and another just north of the Michigan and Huron shores. Both are largely obscured by glacial deposits but the southern is the better developed. It begins with the Garden Peninsula at Big Bay de Noc and continues across the Lowlands to Drummond Island and eastward across Lake Huron as a great series of islands which partially isolate the North Channel and Georgian Bay from Lake Huron

The recession of the ice in this region was from south to north and there is in general an east-west trend to the deposits As shown in Fig. 3, a low moraine runs the length of this province A large moranic tract is also found at the junction of Luce, School-craft, and Mackinac counties and another important topographic feature, aside from the thinly drift covered southern cuesta, is the great swampy plains. The two most important are those which form the major part of the drainage basins of the Manistique and Tahquamenon rivers. These sandy plains have very gentle slopes and are almost featureless, the greatest relief being the small,

3

but frequent sand dunes each crested with a clump of pines which accentuate the grass covered plain. These plains are the result of stream deposition and may be referred in part to the waters escaping from the ice border

The drainage of the Lowlands is very poor and a large percentage of the area is covered by swamps and lakes. In the western part the divide is far to the north, giving a drainage area for the Manistique river of 1,400 square miles. To the east the divide swings southward and separates extensive basins on either side which are drained by the Tahquamenon and Carp rivers. The portion of the Peninsula east of St. Ignace and White Fish Bay is drained mainly into the St Mary's River and Lake Huron. The inland lakes are found among the moraines, on the outwash plains, and along the shores of the Great Lakes, the largest being situated in the low morainic tract south of Seney and McMillan, and along the shores of Lake Michigan near Manistique and St Ignace.

SOUTHERN PENINSULA. The altitude of the Southern Peninsula, Fig. 7, is, in general, much lower than that of the Highlands of the Northern Peninsula and corresponds more nearly with that of the Lowland province. The highest points are found in Osceola county where elevations in excess of 1700 feet have been noted. The lowest altitudes are obviously determined by the level of Lake Erie, 572 feet, in the southeastern part of the peninsula. Ninety-six per cent of the area stands below 1200 feet, and probably the average elevation is not greatly in excess of 800 feet above the sea. The highest area is situated in the northern half of the peninsula, embracing about 1500 square miles largely within Osceola, Wexford, Missaukee, Crawford, and Otsego counties, and exceeds 1200 feet in elevation. Other elevated areas are found in the southern part, chiefly in Hillsdale county.

The Southern Peninsula has been divided into several physiographic provinces which have a diagonal trend in a northeast-southwesterly direction. See Fig 7. Beginning in the southeastern part is a low plain, the Erie Lowland, bordering Lake Erie and to the northwest is the Thumb Upland, extending in a northeasterly direction from Hillsdale county to the Thumb. This gives way to the Saginaw Lowland, to the north of which lies the Northern Upland. The Michigan Lowland follows the Lake Michigan shore and is an exception to the diagonal trend.

The underlying rocks are of Paleozoic age and are closely associated with those of the Lowlands of the Northern Peninsula. Structually the rocks dip towards the center of the State and form a shallow basin which has been bevelled by erosion, distributing the

edges of the various formations in concentric ovals, that is, one
within the other. The formations are of different resistances and
the sandstone in particular yielded slowly to the erosive agents.
The general relief features of this area before the advent of the

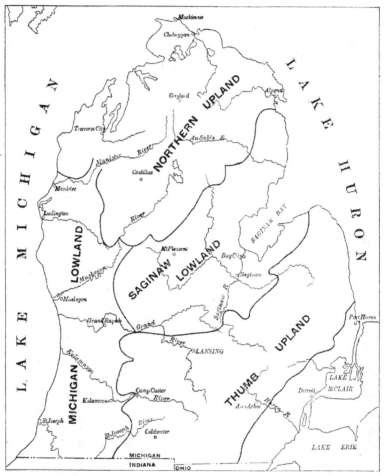

Fig. 7. Map showing physiographic provinces of the Southern Peninsula, (after
Leverett). Note: Erie Lowland not designated.

glacier bore a striking resemblance to the present in that the
larger features were similar in kind and distribution. Thus, there
were upland areas in the northern and the southern parts with lowlands between and on either side. The low area in the northwestern

part between Ludington and Frankfort would now be below sea level if the glacial deposits were removed.

In contrast to the Northern Peninsula, the glacial deposits of the Southern are largely those of an ice invasion just previous to the Wisconsin, or last stage, and form not only the main filling of the valleys but in places prominent ridges The location of the ice of the earlier glaciation was similar to that of the Wisconsin stage and the same areas were, in general, regions of accumulation It is of interest to one engaged in the study of lakes to know that the present surface features are largely due to the veneer of drift left by the last ice recession

During its maximum extension the ice of the Wisconsin stage covered the entire Southern Peninsula and its recession uncovered first an area in the southern part of the State See Fig. 3 Inspection of the moraine numbered 2 on the map shows this area to have been interlobate between the Michigan and the Huron-Erie lobes With further recession two narrow interlobate areas were formed on either side of the small Saginaw Lobe, as shown by moraines 3 and 4 on the map Thus, there were areas of excessive accumulation in the southeastern part, more or less coincident with the Thumb Upland, and in the northern part, coincident with the Northern Upland The latter was an area of especially great accumulation, and here are found extensive moraines, till plains, and broad outwash aprons, the latter constituting the great sand plains.

The apparent coincidence of the pre-glacial physiographic provinces of this peninsula with those of the present time would lead one to infer that the pre glacial topography controls the present relief but such is not the case, since the corresponding areas do not actually coincide except possibly in the Thumb Upland. It is probable, however, that the main influence was the indirect one of determining the positions of the ice lobes and thus the moraines, and that the present topography is due, for the most part, to the distribution of the drift, and near the shores of the large lakes to the working over of this material by the waters of Lakes Algonquin and Nipissing. However, it may be that some of the topography in Hillsdale County and in the region northwest of Thunder Bay is referable to the underlying rocks Stream action since glacial times has modified the surface so slightly that it is negligible

 The drainage of the Southern Peninsula is determined in its larger aspects by the physiographic provinces discussed above, and the sources of the main streams are found in the high interior portions In the northern part the divide is situated near the center of the Northern Upland and the streams flow outward to Lakes

Michigan and Huron. In this locality the headwaters of the Muskegon, Manistee, and Au Sable rivers are in close proximity Many of the smaller streams, however, have their sources on the slopes of the upland province and flow more or less directly into the lakes.

In the southern part the long Thumb Upland forms a veritable watershed and on this are located the sources of the St. Joseph, Kalamazoo, Saginaw (south branches), Huron, and Raisin rivers. As in the northern section, the minor streams head on the slopes of this province and flow directly to the lakes Between the two upland areas lies the Saginaw Lowland which is drained by the Grand and Saginaw Rivers.

Notable and peculiar drainage patterns are shown by some of the streams, especially the Saginaw and Black (Thumb region), but these are due to the distribution of glacial material, more especially the moraines and the uplifted beaches of the predecessors of the Great Lakes In Alpena and Presque Isle counties are many sink holes, and the surface drainage is interrupted by these in some cases From the distribution of the sinks and the presence of "fountains" in parts of Thunder Bay, it has been inferred that there is an extensive underground drainage system, reaching from this region to the vicinity of Black Lake in Cheboygan County, but this has not been carefully worked out as yet

The abundance of lakes in the Southern Peninsula is an indication of the incompleteness of the drainage, and it is noteworthy that many of the larger as well as the smaller lakes are to be found in the morainic districts, for example, in the northern and southern interlobate areas and in the morainic region within Calhoun, Barry, and Kent counties. Aside from the lakes due to the irregular distribution of the glacial material, there are those bordering Lakes Michigan and Huron which are more important in the extreme northern part of the peninsula.

A physiographic study of lakes has as its starting point the origin of the basins, and studies in the past have resulted in a classification according to manner of formation which includes many types The list given, although not complete, will serve to illustrate the diversity of types.

Diastrophism (movements of the
    earth's crust)   New-land lakes
    Slow movements   Ponded lakes   .
    Rapid movements (faulting) Basin range lakes
                          Rift-valley lakes
                          Earthquake lakes

Vulcanism   Coullee Lakes
                          Crater lakes

Gradation   .
    Rivers   Ox-bow lakes
                          Alluvial dam lakes
                          Saucer lakes
                          Crescentic levee lakes
                          Raft lakes
                          Delta lakes
                          Side-delta lakes

Waves and currents   Lagoons
Wind   Dune lakes
Glaciers
    Mountain   Rock basin lakes
                        Valley moraine lakes
    Continental   Border lakes
                        Morainal lakes
                            Marginal
                            Ground
                        Morainal dam lakes
                      Inter-morainic lakes
                      Pit lakes
                      Glint lakes
                      Ice dam lakes
                      Glacial lobe lakes
                      Glacial scour lakes
                      Fosse lakes
Ground water   Sink lakes   ɩ
                      Karst lakes
Gravity   Landslide lakes

It is seen from the list that diastrophism and the gradational processes of rivers and glaciers produce the greater number of types of basins, but of these, glaciers are productive of the greater number of examples, and the lakes thus formed are of greater importance. Although it is comparatively simple in most cases to assign the general cause of origin, there are many cases where it is difficult to determine the specific cause, inasmuch as several factors, each of which may be sufficient to form a lake basin, have been active. For example, basins due to deposition by continental glaciers are easily recognized but it is often a perplexing study to determine which of the various deposits plays the most important part. In cases where several factors enter the most important must be decided upon and the lake classified accordingly. Within the State of Michigan lake basins of the following types have been recognized

Glaciers	
Continental	Glacial scour
	Morainal
	Morainal dam
	Pit
	Inter-morainic
	Fosse
Waves and currents	Lagoons
Diastrophism	Rift-valley
	Ponded
Ground water	Sinks
Rivers	Ox-bow

It is clear from this list that a considerable number of types have been recognized but by far the greater number of examples is due either wholly or in part to glacial action. In fact, there are but few that can be referred to other causes but they are interesting in that they are exceptional, for this State at least, and their characteristics as well as those of glacial origin will be given.

RIVERS. OX-BOWS. Lakes of this class are found in the vicinity of streams which have reached the limit of downward cutting and are meandering. In streams of this age the adjustment between the carrying power and the material in transport is so close that even a slight decrease in velocity will cause deposition of some of the suspended material and, on the other hand, any increase will cause removal. The current of a stream that is meandering on a valley flat is increased on the outside (convex) side of the bend and cor-

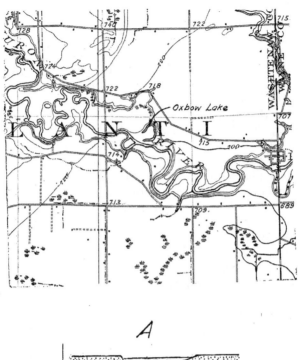

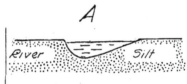

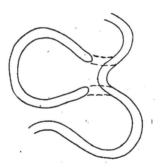

Fig. 8. Map and diagrams showing characteristics of oxbow lakes. Map a part.
of the Ypsilanti quadrangle.

respondingly deceased on the inside (concave). Therefore cutting takes place on the outside and deposition on the inside and at the same rate. This causes the meander to increase in swing, the width of the stream remaining constant, and also deepens the channel next the outside bank. In addition to the increase in width, meanders tend to work downstream, due to the fact that the stream is running down a slope. The neck of the meander is gradually worn away and the stream eventually straightens its course. The ends of the abandoned channel are soon filled by deposition and a lake formed. The characteristics of such lakes are: Its position on a valley flat composed of alluvium, crescentic shape, and greater depth near the convex side. See Fig. 8. An excellent example of an oxbow lake is that shown on the map in Fig. 8, and lies on the valley flat of the Huron River (Washtenaw County) about three miles below Ypsilanti.

GROUND WATER. SINKS. These lakes occur in regions underlain by limestone which is readily soluble in water containing carbonic acid gas in solution. The water with its dissolved gas seeps through the fissures and bedding planes of the rock and carries away much material in solution. The underground openings thus formed sometimes reach large dimensions and are called caves or caverns. The continuation of the process finally causes the roof of the cave to fall, forming a depression on the surface which may become filled with water. Such basins may be irregular in shape but are generally somewhat circular in outline and have no surface outlet, although they may have inlets. The characteristics are shown in Fig. 9.

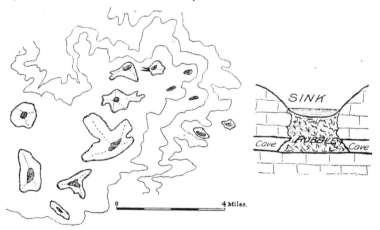

Fig. 9. Map and diagram to show manner of formation of lakes in sink-holes, (after Hobbs).

Lakes of this type are rare in this State and are confined to the Southern Peninsula as far as now known. Ottawa Lake in the southeastern part is ascribed by Lane to this cause. Numerous sinks occur in Alpena and Presque Isle counties but no lakes occupying true sink holes are known. Sunken Lake, a few miles south of Metz in Presque Isle County, is closely related to this type of lake and was visited by the writer. It has little interest except as a type of basin and is now permanently dry. It appears to be a stream channel about one fourth of a mile long which is cut off from the Upper South, a branch of Thunder River, by a dam at its upper end. It ends abuptly at the lower end in a sink which stands above the stream bed and ponded the water which formerly entered this basin at high water stage. A view of this lake bed in shown in Plate I.

DIASTROPHISM. FAULTING. Lake basins due to faulting are exceptional in Michigan and in no case known to the writer can the actual faults be detected. Canyon lake in the Huron Mountain group has characteristics which point so clearly to this origin that it is included in this class. This lake is too small to appear on the map, Fig. 84, but in reality is a most interesting and fascinating body of water. It is scarcely one-fourth mile in length and does not exceed one hundred feet in width. Nevertheless it possesses a charm which lies not in its size but rather in its picturesque location and surroundings. It lies in a narrow canyon of almost uniform width which cuts directly across a hard rock saddle. The shores at the ends are low and swampy but the sides are cliffs which

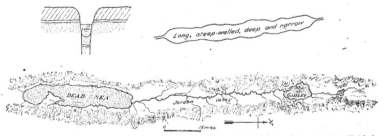

Fig. 10. Diagram and map showing characteristics of rift valley lakes, (After Hobbs).

increase in height from either end to a maximum in the center. The cliffs, while very steep, are not perpendicular but ascend in steps consisting of high risers and narrow treads upon which stand trees and shrubs in precarious positions. The outline of the sides is a somewhat regular zig-zag rather than a straight line, showing the presence of fractures. In addition, the depth of the lake is relatively great and the cliffs descend perpendicularly into the water.

Michigan Geological and
Biological Survey

Publication 30, Geological Series 25,
Plate I.

SINK HOLE, SUNKEN LAKE.

Such characteristics lead one to the conclusion that this basin was formed by the dropping of a portion of the earth's crust, not as one block but several long, narrow blocks, the amount of drop or displacement being progressively greater towards the center of the depression.

The general characteristics of such lakes are shown in Fig. 10 and may be enumerated as follows: Long and narrow, of great depth, and bounded on the sides by rock cliffs.

WARPING. Along the western coast of the Southern Peninsula south of Frankfort many of the streams broaden on approaching Lake Michigan, and the expansion is sufficient to warrant their being classed as lakes, since they have been separated from the main lake by the development of bars. Their separate existence is due to the work of waves and currents but the expansion of the river mouths—the lake basins—is due to a warping of the earth's crust. The warping consists in an uplift of the land to the northeast which is raising the outlets of the Great Lakes and, in the

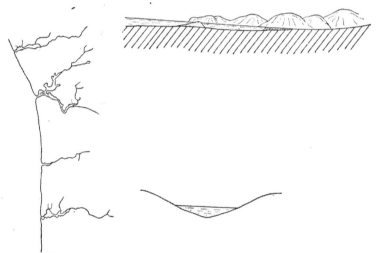

Fig. 11. Diagrams showing characteristics of lagoons of the drowned stream type.

case of Lake Michigan, is causing the water to encroach on the land in the region referred to. This is flooding or drowning the river mouths and, in conjunction with shore action which forms the bars across their mouths, forming lakes of moderate depth whose beds slope gently to a channel formerly occupied by the stream. The shape is usually irregular due to the flooding of main stream and tributaries. In case a single stream is flooded the shape is roughly triangular with the upstream point truncated by a delta-like deposit made by the entering stream. Fig 11 illustrates these characteristics.

GLACIAL LAKES. SCOUR   In some localities the scour of the ice is responsible to a large extent for depressions, although other factors may be important. The scour was a planing action accomplished by rocks held in the base of the ice and was localized according to the topography, structure, and hardness of the rocks over which the ice flowed. Topographic depressions, such as stream valleys running in the same direction as the ice, were deepened by an increase in flow and a greater thickness of ice   Gaps in ridges running transverse to the direction of ice movement were both widened and deepened because of increased flow somwhat analogous to the greater velocity in river narrows   Once through a gap, the ice spread and in some cases flowed along the transverse valley on the far side of the ridge, deepening it locally. It is probable also that the ice in these depressions was the last to melt and outwash was deposited at the ends which accentuated the basin formed by scour. Such lakes are usually long and narrow and the evidence of glacial scour is the presence of striations on the exposed rock surfaces running parallel to the length of the lake   Another structure which facilitates glacial wear is an abundance of fissures in the rocks   Rocks which are easily abraded also were more rapidly worn down by the ice, but regions underlain by such rocks were the locations of stream courses previous to glacial times and the ice merely increased the pre existing relief

DEPOSITION MORAINAL   This term is reserved for the small basins caused by irregularities in the surface of marginal and ground moraines   In marginal moraines the surface is characteristically hummocky and the knobs and basins vary in size and regularity   The size and shape of the lakes occupying moranic depressions are determined not alone by the nature of the individual basins but by the amount of water draining into them   If sufficient water is available to cover several adjoining basins, a lake is formed which is irregular in outline and usually of moderate size   In case a single basin is flooded, the lake conforms to this basin and is often oval in outline and small in extent   The smallest of 'these are mere ponds without outlets and few, if any, inlets, and are rapidly being filled with vegetation. The depth of such lakes is not great and corresponds roughly with the relief of the surrounding country. The shores are frequently strewn with boulders and cobbles and the bottom is composed of a clay mud, where not covered with peat.

In the ground moraines the relief is less pronounced and the lakes are usually very shallow, although they may be of considerable

Fig. 12. Diagrams and map showing characteristics of morainal (marginal) lakes. (Diagrams after Hobbs. Map a part of the Three Rivers, Mich., Quadrangle.)

extent. Houghton Lake in Roscommon County, one of the largest inland lakes in the State, lies mainly on ground moraine and the
depth does not exceed 25 feet. The characteristics of morainal
lakes are shown in Fig. 12.

INTER-MORAINAL. During the recession of the glacier it sometimes
happened that the halts of the ice border were close together,
leaving parallel morainic ridges with a narrow depression between,
composed of ground moraine or outwash. Often such depressions
are below the general drainage level and, if the ends are blocked,
become the sites of lakes of considerable extent. Such lakes are
elongate in the direction of the flanking moraines whose slopes
have the characteristic knob and basin topography, and the ends
are frequently blocked with outwash. The presence of outwash may
be explained by assuming a block of ice which filled the depression
and from whose sides outwash developed in either direction; or
that the outwash aprons developed locally at various places along

Fig. 13. Lake Antoine, a lake of the morainal dam type, (from the Menominee
Special Quadrangle).

the ice front but did not coalesce. This type of basin is very similar to that of morainal lakes situated on ground moraine and perhaps should be considered as a special case rather than a distinct type.

MORANIAL DAM. Although the general statement that continental ice masses such as covered northeastern North America assume a form that is largely independent of the relief of the land is true, yet it is a significant fact that the ice border in its details was extremely sensitive to the topography over which is flowed. At the ice border hills served to divert the flow, and depressions became locations of increased movement especially when their direction was parallel to that of the ice flow. In this way minor tongues were formed in valleys which deposited a series of morainic dams as they receded and above these dams lakes now lie. The valleys must have been present before the final retreat of the ice and may have been pre-glacial or inter-glacial. Lakes of this type are often elongated in the direction of the valley but may be circular or even run transverse to the valley if the dams are close together or low in elevation above the valley floor. They occur frequently in series in the same valley.

In the Iron River district of the Northern Peninsula there are some lakes which are held by drift dams thrown across the valleys between drumlinoidal hills, for example, Fortune, Chicagon, Stanley, while in the vicinity of Iron Mountain an irregular moraine across a pre-glacial valley forms the west border of Lake Antoine, see Fig 13

FOSSE. Fosse, as used in this connection, refers to a long, narrow depression that is sometimes found between a moraine and an outwash plain. It is a remnant of ground moraine upon which the ice stood when the outwash was being formed. The outwash was built up along the steep ice front partially burying it, and when the ice retreated part of the material at the inner edge of the outwash fell back on the ground moraine, forming a very steep slope. A short distance back the moraine was piled up, leaving a depression, as shown in Fig 14

Such lakes may be distinguished by the attenuated form, the presence of moraine on one side and outwash with steep edge on the other, and the absence of outlet or inlets of importance. The water of the lake seeps readily through the sand and gravel of the outwash in lieu of an outlet. Inlets may develop on the side slopes of the moraine but the more important will run in the unoccupied portion of the fosse. Inasmuch as the fosse is a local development, the inlets must necessarily be of little importance and the lake fed principally by ground water. An excellent example of this type of lake is Crooked lake, situated in the group of lakes a few miles west of Chelsea, Washtenaw County.

PITS. The term pit, as here used, signifies a depression in an out-wash plain. It was probably formed by the isolation of an ice block which became covered with debris and melted later, allowing

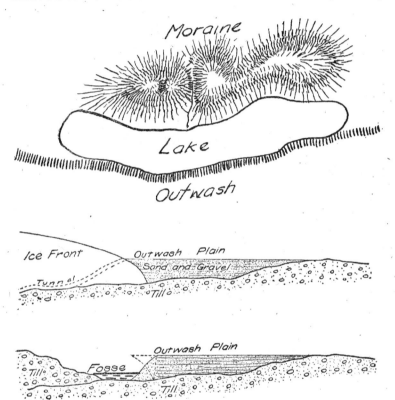

Fig. 14.   Sketch and diagrams to illustrate manner of formation of fosse lakes, (diagrams after Hobbs).

the material above to settle. The important thing in the formation of these depressions is the protective effect of a coating of earthy material on the ice. A small rock fragment on the surface of the ice absorbs enough heat from the sun's rays to become heated through and melts a depression for itself in the ice. Larger fragments or an accumulation of small ones are not able to conduct the heat to the under side and, therefore, protect the ice, and the greater the thickness of the earthy material the slower the melting.

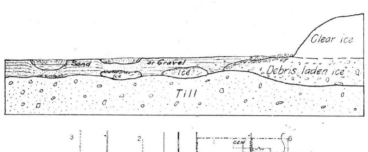

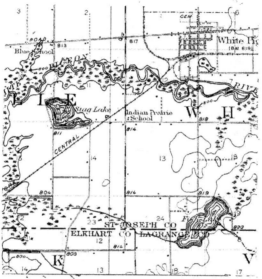

Fig. 15. Map and diagrams to illustrate characteristics of pit lakes. Map a part of Three River Quadrangle. Lower diagram after Hobbs.)

Continental glaciers are characteristically divided into two distinct zones, an upper one comparatively clean and free from debris
and a lower which is heavily clogged with rock fragments. Under
the sun's rays the clear ice of the upper zone melts rapidly but,
when the lower zone is reached, the rock fragments protect the
ice directly below them. The portions of the surface not covered
with debris melt until earthy material is uncovered and finally a
complete rock cover is formed which soon becomes so thick that
melting proceeds at a very slow rate   This difference in the rate
of melting of the upper and lower zones caused the ice of the upper
zone to recede possibly several miles while that of the lower remains
stagnant   Wherever the drainage from the ice was vigorous, the protective cover was removed from the stagnant ice and it melted, but
where sluggish streams were depositing material, the ice was deeply
buried in an outwash plain with an unbroken surface sloping
gently away from the ice   The ice blocks did not underlie all of the
outwash plain but were more in the nature of scattered fragments,
due probably to the uneven distribution of debris in the lower zone
of the glacier   Where the load was exceptionally heavy the debris
accumulated on the surface until a cover was formed which protected the ice beneath so effectively that it persisted until covered
with outwash   At some time subsequent to the formation of the
outwash the ice blocks melted and allowed the material above to
subside slowly, causing pits or depressions in the surface of the
outwash   This process is illustrated in Fig. 15.

The distinguishing features are· The basin is a depression in a
plain, the materials of the plain are water deposits and, therefore,
assorted and sometimes stratified, the slope from the plain to the
water level is steep, the outline is roughly circular, and there is
often no outlet and no important inlets, the lake being supplied
and drained by the seepage of ground water through the sandy
material of the outwash plain.

WAVES AND CURRENTS. LAGOONS. Shore action often isolates a
depression forming a new and usually smaller, detached body of
water. The original depression is due to other causes and the
shore action is responsible for the isolation only. The work of
waves and currents is fully described in Chapter II and needs no
discussion here.

It must be stated that some of the inland lakes studied by the
writer cannot be definitely included in the classes described above
because of the complexity of the origin of the basins and the lack of
data concerning them. In particular, attention is called to a series·
of elongated lake basins along the coast of the northwestern part

of the Southern Peninsula—Pine, Torchlight, Elk, Walloon, etc
These lakes exist in long, narrow valleys whose bottoms are filled
with thick deposits of loose sand. However, on the sides of the
flanking hills at elevations from 100-300 feet above the level of Lake
Michigan are found exposures of clay varying in thickness from a
few feet to more than 100. These deposits have been buried by till,
showing that they were formed prior to the last advance of the ice
over this region. The clays are interpreted by Leverett as lake beds,
inasmuch as they are distinctly laminated, nearly free from pebbles,
and in places show sandy partings between the layers of clay. The
data are incomplete but indicate the presence of great lakes in this
vicinity previous to the last advance of the ice, the extent and duration of which we have merely a suspicion The puzzling thing is
the relation of the valleys in which the present lakes lie to the
ancient lakes as signified by the clays The heavy deposits of sand
in the valleys preclude the possibility of determining by direct
observation whether or not the sand is underlain by the lake clays
found higher on the hills, and it is essential to know this If
underlain by the clays, the basins would be classed as enormous
pits since it would indicate that the clays had sunk from the higher
elevation If not underlain by the clays, it may be assumed that
the deposits have been removed or were never formed in the present
lake basins. If the material has been removed, streams, ice, or both
may have been the eroding agents If the clays were not deposited
in these depressions, we may assume the depressions to have been
filled with blocks of ice, probably stagnant, while the clays were
settling on the beds of lakes which bordered these ice masses

REFERENCES

General
SALISBURY, R. D, Physiography, Henry Holt and Co, N Y
HOBBS, W H, Earth Features and their Meaning, MacMillan, N Y
TARR AND MARTIN, College Physiography, MacMillan, N Y
Michigan
LEVERETT, FRANK, Surface Geology of Michigan, Michigan Geological and
Biological Survey
LEVERETT, F AND TAYLOR, F B, The Pleistocene of Indiana and Michigan,
Monograph 53, U S Geological Survey
VAN HISE, C R, AND LEITH, C K, The Geology of the Lake Superior
Region, Monograph 52, U. S Geological Survey, Chapter 4, Physiography
by Lawrence Martin
ALLEN, R. C, The Iron River Iron-bearing District of Michigan, Michigan
Geological and Biological Survey
LEVERETT, FRANK, Folio 155 (reprint), U S Geological Survey
Lakes, origin of basins
FENNEMAN, N M, Lakes of Southeastern Wisconsin, Wisconsin Geological
Survey, Bulletin VIII
RUSSELL, I C, The Surface Geology of Portions of Menominee, etc An-
nual Report Mich Geological Survey, 1906
LANE, A C, Water Supply and Irrigation Paper, No 30, U S Geological
Survey.

CHAPTER II

THE DEVELOPMENT OF LAKE SHORES AND THE EXTINCTION OF LAKES

CHARACTERISTICS OF WAVES AND CURRENTS

WAVES   Coincident with the filling of a lake basin with water there begins a development of its shores and, to some extent, its bed. Conditions of absolute calm are exceptional and it is seldom that roughened patches do not appear, travel forward, and die out on the otherwise unruffled water surface.   It is a matter of common knowledge that for the most part these patches are caused by the wind, and examination shows them to be composed of a pattern of wavelets which run with the wind and whose crests are at right angles to the wind direction   See Plate II, A   If the wind fails, they disappear but with a freshening breeze the area of the ruffled water soon spreads over the entire lake

From this we might conclude that waves are caused by the friction of the wind on the surface of the water, and further observation will strengthen this conclusion   At any one point, with a freshening wind, it is readily noted that the waves not only increase in height but in length and velocity as well.   This continues until a maximum development is reached which is largely dependent on the strength of the wind and the time it has been blowing   However, a trip along the shore discloses the fact that the waves increase in development toward the lee side of the lake and, if several lakes are observed, it becomes evident that the larger the lake the greater are the waves formed by winds of the same velocity   Thus, in addition to the velocity of the wind and the length of time it has been effective, may be added the factor of the expanse of water across which it blows, or *reach*, in the development of wind driven waves   This development of the wave in height, length, and velocity is due to the fact that an almost continuous push by the wind is effective on the wave from one end of the lake to the other and is, therefore, cumulative   It continues until the friction caused by the differential movement of the water particles is equal to the energy supplied by the wind.   Inasmuch as the storm winds usually steady down at a maximum velocity which is somewhat uniform, a maxi-

mum wave development which is exceeded only during exceptionally
strong winds, may be postulated for a given lake. On the other
hand a decrease in velocity or cessation of the wind allows the waves
to flatten and gradually die out.

Other causes of water waves are possible but it is the wind driven
wave that is effective on the smaller bodies of water. In waves of
this type there are two motions to be considered, the forward motion of the wave itself and the motion of the particles of water affected by the wave. Whenever a wave is running in deep water
where its motions will not be interfered with, it is called a *free
wave* and the motion of the particles is theoretically in circular,
vertical orbits which do not move forward with the wave, the revolution being in the same direction as the movement of the wave.
Thus, in waves of *oscillation,* there is a forward movement of the
particles through the upper half of the orbit during the passage of
the crest of the wave and a backward semi-circle with the trough.
This may readily be observed by watching the movement of a floating
object, and is illustrated in Fig. 16. If all the particles occupied

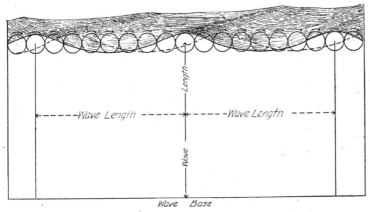

Fig. 16. Movement of water particles in waves of oscillation.

the same relative position in their orbits, or *phase,* e. g., all at the
top, and continued to revolve, the result would be a raising and lowering of the entire surface of the lake accompanied by a forward
and backward movement. This is not the case and the wave pro-
gresses because each impulse is communicated from one particle to
the next adjoining on the lee side. It follows, then, that no two
particles in any wave are in the same phase but are more advanced
in their orbits to the windward. This is represented in Fig. 16 in
which the orbits of conveniently spaced particles have been drawn

and must be considered as representative, the intervening spaces being filled with particles revolving similarly. The particles are represented as revolving in a clockwise direction and, beginning at the left, each particle is more advanced in its orbit (has a more advanced phase) than the next to the right by one-eighth of the circumference of the orbit. By connecting these points a curve is obtained which represents the form of the wave in cross section. This curve* shows the steeper crests and wide troughs, and from this it will be seen that the upper half of the revolution of a particle described during the passage of the crest of the wave must be accomplished in a shorter time and with greater velocity than the lower half, since the forward movement of the wave is uniform.

Both the height and the length of the wave may vary and great variations in the dimensions and velocity of waves are possible. Observation has shown, however, that in general there is a more or less definite relation in fully developed waves between the height, length, and velocity. This varies somewhat in different bodies of water but may be approximately stated as follows: Wave length is five and one-eighth times the square of the period (time between two crests) and the length fifteen times the height. The relationship is shown in Fig 17 in which the phasal difference is the same but the size of the orbits increased.

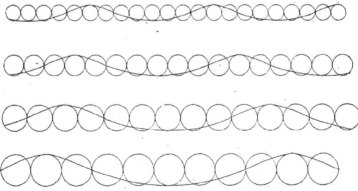

Fig. 17. Diagram illustrating the ideal development of waves.

The agitation of the water particles at the surface is communicated to the particles below, but the motion decreases very rapidly and practically dies out at a very limited depth. See Fig. 18. It is usually stated that the size of the orbits is halved for each in-

*The curve here shown is a trochoid and is obtained from the trace of a point inside the circumference of a rolling circle. A cycloid is formed if the point is on the circumference.

crease in depth equal to one-ninth of the wave length, but this is
only a rough approximation. An illustration may give a better
idea of the rapidity of the decrease in motion with depth. A free
wave which has a height of three feet at the surface is approximately forty-five feet long and the time of passage about three seconds.
At a depth equal to the wave length the diameter of the orbits is less
than one five-hundredth of that at the surface, or in the case cited
seven-tenths of an inch and the time three seconds. The rate at
which the water moves in describing an orbit of this size is about
two-thirds of an inch per second, a very feeble current and in-
capable of geologic work except possibly the transportation of the
very finest sediment. The depth of a wave length below the surface has, therefore, been called the *wave base,* that is, the lower
limit of effective wave action, but observations show that this depth

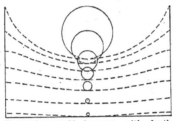

Fig. 18. Diagram illustrating rapid decrease, with depth, of motion of water
particles in a wave, (after Fenniman).

is excessive and probably should be placed at less than half the
wave length.

The relationship in the dimensions of the wave does not hold
under a freshening breeze. Under this condition the height increases faster than the length, and the wave gradually becomes
steeper until a limit is reached which, if exceeded, would cause the
water to describe a loop at the crest of the wave, a condition obviously impossible. Fig. 19, which shows the effect of increasing the
height while the length remains constant, illustrates this point. The
wave is then said to break into a *whitecap,* but it is probable that
the wind which is moving much more rapidly than the wave blows
the crest over into whitecaps before the theoretical limit of steepness is reached.

As stated previously, from a theoretical standpoint there is no
permanent forward movement of the particles of water in waves
but, due to the constant forward push by the wind, it happens, in
reality, that each revolution of a particle finds it slightly advanced
from its former position and there results a drift with the wind.
It is probable that the wind has a greater push on the crest of the

wave than on the trough because the wind and water are moving in the same direction and the steepness of the crest allows the force to be applied to better advantage. Consequently, most of the forward movement occurs during the passage of the crest and an attempt has been made to show this in Fig. 20. By following the course of this continuous line it will be noted that all of the for-

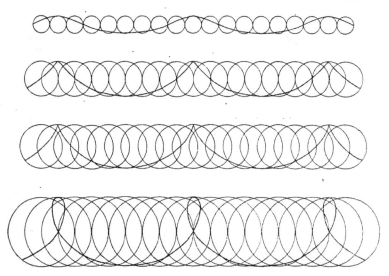

Fig. 19. Diagram to illustrate the formation of whitecaps. For convenience the wave length is kept constant.

ward motion is represented as taking place in the upper half of the orbit. The curve is not accurately drawn principally because there are no data from which to construct it but is presented merely to give some idea of the manner in which a forward drift is set up by the wind.

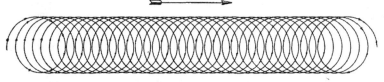

Fig. 20. Diagram of the path of a particle of water affected by a number of successive waves.

In addition to the drift, there are other positive forward movements. Of these whitecaps have already been considered. Another takes place when the waves approach the shore. As the water becomes shallower the agitation extends to the bottom and the lower portion of the wave is retarded by friction. The orbits of the water particles are no longer circles but are deformed into ovals These are more nearly circular at the surface but become flattened with depth until the bottom is reached where the motion is a horizontal oscillation. The retardation of the lower part of the wave is shared by the upper but not in the same degree and results in a decrease in velocity which is less pronounced at the surface The velocity of the wave is continuously reduced as it approaches the beach and is necessarily accompanied by a corresponding decrease in wave length and a steepening of the crests. In addition, the wave height is actually increased, due to the transmission of the motion to a continuously smaller quantity of water as the depth decreases, and the form of the wave becomes steeper on the front or shore side because of the more rapid forward movement near the surface The variations are all progressive and continue until the crest topples forward into foam, or *breaks,* see Plate II, B, which reduces the height of the wave. The storm waves break first at a more or less uniform distance off shore, called the off-shore breaker line, and the reduction in height by breaking is sufficient to allow them to regain their true wave form They then proceed for some distance, in some cases to the shore, without further breaking It is possible to have the slope of the bottom so flat that the waves may break at the off-shore line and continue to the shore with crests a mass of foam, but this usually does not occur In such a case the waves may be dissipated before they reach the shore.

Under the conditions stated above—a very gentle off-shore slope —waves of oscillation are not only modified in the manner described but may in some cases change their character and become a different type, called waves of *translation* The motion of the particles, instead of being in orbits, may become a definite advance accompanied by a lifting and sinking, together making a semi-elliptical path for each particle which does not return to its former position_ Each particle from top to bottom starts simultaneously with the approach of the wave, moves forward and upward until the crest arrives, then sinks in its forward movement, and finally comes to rest when the wave has passed. The forward movement is the same for all particles but the verticle movement is greatest at the surface and decreases downward to the bottom where it becomes zero, that is the movement is horizontal Fig 21 shows the paths of the particles in a wave of this type and Fig 22 the forward and upward movement in the front portion and the forward and downward motion of the particles as influenced by the back of the wave The velocity increases in the forward half of its path from zero

A. WAVES, BURT LAKE.

B. WHITECAPS AND BREAKERS, HIGGINS LAKE.

to a maximum at the middle and then decreases until it comes to rest.

Waves of translation are caused by a sudden addition of a volume of water to a lake or other body of water, each wave representing an addition. Obviously, they are independent of each other and consist merely of crests of water moving forward at a uniform rate of speed. They have neither length nor trough as the terms are used with reference to waves of oscillation, the surface between the crests being flat and the distance variable according to the regularity of the additions of water. When formed in a lake they are caused by the plunging crests at the off-shore breaker line which supplies the additional volume of water and usually run in to the shore in apparently related series because of the regularity with which the waves from the lake enter the breaker zone.

All waves, whether of oscillation or translation, are eventually dissipated on the shore, except in the possible case of an excessively

Fig. 21. Diagram showing paths of water particle in waves of translation, (after Fenneman).

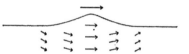

Fig. 22. Diagram showing upward and forward movement in the front part (right) and downward and forward movement in the back part (left of a wave of translation, (after Fenneman).

wide breaker zone. With the final plunge on the shore the true wave motion is lost and the water rushes forward and back over the shore, which acts as an inclined plane. The outgoing water running down the inclined shore meets the next incoming wave but succeeds only in modifying its front, which becomes increasingly convex toward the shore, and increasing its height until it wavers, curls forward, and crashes on the beach. This final breaking of the wave is popularly known as *comber*.

CURRENTS. In the preceding pages it has been pointed out that there is a forward drift of the water in wind driven waves which is further increased within the breaker zone by the partial or total conversion of the waves of oscillation into waves of translation, and that this forward movement occurs mainly at the surface. This transfer of water from the windward to the lee side of lakes necessitates a return. This is accomplished by means of currents, although in large lakes, as Erie and Superior, a small amount of the transfer is accommodated by a piling up of the water at the lee end. The currents are set up when the waves strike the shore and may be

horizontal currents along the shore, *shore currents,* or a vertical
return into the main body of the lake along the bottom which is
called the *undertow,* or both. The nature of the current is determined by the angle at which the waves strike the shore.

When the waves strike the shore at exactly 90 degrees the incoming water runs up on the shore and returns underneath without lateral movement along the shore, forming undertow only. As
stated above, the agitation of the water by waves within the breaker
zone extends to the bottom where it is a forward and backward
horizontal movement having a maximum velocity midway between
two periods of rest. Hence the undertow must be a pulsating
current in which the particles move to and fro but advance slightly
out into the lake with each oscillation. Its strength depends on
the height of the waves and the steepness of the off-shore slope
but decreases as it advances into the lake because it is distributed
through larger amounts of water as the depth increases. In this
way it loses its indentity but may continue throughout the entire
length of small lakes as an inappreciable drift.

But it is impossible for waves to approach all shores at an angle
of 90 degrees. When the waves strike at oblique angles the paths
of the particles of water are as shown in Fig. 23. Instead of a to

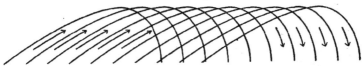

Fig. 23. Diagram to show actual motion of water particles striking shore at an
oblique angle.

and fro motion along a straight line as in the case of the undertow,
the motion is an oscillation on the shore accompanied by a lateral
movement and results in a current along the shore which may reverse its direction because of the variable wind directions. Shore
currents should reach their greatest development when the waves
are running nearly parallel to the shore but this seldom happens.
It may occur where the off-shore slope is very steep and the wind
direction favorable. But where the off-shore slope is gentle the
shore end of the wave is retarded within the breaker zone and the
retardation increases with nearness to the shore. There is, then,
a tendency for the crest of the wave to bend and swing towards a
direction more nearly parallel to the shore, that is strike at 90
degrees. This change in direction may cause oblique waves to
strike the shore at 90 degrees if the obliquity is slight and the off-
shore slope wide.

Two currents, then, are set up on a shore upon which the waves are pounding, the undertow and the shore current, and the relative importance of each varies according to the angle at which the waves strike. With waves running on shore perpendicularly the undertow only is present but any appreciable variation of this angle sets up a shore current which increases at the expense of the undertow as the angle departs from perpendicularity. Considering the entire shore of a lake, the development of waves and currents varies at any given time due to the varying relations between the directions of the shore and the wind at different parts of the lake, and over a period of time, because of changes in wind direction and velocity. Thus, with shifting winds all the shores of the lake may be affected but not equally because the storm winds come usually from a prevailing direction. Under the influence of a wind constant in direction the location of the shore, and the size and shape of the lake are important.

Obviously, the windward side is least affected and the effects increase towards the lee. The size of the lake is important in that as the reach is greater the waves are better developed. As regards shape, the simplest case is a lake of circular outline. The middle of the lee side, A. Fig. 24, receives the strongest waves and at an

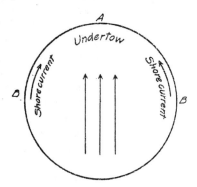

Fig. 24. Diagram to show currents set up on a circular lake.

angle of 90 degrees, therefore undertow only is developed on this shore, and at the sides, B, shore currents are formed. Along the intermediate stretches both shore currents and undertow are present but the former merge into the undertow as they approach A and return underneath. To the windward the waves are inactive and the only current possible is the return below the surface, the continuation of the undertow. On the other hand, if the lake is long and narrow, the condition is not so simple. The most effective

winds are those which blow lengthwise of the lake because of the
excessive reach and develop waves and currents similar to those
established on a lake of circular outline. Cross winds, on account
of their short reach, produce effects of minor significance but similar in character. However, when the wind crosses the lake diagon-
ally, only a short stretch of the shore can be perpendicular to the
wave movement and strong shore currents are developed on the
lee side but the undertow is of minor importance. In this case the
shore current turns the end of the lake and skirts the windward
shore as a return current which has lost its intermittent character
and therefore much of its effectiveness. See Fig. 25.

Fig. 25. Diagram showing conditions under which a return shore current is formed.

THE WORK OF WAVES AND CURRENTS

Waves and currents in the neighborhood of the shores are very
effective erosive agents. They are active not only in tearing down
the land but also in removing and depositing the disintegrated material. The resemblance to rivers is close and is strengthened when
it is realized that they are, in fact, nothing but bodies of water in
motion, obeying the same laws but with strikingly different results. Thus, the transporting power of running water is involved
and with it the presence of tools—suspended material—which are
important in the degrading process. In general, it may be stated
that the waves are the active agents of destruction, and the currents the agents of transportation and deposition. In the final
analysis both are due to the same cause, the wind, and they occur
together. As regards the work accomplished, they may be said to

supplement each other, that is, the currents are dependent on the waves to furnish material for transportation and, on the other hand, the waves would soon lose their force if the material were not removed.

THE WORK OF WAVES. When a wave strikes the shore, there is agitation of the water from the plunge of the wave and at the same time currents are set up, except where a verticle cliff extends into the water to a depth greater than wave base. The range of the direct action of the wave extends approximately from wave base below water level to the greatest height that the waves splash above water level but the effectiveness varies within these limits. The action is greater above water level than below and is greatest at or a little above the water level. The movement of the water is greatest as it makes its final plunge on the shore and during the succeeding in-and-out rush along the inclined beach. Here also is the source of the suspended earthy material which is broken from the shores by the force of the waves with the co-operation of the weathering process. The suspended material is thrown violently against the shore with each incoming wave and acts as a powerful abrasive, which is limited in its action to a narrow zone near the water level. Within this zone cutting is most rapid and the effects are more pronounced where the shores are steep. At first a low cliff develops which recedes and at the same time increases in height. The cliff soon extends above the upper limit of the direct action of the waves and becomes undercut. The overhanging portion must sooner or later fall and, thus, extends the action of the waves indirectly to the top of the cliff and allows the recession to continue. See Fig. 26.

Fig. 26. Farwell's Point, an undercut notched cliff on Lake Mendota, Wisconsin. After a time the overhanging portion will fall by gravity to produce blocks like those in the foreground, (after Fenneman).

Coincident with the recession of the cliff there is formed at its base and below water level a terrace cut in the material of which the cliff is composed and, therefore, known as a *cut terrace*. The terrace itself furnishes the condition necessary for currents which modify its surface to some extent The tools which are so effective in the cutting process are at first too heavy to be carried out of the zone of action of the surf but the continual pounding against the cliff and each other gradually reduces their size until they are carried lakeward by the undertow or along the shore

The distribution of this material along the shore constitutes a *beach* which tends to become smoothed out into straight lines or almost perfect curves. See Plates XII, A and XIII The material of the beach is rounded, except for particles of extreme sizes, and shows a rather close assortment The rounding of the particles is due to the mutual abrasion caused by rubbing Manifestly those particles too large to be moved by waves are unaffected and small particles, such as sand, are so buoyed up by the water that abrasion is not effective. Both waves and currents are active in assorting the beach materials All of the particles which can be moved are picked up and tossed shoreward by the incoming waves but only the finer material is carried away as the water runs back There is, then, a minimum size of particles to be found on a beach but not necessarily a maximum because rocks too large to be moved may be present During exceptionally heavy storms coarse material is sometimes built into surprisingly strong ridges which stand some distance from the shore under normal conditions and are known as *storm beaches*. See Plate XIX.

Other factors in determining the character of beach material are nearness to the source of supply and the nature of the material. Where the material is quarried from a headland, the size decreases and the assortment is better with distance from the source This is due to the more effective wave action on the exposed headland and reduction in size of the particles by abrasion as they progress along the beach If solid rock is quarried, structures such as fractures and bedding are important Thus, with thin beds closely fractured, small flat blocks are supplied which are soon rounded off and constitute a *shingle beach* In Michigan the nature of the glacial deposits is important in determining beach materials, since little solid rock is exposed on the shores of the inland lakes The clay of the till is readily washed away, leaving a strand of cobbles and boulders, while sand and gravel, unless clearly a current deposit, are significant of outwash.

The outward passage in the undertow is a series of backward and forward movements which are far more effective than a steady current of the same average velocity would be. Abundant tools of fine texture enable the undertow to wear down somewhat and smooth off the cut terrace. The modification of the terrace in this way seems to be dependent largely on the time that the process has been active and, therefore, is greatest at the outer edge and decreases to the shore. Consequently the surface of the terrace slopes gradually out to its edge and then drops steeply into deep water. But when the edge of the cut terrace is encountered by the undertow, the current loses its effectiveness due to the sudden deepening and drops its suspended material. This accumulates beyond the edge of the terrace until it reaches the general level of its surface at which time the undertow again becomes effective and extends the terrace into the lake by deposition. Thus, there is formed a *cut-and-built* terrace which is constantly being widened by cutting along the shore and by deposition on the lake side. See Figs. 27 and 28.

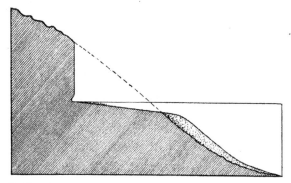

Fig. 27. Profile of a cut and built terrace on a steep rocky shore. The cliff is verticle and notched at the base, (after Hobbs).

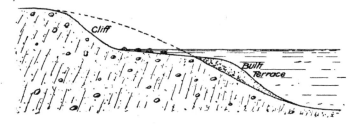

Fig. 28. Profile of cut and built terrace on a steep shore formed of loose material. Note inclination of cliff and the stranded boulders in front, (after Hobbs).

It has a gentle slope away from the shore and drops suddenly into deep water at its outer edge which is limited by the depth at which the water, agitated by the larger waves, loses its effectiveness

7

as a transporting agent—one-half wave length or less. For, a given
locality this depth is fixed by the size of the largest waves and subsequent widening of the terrace serves only to flatten its slope
which, in turn, reduces the action of the waves and currents. The
process, then, is self limiting and the shore eventually becomes
adjusted, at which time the highest waves lose their force as the
shore is reached.

On well developed cut-and-built terraces it is not uncommon to
find a perceptible shoaling of the water just before the "drop off"
is reached, indicating the presence of a sand ridge which may reach
almost or quite to the water level. These sand ridges are nearly
coincident with the off-shore breaker line and their manner of
formation has been referred to the violent agitation of the water
during the breaking of the waves followed by more quiet conditions as the waves regain their true form. In this way the conditions of transportation and deposition are satisfactorily fulfilled.
Similar forms have been described extending above the water level
in large bodies of water and are called *barrier beaches* but in all
cases a lowering of the water level (or elevation of the land) is
involved. It is plausible that the waves might pound such forms
above the water level but as yet no such case has ever been observed.
Barrier beaches are not necessarily attached to the shore, are
composed of sand, and have gentle slopes on the lake side while on
the opposite side the slopes are steeper, Fig. 29. Between the land
and the barrier is a narrow, shallow *lagoon*.

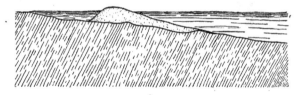

Fig. 29. · Section of a barrier with characteristic steep landward and gentle
seaward slope, (after Hobbs).

In the discussion above it has been assumed that the material of
the shore was uniform but this seldom, if ever, occurs on all shores
even of a small lake. The different kinds of rock vary greatly in the
resistance they offer to the erosive agents and the same kind of
rock may vary from place to place. In addition, certain structures
in the rock serve as lines of weakness along which the erosion
proceeds more rapidly. The more important of these are divisional
planes between beds of stratified rock and joints which are the
vertical cracks so commonly present in all rocks. These variations

in the rocks give rise to a number of transitory forms during the progress of erosion.

Under the conditions stated above (steep slope), cliff formation is one of the first results of wave action. The steepness of the cliff depends very largely on the firmness or consolidation of the rock. The great deposits of sand and gravel which are very numerous and extensive in glaciated regions offer little resistence to the waves and, being but loosely held together, form cliffs of moderate steepness which are not undercut. See Fig. 28. The same statement may be applied to the cliffs cut in clay except that the cliffs are somewhat more steep. However, in solid rock the cliffs may be vertical and overhang the zone of undercutting at the water's edge, Fig. 27.

Of the various forms which are due to wave erosion the under-cut cliff is perhaps the most common wherever hard rock is encountered. In massive rocks the face of the cliff may be very ragged and the undercutting excessive. The same may be true of stratified rocks where the layers are of different degrees of hardness and many picturesque forms result. Wherever a local weakness is present the cutting naturally proceeds more rapidly and a *sea cave*, Fig. 30,

Fig. 30. Sea-caves in process of formation along joints, (after a photograph by C. W. Cook).

is the result. The weakness may be due to a difference in the rock or to the presence of fractures. The fractures or joints may run for long distances along a straight line and often have extremely smooth walls. They apparently run in all directions but study has shown that the more important are grouped in systems which cross each other at right angles. Joints running approximately parallel to the shore may cause smooth-faced cliffs, often without under-cutting if the joints are close together and well developed. They may run oblique to the shore and in this case the cliffs have a buttressed effect. When the joints running at right angles to the shore are followed, caves may develop. Often the joints converge back from the shore and in time a channel is cut through. As the channel enlarges this form is appropriately called an *arch*. Fig. 31.

Fig. 31. A sea arch and small caves on the shore of one of the Apostle Islands, Lake Superior, (after a photograph by the Detroit Photographic Company).

But eventually the arch must fall as the action proceeds and a *stack*, Fig. 32, is left standing entirely separated from the main cliff. And this, too, must give way in time to the irresistable attack of the waves. These forms are all evanescent and represent the early scenes in the development of this particular type of landscape. They are very common features of sea coasts and the shores of large lakes and are an indication therefore, that much of the adjustment of the shores is yet to be accomplished. Inasmuch as the inland lakes lie largely in glacial basins, these features are seldom found.

Waves, as we have seen, are most active on shores with steep off-shore slope but conditions along the shores of any considerable body of water vary and with them the effectiveness of the waves. Headlands are almost universally subject to attack by the waves and to these may be added shores with notable relief, for the surface of the surrounding land is to a great extent an indication of the topography of the bottom, that is steep slopes on land indicate similar slopes beneath the water.

THE WORK OF CURRENTS .

On lakes of irregular outline shore currents must necessarily encounter numerous changes in direction of the shore. The current is able to accommodate itself to many of these but where the bend is abrupt it leaves the shore in the direction it had before the

Fig. 32.   A stack on the shore of Lake Superior, (after a photograph by the Detroit Photographic Company).

bend was reached. As the current leaves the shore its velocity is rapidly decreased because its motive power—waves striking the shore at an oblique angle—is lost and friction is present between the current and the still water of the lake. Deposition, therefore, takes place and is greatest near the point of departure from the shore.

If the bend is caused by a small indentation, the current may carry across the mouth but the velocity is decreased nevertheless and deposition takes place along its path in the form of a narrow submerged *bar,* best developed near the shore. Inasmuch as the currents may reverse their direction along the shore, due to shifting winds, the bar develops from both sides As the submerged bar develops it first reaches the surface of the water at its land connections and is then pounded above the water level by the waves into pointed sand ridges, called *spits,* on either side of the indentation. (See Figs 49 and 50) Spits do not usually develop equally on both sides because of the prevailing direction of storm winds and the varying reach of the waves on different parts of the lake With the formation of spits the currents are able to continue farther beyond the shore and the indentation is rapidly closed by a complete bar which is above the water level This is called a sub-aerial bar or simply a *bar* Plates IX, A, IX, B, XI and XIV. If a considerable amount of water drains into the lagoon, as the cut off indentation is called, a current is set up across the bar which may maintain an open channel It sometimes happens that an island is encountered by the current after leaving the shore and it becomes tied to the land by the bar which developes Fig 65 It is then called a *land-tied island* and the bar is designated as a *tombolo* Bars are composed almost entirely of sand and have a gentle slope on the lake side, due to the action of the waves and undertow, and a steep slope, often as much as one to one, on the lagoon side where wave action is much less intense

In case the indentation is wide the currents may not persist across the mouth and a *hook* or re-curved spit is formed Hooks are closely related to spits in that the material and the manner of formation is the same. The difference is in form, the hook curving back towards the shore See Plate VII Under the conditions necessary for the formation of hooks, the velocity of the current dies out rapidly after leaving the shore and the waves are able to turn it landward. The change in curvature is due in part to a shifting of the wind so that the waves strike the hook more directly or even from the opposite quarter and thus modify its form Also the tendency of waves which are running oblique to the shore to swing to a direction more nearly parallel to the shore may be important in this process The writer has seen waves break along a hook when the retardation of the shore end of the wave was sufficient to swing the crests around the end of the hook and even on the lee side in the opposite direction to the waves on the lake.

In the growth of spits and hooks the varying direction of the winds often causes minor developments in form which are not in harmony with the general growth As has been stated previously, most of the storm winds come from a quarter which causes currents in one direction along a shore and the general development of

hooks and spits is in accord with this. However, high winds do
occur from other quarters and the end of the hook or spit often
grows rapidly during a single storm at an abrupt angle to the
general direction. Such forms are usually very transient, often
being destroyed by the next storm, but may persist on hooks as
prongs extending landward from the sheltered side. See Plate VII
In reality, spits and hooks represent a balance between the currents set up in either direction along a shore and in the normal
development one current usually greatly predominates. All grada-
tions are possible and do occur   The clearest case is where evenly
balanced currents from either direction are forced to leave the
shore at some point   Spits develop from both directions and join
in a point out in the lake forming a triangular or *V-bar*—also
known as *cuspate foreland*—whose base is the shore and whose
sides are equal. If the currents are not equally effective, one side
grows at the expense of the other, the better developed often being
a hook and the smaller a spit   The material is typical shore drift
and the slopes are characteristic except at the tip of the V-bar where
it drops suddenly into deep water. The whole embankment encloses a shallow depression similar in shape and normally filled
with water   Such cuspate forelands seen by the writer were on
long, narrow lakes running north south and, at present, no reason
for the currents leaving the shore can be assigned.

Another case of deposition by currents sometimes occurs along
the shores of wide, shallow embayments between headlands   In
such cases much of the material from the headlands is transported
along the beach by currents into the bay. On account of the shallowness of the bay, the undertow is not effective, and this material
accumulates about the head of the indentation. In this way a sand
flat is built which gradually widens and reduces the indentation.

GENERAL EFFECT OF WAVES AND CURRENTS

In general the tendency of both waves and currents is to make
the outline of the lake more regular   The work of waves has been
described as a process of cutting, which insofar as headlands are
reduced, removes the irregularities which project into the lake
On the other hand, currents are agents of removal and deposition.
Deposition is favored by indentations which are cut off or filled
thereby. However, it must not be inferred that a circular or oval
outline is the final outcome of the work of these agents on all lakes,
although this would seem to be the logical conclusion   The process

of cutting is self limiting and may stop before the headlands are completely reduced Also many indentations are too wide to be crossed by currents, and hooks develop rather than bars, serving merely to make the bends less abrupt V-bars seem to disturb the symmetry of the shores and their complete development would carry them across the lake and divide it into smaller and more nearly circular bodies of water This, however, is unlikely unless great quantities of material are supplied from extraneous sources Another factor is the instability of conditions under which the lake exists The development of lake shores requires long periods of time and changes in conditions may cause new levels or even the extinction of a lake before the work of adjustment is finished

THE WORK OF ICE ON LAKE SHORES

ICE RAMPARTS. On the shores of lakes in regions having cold winters, ice is an effective agent of transportation and deposition. Its action is mainly that of a shoreward movement, accomplished slowly but with great force, which not only carries material forward to the shore but is able to shove heavy rocks in front As the ice disappears in the spring the material affected by it is either piled up in a wall on the shores known as an *ice rampart,* Plate XVII, A, Figs. 51 and 61, or is left stranded on the terrace, to be moved subsequently. The ramparts are best described as walls of rock material and are located a short distance back from the shore They are usually a single ridge but may be compound and the material is of all sizes, including boulders of large size. The slopes are steep on both sides with a tendency for the front slope to be the steeper.

The shove on the shore by the ice is exerted in two ways, by expansion and by ice jams Expansion occurs during the winter when the lake is completely frozen Water is rather exceptional in its properties and behavior under various conditions but, once frozen, acts as any other solid at ordinary temperatures and pressures. Thus, it expands or contracts with a rise or fall in temperature, and this property is involved in the formation of ice ramparts. When a lake first freezes it is enveloped with a layer of ice which completely covers its surface. If the temperature remains constant below the freezing point, the ice merely increases in thickness. But temperatures do not remain constant and the changes are often great and rapid. There is always a lowering at night followed by a daily rise and, in addition, there are the cold and warm waves which sweep over the country. With each drop in temperature the ice contracts but does not pull away from the shores It cracks instead and the cracks are soon healed by freezing, since the temperature is below the freezing point In this way the ice cover is kept intact but actually contains more ice that it did at the higher temperature. If such a condition is followed by a rise in temperature, the ice must expand and it will then be greater in extent than the surface of the lake Repeated alternations in temperature serve to exaggerate this condition The expansion may be accommodated either by overriding the shores or by buckling In the latter case pressure ridges in the ice are formed out from the shore and usually occur in the same places year after year Buckling takes place when the ice is not thick enough to withstand the pressures exerted by the expansion and where the shores are steep enough to prevent a landward movement of the ice edge Even under this condition a slight amount of movement may be possible if the water level is low when the action takes place In glacial material, at least, this results in a cliff embedded with boulders at its base or a boulder lined strand. See Plate VIII, B.

On sloping shores the ice is free to move and, if conditions are favorable, pushes up a rampart. The size of the material plays an important part both in their formation and permanancy As a rule fine grained material such as sand does not freeze into a solid mass and the ice slides over it with little accumulation of debris Also sandy shores are more commonly low and well-developed ramparts are not formed. However, if binding material, such as the roots of trees and mats of grass, is present, the material is pushed into ramparts, Fig 61, but they are soon destroyed by the waves During the winter of 1914-15 the sandy shore at the north end of Whitmore Lake, Washtenaw County, was pushed into a rampart about four feet high but by August of the following summer the rampart was less than a foot in height. Where coarse material is present it offers a good purchase to the ice which carries and pushes it on the shore forming ramparts which resist wave action and are relatively permanent. The fact that fine material is so generally mixed with coarse in ramparts indicates that the shoving action is important. The maximum size of particles moved in this way is not known but boulders of several tons in weight are found in ramparts

Ramparts, formed by expansion, although very common on the shores of lakes in Michigan, require rather specific conditions for their formation and are formed only in winters when these conditions are fulfilled The conditions involve the climatic factor, shore conditions, and the size of the lake. Shore conditions have

already been discussed   Other conditions being equal, the size of
the lake determines the amount of expansion   On small lakes,
possibly less than a half mile in diameter, the amount of expansion
is so small that the ramparts, if formed, are insignificant and soon
destroyed   Larger lakes permit greater expansion but the ice becomes less able to transmit the thrusts caused by expansion, as the
diameters are greater, and it buckles. The ability to transmit the
thrusts depends on the thickness of the ice in relation to its expanse
and is thus controlled by the climate   In this region the maximum
size of lake upon which such ramparts are formed is not definitely
known but probably does not greatly exceed a mile and a half

The climatic factor includes both temperature and snowfall.
temperature changes are essential but they must be large and rapid,
and quickly transmitted to the ice. The excessive temperature
changes of cold and warm waves which occur in this latitude during
winter fulfill the temperature conditions perfectly but the daily
rise and fall does not seem to be adequate   The rate at which the
air temperatures are communicated to the ice depends on the thickness of the snow covering which may form an effective blanket
Absence of snow is, therefore, the most favorable condition

The position of the rampart with reference to the shore is determined by the size of the lake and by the amount and number of
the temperature changes   In general, it is situated just back of
the shore which marks the high water stage   The size depends
on the supply of available material and the number of times the
ice shoves across the shore   If we assume that the ice moves a
definite amount of material at each invasion, it is obvious that the
development of the rampart is dependent on the number of invasions   As a rule, the ice encroaches on the shore but once each
winter, each drop and rise in temperature serving only to push
the ice farther on the shore   More than one advance is possible if
the ice thaws during the winter and loses its continuity, but the
total movement in the several advances is the same as that in a
single advance and, therefore, less effective for each   Within limits,
large particles are more readily moved by the ice than small ones
and a preponderance of such material assures a strong rampart.
However, the supply of this material on a shore may be limited and,
after repeated invasions, may become exhausted, thus limiting
the growth of the rampart.

Inasmuch as the climatic factor is relatively constant over a
period of years, the typical rampart is a single ridge   If the available material is sufficient, the ridge develops until it becomes strong

enough to resist successfully the push of the ice and any further expansion is relieved by buckling of the ice sheet. The growth from this time on, if any, must be in width and from the lake side. On lakes whose levels are gradually lowering the overriding of the shores by the ice is not materially decreased but the position of the ice edge after expansion becomes less and less advanced as the shores recede and a series of ramparts are formed to which the name *ice-push terrace* has been given. Another factor in their formation is that with the lowering in level fresh areas of the bottom are brought into the zone of ice action and the supply of material is replenished.

Ice ramparts of the expansion type, then, are limited to regions whose winters are severe and are punctuated by frequent cold and warm waves and to lakes of moderate size with absence of snow covering. Of these conditions the frequency and amount of the effective temperature changes, the amount of snow, and even the thickness of ice vary considerably, and it is only during winters when all of these factors are favorable that the expansion is effective in forming ramparts.

ICE JAM. The explanation of ice ramparts on the basis of expansion is only half of the story. Ramparts almost identical with those known to have been formed by expansion are common on lakes which do not fulfill the conditions necessary for this type. These lakes may exceed the maximum diameter postulated for expansion many times and are covered for the entire winter with a thick layer of snow. In fact, it is known from observation that the ice does not expand on the shores of the larger lakes, and the ramparts have been accounted for by the action of ice jams which occur during the final melting of the ice in the spring.

The melting of the ice at this time proceeds most rapidly at the shores, due to the more rapid heating of the land than the water under the influence of the rays of the sun, and a lane of open water of considerable width is formed next the shore. After the lane is formed weather conditions are of great importance. Some springs a prolonged warm spell is accompanied by calms or light breezes and the ice melts rapidly with little disturbance. It may disappear entirely in this way or become porous or "rotten" so that subsequent winds reduce it to slush. If, however, a storm develops after a lane is formed but before the ice has become porous, the mass of ice is blown before the wind and moves slowly to the shore with an almost irresistable force which carries everything in its path. See Plates X, A and XII, B. The storms in this latitude are cyclonic in nature and may best be described as vast whirlwinds which revolve in a counter-clockwise direction and at the same time travel from west to east across the country They are especially frequent in Michigan because most of the storms tracks unite in the Great Lakes region   They are accompanied by winds which shift from an easterly direction usually through the south to the west and northwest, but occasionally in southern Michigan shift through the northern half of the circle   The velocity of the winds increases with the shifting and reaches its maximum with the westerly and northwesterly winds at which time it often reaches the intensity of a gale   These storms travel eastward at the average rate of about 700 miles a day but the rate is variable and they may halt for 24 hours or more   Inasmuch as they affect areas often 1500 and more miles across, their effects may be felt for several days in a given locality. All shores of a lake may thus feel their influence but the eastern and northeastern sides are in the lee of the strongest winds, at least for southern Michigan

Where shore conditions are favorable ice jams bring in and pile up material in ramparts almost identical with those formed by expansion   Boulders of several tons in weight are moved shoreward in this way, leaving a trench between them and the lake and having a pile of rubble in front. Several such rocks were found on the northeast shore of Long Lake, Alpena County, (See Figs 77 and 78) As in the case of expansion ramparts those formed by ice jam are self limiting for they finally must reach a strength which is able to stop the advance in the lower portion of the ice and the top shears over   Repetition of the process may form an ice push terrace, see Plate III (Athabaska), and this may possibly occur during one season as the ice is buffeted back and forth by the shifting winds or by a close succession of storms

The size of the lake is also of importance   Permanent ramparts of this type are not found on very small lakes because the momentum of the small ice masses is not sufficient for large effects   On very large lakes they are formed but, the material of the shores is usually fine and wave action excessive so they are soon destroyed, e. g , on the Great Lakes. The size of lakes on which the maximum push is exerted is not known but it is much larger than that for the expansion type   Practically all of the larger inland lakes of Michigan show evidence of ice action which is roughly proportional to the size. On many of the lakes of intermediate size it is certain that the push is exerted in both ways and the ramparts are thus intensified.

A.   ICE-PUSH TERRACE, ATHABASCA.
Courtesy Canadian Geological Survey.

B. LAKE NEARING EXTINCTION BY VEGETATION, SECOND SISTER LAKE,
NEAR   ANN ARBOR.

Another effect of ice occurs when a great number of floating cakes of ice are present These drift with the wind to the shores and, instead of being pushed up on the shore, some drift along the shore with the waves and currents. The action of these agents is increased by the ice especially as regards the transportation of large material Some of the material may be supplied by rocks frozen into the ice which are released on melting but some shore material is moved along by the ice blocks and arranged into forms similar to spits or V-bars A V-bar formed in this way was noted on Long Lake, Alpena County, Plate XIV, B. The form, the depression in the center, and the slopes are characteristic of current action but the material is angular limestone blocks having in some cases a largest dimension of as much as eighteen inches.

A similar form is shown in Plate XV, A. This feature resembles a spit in its position at the neck of an indentation but differs in form and material Normally the outline of a spit is very regular but in this case the curvature is serpentine in character (the main body of the lake is to the left of the spit in plate) Also the material is angular and of relatively large size on its surface, although much of the submerged portion is composed of sand It is probable that current action is largely responsible for its formation but floating ice blocks have added some material and have succeeded in modifying its form

THE EXTINCTION OF LAKES

With the birth of a lake the forces which were responsible for its formation leave it unprotected to the action of certain agents which remodel its outlines and, to some extent, its bed. In addition, another set of agents becomes active which inevitably results in the extinction of the lake if existing conditions prevail All of these agents work rapidly from a physiographic standpoint and support the idea that lakes are temporary features of the earth's surface.

The processes which are working towards the extinction of lakes are filling, draining, and evaporation. The filling of a lake basin may be achieved by sedimentation, by animal and vegetal remains, and by chemical precipitation. Sedimentation is active in lakes whose entering streams bring in great quantities of silt which is deposited near the shores to be worked over later by waves and currents, and to which may be added the material torn from the cliffs by the waves The working over of this material into bars and barriers also favors the accumulation of vegetation

Some of the lakes are inhabited by innumerable minute animal

organisms whose hard parts are composed of calcium carbonate.
When the animals die the fine shells drop to the bottom and become
a part of beds of a white, powdery substance known as marl. Marl
is usually considered to be a mixture of calcium carbonate material
from several sources which, in addition to animals, include vegetation and chemical precipitates Marl beds as much as forty feet
in thickness have been found in Michigan lakes and are being utilized
in the manufacture of Portland cement The bed shown in Plate
IV, B, is from three to four feet thick and is exposed along the artificial channel of the Sturgeon River near Indian River. Thicknesses
of seventeen feet obtained by borings have been reported along
Crooked River in the same vicinity

Vegetation is another source of filling Numerous water loving
plants analogous to the leaves and stems of deciduous trees die at
the close of the growing season and sink to the bottom These dead
parts, being covered with water, are protected from the gases of
the atmosphere and only partially decompose. The yearly residue
accumulates as deposits of peat, a light-brown to black porous substance composed very largely of vegetal remains, many of which
are well preserved This material burns readily but with poor
heat values and is not used to any great extent as fuel in this
country at the present time The abundance of better fuel has held
back the exploitation of peat but, as the supply of coal diminishes,
the importance of the great peat deposits will become more and
more appreciated.

The plants which enter into the formation of peat may or may
not be attached to the bottom but in either case probably do not
grow in water exceeding twenty-five feet in depth, due to unfavorable conditions of heat and light, and usually are within from two
to six feet of the surface The floating forms are important in
lakes which are protected from strong winds and may sink and
form a deposit over the entire lake bottom Those attached to
the bottom start in the shallow water along the shores and grow
outward into the lake as the accumulation of their remains decreases the depth However, these forms, growing most abundantly
near the surface of the water, are not entirely dependent on shallow
water but extend outward over the surface as a floating bog, composed of the felted and intertwined stems and roots. These bogs,
often tenacious, are elastic and give under pressure, hence the name
quaking bogs They may develop so rapidly as to cover the surface
of the lake before the basin is completely filled and are thus underlain by clear water. The development from this time on is accom-

plished by droppings from the under side of the bog, and in this way the water is crowded out of the space below. The bog becomes firm, first along the shore and progressively outward. When a lake is filled with peat the growth of vegetation on its surface continues for a time. But exposure to the air is unfavorable for preservation of the plant remains and the accumulation ceases a short distance above the former water level.

The encroachment from the shores in typical cases is quite regular and shows an interesting zonal relationship between the different kinds of plants. The constitution of the zones may vary but for southern Michigan the first plants to develop are the floating forms and the pond weeds. As these grow outward a zone of water lillies starts at the shore and is closely followed by the floating sedges which form the floating bog. With the filling of the clear water

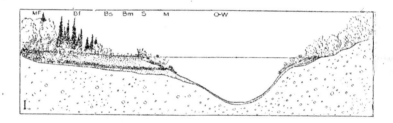

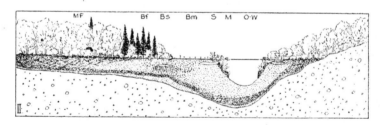

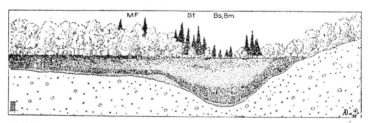

Fig. 33. Diagrams illustrating the filling of a lake by vegetation. The several plant associations of the Bog series, displacing one another, belong to the following major groups:—(1) O. W.—open water succession; (2) M.—marginal succession; (3) S.—shore succession; (4) B.—bog succession, comprising the bog meadow (B. m), bog shrub (B. s) and bog forest (B. f); and (5) M. F.—mesophytic forest succession. (Reproduced from Bulletin 16, Geological Survey of Ohio.)

under the floating matt, shrubs and other plants develop on the surface of the matt which crowd out the sedges. Next come the conifers, usually tamarack and spruce, and the last to propagate are the deciduous trees, especially poplar, willow, and maple. See Fig 33 and Plate III, B Such is the typical succession when fully developed but in the intermediate stages the later zones are absent.

In this manner lakes are filled by vegetation but the process varies in importance in different lakes. Quiet water is essential for plant growth, hence small lakes and lagoons are most affected. Shore conditions also have an effect Gentle off-shore slopes are favorable because wave action is less intense and depths are suitable for vegetation, but are often composed of sand in which plants take hold with difficulty. Frequently there is found a heavy growth of weeds in the mud just beyond the edge of the terrace but the sandy terrace itself supports a sparse growth of reeds. Dead lakes, as lakes filled with vegetation are frequently called, are characterized by a monotonously flat surface composed of black soil and covered with a thick carpet of moss and shrubs above which is growing a thin stand of timber See Plate XVIII.

Lakes may become filled to some extent by chemical precipitation but this process is limited in its application. In this climate it may have been of importance in the formation of marl where cold springs enter the lakes, but in dry regions it plays a more important role. In such regions the lakes are typically without outlets, due to the fact that evaporation is excessive and prevents the waters from rising to an avenue of escape. The loss of the water by evaporation allows the dissolved material brought in by streams to accumulate and, when sufficient concentration is reached, to precipitate on the shores and bottom. Among the substances deposited in this way are salt, borax, calcium carbonate, etc.

The draining of a lake is accomplished by cutting down of the outlet. Inasmuch as lakes act as settling basins, the outlets are relatively free from sediment and in general cut very slowly. The size and velocity of the outlet, and the resistance that the material over which it flows offers to abrasion, determine the rate of down cutting. Certain lakes, on account of their depth reaching below sea level, cannot be drained under existing conditions but, with the cooperation of filling, extinction is always a possibility.

Changes in climate are necessary for the extinction of lakes by evaporation and the change must be such that the supply of water is decreased or the evaporation greatly increased. A more arid climate supplies both conditions and is usually accompanied by an increase in temperature Many examples of partial or total extinction from this cause are to be found in the arid west but none in Michigan Great Salt Lake, which has been greatly lowered in level in this way, is one of the best known examples

The relative importance of the different methods of extinction varies greatly in different regions and with individual lakes. In general, the outlet is deepened rapidly in unconsolidated rocks, but even in hard rock this may be true if the down-cutting is due to the recession of a waterfall, such as Niagara Falls in the outlet of Lake Erie. As a rule deposition is more important than draining but in Michigan this is probably not the case Down-cutting of the outlet is important because the great majority of the outlet streams run over unconsolidated glacial material which is readily eroded without the help of tools On the other hand deposition has been slight Many of the lakes are fed by springs and the drift deposits have as yet been only slightly trenched by streams, in most areas the original slopes being almost intact. In addition, the streams are usually short and the areas draining into the lakes small. An exceptional case is Torch Lake near Houghton where the Sturgeon river has built a large delta at the southern end of the lake. A more important source of material in our lakes is the cliffs which sometimes form a large part of the shores. The cliffs, composed almost entirely of unconsolidated material, are easily eroded by the waves and the debris is distributed along the shores and bottom. It is possible that the enlargement of the lake by shore recession may equal the amount of filling. Where cliffs form a considerable part of the shores the filling must be greater; and the ratio increases according to the height and preponderance of the cliffs It is probable, however, that the amount of deposition in the lakes of Michigan so far has been a matter of a few inches only on the bottom.

At the present time, draining is probably more important than filling, but with future development the down-cutting of the outlets will gradually decrease as the streams approach grade, and the sediment brought in by tributary streams must increase as these streams extend their courses. At the same time the material deposited by waves and currents will decrease as the terraces widen. The deposition of part of this material in shore-forms reduces the size of the lake by cutting off indentations and thus facilitates filling, both in the main body of the lake and in the lagoons.

Vegetal accumulation seems to be more important in the extinc-

9

tion of lakes in Michigan than either of the two processes discussed
above and is especially effective in the smaller lakes and lagoons
It is impossible to give an estimate of the amount of filling that has
been accomplished in this way, but the prevalence of "dead lakes"
and quaking bogs indicates that vegetal accumulations are of frequent occurence All peat deposits are not necessarily evidence
that a lake basin has been filled, and it is only by a determination
of the depth and distribution of the peat and in some cases a
recognition of plant zones that the extinction can be proven

As regards chemical precipitation, marl is practically the only
deposit of any significance in the lakes of the State and it may be
formed in other ways Three factors may be active in its formation,
plants, animals, and chemical precipitation, and their relative importance is not known In general, marl is one of the first deposits to be formed on a lake bottom and is often covered with peat
It may be sufficient in itself to fill a lake basin but no cases of such
filling have been described in the knowledge of the writer.

THE CYCLE OF SHORE DEVELOPMENT

In the preceding pages the development of lake shores under the
influence of waves and currents has been traced This development
is gradual and systematic, and the various stages are marked by
definite topographic forms In other words, the shores pass through
a cycle of events which begin with the birth of the lake and termi-
nate when the waves and currents are impotent to further modify
them A change in water level, either up or down, institutes a new
cycle which may or may not interrupt the previous one before it
is completed Following the practice with regard to streams, the
stages in the cycle have been likened to the life cycle and are termed
youth, maturity, and old age These terms, in a general way only,
indicate corresponding lengths of time during which the forces
have been active, but conditions, both as to the constitution of the
shores and the force of the waves and currents, are so variable that
the emphasis should be placed on the stage of development rather
than on the time element

The youthful stage is a period of active erosion The shore is
marked by irregularities above and below water level, and a general
lack of adjustment to the movements of the water The presence of
frequent headlands necessitates numerous bays with sharp curves
and the shore currents are consequently poorly defined and discontinuous As the headlands are reduced and irregularities of the
bottom filled, the currents increase in strength and continuity, and

eventually simplify the shoreline by cutting off re-entrants Youth, then, is a time of relatively rapid changes and is brought to a close when all possible cut-offs have been accomplished

The progress from this time on is gradual in contrast to the rapid changes of youth and characterizes maturity The shore line as a whole either shifts landward or lakeward depending on the efficiency of the currents and the material available Where abundant material is supplied by incoming streams, the shore will advance lakeward If little or no material is supplied, the shore must progress landward but the recession becomes increasingly slower until an end point is reached Shores of most lakes probably never reach a stage beyond maturity because of the interference of the process by extinction or by the inauguration of a new cycle The inauguration of a new cycle by a rise in level gives conditions of the same nature as those present when the lake basin was first flooded In case the water level sinks, shore action will be influenced more or less by the topographic forms developed during the previous stage, and the development may consist largely in a remodeling of these features. The latter condition is of common occurrence on the inland lakes of Michigan. On practically all the lakes, at least one higher level may be recognized, unless the level has been raised by dams, and in some cases as many as four have been found.

REFERENCES

Waves and Shore Action.
FENNEMAN, N M, Lakes of Southeastern Wisconsin, Wisconsin Geological Survey, Bulletin VIII
GILBERT, G K, Topographic Features of Lake Shores, U S Geological Survey, Fifth Annual Report Lake Bonneville, U S Geological Survey, Monograph I
STOKES C G, On the Theory of Oscillatory Waves, Cambridge Transactions, Volume VIII
RUSSELL, J SCOTT. The Wave of Translation, London, 1885
CORNISH, VAUGHAN, Waves of the Sea and Other Water Waves, Chicago
Ice Action
BUCKLEY, E R, Ice Ramparts, Transactions of the Wisconsin Academy of Science, Arts and Letters, Vol XIII
TYRRELL, J B, Ice on Canadian Lakes, Transactions of the Canadian Institute, Vol IX
JOHNSON, D W, Shore Processes and Shoreline Development N Y, 1919
Also general references cited at end of Chapter I

CHAPTER III

LAKES OF THE CHEBOYGAN RIVER BASIN

In the basin of the Cheboygan River lie several of the larger inland lakes of the State, which, on account of their grouping and manner of formation, may well be discussed together. See Fig 31. About three miles upstream from the city of Cheboygan the river branches, one branch leading from Black Lake on the borders of Cheboygan and Presque Isle counties, and the other draining a chain of lakes known as the "Inland Route." The lakes of the Inland Route and their connections are navigable for boats of small draught and a regular passenger service is maintained during the summer months from Cheboygan on the Straits of Mackinaw to Conway on Crooked Lake about three miles from Little Traverse Bay. The lakes included in this route are Mullet, Burt, and Crooked Douglass, another lake of considerable size and importance, lies directly north of Burt, and is also included in this drainage system.

So far as known these basins lie entirely in glacial deposits which are somewhat complicated in this interlobate region. On the northeast side the moraines deposited by the ice of the Michigan and Huron lobes have a northwest-southeast trend and consist of a number of ridges which overlap in some cases. The best defined is probably a narrow ridge which parallels the shore of Lake Huron from Mackinaw to beyond Cheboygan, the only break being that through which the Cheboygan River flows. On the western side the moraines were deposited by the Michigan lobe and should be more nearly north south in trend but are poorly developed. Little Traverse Bay caused a small lobe of the ice which penetrated as far as Crooked Lake and left the weak morainic ridges that cross this lake. The puzzling topographic feature is the extensive lowland area which is irregular in outline and extends from the head of Little Traverse Bay nearly to Cheboygan. This depression is crossed by similar depressions running northwest-southeast. The latter apparently lie between the moraines but the main depression runs transverse from Little Traverse Bay to Cheboygan, near which place the depression is terminated by the Cheboygan moraine mentioned above. It seems certain that the depressions existed

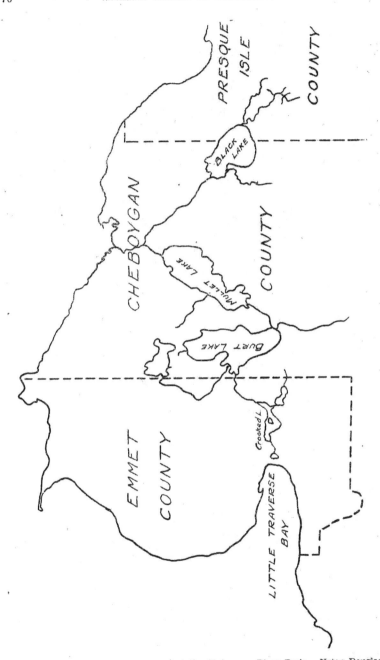

Fig. 34.   Outline map showing lakes of the Cheboygan River Basin.   Note: Douglass
Lake, north of Burt Lake, is undesignated.

prior to the last retreat of the glacier and may have been caused
by stream action previous to the advance of the ice, by the scour
of the ice in its advance, or by both. During the retreat of the ice
these depressions were filled with small lobes of ice which melted
more slowly than the main ice sheet and prevented heavy deposition in or across them. Also this region is underlain by a pure
limestone which has been dissolved to a considerable extent east of
this locality forming numerous sinks, and it is probable that some
of the deep holes in these lakes were formed in this manner.

All of these lakes lie in parts of this irregular depression whose
slopes are strikingly marked by shore lines of former lake levels
higher than the present. One of these shores stands on the average
about 90 feet above Lakes Michigan and Huron and marks the
borders of Lake Algonquin which in this region may best be described as a great archipelago. This archipelago covered all of the
present inland lakes of this group and large areas of the adjacent
lowland as well, leaving a heavy veneer of sand on the slopes now
exposed. Below the Algonquin beaches at elevations varying from
thirty-five to forty-five feet above Lakes Michigan and Huron, is
another well defined shore line, that of Lake Nipissing. It stands
below the level of Douglass and Black Lakes but is present around
Burt, Mullet, and Crooked Lakes, a short distance back from the
shores and at elevations varying from fifteen feet above Crooked
Lake to twenty-five feet above the Cheboygan River at Cheboygan.
Thus, with the sinking of the level of Lake Algonquin, Douglass and
Black Lakes become isolated basins while the lower part of the depression, in which the lakes of the "Inland Route" lie, was still submerged and separated a large island to the northwest from the
mainland. During Nipissing time the opening at Little Traverse
Bay was partially closed by a bar the sands of which have been
heaped into dunes, see Plate IV, A. These dunes rise gently on the
western sides to heights of one hundred thirty to one hundred
forty feet and then drop steeply on the eastern sides, showing
clearly the predominance of westerly winds. Near the shore of the
bay small dunes are now in process of formation and are migrating
eastward. Farther inland, however, the large dunes have been
clothed with vegetation which has prevented further movement.
This row of dunes forms the divide which forces the water to run
eastward into Lake Huron and is narrowest and lowest at Kegomic,
having a width of slightly more than one-fourth mile and a height
of thirty-four feet above Lake Michigan.

The recession of Lake Nipissing to the present Great Lakes level isolated a large inland lake which at first occupied all of the depression between the bar at the head of Little Traverse Bay and Cheboygan. Later it was divided by a bar at Indian River and then lowered to the present condition as the Cheboygan River deepened its channel. The variation in elevation in this part of the Cheboygan River drainage is very small, the total drop being less than twenty feet in thirty miles, and most of this occurs in the last mile of the river. The difference in elevation between Crooked and Mullet lakes is less than sixteen inches but this is in part due to a ponding of the water by a dam across the river at the mill of the Cheboygan Paper Co

CROOKED LAKE

Crooked lake is the western member of the "Inland Route" and is readily reached by the G R & I R R which skirts its northern shore The name is none too appropriate if applied to its outline, which is roughly triangular and is nearly divided by Oden Island slightly east of the center. The lake is shallow for the most part but contains a good sized basin which drops to sixty-one feet in depth west of the island.

The irregular basin of Crooked Lake lies in a trough which crosses the general trend of the morainic ridges having northwest-southeasterly trend The constriction in the outline caused by Cincinnati Point is due also to morainic material This persists as a submerged ridge across the lake, with a maximum depth of less than twelve feet, and is flanked by deeper water. A similar ridge but better developed almost divides the lake at Oden Island It seems probable, then, that the main depression existed before the last retreat of the glacier and may have been formed by a small lobe of ice which pushed through Little Traverse Bay. As the ice retreated, small morainic ridges were deposited across the trough and are largely submerged at the present time. The deep basin west of Oden Island was probably filled by a protected mass of ice which left this depression on melting The whole depression was later covered by the waters of Lakes Algonquin and Nipissing, which deposited a veneer of sand over the morainic material In fact, this sand covers the lowlands bordering the lake, and the till is exposed only where the sand has been removed along the headlands by wave action

Three former levels are easily recognized along the shores of Crooked Lake. The Algonquin and Nipissing lakes have already been mentioned and their shores are found at levels of seventy and

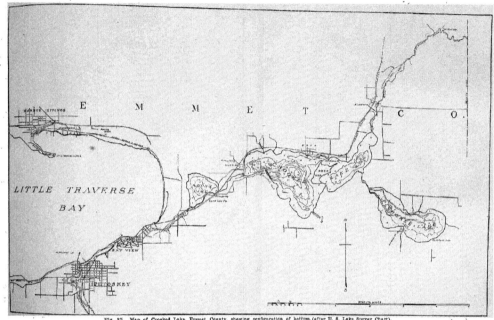

Fig. 35. Map of Crooked Lake, Emmet County, shewing configuration of bottom, (after U. S. Lake Survey Chart).

A. SAND DUNES, LITTLE TRAVERSE BAY, ROUND LAKE IN FOREGROUND.

B. MARL BED, STURGEON RIVER NEAR BURT LAKE.

fourteen feet respectively above the present level. The third level occurs between four and five feet above the present and is but moderately developed, in places dropping out entirely. The faintness of the shore lines of this Post-Nipissing level may be due in part to the greatly reduced size of the lake and the consequent weakened shore action, but also to the fact that this level was maintained for a short period of time. The drop to the present level was due to the cutting down of the outlet, which runs through loose sands and therefore worked rapidly.

The shore adjustments of this lake are interesting and have taken place largely at the lower levels. Much work was done during the Post-Nipissing stage but adjustments are still taking place that will make important changes in the lake if allowed to continue. These may best be appreciated by a description of the shores in the order of a traverse.

Conway, situated at the west end of the lake, see Fig 35, lies on a sand flat but slightly above the level of the lake. This flat is interrupted by a shallow, swampy trench through which the outlet of Round Lake reaches Crooked. The beach at this end is of sand and the lake bottom slopes gently outward, making an excellent and safe bathing beach. South of the outlet of Round Lake, the land slopes gradually upward to the Nipissing beach which follows the lake shore to Cincinnati Point. Along this shore the Nipissing terrace is well developed at an elevation of fourteen feet above the lake, averaging about one hundred yards in width, and above this an abrupt cliff fifty to fifty-five feet in height rises to the Algonquin terrace. The beach is of clear sand and even in contour except where littered with drift wood. The material of this beach is working eastward and is being deposited in a spit attached to the west side of Cincinnati Point.

The point is caused by a till knoll which stood as an island at the beginning of the Post-Nipissing stage but was connected with the mainland by a bar along the western side behind which was a lagoon. This bar now stands from eight to one hundred feet back from the beach. Inasmuch as the present wave action on the east side of the point is slight, in place of a bar a terrace is found. Along this side the ice has pushed a strong rampart where shore conditions were favorable. It is especially noticeable at the end of the point and near the mainland, but fails between these places. East of Cincinnati Point the Nipissing terrace is narrow, but of sufficient width to allow the building of a wagon road. Above this terrace a steep cliff, fifty feet high, rises to the Algonquin terrace

which ends in a well defined shore line one hundred or more yards
to the south Along the present shore there is no indication of the
Post-Nipissing level and the beach is of coarse material as far as
the blunt swell which marks the southeastern limit of the point
Here the Nipissing terrace widens and slopes gently to the shore

The bay beyond Cincinnati Point is caused by a long, narrow,
swamp which swings back towards Round Lake Beginning on the
point and extending about one-third the distance around the bay is
a continuous rampart which reaches a height of six feet in places
and was formed during the Post-Nipissing stage Near its southeastern extremity it encloses a lagoon, indicating that both currents and ice have been active in its formation The bay terminates
in a broad point which is lined with a beach of coarse material, an
indication that the material is still covered with sand Along this
point the ice has pushed up a rampart which continues around the
southern end of the lake as the most prominent shore feature as far
as the Minnehaha River North of the river the land is low and
flat but not swampy The rampart is present, but poorly developed
along this shore A short distance inland a faint terrace and shore
of the Post-Nipissing stage can be distinguished Shore action
has been slight here, in spite of the fact that the waves which
strike this shore have the longest reach on the lake and are driven
by the strongest winds The explanation is that the off-shore
slope is very gentle around the entire southern end of the lake and
the force of the waves is largely dissipated before they reach the
shore. The adjustment is not complete, however, because currents
are actively transporting the shore material northward and have
built a spit more than one hundred yards in length opposite Oden
Island This spit extends outward under water and meets a long
slender spit which has grown from the southeastern end of the
island The opening between the island and the mainland, which
was originally more than one-fourth mile in width, is now less than
two hundred feet and is so shallow that only boats of very
small draught can pass The two spits are not exactly in line at
present, the direction of that attached to the island being almost
due east They will eventually swing into line, and, once this is
accomplished, the tying of the island to the mainland to the south
will be a matter of a few years only

The till of the island is largely masked with sand, but an indication of its presence is found in the cobble beach along the south
shore This island was evidently a shoal during Nipissing time
but was partly above water during the Post-Nipissing stage At

this time most of the area was planed off to a sand terrace with the
exception of a small part near the south side. At the Post-Nipissing
stage the lake ice was very active on the small island and pushed
up a prominent rampart on all shores. Wave action has been
especially active on the west shore and to a lesser extent on the
south shore. This resulted in the transportation of the shore material around the north and south ends and its deposition in the
form of spits, of which the one at the southeast corner has already
been described. The counterpart of this spit occurs on the northwest corner and is actively growing at the present time. It has extended some distance beyond the original shore of the island and
encloses a lagoon to the east. The outline of the tip of this spit as
shown in Fig. 36, presents a sudden jog to the east. Undoubt-

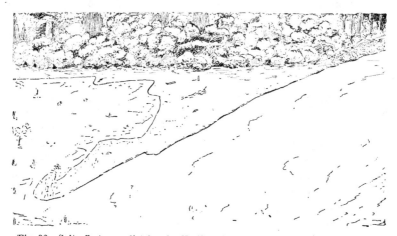

Fig. 36. Spit offset near distal end. Northwest end of Oden Island, Crooked Lake.

edly this jog represents a slight elevation of the level of the lake
or at least a holding up of the water to a more uniform level
throughout the year than it naturally would have. The only explanation the writer can offer is that the waters are ponded to some
extent and kept at a more constant level by the presence of the
dam at Cheboygan, which is but five feet lower than the level of
Crooked Lake. Unless the channel at this point is kept open artificially, the island will be tied to the mainland from this end as
well as the south. No data could be obtained concerning the
date of construction of the dam, and this is very unfortunate for,
with this at hand, some estimate of the time necessary for the completion of the bar might be made, if the interpretation of the break
in the outline of the spit is correct.

East of the island the shore is low and shows a faint beach of the Post-Nipissing level some distance back from the shore Wave action is slight here, but currents are set up which have formed a spit about one hundred feet long on the south side of the small bay into which the outlet of Pickerel Lake enters Beyond this bay the land rises to the Nipissing terrace which is rather wide and slopes gently toward the lake The beach is of sand which is being carried northward and deposited in a well developed hook at the somewhat prominent projection Along this hook the trees line the shore in places, and the roots are gradually being swept free from sand, which is added evidence of an abnormally high level for the lake Back of the hook just mentioned stands a lagoon which connects with the north end of the lake and is in process of filling by vegetation.

Crooked River, which discharges the water of this lake into Burt, is a very sluggish stream, having a drop of slightly more than six inches in over four miles The valley runs between the edges of the Nipissing terrace and gradually narrows until at Alanson it just allows the passage of the stream. This is the only place on the river where a road-crossing has been made Below Alanson the depression widens somewhat and the river expands into Hay Lake, now so filled with vegetation that it has been necessary to dredge a channel. Leaving Hay Lake the stream takes a straight course through a low sand flat, but suddenly begins to meander at the Devil's Elbow. This seems to be the highest place in the depression between Crooked and Burt lakes, and the banks correspond closely in elevation with the Post-Nipissing level as found on Crooked Lake It is evident from this that the drop to the present level is due to the cutting of the outlet through these sands. The stream with its present current could hardly have cut this channel, but at the higher level the gradient was somewhat steeper and there were no artificial obstructions in the drainage system

Returning to the lake, the north shore presents little of interest until Ponshewaing is reached Here the Post-Nipissing terrace is well shown, and upon this an ice rampart is found somewhat west of the point Currents from the west have been active along this shore, but the resulting forms are obscured by docks and "made ground" However, at Oden a well developed spit was formed at the Post-Nipissing level, running to the east and partially enclosing a narrow lagoon which has been dredged and is now used as a harbor for small boats The town of Oden is built on the Nipissing terrace, the front slope of which has been cut into low cliffs by the waves of the present lake   Farther to the west, this terrace is relatively narrow and the Algonquin terrace above is the more prominent   As the west end of the lake is approached, both terraces leave the lake and continue to the north side of Little Traverse Bay. Along this shore the terrace of the Post-Nipissing stage stretches from the foot of the Nipissing terrace to the beach and is wet and swampy.

From the description above it should be clear that Crooked Lake as an isolated basin has stood at a level some four feet higher than at present.   Considerable adjustment of the shores has taken place at the higher level and is still going on   A notable change that may be expected is the tying of the island to the mainland both at the southeast and northwest ends.   This will probably be accomplished first at the southeast and later will have to be prevented artificially at the northwest end of the island if the lake continues to be navigable to its western end.   The "drop off" is well defined on shores exposed to the storm winds, such as the west side of the island, the large embayment on the south shore, and the north shore near Oden   The depth at the "drop off" is approximately four feet, and in most places it is evident that the slope of the submerged terrace is very flat.   This depth seems very small for a lake of this size, and it is probable that this terrace is largely the result of wave and current action during the Post-Pipissing stage, at which time the depth over the terrace was double that at present.   This flat off-shore slope must greatly reduce the force of the waves, but complete adjustment has not been accomplished as yet   In the future, more is to be expected from deposition than from cutting, although the slight flooding of the lake has increased the latter   Ice action has been of some importance, and in several cases excellent ramparts have been formed   Yet, as a rule, the material and topography of the shores are not favorable for their development

As to the extinction of this lake, it is certain that it cannot be drained unless the level of Lake Huron is materially lowered   It stands 14 6 feet higher than Lake Huron and there are three "holes" which have greater depths than this.   Tributary streams are few and deposit little sediment, so this method of extinction may be considered of slight importance.   Filling by vegetation is of much greater importance.   In many places marl is being deposited, and beds of seventeen feet in thickness have been reported in the outlet south of Alanson.   In addition, heavy stands of reed grow each season on parts of the submerged terrace, particularly in the east arm and along the south shore where some protection from the waves is afforded, and aid the process of filling

BURT LAKE

The second member in this group of lakes is Burt Lake, which with an area of 26 5 square miles is one of the largest inland lakes of the State This lake is oblong in shape and extends north-south Its length is slightly less than ten miles and its width reaches about five miles, although the average is probably nearer three. See map, Fig 37 It is easily reached by the Michigan Central R R which crosses the outlet at the town of Indian River, situated on the outlet one-half mile from the lake

As far as known, no hard rock outcrops on the shores of this lake, the surrounding land being composed entirely of glacial deposits In general, it is flanked with moraines which run slightly oblique to the length of the lake One of these moraines, which causes Colonial Point on the west side, ends abruptly at the point, and irregular deposition of the morainic deposits on the east side has given rise to Greenman point near the head of the lake The north end of the lake heads in a swamp beyond which is the outwash plain extending to the east end of Douglass Lake On the west side, Crooked River enters the lake through a low sand plain and Indian River drains the lake through a similar depression at the south end The basin is consistently regular, usually reaching depths of forty to forty-five feet, but is somewhat deeper towards the south end Two exceptions to the evenness of the bottom are present A small pit east of Colonial Point which drops to more than seventy feet in depth, and a shallow depression near the south end fifteen to twenty feet below the general level This basin seems to lie in a depression between morainic ridges which on the west side especially are irregular in distribution and continuity, and were deposited by the ice from the Lake Huron basin The ice in this locality did little abrading, and this basin probably existed before the last retreat of the ice The complication of the morainic system makes it seem plausible that Burt Lake was filled with ice after the general ice front had retreated, and around parts of its borders outwash was deposited which now lies well above the lake level, e g, the outwash at the north end. The "holes" in the bottom of the basin may be due to exceptional thickness of the ice or may possibly be sink holes

Burt Lake, on account of its size, the excellent development of the Nipissing terrace and cliff, freedom from swampy shores, and

Fig. 37. Map showing outlines and configuration of the bottom of Burt and Mullet l
(After U. S. Lake Survey Chart.)

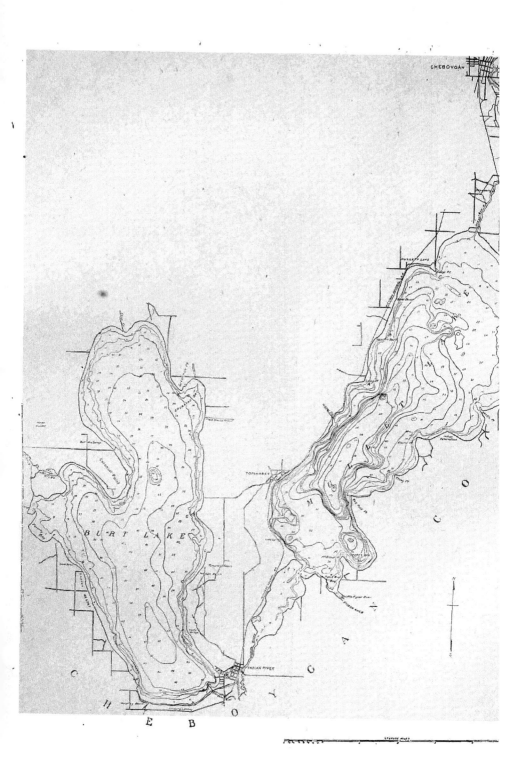

its accessibility shares the popularity of the lakes of the "Inland Route" as a place for recreation   At the present time the summer homes are largely near the south end of the lake and along the west shore south of Crooked River   These locations are near Indian River, the source of supplies, and along the route of the passenger service from Conway to Cheboygan.   There are abundant cottage sites all along the shores, and the writer confidently looks forward to a much greater development of this lake as a summer resort in the future

Indian River leaves the lake at the extreme southeastern corner and flows through the north side of a break in the upland which is about a mile in width and extends to Mullet Lake.   This rather broad channel is flanked on either side by the high cliffs of Lake Nipissing.   Its bed, where not trenched by Indian and Sturgeon Rivers, rises gradually to a sand bar which extends from cliff to cliff through the town of Indian River in a regular curve concave to the west   This bar grew from the west and practically separated the Burt and Mullet lake basins, forcing the outlet to the north On the gentle front slope of the bar are several minor beaches which were formed during the recession of Lake Nipissing and probably mark levels of short duration, since small terraces and cliffs at like elevations are found along the shores of Burt Lake   In the lagoons behind these small beaches swamp conditions prevailed, and beds of marl were laid down one of which is shown in Plate IV

Until thirty-five years ago, the Sturgeon River flowed behind this bar into the Indian River and choked the channel with its heavy deposits of sand   When the necessity of navigating Indian River arose, the results of this deposition were recognized and an artificial channel was dug which turned the waters of Sturgeon River directly into Burt Lake   Some idea of the amount of material deposited by the river may be obtained from the delta which has been built into Burt Lake since that time.   It projects fully three hundred yards beyond the general curve of the shore and at present has split the stream into two distributaries.   The west shore of the delta curves outward gently but the turn on the east is abrupt, showing that westerly currents prevail now as in former times   The delta extends outward under water a short distance only and drops rapidly from about ten feet to nearly twenty   The sub-aqueous terrace continues around the south and west sides of the lake to the vicinity of Saegers Resort, where it is much less definite, and disappears in the bay to the north

To the west of the delta the Nipissing terrace narrows, and the

cliffs which rise above it to a height of thirty-five feet gradually approach the shore. At Pittsburg Landing this terrace stands sixteen
feet above the present lake level and is wide enough to afford an
ideal location for cottages, see Plate V, A. The lake side of the
terrace in places merges into a lagoon and marks a level of the lake
between Nipissing and the present. This shore is exposed to the
northerly and northeasterly winds, and the effect of the waves of
long reach is seen a short distance to the west, where the Nipissing
terrace has been entirely removed and bare cliffs in excess of fifty
feet in height reach from the shore to the top of the Algonquin
terrace At Kingsley Beach the Nipissing terrace reappears with
moderate width and is backed by a low cliff rising to the Algonquin
terrace. This condition persists as far as Saegers with slight
variations in the width of the Nipissing terrace and the character
of the material of the present beach. For the most part, sand
beaches prevail, but at the Saw Mill and at Saegers where the
moraine comes to the shore the beach is strewn with boulders. The
low cliff between the present shore and the Nipissing terrace is,
as a rule, covered with grass, but in a few places fresh scars boldly
announce a renewal of wave work At Saegers it has been necessary to dump boulders along the shore to prevent the encroachment of the waves, in other places the cutting has not as yet obliterated a small terrace between the Nipissing and the present level.

Beyond Saegers the Nipissing terrace widens and slopes gently
to the lake Trees growing to the water's edge are being undermined by wave action and thrown over on the shore either by winds
or ice As the shore swings into Poverty Bay the prevailing currents leave the shore and have built a spit running into the bay.
This spit has grown at least one-hundred yards from the shore and
supports a row of trees on its surface Behind the spit is an excellent example of the filling of a lagoon by vegetation, mainly
rushes and cat-tails. Here again we find evidence of flooding, for
the outline of the spit has not the characteristically even contour
and is lined with tree roots partially excavated by the waves.

Around the bay, called by some Poverty Bay, the shores are low
and swampy, and show little wave action The bottom here is
muddy, and in the shallow water vegetation, protected from the
strong winds, is growing outward from the shore, giving practically
no beach. Crooked River has built a small delta into the bay but
at present is flowing through an artificial channel. At the head
of the bay, however, Maple River has built a large projection
through which it flows in a series of distributing channels It will

A. PITTSBURGH LANDING, BURT LAKE.

B. BOULDER-PAVED BANK, BURT LAKE.

be noted from the map, Fig. 37, that the branches of the river avoid the main part of the delta and now empty into small bays on either side This will result in the filling of these bays until the present channels become so clogged that further shifting is necessitated The even shore line of the bay northeast of Maple River is quite in contrast to that to the southwest, and examination shows that a low sand bar has developed from the east side of Colonial Point, extending to the mouth of the river and cutting off a part of the low swamp about its lower course

There is a sudden transition from the swamp of Maple River to the higher ground of Colonial Point This point is a morainic hill whose top was planed off during Algonquin time. The Nipissing terrace is very well developed along the point but becomes faint inland as it converges from the shores to the northwest. It was impossible to trace the shore completely around the hill, but from the elevation of the land to the northwest it is safe to conclude that this point was a peninsula with a very narrow neck, or possibly a land-tied island in Lake Nipissing. The terrace is wider at the end of the point than at the sides, due to protection on the west side and excessive wave action on the northeast which has removed part of this terrace since Nipissing time A Post-Nipissing terrace is well preserved on the bay side, forming a low, swampy zone next the shore which never exceeds twenty feet in width.

Off the end of the point and continuing northward the subaqueous terrace is narrow and the "drop-off" sudden at about ten feet. This continues, but gradually widens and loses its identity towards the north end of the lake The shore features on the east side of Colonial Point are rather uniform, consisting of a well-developed but narrow Nipissing terrace the outer edge of which has been cut into low cliffs by waves at the present level, and a beach of coarse material, residual from the disintegration of the till One interesting exception occurs at the small projection on the east side of the point near the end. At this place the Nipissing shore recedes from the present shore a distance of two-hundred fifty yards in a slight indentation into which the currents are able to swing However, at one of the lower intermediate levels the currents left the shore and built a bar across the head of this bay, enclosing a shallow lagoon which is now dry and supports a growth of large trees This bar may be recognized on the present beach by the change from the coarse material to sand.

North of Colonial Point the low ground which runs southwestward to the Maple River swamp comes to the shore. The trees grow

11

to the water's edge and are being washed away at high water, giving alternate stretches of partly excavated tree roots and sandy beaches This low tract is somewhat over a mile in width and gives way to morainic hills on whose slopes the features are so similar to those found on the east side of Colonial Point as to need no further description Near the north end of the lake the cliffs leave the shore which is then bordered by a swamp through which Carp Creek runs The contour of the sand beach has a scalloped effect, due to the prominent delta built by Carp Creek. Currents are active here, coming from opposite directions in each re-entrant, but have not developed distinguishable bars at the present shore. It is possible that bars may have been built at higher levels, but the nature of the swamp and the heavy undergrowth makes their determination an uncertain task under the conditions

On the east side of the lake the swamp gradually narrows and is replaced by a morainic ridge of hard, red till, running slightly east of south and ending abruptly at Greenman Point Along this shore the Nipissing level is represented by a prominent cliff but the terrace is narrow and steep, indicating a small amount of wave action during Nipissing time This is to be expected from the location of the shore which precludes the possibility of waves of long reach striking it except at a very oblique angle The present beach contains much coarse material which is quite generally pushed up above the strand, and in places patches of ice ramparts are to be seen, best developed at Greenman Point. Evidence of ice action is not common on the shores of this lake, and its presence on the northeast shore leads to the conclusion that ice jams are the cause of the shove rather than expansion In addition, the size of the lake is in excess of the maximum on which expansion is considered to be effective

At the end of Greenman Point an interesting hook discloses considerable current action along this shore The hook, a sketch of which is given in Fig 38, rounds the point and doubles back on itself almost parallel to the main shore, extending well into Bourassau Bay and enclosing part of the swamp into which this bay heads The material is finely graded from cobbles four to five inches in diameter near its land connection to fine sand at its end, and has been supplied entirely from the cliffs to the north The weak currents moving south are unable to cross the broad entrance to the bay and deposit material which is subsequently worked into the bay by the strong southwesterly winds At the head of the bay the only effect at present of wave or current action is the under-

mining of trees which grow to the water's edge, and this is probably
due to a recent elevation of the water level. On the east side of the
bay, however, material from the south is being worked into the bay
by southwesterly winds, here the most powerful on account of
reach, forming a sand beach.

Fig. 38.   Hook at Greenman Point, Burt Lake.

South of the bay the moraine approaches the lake and for a short
distance has the characteristic profile of this region,—a flat terrace
surface at the top referred to Algonquin time, a cliff and terrace of
Nipissing stage below this, and the final descent to the lake which
may be notched in places by the Post-Nipissing terrace (see Fig. 39).

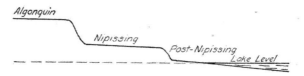

Fig. 39.   Diagrammatic profile of the exposed terraces of Burt Lake.

For a distance of about a mile the Nipissing terrace is narrow and
steep but then widens considerably beginning at the point below
Fresh Breeze Resort. Along the present shore coarse material on
the beach occurs almost uniformly and occasionally numbers of
boulders are found. The boulders invariably stand high on the
beach and in some cases have been forced back into the clay cliff.
This indicates strong ice push, but conditions are not favorable for

the formation of definite ramparts The small point about midway
between the ends of the lake, A on map, is an almost isolated mor-
rainic hill which may have been an island during Nipissing time
since the main cliff runs back of it It is virtually lined with
boulders, large and small, which are shoved up into a wall See
Plate V It is possible that some of these have been cleared from
the adjoining farm and dumped here, but the regularity of the
wall and the presence of drift logs four and five feet above the
present level shows clearly that ice push is intense at this point.
The Nipissing terrace here is relatively wide and strewn with
boulders. This shows that the action of the waves was strong in
this locality during Nipissing time, and the terrace is cut rather
than built A glance at the map shows that the strong northwesterly winds have considerable reach here and that the direction of
the shore is favorable for heavy pounding by the waves and for
efficient current action to remove the disintegrated material. South
of the point the land is low and was covered during Nipissing time.
Three definite bars below the Nipissing level were found in this
swampy depression, each of which cuts off a crescent shaped lagoon
The lower one was formed at the present level, but the remaining
two stand higher and mark levels intermediate between the
Nipissing and present The material in these bars was derived from the north and was distributed as far as the point just
north of Tuscarora Beach. The present shore at this point shows a
hook-like form which is being built largely from the south. In
reality, this form is being built more after the fashion of V-shaped
embankments, for material is supplied both from the north and
the south, although there is no enclosed depression The currents
from the south are the stronger and the hook is consequently turned
to the north The point itself is caused by the projection of bouldery drift, some of which has been pushed northward into a spit of
coarse material at a level above the present From the size of the
boulders this evidently has been formed largely through the push of
drifting ice blocks See Long Lake, Alpena County, for similar
forms South of the point the waves are actively cutting the Nipissing terrace and have formed a low, freshly cut cliff from which the
material of the hook is derived Along Tuscarora and Wautan
beaches the waves are cutting the outer edge of the Nipissing terrace, in places exposing the boulder clay. The terrace here has,
therefore, been cut Large boulders have been lined on the beach
by ice, but their paths on the lake side are obliterated.

South of Wautan Beach the Nipissing shore continues almost

south instead of following the present shore, and the terrace widens to some extent. At the somewhat prominent projection about one mile south of Wautan Beach, both the shore and the outside edge of the terrace of the Nipissing stage are back some distance from the shore, the intervening area being swamp except at the somewhat higher ground of the point. North of the point this swamp is cut off from the lake by a complete bar at the present level, but to the south two definite bars are to be found at the Post-Nipissing level during which stage the point, then an island, was connected to the mainland. From this point to the outlet the slopes have the characteristic profile, and the shores are lined with the coarse material commonly present where waves have cut into boulder clay One place of interest is a narrow swampy area a short distance north of the outlet, lying adjacent to the shore and backed by a low cliff rising to the Nipissing terrace which is here poorly developed. This swampy area may be a terrace of the Post-Nipissing level but, if so, indicates considerable wave action at this point. The poor development of the Nipissing terrace here seems to show slight wave action, and the swamp is more likely the bottom of Lake Nipissing beyond the zone of wave action

From the above description it will be seen that the physiographic features of Burt Lake are comparatively uniform, so much so, that their description is somewhat monotonous Shore adjustments, past and present, have been few and consistent for the most part in the development of a cut and built terrace bordered with cliffs, and a limited amount of deposition. The most notable changes occurred during Nipissing time when the basins were cut off from the main lake and partially isolated. The change from Nipissing to the present level was accomplished slowly and with at least two intermediate levels, as shown by beaches and by slopes notched by wave action. The dropping in level was due to the cutting down of the Cheboygan River which varied in rate, due probably to variations in the constitution of the material of the moraine near Cheboygan. A closer packing of the till or heavy accumulation of boulders in the channel would hold up the waters for a time, but, with their removal accomplished, the downward cutting would be renewed.

The intermediate Post-Nipissing levels were of short duration and little work was done The cliffs and terraces are faint where present and for the most part have been entirely removed by wave action during the present stage. In general, deposition was active in the past in the same localities as at present, but no important

reduction in the size of the lake was accomplished by the development of bars across indentations In fact, under the present conditions it is unlikely that any great changes in outline due to this
cause will occur, except possibly at Greenman Point. Here the
southerly winds seem to be able to distribute the material brought
along the point, and the bay may be filled but not cut off The
only other large point, Colonial, is being attacked by the waves
Possibly the greatest development will be the delta of the Maple
River which may fill the bay into which it flows. This depends
largely on the rate of deposition, for it seems likely that this stream
will be abandoned as an outlet of Douglass Lake (see description
of this lake).

Wave action has predominated on this lake and the terraces
are the prominent features on the slopes facing the shore In some
cases the Nipissing terrace is complete but, for the most part,
has been cut into at lower levels. Under existing conditions, wave
action is also the prominent agent, and a relatively narrow terrace
and "drop off" is present, especially well developed along the sides
and at the south end The depth of water at its outside edge is
between ten and eleven feet and this is much less than the wave base
for this lake, which reaches a depth of at least thirty feet In this
case the submerged terrace has been formed mainly at the present
level and indicates that the depth at which effective transportation of sand ceases is about one-third of the wave length during the
greatest storms

Burt Lake, on account of its size, depth, regular outline, and
slight elevation above Lake Huron will become extinct very slowly
Filling by vegetation, although in progress, is not effective due
mainly to the lack of protected shores It is most active in the
bay west of Colonial Point and in Bourasau Bay on the east side
Both of these bays support a heavy growth of rushes during the
summer, and in the former marl covers much of the bottom. Considerable sediment is brought to the lake by streams but they
supply only the minor part of the water of this lake. The presence of extended areas of sand in this locality increases the importance of ground water over surface drainage, and much of the
water is supplied from this source In fact, there are but three
streams of any importance which enter the lake—Sturgeon, Maple,
and Carp—and of these Maple River may possibly be abandoned.
There is the possibility that these streams will develop and drain
much larger basins in the future, and make sedimentation a factor
of importance. Deepening of the outlet at the present time is at

a stand-still, due to human interference, and it seems probable that this will continue indefinitely However, ignoring the human side and assuming that no obstruction will be present in the outlet, the amount of draining must necessarily be limited by the level of Lake Huron, whose present level is but fourteen feet lower than Burt Lake Lowering of Burt Lake by fourteen feet would decrease its depth more than one-third, but the reduction in area would be relatively slight Still, the shores would be much lower than at present and the muds of the present bottom would afford excellent conditions for a heavy and rapid growth of vegetation Another possibility lies in the fact that the land is here rising very slowly, and the consequent dropping in the level of the Great Lakes would allow complete drainage of the lakes of the "Inland Route," provided the uplift continues for a long enough period of time

MULLET LAKE

A short distance east of Burt Lake and connected with it by the Indian River lies Mullet Lake, see map, Figure 37 These two lakes are very similar in shape and size, the greatest difference being in the orientation. Disregarding the extinct arm at the southwest end, Mullet Lake is almost identical in length with Burt Lake, and the average width and size, 26 8 square miles are not materially different. The outline of the shores shows considerable irregularity especially on the southeast side The points for the most part run directly out into the lake and have about the same general direction as Colonial Point and the northeast shore of Burt Lake

The surrounding country stands well above the lake and has a somewhat northwest-southeast trend, although this is none too apparent. Across this topography the deep basin of the lake extends as a part of the peculiar depression in which the "Inland Route" lakes lie Curiously, the deepest part of Mullet Lake is situated in the constricted central portion, whereas the broad expanse at the north end is relatively shallow. Northeast of a line connecting Dodge and Needle points, the water rarely exceeds thirty feet in depth and is, furthermore, marked by several shoals more or less in line with these two points The drop to deep water is gradual towards the southwest until a deep trough which runs along the narrow part of the lake is reached This trough is in excess of one-hundred feet deep throughout and extends southwestward to a steep upward slope which follows a sinuous course northwesterly from McArthur Point It is well defined and is bounded by steep slopes on all but the northeast side. Several "holes" exist in the bottom of the lake, the deepest lying off Long Point and reaching a depth of one hundred forty-five feet Another is Scotts Bay which drops to more than eighty-five feet

The origin of the depression in which this chain of lakes lies has been discussed at the beginning of this chapter and in Chapter I. The pecularities of the shore line and the bed of the lake are explained by the distribution of the glacial formations The last ice sheet covered this lake from the northeast and retreated in the same direction. The main depression was in existence previous to the advance of the ice and caused a local advance of the ice front As the ice retreated over this country its front halted in the vicinity of Red Pine Point, building a moraine The ice still filled the lake basin at this time, therefore the moraines do not cross the lake. On the west side of the lake, clay hills are present which are in line with Red Pine Point and the morainic ridge near the northeast end of Burt Lake, making it probable that this line marks a position of the ice front. In width the moraine reaches to Round Point and thus accounts for the narrow central part of the lake. This moraine is not of the distinct knob and basin type for it was deposited under the waters of a lake which washed the ice front and, therefore, shows much less relief Furthermore, it was covered by Lake Algonquin, and, in addition to the planing off of the hilltops, a veneer of sand or clay, depending on the proximity to the shore, was deposited over much of this territory This moraine is traced with difficulty and some doubt may be expressed as to the correctness of the interpretation given above It may be that a stagnant block of ice occupied the deep trough of the lake, but at any rate, its border stood at one time at the steep slope running northwestward from McArthur Point. Two moraines also cross the course of the Cheboygan River, running in the same northwest-southeasterly direction. The first moraine crosses the river soon after leaving the lake and is bordered by an outwash plain which extends to the southwest and accounts for the shallow lower end of the lake. The Black River flows between this moraine and a narrow ridge in the vicinity of Cheboygan.

Upon leaving Burt Lake via Indian River, the amount of artificial control of the stream is somewhat surprising and bears strong evidence of the popularity of these lakes as summer resorts, for the main traffic through them is by resorters and tourists. The long piers, the dredged channel, and the diversion of the Sturgeon River into Burt Lake from Indian River are readily explained when it is realized that the drop from Burt Lake to Mullet is less than one

foot, most of which occurs in the first mile and a half. Also, the
valley spreads to a width of more than one-half mile south of
Indian River and becomes a swampy mud-flat through which Indian
River meanders. The stream was unable to keep a channel open at
its mouth and in its lower course, which was undoubtedly a shallow arm of Mullet Lake now filled by the silt carried down by
Sturgeon River before its diversion.

At the entrance to Mullet Lake proper a striking shore feature
presents itself on the west side. Currents swinging along this shore
from the north have deposited their load of sand in a long, narrow
spit which extends fully half way across the opening. At the end
it turns back abruptly, and many of the trees which line it stand
in water. These facts indicate an accident in the history of the
lake,—the artificial raising of the water level by a dam at Cheboygan. Under normal conditions the spit would have continued
straight across the indentation, forcing Indian River to the extreme south side. Under the present conditions the spit must become adjusted to the higher level, and the probable course of events
will be a slow increase in the irregularity of its contour until the
trees are removed. Then the work will proceed more rapidly, and
the bar be re-formed farther back in the swamp, probably in line
with the sharp point on the opposite bank, as indicated by the direction of the hook. Mullet Lake illustrates excellently the renewal of activity on lakes whose level has been raised, and further
evidence may be found within sight of the bar in the freshly cut
cliff to the west which is pounded by the waves driven by the powerful north and northeasterly winds

Along this shore the rolling topography is covered with sand,
but, where sections are exposed, boulder clay, or till, is usually exposed underneath. The till is seen on the cliffs and is much more
resistant to wave action than the sand which comes to the shore in
the depressions, giving rise to small projections of the shore, as at
Cold Springs. The cobbles and boulders of the beach, indicate
till from which the finer particles have been removed. North of
Cold Springs a depression extended below lake level and has not
only been isolated by a bar but filled. Across this extinct lagoon
the Michigan Central R. R has built an embankment The raised
water level is very evident on this shore from the presence of great
quantities of driftwood and from the trees whose roots are washed
by the waves

Near Topinabee, however, the slopes of the main depression in
which this lake lies approach the shore, and the banks are some-

what higher The slopes are composed of till and much coarse material is found on the beach, which has been pushed into a feeble
rampart or lined along the shore by ice action. Topinabee is one
of the important resorts of the lakes of the "Inland Route" and
there is a geographic reason for this Along the shore are found
a series of terraces and cliffs which mark the higher levels at which
the lake formerly stood. The diagram of the terraces on Burt
Lake, Fig '39, will perhaps give an adequate idea of the relations
of these terraces Next the shore a low cliff is found locally which
is receding into a terrace about four feet above the present level.
This terrace reaches a width of fifty feet at Topinabee and is
flanked on the land side by a low grass-covered slope, the bottom
of which marks the shore line at the time when the lake stood at
this level Above this cliff is a much wider terrace which gradually
rises to a height of sixteen to seventeen feet above the lake and
ends abruptly in a steep cliff more than forty feet high. This cliff
and terrace were formed by Lake Nipissing and are continuous
with those found at approximately the same level on Burt and
Crooked lakes. Near the top of the high cliff is a slight notch, indicating a level of short duration Above this stands a broad terrace upon which much of the town is built The highest terrace
terminates at the base of a cliff and was formed by the waves of
Lake Algonquin Quite generally the terraces are sandy, the result of the action of the undertow, and the cliffs are in clay and
stand at a steep angle The sandy character and the nearly level
surface of the terraces insures dryness and affords excellent locations for buildings. The Nipissing terrace is the usual choice of
location for summer homes, on account of its proximity to the
lake and the excellent water supply derived from flowing wells
Another factor is that the railroad has taken advantage of this
level strip which persists the entire length of the lake, making the
resorts readily accessible

Such are the terraces that practically surround Mullet Lake and
much of the interest from our viewpoint centers around them As
already stated, the Algonquin and Nipissing shores are continuous
around Burt and Mullet lakes, the former standing well back and
above the present lake That is to say, there was a continuous body
of water in this region, and the tracing of its shores with their
varied topographic forms is a profitable and pleasing study. The
level below the Nipissing, which we shall call the Post-Nipissing
stage, stands at about the same level as on Burt Lake, four feet
above the present, but the lakes were probably separated by a bar

A. NIGGER CREEK, MULLETT LAKE.

B. STONEY POINT, MULLETT LAKE. a, NIPISSING TERRACE, b, ICE
RAMPART, c, POST-NIPISSING TERRACE.

at Indian River   The Post-Nipissing stage was of relatively short duration and the terraces are narrow or absent except at the ends of the lake   The absence of this terrace in many places indicates that it has been destroyed during the succeeding stages

Northeast of Topinabee the Post-Nipissing terrace widens and is followed by the railroad. It slopes gently to the water's edge where the trees are washed by the waves   The inefficiency of the waves here is due to the protection afforded by the vegetation and the lee position of the shore with reference to the prevailing strong winds. Conditions soon change, and south of Nigger Creek the Post-Nipissing terrace has been entirely removed   In its place is a cliff in the outer edge of the Nipissing terrace. The section afforded by this cliff shows till covered by stratified sand and furnishes the key to the nature of the terrace. At first waves were active and carved a cut terrace but, as the cutting advanced landward, more and more of the outer portion of the terrace came into the zone of deposition by the undertow, hence the covering of sand   Beyond the cliff the Nipissing terrace recedes from the shore, following the depression in which Nigger Creek flows, and a narrow terrace of the Post-Nipissing stage is present at the shore   Currents are active at the entrance of Nigger Creek and have built spits from both sides at the present level. The spit on the north side is the better developed and has forced the stream to make a sharp bend to the south before entering the lake. Near the lake, Nigger Creek is an almost stagnant pool, Plate VI, A, which is being filled with hydrophytic (water loving) vegetation, through which stand trees with submerged bases   This condition is due to the raised water-level and will soon kill the trees, making this an unattractive, mosquito-breeding swamp   For about a quarter of a mile north of Nigger Creek the railroad embankment interrupts the natural contour of the shore but runs farther inland at the blunt point beyond.

Along this point the greater efficiency of the northerly winds is again apparent. On the southern side of the point the Nipissing cliff is perhaps a thousand feet from the shore, the intervening space being occupied by both the Nipissing and Post-Nipissing terraces   Along the present shore a well-developed rampart has been pushed up by the ice to a height of four feet, one of the strongest on this lake. The northeast side of the point is quite in contrast to this, for the waves have reduced the low terrace and are actively cutting into the Nipissing, exposing fresh cliffs of boulder clay. In the bay between this point and Long Point, both the Nipissing and Post-Nipissing terraces are present and are relatively wide. A railroad embankment obscures the conditions along the present shore but this wide indentation probably was never cut off by a bar. Near Long Point a small ice rampart indicates a moderate amount of ice push.

Long Point is interesting in that it is a region where wave action has been excessive with practically no evidence of deposition except on the sub-aqueous terrace. The Nipissing and Post-Nipissing terraces are present on both sides and contrary to expectation, are better developed on the north side. Combined they reach a width of more than one-fourth mile, but off-shore is a submerged terrace of almost double this width. The submerged terrace is well defined all along the northeast shore facing the deepest portion of the lake and drops off at about twelve feet, slightly lower than in Burt Lake. Both lakes are similar in size and shape and the greater depth of the "drop-off" in Mullett is to be ascribed to a greater rise in the water level than to any considerable difference in the force of the erosive agents. This is also shown by more active cutting on the present shores of Mullet.

From Long Point to Dodge Point the shore is comparatively straight with the exception of a shallow indentation south of Hiawatha Beach. Conditions are very uniform along this stretch, the features consisting of the Nipissing and Post-Nipissing terraces which are relatively constant in width and extend more than a quarter of a mile back from the shore as a rule. The blunt point near Hiawatha Beach is an exception. Here a hill of resistant material has increased the work of the waves, and, although the terraces, exposed and submerged, are well developed, the projection of the shore line reflects the difficulties encountered. For a similar reason the shore projects slightly at Silver Beach but, in this case, the cause is an accumulation of large boulders. For the most part the shores are sandy but are often obscured by driftwood and vegetation growing in the water. In a low cliff below Hiawatha Beach and at other places along the low shore where trees have been uprooted, accumulations of marl are present, furnishing a hint as to one method by which the lake is being filled. Ice action is effective along the shore and has piled up ramparts at various places, notably near Hiawatha Beach. Even on the low sandy shores small ramparts are found, but always where vegetation acts as a binder.

The shores are somewhat higher and the beach is of clear sand along the sharp bend in the shore line towards Dodge Point. Favorable shore conditions and the protection from storm winds

afforded by the point make this an ideal location for the summer
resort of Mullet Lake. Also the topography of the point is such
that it is not necessary for the railroad to follow the shore, and
the inconvenience of the tracks and danger of accidents is partially eliminated. One of the landmarks of this part of the lake is the
sharp knoll above the point crowned with a clump of pines which
are elsewhere lacking. The Nispissing terrace surrounds this hill on
all sides except the northwest, where the island rises just enough
to make it uncertain as to whether this height was an island or
a narrow-necked peninsula at that time. By using this sag, the
railroad is able to keep its tracks straight and at the same time
follow the terrace. On the lake side, the knoll was cut into
a steep cliff at the foot of which lie quantities of coarse beach material. The beach pebbles have been quarried to some extent but
their use was not ascertained. The Nipissing terrace is broad
and near the lake is sandy, furnishing excellent sites for the buildings of this deservedly popular summer resort. The Post-Nipissing level is here represented by a terrace which does not exceed
fifteen feet in width and whose edge is pushed up into an ice rampart at the tip of the point. Little, if any, deposition by currents
is to be found here.

Beyond Dodge Point, the Nipissing terrace fringes the hills
which run to the northwest and is narrow, but the Post-Nipissing
terrace widens and extends around the foot of the lake. This lower terrace stretches along the course of the Cheboygan River in
a V—and ends in a low outwash plain immediately in front of a
narrow moraine, the hilltops of which were bevelled by the waves
of Lake Nipissing. The evidence of this is to be seen in the river
banks where stratified sandy material gives way to hard clay cliffs
about sixteen feet high before Strawberry Island is reached.

The shores on either side of the outlet are low and sandy but,
except for local patches, are covered with drowned vegetation which
offers passive resistance to the onslaught of the waves. This is
well illustrated along the shore in one locality between Dodge
Point and the outlet where the vegetation has been cleared from
the shore. The result, shown in Fig 40, has been a recession of
the shore line of forty to fifty feet but unfortunately the time during which this was accomplished was not learned. From this we
can realize what may be expected from wave action when the trees
bordering the shores are killed and removed.

The Post-Nipissing terrace narrows after leaving the outlet
and becomes a narrow strip of variable width along the north-
south trending shore of the east side, as far as Needle Point. Its

width varies with the topography, widening in the depressions
and narrowing at the points, and is always flanked by the Nipissing terrace which developed to a much greater extent on this shore
than on the opposite side of the lake. This is due to some extent
to the flatter topography on the east but also to the exposure to
storm winds from northerly and westerly directions. This development of the Nipissing terrace is well shown north of Aloha
where its width reaches nearly one mile. Beneath the lake in this
shallow portion the submerged terrace is poorly developed, and
from Dodge Point to beyond Needle Point the bottom slopes gradually to moderate depths. Along this same shore, adjustments by
both waves and currents are slight. The broad terraces are sand
covered and often are composed entirely of this material on the

Fig. 40. Recession of a flooded shore line due to removal of vegetation, Mullett Lake.

outer or built portions. Consequently, they are easily removed
by the waves and the shore is generally receding except where
held up by vegetation. In fact, the recession of the shore is greatly retarded here both by trees still standing and large quantities
of driftwood which line long stretches of the beach. The projections of the shore line are slight and blunt, and are due to irregularities in the original topography rather than to differences in the
resistance of the material. One exception to this statement occurs
at Point A, on the west side of Mullet Lake, see map, Fig. 37, which
is lined with boulders and is probably composed of till.

As in the case of the Michigan Central, on the west side the
Detroit and Mackinaw R. R. uses the terraces for its roadbed as
far as Aloha. This town is favorably located for resort purposes

but is more exposed to storms than locations on the west side of the lake.

From Needle Point on, the irregularities of surface and differences in resistence of the material cause a much more broken shore line, in fact a narrowing of the lake. It is probable that a moraine, laid under water and later covered by Lake Algonquin, crosses or runs to the lake shores here. Needle Point is composed of compact boulder clay which in itself is resistent to erosion and also furnishes many boulders to act as a breakwater. It was formerly less sharp and extended about eight hundred feet farther out into the lake. The contrast between the north and south sides of the point, in accordance with practically all similar features of the lake, illustrates very strikingly the importance of storm winds, here northerly, in the erosion of the shores. The north side is rapidly being worn back and for a short distance near the tip a storm beach has been piled up, enclosing a narrow lagoon. The tip of the point is kept sharp by the recession of the north side, and directly in line with it is a small island which was formerly a part of this point. This is clearly a remnant or outlier and was never a land-tied island, for the remnant of the connection is now a submerged boulder ridge. On the south side of the point evidence of cutting at present is not to be found, but instead the beach is of even contour and composed of assorted material which decreases in size with distance from the point, its source. The bay southwest of Needle Point is bounded by swamp and the shores lined with driftwood, stumps, and standing trees. The beach, where not obscured, is of sand but no indications of a bar were found.

The broad projection culminating in Round Point is due to hills of resistant clay in proximity to the shore. At the Indian Reservation the Post-Nipissing terrace is obliterated and the waves are now cutting into the Nipissing terrace, exposing boulder clay in a cliff eight to ten feet high. A sandy depression to the west accounts for the smooth beach of wave-worked material which soon gives way to a knob rising sixty feet above the lake. This hill is flanked by the cliffs and terrace of the Nipissing stage on all but its landward side and was an island at that time separated from the mainland by a shallow strait, almost duplicating the hill at Mullet Lake Station. On its northern exposure, wave action is excessive and is cutting a cliff in the Nipissing terrace. The tip of the point is low and is a triangular remnant of the Post-Nipissing terrace. It does not show the wear that takes place on either side, and probable some deposition took place here when the lake level stood lower than at present   Ice action has formed a small rampart on the tip.

Along the shore between Round and Stoney points, the Nipissing terrace is again in evidence and the adjustment of the shore is broken only by one minor point of boulders   The Nipissing cliff rises to the high Algonquin terrace a few rods back of the shore. Stoney Point is merely a repetition on a smaller scale of the majority of the points on the lake. The clay of the Nipissing terrace is cut into a cliff six to eight feet high on the north side, but around the point there is little wave action, leaving intact both of the lower terraces   However, the end of the point shows the relations of the different levels so well that a photograph is reproduced in Plate VI, B   Note the beach of coarse material with many large boulders and the till cliff of varying height   Near the end of the point (center of view) the cut terrace of the Post-Nipissing level is present and has been cut into a low cliff by the waves at the present level.   This ends abruptly at the left in an ice rampart which contains many large boulders and was formed during the Post-Nipissing stage.   Beyond the rampart is the surface of the Nipissing terrace, here in the cut portion

The bay between Stoney and Red Pine points almost exactly repeats the conditions for the bay north of Stoney Point and need not be described. Red Pine Point, however, is an extended morainic hill which compares favorably in height and is in line with the highland extending beyond Topinabee towards the northeast end of Burt Lake. This is probably an extension of a moraine but did not continue across the lake basin. It is heavily wooded and is altogether one of the finest locations on the lake. It is one of the few points that show any tendency towards growth from current action. At the present level a small spit is extending to the northwest but apparently very slowly   The position of the drop-off gives us some idea of what has gone on in the very recent past and shows a much greater deposition than at present. The growth of the spit to the northwest is unique for this lake and requires explanation.   The wind directions which may affect this point are about equally divided between the two sides, but in violence those from the northerly quadrant are the more important. Yet the force of the waves tossed by these winds is lessened by their passage across the gradually shoaling bottom, but on the southwest side the submerged terrace is narrow and the waves strike the shore with but slightly diminished intensity. Also the regular shore to the southwest with its nearly continuous cliffs furnishes abundant material and allows the development of a far more efficient current than is possible on the irregular, low shore north of the point

The end of the point is the key to the events that have happened here. A fragment of the Post-Nipissing terrace is present whose cliff has been pushed into an ice rampart. Landward from this there is the distinct Nipissing terrace of moderate development On this terrace, closely paralleling the ice rampart, is a strong bar which runs to the southeast, gradually crossing the terrace and merging into the Nipissing cliff. The cliff at the present level on the north side of the point cuts the bar at a sharp angle, furnishing an excellent cross section from which the relations are easily seen. The southeastern side has therefore been a point of departure of currents since the point has existed as such The Nipissing terrace is narrow but distinct along this shore, and the cliff above it rises steeply to remnants of the Algonquin terrace on the hill top The Post-Nipissing terrace has for the most part been cut away and the waves are now attacking the terrace above, forming cliffs five to eight feet high.

Scotts Bay is a deep depression and continues to the southeast as a low swamp which supports a heavy growth of vegetation A narrow lagoon has been formed at the present level by the formation of a low storm beach, but the swamp as a whole was probably never cut off, although it is possible that a bar, thoroughly hidden by vegetation, may exist farther back The Nipissing terrace swings far back around the swamp but reappears again at McArthur Point where hills of boulder clay stand near the lake This point was originally of gentle slope towards the lake and the waves of Lake Nipissing quickly reduced it to an elongated terrace fully a half-mile in length. The depression in which the Pigeon River flows is so badly flooded that little could be determined as to the shores except on the south side where we leave the lake with the waves cutting back into the familiar Nipissing terrace.

A reading of the above description has no doubt left the impression that wave cutting is the important work being done on this lake at present Current action at the present level assumes importance only on the west side of the inlet and at Nigger Creek. The latter probably will be able to maintain a channel through the bar but there is a possibility of greater growth at the entrance of Indian River. This bar should adjust itself to the higher level and extend to the other side, leaving a gap large enough to accommodate the flow of the stream. Undoubtedly other adjustments were made but have been destroyed in recent times, as may be inferred from the study of Red Pine and Stoney points The effects of the

13

lifting of the water level are excellently illustrated on, this lake. The flooded bays and inlets, the fresh cliffs and the trees standing in water, together with great quantities of driftwood which line the exposed shores stand as evidence of this fact. The future development of the shores of this lake must result from the increased activity of the waves and will consist at first in a recession of the shores At present this is proceeding somewhat slowly as the shores are protected by vegetation, but it will increase when this protection is no longer available. Adjustment should occur first along the low shores and indentations since here the waves are working in the veneer of sand which covers the entire depression in which the lake lies Still, such places are regions of deposition rather than degradation, and we may confidently look for a gradual building out of the beaches in such places, except in the limited number of bays where currents may leave the shore and form bars.

Evidences of ice action on this lake indicate moderate effects. Ramparts are found mainly on the points and are discontinuous and poorly developed In the bays the material is sand and ramparts are not developed or, if so, are quickly reduced by the waves at the present period of excessive activity. We are uncertain as to the shore features of this lake under normal conditions, and encounter difficulties in attempting to discuss the relative importance of expansion and ice jam In some of the bays expansion should be active, but in general the lake is too large for expansion and powerful ice jams are to be expected

The agencies working towards the extinction of this lake are apparently making little headway. Filling of any sort is insignificant, especially since the diversion of the Sturgeon River into Burt Lake Vegetation has made little progress in the main body of the lake on account of the excessive wave action, and there are few localities where it is likely that it can establish itself in the future. Some deposits of marl are present on the shores, it is true, but we can hardly look to this alone to fill such a large basin The tributary streams are few and as yet have deposited little material. As these streams lengthen their courses, more sediment will be brought to the lake and filling from this source will increase. Aside from a change in climate which cannot be foreseen, there remains the cutting down of the outlet With conditions as they are at present, this is impossible but might succeed in lowering the level to that of Lake Huron, fourteen feet lower, provided the dam at Cheboygan is not maintained. This would bring the level just low enough to expose the present submerged terrace and would not materially change or reduce the size of the lake except at the north end. However, the rising of the land to the northeast of the Great Lakes, in itself a slow process, increases the importance of the incision of the outlet, but an uplift of seventy-five feet or more is necessary if the lake is to be drained

BLACK LAKE

Slightly over three miles from its mouth the Cheboygan River divides, one branch connecting with Mullet Lake and the other taking a southeasterly direction   Some difference exists as to the name of the latter and it is designated on different maps as the Cheboygan and as the Black River   The same is true with reference to a large lake which is drained by this river, situated some ten miles above the forks   This question has been referred to the United States Board on Geographic Names and we will follow its decision by using Black for both the river and lake

Black Lake is somewhat elongated in a northwest-southeasterly direction and has a length slightly greater than six miles   Its greatest width is approximately three and three-quarters miles and its area fifteen and seven-tenths square miles   The exact elevation of the lake is not known but is estimated at six hundred forty feet above sea-level or forty-five feet above Mullet   The shores are of relatively even contour, as compared with the other lakes of this system, and are noticeably interrupted only where the Upper Black River enters on the southwest side and at the quarry near Bonz Resort on the south side, see map, Fig. 41. The topography of the surrounding country shows a tendency towards a northwest-southeast trend caused by the deposits of the glacier which occupied the basin of the northern part of Lake Huron. Much of the northeast side of the lake is bounded by highland which varies in height and distance from the lake and continues in the same general direction beyond the southeastern end of the lake. On the opposite shore the highland runs along the south end approximately parallel to the cliffs of the northeastern side but is composed to some extent of hard rock which outcrops at the quarry near Bonz Resort This highland is broken by an extensive depression, through which the Upper Black River flows, and does not reappear until near the outlet. If the directions assumed by the lake itself, its outlet, and the inlets at the southeast end are taken into consideration, the northwest-southeast trend is rather striking, and there is a tendency to attribute the basin to a sag between the fragmentary morainic ridges which trend in this direction. However, the presence of hard rock outcrops and the broad depressions in which the Upper Black and Mud Creek flow make the problem much more complex. In

addition, the lake has not been systematically sounded and, although probably deep, little is known of the nature of the basin
covered by the lake. Therefore, it seems best to leave the origin
of the basin as unsettled until sufficient data are known.

This region was covered by the waters of Lake Algonquin which
stood more than one hundred feet above the level of Black Lake.
The sands and clays deposited under water at this time cover
the land surfaces in the vicinity of the lake, and the sands, especially, have been worked over subsequently by waves and the wind,
furnishing many interesting features. Black Lake stands above the

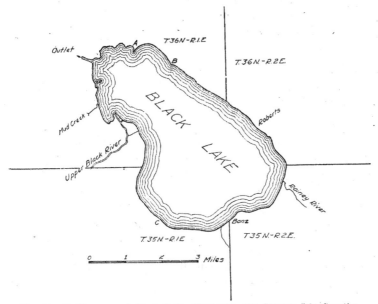

Fig. 41. Outline map of Black Lake, Cheboygan and Presque Isle Counties.

level of the Nipissing beaches and, therefore, was not a part of
that lake. Two levels higher than the present may be clearly
recognized along the shores but must be referred to transitory
stages of the Great Lakes while the water was dropping from the
Algonquin to the Nipissing level. This is certainly the case for the
higher level but other causes may be advocated for an intermediate
level about four feet above the present.

Black Lake lies some distance from the railroad and compares
unfavorably with some of the other lakes of the system in this
respect. It may be reached either from Cheboygan by automobile
or from Onaway. The former is the more generally used, although
it necessitates a longer journey and lands one at the outlet. The

first impression the physiographer gets is that the lake is flooded
The virgin hardwoods on the low flat that borders the river stand
in water near the stream, and. the same conditions hold for the
small islands which rise barely above the lake just off the outlet
This flooding is probably caused by a dam thrown across Black
River six miles below, which has a head of eighteen feet

The flat which lines the river rises gently to low cliffs on either
side but is more extensive on the north side This flat is interpreted as the terrace of a higher water level and the conclusion
may be verified at almost any point on the shores of the lake It
will be referred to as the Upper Level. The flat continues on the
north side and shows little of interest except the marly constitution of the shores, indicating a method of filling

The irregular shore which fronts this terrace ends abruptly at
point A, see map, Fig. 41. This point is a sharp spit which continues approximately a quarter of a mile outward into the lake as
a distinct submerged bar in line with the shore of the east side of
the spit The material on the west side of the point is pebbles, but
that of the east is sand It is evident from this that the waves are
especially active on the west side and that currents have built the
fine sand beach of even curvature on the east It may be inferred
that the waves are more powerful on the west but this is not the
case It is the relative strength of wave and current action which
determines the character of the beach. Southeasterly and southerly
winds, although less powerful than the westerlies, have a long fetch
at this end of the lake and set up strong currents on the northeast
shore, causing deposition to predominate over cutting on the east
side of the point On the west side waves of less power have been
able to throw up a strong storm beach because the shore is not
choked by debris carried by currents of very limited development
along the irregular shore to the west. Inasmuch as the configuration of the bottom of the lake is not known, no cause for the current
leaving the shore at this point is advanced.

East of the point the sandy shore sweeps in a smooth curve to
point B. This point seems to have thrown the currents out a short
distance from the shore and a low bar enclosing a narrow lagoon
has resulted This swampy lagoon terminates at the foot of a steep
bluff, which gradually approaches the north shore of the lake from
the northwest, and marks the shore of the Upper Level This level
shows that considerable adjustment in the outline of the lake occurred, and in many places the drop to the present level has exposed a terrace of considerable width which is well shown along this
shore.

Point B is due to a local accumulation of boulders and immediately gives way to a sandy terrace The effects of the flooding of the lake are here apparent in the increased activity of the waves which have cut the edge of the terrace into a low cliff. This cliff is rapidly receding, necessitating the building of breakwaters. Near point B the numerous springs issuing from the high cliff cause a swampy condition of the terrace, although it is well above the water level Where dry, the terrace proves a suitable location for summer cottages which are furnished with excellent drinking water from the springs The cliff back of the terrace has its greatest development in this locality and rises generally sixty feet or more above the lake. At the top of the cliff is a flat terrace formed during the existence of Lake Algonquin whose shores stood some distance to the northeast. Above this level now stand a few sand dunes which, in some cases, form part of the cliff, making a sheer drop of nearly one hundred feet, the highest on the lake

To the east along the lake shore the highland drops suddenly to a low swamp and beyond this is a lowland composed of clay hills with infrequent sags The terrace is narrow and the shore lined with small boulders, the product of selective wave action on the boulder clay. Beyond Roberts, the hills recede sharply and the low terrace widens into a swamp which encircles the southeastern end of the lake A stream entering the lake in this vicinity has been turned to the southeast and shows the predominance of westerly winds on this shore At the Upper Level the eastward moving current left the shore and built a complete bar from the mainland to a narrow island which lies adjacent to the present shore near the bend to the southwest around the upper end of the lake

The northwest shore beyond point A has been the scene of intense wave action throughout the history of the lake, as is shown by the preponderance of cliffs which in places are prominent features of the landscape In addition, the submerged terrace is well developed and was estimated at fifteen hundred or more feet in width It drops quite regularly to deep water from depths of eight feet, except in one locality a short distance northwest of Roberts. The soundings here showed a terrace which slopes gradually outward to eight feet upon the outer edge of which was found a submerged bar three feet in height Such a ridge is probably due to the violent agitation of the water where the incoming storm waves first break and may be the forerunner of a barrier. The depth of the water at the "drop off" is certainly less than one-half the wave length of the storm waves on this shore but cannot be taken as indicative of any relationship between the two factors, since uncertainty exists as to the completeness of adjustment to the present level. Inasmuch as the adjustments were so great during the Upper Level, it is probable that the submerged terrace conforms more nearly to conditions at that time than to those existing now.

The low ground through which the Rainey river flows extends to the southeast and is an exposed sandy terrace. At the shore a sand beach curves evenly towards the limestone bluff east of Bonz Resort, and below water the terrace slopes gradually out to a well defined "drop off" more than one fourth mile off shore. The exposed terrace back of this low ground and beach is poorly drained except on two sand bars which are best seen where the river cuts through. Both bars are attached to the shore near Bonz Resort point and run to the north around the end of the lake. They diverge somewhat as they leave the point and finally play out beyond Rainey river. The bar nearer the lake stands at a level which corresponds to the Upper Level along the northeast shore. Back of it is a narrow swamp above which rises the second bar at a slightly higher level. This bar clearly indicates a water level intermediate between that of Lake Algonquin and the Upper Level. This probably was a transitory stage and, owing to the lack of accurate elevations, it seems best not to attempt to show its relation to any of the Great Lakes stages.

In the early stages of the highest level the lake was of much greater extent with large bays at the southeast end, west of Bonz Resort, at the Upper Black basin, and at the outlet. Adjustments of the shore were few and incomplete. Shore action was of greatest intensity in the Rainey River bay but here the bar was not completed. No such features were found in the other bays. It is interesting to note that the development of the bars in the Rainey River bay was from the west. The reason for this lies in the configuration of the shore rather than in the difference in exposure to storm winds. At this time the northeast shore was irregular and gave little opportunity for the development of currents. On the other hand, Bonz Point was the scene of great wave action and furnished abundant material.

As the point near Bonz Resort is approached, the material on the beach rapidly increases in size and the shore becomes rocky. The exposed terraces gradually reduce in width and are very definite. The Upper Level shore is here surmounted by a rock cliff ten to fifteen feet high above which stands the flat terrace and cliff of the highest level. The point is caused by the only exposure of hard rock found on the lake shores, a closely fractured limestone. It stands in a bold cliff thirty or more feet high, which does not

come to the water's edge, indicating its formation at the higher
levels of the lake The cliff shows no indication of the highest level,
but the weathering of the closely fractured rock would have quickly
obscured the poorly developed terrace that may have been formed
during this short-lived stage. Along this shore evidence of ice push
is seen in the line of large rocks along the present strand This
point is in reality a hard rock ridge which runs northwest-southeast
and formed a promontory during the higher levels. To the west
stood a broad bay which was separated from the lake by a complete
bar during the Upper Level This shallow lagoon was soon filled
with vegetation and now exists as a flat swamp above which rises
the bar near the present shore This bar is the only dry ground
near the lake in this vicinity and upon it are built the cottages of
Bonz Resort The maximum width of the swamp is about one-
fourth mile and it is bounded by cliffs on the land side To the
west it narrows and the cliffs stand nearer the shore. At locality C
(see map) they come within one hundred feet of the shore and
form the western attachment of the Bonz Resort bar The cliffs
again recede and another bar continues towards the outlet of the
Upper Black. This bar also stands at an elevation corresponding
to the shore of the Upper Level along the northeast shore and the
lower bar in the Rainey River embayment. It lies some distance
back from the shore and splits to the north, assuming the form of a
large hook rather than that of the simple spit.

The bars run almost to the present channel of the Upper Black
on the surface of a broad delta. This delta causes a large projection
of the shore line and is one of the best examples of this feature
to be found in Michigan lakes The river reached the lake by a
series of distributaries, some of which still flow during the flood
season The effective currents along this shore are northerly,
formed by the easterly and southeasterly winds of long sweep, and
have caused the unsymmetrical development of the delta towards
the northwest. At present, the shores are being cut away and the
material shifted towards the west, turning the present channel of
the river in this direction The movement of the material is so
rapid that it is necessary to keep the channel of the river open
artificially. The submerged portion of the delta is correspondingly
large, and the submerged terrace consequently reaches its greatest
development here, fully a half mile in width

Beyond the delta the low ground persists nearly to the outlet as
a swamp. When the lake stood at the higher level this was a
locality of great current action, and the results are to be seen in a
series of bars standing near the shore on the exposed terrace. Near

the delta a single bar cut off the swamp to the west, but this bar splits three times in its course to the north, forming four distinct bars They are especially well developed north of the mouth of Mud Creek and lie within forty rods of the shore. The direction of the currents, as shown by the bars and the deflection of Mud Creek to the north, conformed to the general direction along the south-west shore None of the bars along this shore were complete, but the best developed is that standing next the present shore and reaches to within a few yards of the high ground near the outlet The end of this bar forms the small hook in the present shore line just south of the islands

The half mile of shore south of the outlet is bordered by a low, swampy terrace above which a cliff rises to high land. Wave action was active here at the time when the bars to the south were being deposited, and a terrace of moderate width was formed. The small islands at this end of the lake are all flat-topped and stand at a level slightly above the lake. It seems probable that they were small islands during the early stages of the Upper Level but were completely bevelled during that stage.

In brief, we may state that Black Lake first came into existence as a separate body of water during the recession of Lake Algonquin A high level is recorded in one locality only, the land form being the higher spit attached to Bonz Resort point and extending east around the Rainey River bay. The lake at that time was much more irregular in outline and larger in size than at present. The lack of adjustments of the shoreline indicates that this level was of short duration. Following this the lake halted at a level a few feet higher than the present, which we have called the Upper Level This level was probably the most important one for the lake, and the shores were maturely adjusted to the waves and currents. Great bays were separated from the main body of the lake by currents and bold cliffs cut by waves. In addition, the Upper Black deposited great quantities of silt forming a large delta at its mouth. In general, the present outline of the lake was determined at this time

Only minor adjustments have been accomplished since the lake receded from the Upper Level; in fact, there remains little to be done Of recent years, the ponding of the waters has increased wave action and some readjustment will be the result. It should be largely in the form of cutting back the exposed terrace of the Upper Level. This will continue until equilibrium is established and should progress rapidly, since the material is largely sand. The small points will be reduced more and more by wave action, but

the delta of the Upper Black will continue to increase to the north
The growth of the delta must eventually fill the lower end of the
lake, after which two possibilities arise. A shifting of the distributaries may pour the silt into the main body of the lake and the
filling proceed without interruption, or the Upper Black may connect directly with the outlet. The latter seems the more probable
to the writer, since the delta is growing in this direction. Filling
by marl or vegetation must be limited to the shallower portions
of the lake and will not be important until a great amount of filling
by other means has taken place. Another factor in the extinction
of the lake is the cutting downward of the outlet. This has probably caused the drop from the Upper Level to the present, and, if.
unimpeded artificially, would eventually lower the lake level to
that of Lake Huron. Inasmuch as the depths are not known, it is
impossible to state whether this would completely drain the lake.
At present, the filling of the lake by the silts of the Upper Black
River is the most important

DOUGLASS LAKE

Douglass Lake lies on the western border of Cheboygan County
in Munroe township, T 37 N, R. 3 W., and is about fifteen miles
due south of Mackinaw City. A mile and a half to the south is
the north shore of Burt Lake whose level lies one hundred eighteen
feet below that of Douglass. It is reached from Topinabee on the
Michigan Central R R or from Pellston on the G. R. & I. R. R.
by a drive of several miles over a pine "slashing", now grown up to
poplar and associated trees At present, it is the home of the summer stations maintained by the department of Surveying and of
the Biological Sciences of the University of Michigan, whose camps
are located on South Fish Tail Bay. In addition to the University
camps, there are several resorts, so that the lake is fairly well populated during the summer months but less so than some of the more
accessible lakes in the vicinity

Douglass Lake stands at an elevation of seven hundred thirteen
feet above sea level and one hundred thirty-two feet above Lake
Michigan, into which it drains Its greatest length is somewhat
less than four miles, and greatest width does not exceed two and
one-half miles, the area totaling 6 2 square miles Two constrictions
appear in the outline of the lake which divide it into three basins
united by broad connections However, if the configuration of the
bottom is considered these basins are not so evident. The western
end is a true basin which drops to a depth of eighty feet, but the
central portion is less than thirty feet in depth and would hardly

be called a basin. The eastern arm is peculiar in shape and contains two deep holes in North and South Fish Tail Bays which connect with a pit off Grape Vine Point and are separated from each other by a broad shoal which extends to the eastern end of the lake. The greatest depth is eighty-five feet and occurs in South Fish Tail Bay.

The material surrounding the lake is all of glacial origin and is composed of sand, except at the headlands. These headlands are caused by till, which is much less readily attacked by the waves, and it will be seen from the map, Fig. 42, that, in general, they are

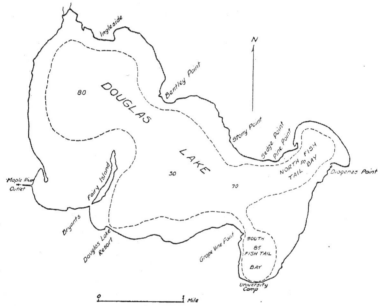

Fig. 42. Outline map of Douglass Lake, Cheboygan County. Broken line indicates approximately the edge of the off-shore terrace. (After U. of M. Surveying Department map.)

opposite each other. There seem to be two small till ridges here which cause the constrictions in the outline of the lake but do not persist across the basin unless possibly in the case of the more westerly. On either side and between the ridges are heavy deposits of sand which partially filled the depressions except where the lake now lies. The eastern end of the lake is surrounded by outwash but the sands of the central and western basins, although possibly outwash, were deposited, in part at least, on the bed of Lake Algonquin which formerly covered this region.

The basin of Douglass Lake lies in the region covered by the ice

from Lake Huron which moved in a southwesterly direction in this
locality, as shown by the northwest-southeasterly trend of the
moraines A large moraimic tract lies to the northeast of the lake
and on the southwest the Colonial Point moraine of Burt Lake
extends to the vicinity of Fairy Island, so that, in a way,
the basin is situated between moraines Yet the peculiarities of the
lake, both as to form and basin, cannot be accounted for in the
simple inter-moraimic type of basin which is usually more or less
regular in outline and shallow in depth The proximity of moraine
on the northeast and the presence of outwash at the eastern end of
the lake, however, lead to the conclusion that the basin was caused
by the burial and subsequent melting of one large but very irregular block of ice or three separate blocks of which that occupying the
central position was relatively thin

One of the striking physiographic forms to be seen near this
lake is a well-defined cliff and terrace about twenty feet above the
present level It is not continuous but appears at varying distances
from the shore on the higher elevations which have been planed
off in some cases and have flat tops The elevation of the base of
the cliffs corresponds with that of Lake Algonquin in this region,
and the general distribution of the beaches of that lake shows
that Douglass Lake was at that time a depression in the bottom of
one of the inlets of a great archipelago The Nipissing beach which
appears commonly on the shores of neighboring lakes is not present
here, Douglass Lake being more than a hundred feet above its
level This lake, then, must have come into existence with the
subsidence of the waters of Lake Algonquin and the present shore
features are due to the forces which have been acting since that
time

In South Fish Tail Bay the material of the outwash plain is easily
eroded, and a clearly marked cliff and terrace stand back of the
present shore at the Algonquin level The present beach is gravelly,
indicating rather strong current action, and beneath the water a
built terrace of sand extends outward a short distance, dropping
suddenly into deep water at a depth of four feet. Wave lengths
of three and four times this figure are common on the lake, thus
making the rather low value of one-third to one-fourth the wave
length as the limit of effective transportation by the undertow.
There is, however, a probability that this terrace was formed largely when the lake level stood about four feet higher than at present,
as shown by elevated beaches, and has not yet been adjusted to the
changed conditions.

Grape Vine Point to the west is caused by moraimic material

which is less readily attacked by the waves, but this position is exposed to the westerly and northwesterly storm winds and shows considerable cutting The Algonquin cliff and cut terrace is well developed on the headland The submerged terrace widens at the point and the shoreward portion is clearly formed by wave cutting Some deposition has taken place on the east side of the point, but the waves are able to swing around the headland for the most part and the point is therefore blunt. Westward the material again becomes sandy, and the recession of the Algonquin cliff indicates excessive cutting in Algonquin time. The submerged terrace continues wide, and its limits are sharply defined by a line of demarcation where the yellow of the sand gives way to the dark blue of the deep water.

Along this shore at the present level deposition is taking place, and the shore has been straightened in some instances Just west of Grape Vine Point is a narrow lagoon a hundred yards or more in length, which has been separated from the lake by a sand bar between one and two feet high In general, the south shore as far as Bryants is a succession of small projections and indentations. The projections are caused by local accumulations of coarser material and are marked by cliffs in close proximity to the shore and by gravel or pebble beaches. The beaches show coarser material on the north and northeast sides of the points but change rapidly to sand on the sides facing the west. The north and easterly winds are the more important on this shore because of the protection from the westerlies offered by Fairy Island. The indentations are lined with sand beaches and the cliffs recede from the shore. The bases of the cliffs referred to here are probably washed by the waves at high water stage in the spring along the projections, but in the indentations they stand about four feet above the present water level marking a higher level of the lake in the past. That this former level, which we may refer to as the Upper Level, was maintained for a considerable time, is shown in the rather large indentation a short distance east of Douglass Lake Resort This indentation was entirely cut off by a bar at the Upper Level and, with a lowering of the water, dried up and grew up to forest which has since been cut.

At the Resort the cliffs run close to the lake and the terrace of the Upper Level has been cut away In the small bay to the west they again recede Along the shore of this bay was noted a small sand spit, rather blunt in shape, which is being built by currents propelled by northeast winds since the "drop off" runs close to the shore on its northwestern side Fairy Island is a narrow strip of

morainic material which is tied to the mainland by a bar from the
west side at low water but probably is not completely attached at
high water. At the Upper Level, the connection was less pronounced or was not present, for on the projection of the mainland
opposite the island a blunt spit has been built about four feet
above the present level which does not extend to the present shore
This spit is more in the nature of a V-bar and encloses Bryants Bog

The Island presents an interesting profile. The essential feature
is a flat top surrounded by a cliff from the base of which a terrace
slopes gently to the water's edge. This terrace shows a much greater
width at the ends than along the sides. The flat top was planed off
by the waves of Lake Algonquin, and the cliffs and terrace below
were cut after the water had subsided to the Upper Level At this
level, ice action built strong ramparts which begin at the base of the
cliff and extend out on the terrace The submerged terrace off the
north end of the island is wide and was formed largely by wave
cutting, as is shown by the large boulders scattered on its surface
However, to the southeast the bench swings outward in a broad
curve and is built of sand transported by currents set up by westerly winds. West of the island the bay is shallow and the bench
not well marked

Westward from the island the shore is sandy and of perfect curvature for perhaps a quarter of a mile. It is in fact a bar which ends
in a small hooked spit and behind which is a lagoon supporting a
heavy growth of rushes. From the map, Fig 42, it will be noted
that this shore conforms in curvature with the west shore of the
island, from which most of the material composing the bar has
been derived. The land west of the lake is low and sandy and was
covered with water during Algonquin time. During the early stage
of the Upper Level this end was considerably greater in extent, but
before the water receded to the present level a strong bar developed,
forming a large lagoon to the west which is still wet East of Maple
River the bar was built by shore-drift from Fairy Island under
northerly winds, or by return currents when the winds were from
a more westerly quadrant North of the river the bar continues
around the entire west end of the lake but was built by southerly
drifting currents, clearly shown by the spit just north of the river
It is poorly developed around the bay at the northeastern extremity
of the lake and cut through by small streams but persists as far
as Ingleside where cliffs line the shore. The "drop off" in the west
arm of the lake is sharply defined, except in the shallow water of
the south side, and the terrace is wide The sandy material in this
locality obscures the manner of formation of this terrace but the

presence of the great bars along the shore seems to indicate that it has been built rather than cut.

At Ingleside the moraine comes to the shore, forming a point which is now being attacked by the waves. The Upper Level terrace has been obliterated and the finer material of the till carried away, leaving a beach of rather coarse material. The bay between Ingleside and Bentley Point is caused by a sag in the moraine which has been partly filled with sand. The head of this indentation was completely cut off by a strong bar at the same level as those on the west arm. At the present level a small ice rampart has been formed twenty to thirty feet in front of the bar. The shore of this bay is rather irregular at the low water stage of mid-summer, a condition not to be expected in front of a bar. Examination of the materials of the shore, however, discloses the fact that the waves have entirely stripped the sand covering in places from the hard clay of the moraine which holds up wave action, causing minor projections.

Some peculiar forms built of sand, called cusps, were noted in this bay which, although similar to spits, differ materially and cannot be explained in the same way. They consisted of sharp points of sand built out from the shore at an oblique angle, extending above the surface at low water and continuing outward below the water level as bars. In some cases they turned back to the shore abruptly similar to V-shaped bars, but in all cases their direction was towards the median line of the bay; that is, if extended outward, those on opposite sides of the bay would meet approximately along a line drawn from the head of the bay out into the lake. A possible explanation is that during moderate storms at low water stage small storm beaches are thrown up over which the waves break. At first the storm beach is continuous and the water collects behind it in a narrow lagoon. If more water is supplied to the lagoon by the waves than can seep back through the sand, the level of the lagoon rises and eventually the water flows back to the lake over low places in the beach. Thus, channels are cut through the storm beach, each channel draining a portion of the lagoon. Such channels will be maintained only where the streams are able to overcome the tendency of the waves and currents to obstruct them. The power of a stream is dependent on its velocity and in this case is determined by the amount of water in the lagoon; that is, the size. Since the width of the lagoon is practically uniform, the size is directly proportional to the length. During the early stages of a storm, many such channels may be formed and obliterated, but eventually the lagoon is divided into sections of more or less uniform length, which are able to maintain an open channel to the lake. The streams in maintaining these channels are constantly carrying out and depositing sand which is worked over by the waves and currents into spit-like forms. See Figs. 43 and 44.

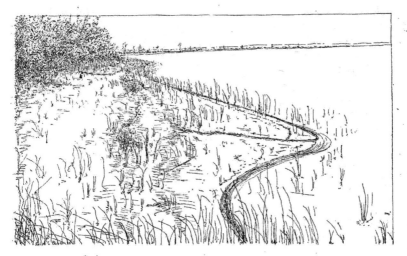

Fig. 43. Sand cusp, Douglass Lake.

Fig. 44. Sand cusp, Douglass Lake.

These features are formed when the waves run directly into the bay. At such times the waves enter the bay with straight crests but are retarded at both ends as they progress, causing a curvature of the

crests, see Fig. 45. On the sides of the bay the waves strike the
shore obliquely and set up currents running towards the head of the
bay, where they merge into the undertow. Thus the cusps point
towards the center of the bay. The fact that such forms occur on
flat shores and at low water suggests that the forces of degradation
and deposition are so evenly balanced that once the balance is overcome, the predominant force will continue its work. In this case,
the deposits made by the outlets of the lagoon are able to force the
currents from the shore, but at the same time are remodelled into
cusps, whose directions conform to the course of the currents.
However, at high water and during heavy storms the balance is
destroyed and the forms are obliterated.

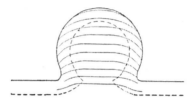

Fig. 45. Conventional diagram illustrating the increase in curvature of waves
within an embayment. Broken line indicates edge of off-shore terrace.

At Bentley Point wave action is heavy, as is shown by the coarse
material of the beach. Currents are also active and have built a
spit running to the southwest, which is about one hundred feet
long at low water. The reach of the waves is here more important
than the strength of the wind and the currents from the east are
stronger. The broad bay east of Bentley practically duplicates
the shore features found between Ingleside and Bentley, except
that the cuspate forms are not present. The ice rampart here is
somewhat better developed and reaches a height of four feet in
places.

The blunt headland opposite Grape Vine Point is caused by a
projections of the same moraine and has similar features in general.
Cliffs rise from the shore to a flat topped area, somewhat less than
twenty feet above the present level, which extends nearly a mile
to the north, terminating in the Algonquin beach. This flat topped
area is the cut-terrace of that time. On either side of the cliff at
Stony Point the terrace and cliff of the Upper Level are present,
and upon the terrace spits, formed during this stage, run both to
the east and the west. These forms are steep and narrow near the
cliffs and are composed of coarse material, including boulders up to
a foot in diameter. Farther from the cliffs, the material decreases
in size and the spits broaden, reaching widths of nearly one hundred

15

feet at the ends where the material is sand. The elevation near the cliffs is in excess of five feet above the terrace but drops to less than three feet at the ends. Currents have been largely instrumental in the formation of these spits, but ice action has aided near their land attachment where the forms are more characteristic of ramparts than of current deposits.

Farther to the east, at Sedge Point, the currents again left the shore at the Upper Level and built a recurved spit that cut off low ground to the north, which is still swampy. At the present level the currents are depositing in front of the fossil spit and have built a series of recurved spits which enclose triangular lagoons, as shown in Fig. 46. At Pine Point, a short distance east of Sedge

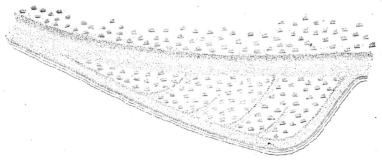

Fig. 46. Diagrammatic plan of bars and lagoon at Sedge Point, Douglass Lake.

Point, a spit similar to that just described appears. Entering North Fish Tail Bay the shore turns abruptly to the northwest and the currents, being unable to follow the shore, have formed a perfect example of a compound hook which is reproduced in Plate VII. This bay is a deep pool, showing depths in excess of fifty feet, but presents little of interest along its shores until Diogenes Point on the east side is reached. At this point the currents swinging into the bay from the south have deposited a complex series of recurved spits at the present level, which enclose irregular shaped lagoons now being filled with vegetation. A sketch of these is presented in Fig 47, the lagoons being numbered in the probable order of their formation.

The eastern end of the lake is a long sand beach above which small sand dunes have been piled by the wind. The peculiar widening of the submerged terrace along this shore is of considerable interest. It projects lakeward suddenly just below Diogenes Point and gradually widens until the deep hole in South Fish Tail Bay causes it to double back and run close to the shore. The entrance to North Fish Tail Bay is wider than that of its

A. HOOK, DOUGLASS LAKE.

B. RAISED BEACHES, PINE LAKE.

counterpart to the south, which may account for the better developed forms along its shores. The wide terrace in this part of
the lake is composed of large rocks at its outer edge but shoreward
these give place to clear sand. The explanation is that an island
or at least a shoal, similar to Fairy Island in shape and material,
but larger in size, existed formerly at this place and has been destroyed by wave action which was able to transport the finer material only. Thus, an accumulation of boulders was left under
water at a depth which marks the lower limit of effective wave
action, and this part may be considered a cut terrace. The finer
material was washed shoreward and completely filled the depression, making the terrace continuous to the shore. Clearly, the

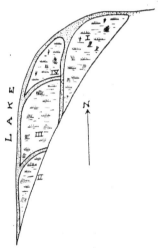

Fig. 47. Diagrammatic plan of bars and lagoons at Diogenes Point, Douglass Lake.

westerly winds both on account of their strength and reach have
played the prominent part in the formation of this exceptionally
wide cut-and-built terrace.

HISTORY. During Algonquin time the lake did not exist as a
separate basin but rather as a depression in an arm of a great
archipelago. With the recession of the waters to the Nipissing
level, Douglass Lake became an isolated basin and stood at a level
approximately four feet higher than at present. At this level
most of the shore adjustments were made, the most notable being
the development of bars along the west end, across the indentations on the north side, and also near Bryants on the south side.
Inasmuch as the adjustments were so largely made at the higher
level, it is felt that the submerged terrace, which is so well developed on this lake, was formed at that time with a depth of water

at its outer edge of from seven to eight feet, or about one-half the wave base during the greatest storms, rather than the low value as shown at the present level The adjustments now in progress are minor in importance and consist mainly in cutting back the headlands and in some current action Wave action on the headlands has succeeded in obliterating the terrace of the Upper Level in most places Current action is slight because much of the adjustment of the shore had been completed at the higher level, and the amount of material supplied by waves and tributary streams is small No large indentations are now in the process of being cut off except possibly a portion of North Fish Tail Bay The other current deposits are small in size and formed mainly during the low water stage to be re-formed or obliterated during the flood stage The most significant of these is the bar which connects the island to the mainland. Evidence of ice action is present but shows no exceptional development of ramparts, due for the most part to unfavorable shore conditions both as to topography and material rather than insufficient ice push.

With the shore adjustments largely completed, the interest in the future development lies mainly in the possibilities of extinction Up to the present, vegetation has played little part except in the filling of the lagoons which has reduced the area of the lake considerably. The vegetation in the main lake is principally rushes and is limited to the submerged terrace and mainly to that part which is exposed at low water This filling is most important in the shallow water between Fairy Island and the west shore. Filling by sediment is so small that it may well be neglected. Cutting down of the outlet has been of some importance in the past and accounts for the dropping in level from the Upper Level to the present Since the outlet flows through unconsolidated sand, this method of extinction may continue to be effective, but underground drainage may greatly interfere.

Somewhat less than a mile southeast of South Fish Tail Bay is located Big Springs, the source of Carp Creek which drains into Burt Lake The lower portion of this stream flows through a swamp but the upper course heads in a gorge cut to a depth of sixty to seventy feet in sand. Near its head the gorge ramifies and at the end of each ramification is a spring The supply of water from these springs is large and constant, but unfortunately the writer had no means of comparing the amount with that discharged by Maple River, the surface outlet of the lake Between Big Springs and the central basin of the lake are several sinks in the outwash plain which may be interpreted as indicating an underground seepage line rather than the result of the melting of

buried ice blocks. Further evidence is supplied by a well record
at Bogardus Camp which shows a dropping of the ground water
level to the south. From this it seems reasonable that a considerable portion of the water of Douglass Lake drains southward underground and issues at Big Springs   Also it is evident that the
gorge has been formed by sapping at the springs and is gradually
working backward towards the lake. If this is correct, the lake
probably will be tapped and the outlet will be shifted to a point
just west of Grape Vine Point. The gradient of the new outlet
will be much steeper than that of Maple River and down cutting
will proceed at a more rapid rate than at present   The level of
the lake will then lower with minor changes in outline until the
outlet has cut down twenty feet   The east and west basins will
then exist as isolated basins sixty to sixty-five feet in depth separated by the dry bed of the central part   These lakes will still drain
through the new outlet and may be completely drained since the
greatest depths are above the level of Burt Lake   Yet, the process
becomes progressively slower as the gradient of the outlet flattens
and vegetation will probably accomplish the final extinction

CHAPTER IV

LAKES OF THE GRAND TRAVERSE REGION

In what is known as the Grand Traverse region, situated in the northwestern part of the Southern Peninsula, are a number of most excellent lakes of considerable size. Most of the more popular of these lakes border Lake Michigan and, in fact, were once a part of it, having been isolated by great bars which developed in either Algonquin or Nipissing time The only exception among the lakes visited in this region is Walloon which became an independent basin when the Great Lakes subsided to the Algonquin level The popularity of these lakes is due not only to their natural beauty and adaptability for summer resorts but as well to the proximity of Lake Michigan to the west, which considerably tempers the summer heat.

The lakes included in this chapter—Walloon, Pine, Torchlight, Elk, and Crystal—are typical for the region and are all attenuated in form, in which respect they resemble the famous "finger lakes" of central New York In addition to their attractiveness as summer resorts, the situation of these lakes in an excellent fruit-growing region makes them all the more important. In such regions transportation is always a problem and, in this case, may be solved partially by navigation Pine Lake has for some time been connected with Lake Michigan by an artificial channel through which boats of considerable draught may pass without difficulty. In fact, Charlevoix is a regular stop for some lines of navigation during the summer months. The lake itself is navigable for boats of heavy draught for its entire length, and this cheap means of transportation should lead to an increased development of the agricultural possibilities of the region, already well started. Of the other lakes, Elk and Torchlight offer similar possibilities but at greater cost, since locks at Elk Rapids and considerable dredging between the two lakes would be necessary An illfated attempt was made to make a navigable waterway from Crystal Lake to Frankfort but the result was merely to lower the level of the lake This proved so serious that a dam was built at the outlet to hold the water at somewhere near its natural level.

With the possible exception of Crystal, these lakes are also simi-

lar in the nature of the basins which they occupy. As discussed
at the close of Chapter II, the basins are large troughs running
more or less parallel to the direction of ice movement during the
last glaciation, but present difficulties of explanation as to manner of formation which have not yet been solved.

WALLOON LAKE

Walloon Lake is the most easterly in position of the lakes of
this group and is situated in north-central Charlevoix County, a
few miles east of Pine Lake. It is easily reached by the Grand
Rapids & Indiana R R, which follows the broad valley of Bear
Creek south from Petoskey and runs a short spur from the main
line to Walloon Lake Station at the south-eastern end of the lake.

Walloon Lake is one of the most popular in the State. It is
of sufficient size to warrant a large fleet of motor boats, and the
irregular shore line lessens the fetch of the waves that would otherwise become of dangerous size during storms and sudden "blows"
The abundance of high ground along the shores insures excellent
locations for cottages and its nearness to the railroad makes it easy
of access. The fishing is also an attractive feature. Unfortunately, from the standpoint of the resorters, the level of the lake has
been subjected to serious fluctuations by the use of the water for
power. A dam was constructed to regulate the flow of water
throughout the year, and the result has been a serious lowering of
the level during the summer months. This has been done since the
lake developed into a summer resort, causing great inconvenience,
and loss of property to the cottagers, and has been the subject of
long litigation. The height of the dam has been fixed by law but
the lake has not been visited by the writer since that time

The outline of this lake is very irregular and, although over nine
miles in length, has an area of only 8 35 square miles In the
figure given for the area is included the North Arm which covers
slightly more than one square mile Thus, the width on the
average is about three-fourths of a mile and rarely exceeds one
and a half miles.

From the map the idea may be gained that the lake has a general northwest-southeast trend which is interrupted by the North
Arm However, from the physiographic standpoint, it may be
better described as occupying parts of two elongated basins of the
type mentioned earlier in this chapter. The trough occupied by
the main lake has a northwest-southeast direction for the northern
half of its extent. It then swings more nearly eastward and connects with the Bear Creek valley a mile or more beyond the lake.

Near the southeastern end of the lake the second trough, in which the North Arm lies, crosses the main depression and causes the deep bay on the south side of the lake opposite the North Arm. South of the lake it turns to the southeast and unites with the Bear Creek depression some three miles below the main trough.

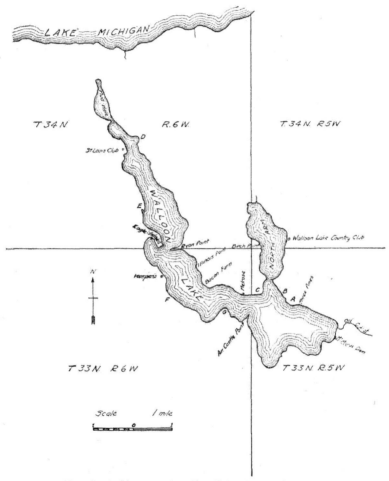

Fig. 48. Outline map of Walloon Lake, Charlevoix County.

The surface features of the region are relatively simple with the exception of the depressions mentioned above. The greater part of the lake is surrounded by morainic deposits composed of a rather sandy till. To the north lies a till plain which borders about three miles of the north end of the lake and a much smaller

part of the extremity of the North Arm. The surface, then, is
composed of knobs and basins, or sags and swells, except at the
continuations of the intersecting troughs Both of these types are
descriptive of a rolling topography, the chief difference being in
the amount rather than in the character of the relief Naturally,
a very irregular shore line of minor headlands and embayments
is the result

The northern end of the lake lies within a mile of Little Traverse
Bay and is separated by a low divide about one fourth mile north
of the lake Nearby and but a few feet below the crest of the
divide stands the shore of former Lake Algonquin Thus, the
Walloon lake basin was not connected with this predecessor of
Lake Michigan at the north end, and, if any connection existed, it
must have been at the present outlet The latter is uncertain but,
at any rate, the lake was practically isolated at this time

According to the original land survey, the outlet of Walloon
Lake was at the southeastern end on the north side of the valley
leading eastward to the Bear Creek valley At present, the lake
drains over a dam and through a newly cut channel at the south
side of the flat The town of Walloon Lake is built on the flat
and much of the topography is thereby obscured It seems reasonable, however, that the present channel is artificial and that the
outlet, as shown on the early maps, represents the conditions as
regards shore action in this locality The shore along the valley
floor is an adjusted sand beach where not interfered with by structures Under the present conditions no trace of a bar could be
found and it is probable none was formed Material is carried to
this shore from both sides during westerly "blows" and is largely
redistributed by undertow. If we accept the position of the outlet
as shown on the early maps as correct, shore currents have affected a transfer of material to the north along this shore, in spite of
the fact that the irregular south shore is not favorable to the
formation of strong currents

Along the north shore to the entrance of the North Arm the
morainic knobs and basins drop gently to the lake Thus, the
shore is a succession of flats and lens-shaped cliffs which reach a
maximum height of nearly forty feet at Three Pines. No distinct
submerged terrace is present, and the only depositional form noted extends eastward from the cliffs at A, see map, Fig 48 This
form is a 'blunt hook about forty feet in length and is composed
largely of shingle The coarse material has been shoved into a
distinct rampart near the attachment to the cliffs by the expansion of the ice during the winter Further to the east the ram-

part splits into three distinct ridges which decrease in height and play out as the end of the hook is reached Shore action is constantly supplying material to the hook, which is being reworked by the periodic ice shove into a series of ramparts, that is, a local ice-push terrace Ice push is also in evidence at B, where boulders have been forced into the cliff. In general, the shore forms are the result of wave action in this locality, due largely to the lack of sufficiently large embayments The effective winds are from the west, and strong eastward moving shore currents develop almost to the exclusion of undertow These currents are virtually uninterrupted for more than two miles and are able to transport relatively coarse material which is ground to smaller sizes as it travels along the beach Thus, there is a noticeable grading of the beach material which decreases in size to the east and becomes sand at the lower end of the lake It is here distributed by the undertow into which the shore current merges See Chapter III

Another interesting feature found along this shore is the combination of narrow terrace and low cliff which borders the low parts of the shore The terrace supports a heavy growth of vegetation, including trees of considerable size, and may, therefore, be taken as an indication of a stage of the lake which stood two feet above the level of the water in the summer of 1913, and not merely a high water mark It must have been continuous when the water subsided and has been removed since by wave action except along the low, protected parts of the shore

At the narrow entrance to the North Arm, conditions are rather abruptly changed Current action here assumes the prominent role, and the wind directions which were so important on the shore just described are secondary It will be noted from the map that the shores of the approach to this bay gradually converge to two opposite points, forming a channel a quarter of a mile in width Within the bay, the shores recede rapidly and increase the prominence of the points. The significant fact is that the currents on both sides are not only forced to leave the shores at these points but are able to maintain their courses across the channel. Furthermore, the winds from both the northerly and southerly quadrant are effective and have about the same reach. Therefore, the spits which developed from these points are not unexpected.

These spits, shown in Figs 49 and 50, restrict the channel more than one-fourth of its original width and are connected by a submerged bar which is within eight feet of the surface at its lowest part. Within the memory of settlers this depth was as great as

eighteen feet, therefore, the bar is developing rapidly and the
channel will soon have to be kept open artificially, if it is to be
maintained. As seen in the sketches, these spits are triangular in
shape and are of regular curvature on both sides, indicating that
currents from both the main lake and the North Arm have been
instrumental in their formation. Yet, if the attachments and

Fig. 49. Spit at the west side of the entrance to the North Arm, Walloon Lake.
(Sketch from photograph).

Fig. 50. Spit at east side of the entrance to the North Arm, Walloon Lake.
(Sketch from photograph).

curvature of the spits with reference to the adjoining shores are
considered, it is clear that the greatest development has been from
the main lake. This may be due to several causes: The prevalence of storm winds, the depth of the water affected, and the
nature of the shores. Of the first two, we are not certain, but it
is probable that the main lake is the deeper, and that the storm

winds shift more frequently through the southerly quadrant than the northerly. As to the nature of the shores, we find a greater prevalence of cliffs along the converging approach than in the bay, although the shore affected is shorter. This is probably due to the intensification of the waves and, therefore, current action in the narrowing approach It appears, then, that all three factors are favorable to growth from the main lake, but detailed study is necessary for a decision.

Furthermore, it is apparent that the spit on the east side is the better developed This is clearly due to the greater shore line affected and the unquestionable prevalence of storm winds having a westerly component. It is also apparent from the sketches that a considerable part of these spits developed during the higher stage The drop to the present level was so slight that conditions were unchanged and the present growth is a continuation of that of the previous stage

As regards shore action, the North Arm acts as an isolated basin. Shore conditions are similar on both sides and resemble those of the north shore between the east end of the lake and the entrance to this bay Moraine borders the southern part of this embayment but drops to a till plain which skirts the shores of the northern half The characteristic shore features, therefore, are the now familiar cliffs and terrace in front of which runs a sandy beach interspersed at the small points with boulders Wave action is prominent but the cliffs are considerably lower than on the main lake. Current action, however, has not been productive of any decided effects unless it be a gradual building out of the flats to the line of the cliffs This could not be determined on account of the heavy growth of vegetation which obscures the surface of the lowlands In but one locality, aside from the spits at the entrance, are currents actively depositing and this occurs on the south side of Birch Point Here a small spit composed of well assorted pebbles extends southward from the point and continues under water as a sand terrace The relief is much less near the north end, and much of the shore is swampy Continuous swamp fringes the north end with the exception of a low but conspicuous swell west of the inlet. The vegetation of this swamp is creeping outward over the marl-covered bottom, indicating the inception of the final stage in the development of this embayment—its extinction by vegetation Ice shove of the expansion type is active here, but shore conditions are not favorable for decided results. Ramparts of local extent are present on the low cliffs near the

Walloon Lake Country Club but are much inferior to those found on the main lake.

In general, it is evident that shore action within the North Arm is much less intense than on the main lake and the adjustments are correspondingly weaker, as may have been inferred from the discussion of the spits at the entrance

Outside the North Arm the increased activity of shore forces is apparent Interest centers first at point C, where the shore makes a right-angled bend to the west Ordinarily, one might expect the currents set up by westerly winds to leave the shore at this point and deposit their suspended material in alignment with the north shore Instead, however, we find bold cliffs below which stands a narrow terrace of the higher level. Around the point this exposed terrace widens and upon it a well-developed spit, which has been modified by ice shove, swings from the shore, enclosing a narrow lagoon, now drained. From this it is evident that the south and southeasterly winds which sweep without interruption across the widest part of the lake are the most effective. It is probable that the currents flowing eastward along the north shore deposit material at the point, since lagoons are found further to the west, but any such deposits are subsequently worked around the point by the southerly winds.

The lagoons referred to above are found between C and Bacon farm The depressions are sags in the moraine, closed by bars at the higher stage of the lake These bars have been remodelled by ice-push to such an extent that somewhat close observation is necessary to detect current action The assortment and gradation in size of the material along the bars are the deciding characteristics The first bar encountered from the east shows two distinct ramparts which rise in steps away from the lake The elevations of the ramparts correspond with the present and higher levels of the lake, and the ramparts were, therefore, formed during these stages. Farther west the bars across the mouths of the small indentations have been remodelled into single ramparts

Beyond Bacon farm an almost continuous cliff faces the lake and extends back of Ryan Point to the north part of the lake The principal break occurs at the slight recession of the shore north of Illinois Point The gentle slopes which come to the shore here were carved into a distinct terrace at the former level and are now heavily wooded The smaller initial adjustments by both waves and currents have taken place along this shore, and the shore-line, although sinuous, extends with little variation from the cliffs to flats The adjustments are far from complete, however, since the submerged terrace is almost entirely lacking at the present level and was poorly developed at the higher level. Near Ryan Point an outcrop of black shale rock was found in the cliff above the lake. This rock offers little resistance to eroding agents, in fact, less than the adjacent boulder clay, and weathering is disintegrating it so rapidly that it exhibits none of the characteristics of rocky shores. Rock outcrops are so infrequent on the shores of Michigan lakes that it is mentioned in passing. The most noticeable shore activity is due to ice-shove. Expansion must be very active on this shore for its effects are seen on virtually every cliff and flat where conditions are at all favorable, and the enumeration of each rampart and boulder-paved cliff would become monotonous.

At the narrows formed by Eagle Island and Ryan Point the adjustments are of striking proportions. Currents have left the shore on both sides of the lake and have developed spits which have reduced the width of the narrows relatively more than those at the entrance to the North Arm, although the channel is not so restricted nor so shallow. Naturally, we compare these two localities and find that the spits on the east sides show the greater development in both cases, due to the same cause—the greater strength and the prevalence of westerly winds. Ryan Point, however, whose north side has a curvature in conformity with the shore to the north, has been built to a large extent by currents from the north, a fact readily accounted for by its position near the south end of the extended west shore. This spit, which extends almost half way across the narrows, is of clear sand and was built mainly at the abandoned level of the lake. Thus, its surface stands two feet or more above the present level. As the spit developed, grasses and, later, trees took root, forming a mat over its surface. Ice action was then able to form a series of low ramparts parallel to both shores but better developed on the north side. When seen by the writer, this point was being eroded on the north side and built up on the south, a process which, if it continues, will shift the position of the entire spit to the south. This shifting was well shown at the tip of the point by a sudden jog in the shore-line which occurs at the attachment of a recent extension of the spit.

On the opposite side of the lake conditions are similar but the results are on a much smaller scale. The currents leave the shore at the extremity of Eagle Island but are relatively feeble, due to the infrequency of strong east winds and the irregular shore to the north. The blunt sand spit which reaches southward from the end of this point consists of two parts: A swampy, grass-covered flat next the cliffs and a bare outer zone bordering the lake. There is practically no difference in the elevation of the two parts, but the failure of the grass cover forms a sharp line of division It is possible, of course, that the vegetation is gradually creeping outward and that the development of the spit has been continuous. Yet, from conditions found elsewhere on the lake, it seems more probable that a broad bar, for the most part submerged, developed during the higher stage, and that the slight lowering of the level exposed a portion of this bar upon which vegetation soon took hold If this is correct, the bare portion must be an extension of this bar formed under the present conditions At any rate, it is evident that the currents from the north are the more potent.

On the east side north of Ryan Point, the more or less regular alternation of cliffs and flats again appears. Shore conditions, even to the frequent evidences of ice shove, are very similar to those below the point, but show, in general, greater activity of waves and currents Thus, a persistent submerged terrace is present which reaches a width of one hundred feet or more on the southern stretches of this shore and drops into deep water at a depth of four or four and a half feet Opposite the St. Louis Club two small hooks which extend southward from minor projections indicate the prevailing movement of the shore currents It is evident that here wind direction is more important than reach in the development of currents.

The conspicuous embayment, D on map, in the rather regular shore along the northeast side, is caused by a large amphitheatre-shaped basin, a sag in the moraine. North of this the even slopes of the till plain dip gently to the lake, forming shores which are low but not swampy

The north end of the lake is called the Mud Hole True to its name the bottom is covered with an ooze of marl upon which is accumulating the yearly residue of a heavy growth of rushes It is a distinct basin with a shallow, narrow entrance, which is further constricted by the development of a spit on the west side. Within the Mud Hole shore action is limited to the expansion of the ice, and this is not important at the present level. However, a distinct rampart, containing boulders of considerable size, stands at a higher level near the north end where the width of the bay was not greater than one fourth mile. See Fig 51. This observation is interesting in view of the rather prevalent opinion that ramparts are not formed on lakes of much less than a half mile in diameter The north shore of the Mud Hole is fringed by a

swamp which extends northward to the low divide which stood
between this lake and Lake Algonquin. It seems certain that Walloon Lake stood at the higher level at that time and covered this
swamp. This being the case, the divide was but a few rods in
width.

Fig. 51. Ice rampart, Mud Hole, Walloon Lake. (Sketch from Protograph.)

The west shore above Eagle Island is much more broken than
that of the opposite side and, although shore action is relatively
feeble, more deposits are found. The first to be encountered is
the spit at the entrance to the Mud Hole, already mentioned. This
spit is turned to the northeast and, therefore, is being built by
currents from the south. The material for this spit is quarried
from the short stretch of shore in the bay to the south and is
limited in amount. Nevertheless, the spit is developing rapidly,
on account of the small amount of filling necessary to close the
channel and the fact that the currents are quickly brought to a
halt. Ice push is strong in this locality and has formed a rampart on the south side of the spit which merges into a boulder
paved cliff at its attachment.

Again at the north end of the blunt point upon which the St.
Louis Club is located, the currents have held to their course at
the present level, even though the bend in the shore is not pronounced and the hook, thus formed, shuts off a narrow lagoon
which is open at the north end. This lagoon supports a heavy
growth of lily pads, rushes, and grass and will soon become filled.
Ice action does not seem to be effective at the present level but its
effects are evident at the ramparts along the old shore. However,

17

in the bay to the south of the St. Louis Club ramparts are found at both levels, but that at the present shore is of moderate development and is not continuous

Below this bay the waves are working on the lower slopes of the hills and have formed low cliffs along a stretch of shore a half mile in length Currents are also of considerable force and have carried away the finer particles, leaving coarse material on the beach The effective drift is to the south and much of the debris has been deposited in a hook and an extended submerged terrace, E on map, which are detaching a narrow lagoon to the rear.

Before Eagle Island is reached the slopes drop to a narrow swamp which runs directly south across the neck of this projection to the decided embayment on the south side This swamp is barely above the present water level and was evidently covered during the higher stage of the lake, therefore the name, Eagle *Island* The swamp borders the north shore of the bay partially enclosed by Eagle Island, and dense vegetation has obscured the beach A small spit on the east shore of this bay at the edge of the swamp is interesting in that it is an index of the power of the winds from the southwestern quadrant. The spit is turned to the northwest and derives its material, therefore, from the short stretch of shore between it and the end of the point The fetch of the waves is short and must be driven by strong winds to be of any significance The shallowness of the bay is, however, an important factor in the formation of this spit, on account of the small amount of filling necessary and the rapid decrease in intensity of the waves as they progress towards the beach As in other shallow parts of the lake, heavy deposits of marl cover the bottom upon which reeds are now taking hold

The protected west side of the bay is bordered by gentle slopes which have been carved into a low terrace at the higher level but show little evidence of wave action at the present level. As a matter of fact, conditions along this shore are reversed for the higher and present levels, and currents are now the important agent of adjustment They leave the shore in two places along this side, due probably to the shoaling of the water, see Crystal Lake, and have formed small sand spits which point northward Easterly winds are, of course, the most effective, since the bay is well protected on the north by Eagle Island

Near Harpers, ice action is well shown by ice ramparts across the mouth of a ravine at the present and higher levels As usual, the older rampart is the better developed The embayment south of

Harpers is lined by a sand beach of even curvature in spite of the alternation of cliffs and sags, and the effects of ice action are evident as ramparts or boulder-paved cliffs From F to G wave action has predominated and cliffs of variable height face the lake, with the exception of a wide depression on the west side of point G During the higher stage a bar developed across this depression, and the elongated lagoon was filled with vegetation The growth of the bar must have been from the west under the influence of northerly winds Ice action piled up a rampart along the old shore previous to the development of the bar and later has been active along the bar The sandy character of the bar is not favorable for decided effects and the present rampart is inferior in development

Again at G conditions were reversed with the sinking of the water to the present level, and a broad terrace is being built at the foot of the cliffs by currents from the west The point of departure of the currents is not definite and a blunt point is the result A large amount of material is dropped at this point since it extends three hundred feet or more into the lake as a submerged terrace, dropping into deep water at four feet The turning of the currents from the shore at G and the very shoal water between G and Air Castle Point have effectively prevented adjustments along the intervening shore

But at Air Castle Point, the constructive work of shore agents is shown on a scale comparable with that at the entrance to the North Arm and at Ryan Point This great spit is irregular in outline on the west side but has an even curvature in accordance with the trend of the east shore. Clearly it has been built by currents from the south Deposition is still taking place, and a submerged portion is growing into the lake as a relatively narrow bar with a somewhat greater curvature than the subaerial part, a form in striking contrast to the re-curved spits or hooks which are usually formed when currents are dissipated in deep water. The increase in curvature occurs along the part of the bar which has grown into deep water and is exposed to the force of the waves from the west, undiminished by the projecting point G and the intervening shoal Under such conditions the spit will increase in curvature as it grows, and its position will represent the relative strength of the forces acting on either side. It is probable that this spit will develop to the west of point C and, therefore, will not divide the lake, but it is impossible to make a definite statement on this point considering the present development of the spit The greater part of the spit was built during the higher level and, after the establishment of vegetation, a continuous ice rampart was pushed up on the east side.

Below Air Castle Point cliffs, unbroken save for a narrow valley
which is blocked by ice ramparts, line the shore to the head of the
large embayment which forms the southern extremity of the lake
As already stated, this bay is caused by the continuation of the
North Arm trough which extends several miles to the south and
southeast The shore is, therefore, low and swampy· The noticeable features are the well-developed submerged terrace and the ice
ramparts The ramparts are three in number and are especially
well developed and distinct They increase in elevation, size, and
continuity with distance from the shore The best developed, the
one farthest inland, stands three to five feet above the adjacent
land and encircles the bay with but a single break where a small
stream crosses. The middle rampart is inferior in development but
still is a decided ridge, the lowest is discontinuous and poorly
defined in places Two ramparts are common and may be correlated
with the two stages of the lake The presence of the third rampart
in this one locality is, however, somewhat puzzling

The lake attains its greatest width opposite this bay but still does
not exceed the maximum limit for ice expansion The expansion,
then, is greatest in this locality, and the ramparts are exceptionally well developed From its elevation, the rampart farthest inland
may be considered the equivalent of the higher rampart formed in
other favorable localities where two are present Also it is evident
that the ramparts nearest the shore are in process of formation at
the present time and are correlatives But a lake stage, corresponding in level with the intermediate rampart, cannot be assumed
since corroborative evidence at other localities on the lake is entirely lacking To the writer this series of ramparts seems to have
been formed in a manner similar to that of an ice-push terrace but
on a shore of such flat slope that the ramparts are separate and
distinct ridges The cause of the lowering of the lake level was the
gradual deepening of the outlet by natural processes The earliest
and largest rampart was formed at the highest stage after vegetation had become well established and served to bind the loose sands
The size indicates that the higher stage must have been of relatively
long duration During the lowering of the level the vegetation
slowly encroached on the emerging lake bottom and was not disturbed by the ice which, under normal conditions, expanded to
positions less and less advanced as the shore receded But under
especially favorable conditions such as high water, light snowfall,
and numerous alternations of temperature during the winter, excessive expansion took place, and the ice advanced into the zone of
vegetation and pushed up the rampart The slope seems to be the

most important factor in this consideration since the rate of recession of the shore and, therefore, the advanced position of the expanding ice is dependent on the flatness of the slope. Another possible cause for the intermediate rampart is that the lowering of the level was temporarily halted by an obstruction in the outlet, which was sufficient for the formation of a rampart but not for distinguishable effects of the other shore agents.

The shores from this bay to the outlet are of the cliff and sag type, modified locally by ice action. This type has been so frequently mentioned in connection with other localities that repetition is not necessary and the description of the shores may be left at this point.

In resumé, the episodes in the history of this lake are but two, the present level and a stage a few feet higher. This may seem somewhat meager when compared with the numerous stages of several of the nearby lakes, but the many adjustments of the shores, begun at the higher level and continuing at the present, are of sufficient interest to compensate for the deficiency.

Walloon Lake stands well above the levels of the predecessors of the Great Lakes since Algonquin. There is a possibility of a connection with Algonquin at the southeastern end and a certainty that the higher stage was in existence at this time. Whichever may have been the case, the agencies affecting the shores of the higher level were similar in intensity to those active today, since the reduction in area has been slight and the lake was practically enclosed.

The irregularity of the basin and the adjacent slopes afforded many opportunities for large and significant adjustments of the shores, but on the other hand, effectively reduced the intensity of the forces by which such adjustments are accomplished. The limited reach of the winds and the irregularities of the shores permit a moderate development of waves and currents and the results, in general, correspond. Waves have cut back many of the minor salients, reducing the smaller sinuosities of the shore line, but the very limited development of a submerged terrace shows a relatively small amount of wave action. And the currents can neither be of great power nor continuity on account of the short stretches of even shore. The striking thing, however, is the localization of their effects at critical points, which greatly increases their importance. Thus, a continuation of their activity at the entrance to the North Arm, at Ryan Point, at the channel to the Mud Hole, and possibly at Air Castle Point will lead to a division of the lake into smaller members, and this, in turn, will greatly hasten its extinction by the processes already well started. Ice expansion is active to a remarkable degree on the shores of this lake. The series of ramparts, the boulder-paved cliffs, and the ice-push terraces are unequalled on Michigan lakes.

By far the greater development of the shores occurred at the higher stage   The slight lowering of the level has caused a reduction in the activity of the waves which in some localities has been sufficient to reverse conditions from cutting to deposition.   The decrease in wave action furnishes less material to the currents, and all of the shore adjustments are necessarily taking place more slowly   Nevertheless, it is evident that the Mud Hole and the North Arm will soon be separated from the main lake, to be followed later by the division of the remainder of the lake into two basins by the growth of Ryan Point   Shore activities will be further reduced in the separate basins and in the meantime vegetation, which has already accomplished considerable filling in the partially enclosed bays, will increase   Thus, it may be suggested with some confidence that this lake will become extinct before the completion of the adjustment of its shores takes place

PINE LAKE

Pine Lake, called Long Lake on the earlier maps, is elongated in a northwest-southeasterly direction and at Charlevoix lies within a mile of Lake Michigan   See map Fig 52   The main body of the lake is slightly over thirteen miles in length and probably does not exceed one and one-half miles in average width   Where greatest, the width is but little more than two and one-half miles, and in one place only, near the upper end, does it contract to less than a mile   Thus, the main lake may be considered rather uniform in its dimensions, with only minor bays and projections relieving the regularity of its shores. However, an important exception is found in the narrow South Arm which extends nine miles in a direction slightly east of south   The South Arm is much narrower than the main lake, its average width being estimated at less than a half-mile, and is constricted to five hundred feet in the narrows near its entrance. The total area of the lake is 26 7 square miles   On account of its peculiar shape and navigability, the lake has influenced to some extent the grouping of population about it, and we find the cities of Charlevoix, Boyne City, and East Jordan at its extremities

The region in which Pine Lake lies is one of the few localities in Michigan where drumlins are found   More than half of the main lake and virtually all of the South Arm lie in longitudinal depressions which are surrounded by these peculiar hills of hard boulder

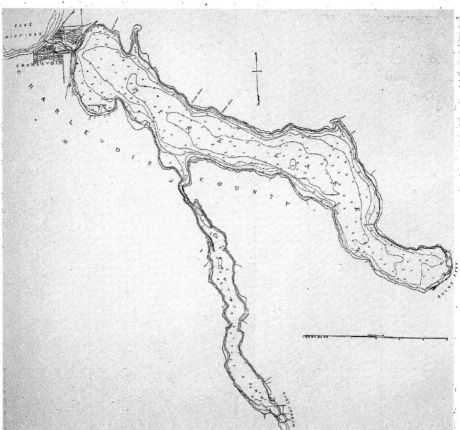

Fig. 52. Map showing outline and configuration of the basin of Pine Lake, Charlevoix County. (After U. S. Lake Survey Chart.)

clay. The remainder is morainic material of sandy character. The drumlins are characterized by smooth slopes and a general parallelism of their longer axes and were formed under the glacier, the longer axes indicating the direction of the ice movement. The smooth slopes adjoining the lake are high, rising in places to heights of three hundred feet above the lake. In many cases, the drumlins are roughly parallel to the basin of the lake, but considerable discordance is found, especially in the South Arm, and the basin is considered to have been independent of the ice movement at the time when the drumlins were formed. This idea is further strengthened by the fact that the basin of the lake is exceptionally free from islands, shoals, and deep holes.

The physiographic history of Pine Lake shows four distinct levels, in which respect it is not exceeded by any of the inland lakes of the State. The shore lines of these levels, especially the two highest, are conspicuous on the slopes above the lake and stand usually at moderate distances from the present shore, see Plate VII. The highest terrace stands about eighty-five feet above the lake at Charlevoix and was formed by Lake Algonquin. In contrast to the lakes of the Cheboygan basin, Pine Lake was not greatly extended in area during this stage except at Horton Bay, Boyne City, and in the South Arm. The latter was connected with the series of narrow troughs which lead to Grand Traverse Bay and in which lie Intermediate, Torchlight and Elk Lakes.

The next lower level is that of the Nipissing Lakes, and the beach stands twenty-seven feet above Pine Lake at Charlevoix. The sinking of the water to this level was accompanied by considerable constriction of the lake at the extremities, and the basin was isolated except for a narrow strait at Charlevoix. Following the Nipissing stage, a drop of eighteen feet brought the level to nine feet above the present. This level may be designated as the Post-Nipissing, and the basin was completely isolated for the first time. The drop from the Post-Nipissing stage to a level four feet above the present, which we shall call the Upper Level, probably accompanied the downward cutting of the outlet. This level was abandoned when the lake was connected with Lake Michigan by an artificial channel in 1873, the amount of lowering being 3 62 feet, according to the United States Engineer.

The interesting history of the lake may be profitably supplemented by a study of the shore features at the various levels. In general, it may be stated that the regularity of the basin and the smoothness of the surrounding slopes have not furnished conditions for large adjustments of the shore lines. Also, on account of the greater power of the waves and possibly longer periods of action, the adjustments at the higher levels were of greater magnitude.

The narrow neck of land which separates Pine Lake from Lake Michigan is less than a mile in width. Its surface is composed of a flat terrace, the Nipissing, standing at an elevation of slightly less than thirty feet above Lake Michigan, and above this on either side rises a steep cliff to the Algonquin terrace, more than eighty feet above the lake. A rather deep depression, occupied by Round Lake, breaks the monotony of the Nipissing terrace and connects with Lake Michigan by a narrow channel, artificially deepened and widened. The connection with Pine Lake is now by an artificial channel which isolated Park Island the north side of which is formed by the Old River, the former outlet of Pine Lake. The channels are dug to a minimum depth of twelve feet and allow the entrance of large vessels into Round Lake, which makes an excellent harbor. The town of Charlevoix is built on the higher terraces but largely on the Nipissing terrace west of Round Lake. This thriving town is one of the most popular summer resorts of the State and is by far the best location on the lake. The extension of the lake towards the southeast is almost directly away from Lake Michigan, and the cooling effect of the lake breezes is slight at the farther extremities. Consequently, the lake as a whole is not so extensively patronized by summer visitors as are some others in the State.

On the Lake Michigan side of the Nipissing terrace at Charlevoix stands a narrow sand bar which developed from the southwest and must have crowded the outlet to the north, although it probably did not completely close it. Towards Pine Lake the Nipissing terrace is bordered by a cliff which drops to the Post-Nipissing level. In the early part of this stage Round and Pine lakes were connected by a strait about five hundred feet in width, but this connection was gradually narrowed by a bar which developed in a northeasterly direction from the cliffs on the south side of the present channel to the large bend in the Old River. Sufficient water passed through the channel to keep it open, but the bar was able to force the stream to the cliffs on the north side. Above the shore of Pine Lake in this vicinity, the Upper and Post-Nipissing shores are well defined, the former having an especially fresh appearance. Thus, in the vicinity of Charlevoix the four main stages of the lake may be readily distinguished.

Along the north shore the Nipissing terrace narrows and soon disappears. At the present shore are found storm beaches indicating the existence of powerful waves which develop with a fetch of several miles when the wind is from the southeast. At the most northern tip of the lake is a lowland extension which was the scene of strong current action in former times   The present shore swings in an even curve towards Pine Point and is bordered by a flat which slopes gently upward to a distinct sand bar about one hundred yards from the shore   Behind the bar, the crest of which stands four feet above the lake, is a swampy lagoon, which gradually becomes drier to the north.   The depression is again interrupted beyond by a strong bar which stands twenty feet above Pine Lake.   In both cases, the bars extend completely across the depression and, since their elevations correspond to the Nipissing and Upper Levels, we may conclude that portions of this bay were cut off from the main lake at those levels   The present conditions at Pine Point show moderate wave and current action from the west, thus enabling us to determine the direction of the development of these bars

Pine Point was formerly much more prominent than at present because, in addition to the bay just discussed, there existed a narrow indentation east of the point, which extended fully a quarter of a mile inland.   This bay persisted until the Upper Level, during which a bar was built near the present shore   An attempt at draining the lagoon, thus formed, was made by digging a ditch through the bar, but with mediocre success   At the present level the only shore action is accomplished by waves which have thrown up a storm beach of sufficient height to enclose a narrow, crescent-shaped lagoon   Along this shore the waves have laid bare considerable marl which was deposited during earlier stages.

On either side of Oyster Bay drumlin-like projections of nearly north-south trend reach the lake shore and are responsible for its irregularity. On the lake side of the promonotory west of the bay the waves are actively cutting as they have been in the past   The effects are seen in a beach of rather coarse material and in distinct, but narrow, terraces of the Upper, Post-Nipissing, and Nipissing levels   Oyster Bay occupies a shallow sag that continues northward forty rods or more beyond the present shore   During the Upper Level, the greater part of this depression was covered, but a distinct bar within two hundred feet of the present shore indicates the formation of a lagoon at the head   The extinction of this lagoon was caused by accumulation of marl, heavy deposits of which may now be seen

The long stretch between Oyster Bay and Horton Bay is noticeable mainly for the perfection of the terraces of the former levels of the lake, shown diagrammatically in Figure 53. The least developed of the terraces is the Post-Nipissing which has been cut away in places   The minor projections, for example Wilson Point, all show active cutting by waves on the west side and a tendency towards deposition on the east   Thus the beaches are stony to the west but of fine ma-

terial or of marl on the opposite sides. The coarser beaches are
in places pushed into low ice ramparts. One mile beyond Wilson
Point is the Shale Dock which marks the location of the only outcrop
of rock near the present shore of the lake. It is a dark-colored, soft
shale and was formerly used by the Bay Shore Lime Co., which
operated the quarry and shipped the rock by water to its plant at
Bay Shore. This outcrop does not reach the present shore but was
undoubtedly carved by waves in the past. However, the rock
weathers so easily that the characteristic shore forms have been
destroyed.

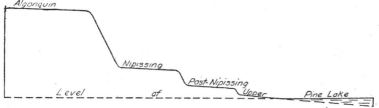

Fig. 53. Diagram showing exposed terraces along the shores of Pine Lake.

The shore west of Horton Bay shows an extension of the Upper
Level terrace which continues to the bay. This bay lies in a depression which caused a large expansion of the lake during the stages
previous to the Upper Level. This was especially marked during
Lake Algonquin and extended several miles up the Horton Creek
valley. The rounded projection of land on the west side of the bay
was covered until the lake stood at the Post-Nipissing level. During
this stage it was a narrow promontory and was severely pounded
by the waves on the lake side, forming a beach of coarse material.
This rubble was pushed into a decided ice rampart which still stands
four to five feet above the beach and contains many good sized
boulders. The Upper Level is well shown by a definite beach which
swings around the point and into the bay as a bar, cutting off the
swampy hinterland. On the east side of the bay the high ground
lies from one-eighth to one-fourth of a mile from the shore, and a
similar bar at the same level cut off the lowland at the foot of the
hills. This bar developed from the east, as is shown by the westward
turning of Horton Creek before entering the bay. From Horton Bay
to Boyne City and beyond the surrounding topography is morainic
rather than drumlinoidal, and the material is sandy till. This is
readily detected by the change in the beach material from rubble to
sand about one-half mile beyond the bay. This shore is exposed to
strong westerly winds and the wave action is intense. The former
levels are well shown with the exception of the Post-Nipissing which

has been cut away. The absence of this terrace in a locality of strong wave action, while those above and below it are well developed, may be interpreted to mean that this stage was of short duration.

The configuration of the lake is such that the fetch of the waves driven by westerly winds, the most important here, decreases to the south and currents become relatively more effective. Therefore deposition is to be expected where shore conditions permit. This is well illustrated as Horse Point is approached from the north, where a broad indentation formerly existed. At present, the beach is of fine sand and of even curvature to the end of the point. Inland at the Upper Level is a narrow spit which almost parallels the present shore and encloses an elongated lagoon. Similarly on the landward side of this lagoon is another spit at the Post-Nipissing level, which likewise has cut off a lagoon but of smaller proportions. At the tip of the point, however, wave action again predominates, and the Upper Level terrace has a width of from one hundred to two hundred feet. In addition, the coarse material has been forced up into a decided rampart at the present shore. Ramparts on a lake of this size must be largely of the ice jam type and are a further indication of the power of the waves. South of the point the hills recede from the shore, and broad terraces of the Upper and Post-Nipissing levels are present. The width of the terraces is due to the flatness of the slope rather than excessive shore action. At the present shore wave action is cutting into the Upper Level terrace. This cutting is slight as a rule, but at A (see map) the waves have reduced the Upper Level terrace and are cutting into the sand of the Post-Nipissing. As Boyne City is approached, the upland stands nearer the lake and the terraces are narrow but distinct.

At Boyne City the lower levels follow the present shore but are obscured by buildings. The Algonquin shores run to the southeast as far as Boyne Falls and it is on the terraces of this and the Nipissing stages that most of the city is built. Along the southwest shore from Boyne City to the entrance of the South Arm the upland slopes somewhat steeply to the shore, and consequently the terraces are narrow. The Algonquin and Upper Level terraces are well defined, but the intermediate ones vary in development and are obliterated locally. Shore action is limited in this part of the lake and is mainly by waves which have made a stony beach. Inferior local ice ramparts on the beaches of the Upper and present levels are evidence of an ice shove of moderate force. The moderate wave action is somewhat intensified on the southeast sides of the points which, with the exception of that at Platten Dock, are due to the glacial topography On the northwest sides of points, current action has enclosed small lagoons in some cases, as at B At Platten Dock a stream entering the lake has built out a delta of considerable proportions This delta was formed during Nipissing times and since then has been degraded by wave action on its borders, forming terraces at the Post-Nipissing and Upper Levels The terrace of the latter is now swampy, due to the presence of a storm beach at the present shore In places along this shore wave action at the present level has cut low cliffs, which often expose marl Such localities are easily recognized when waves are running by the milky appearance of the shallow water

The broad point between the main lake and the South Arm is exposed to the heavy seas of the northeasterly winds and wave action is powerful In addition, the original slopes were low, consequently all the terraces are well developed and wide Ice has also been active in this locality, having formed distinct ramparts on the beaches of the present and Upper levels on the west side of the point The intensive work of the waves on this point may be appreciated by a trip of somewhat over one-fourth mile eastward from the narrows of the South Arm to a drumlin, the top of which was completely bevelled during Algonquin time The drumlins are, perhaps, best developed along the South Arm but as a rule lie beyond the borders of Lake Algonquin

The entrance to the South Arm is almost closed by an abrupt projection of the shore from the east side The south end of this projection makes a sharp re-entrant and affords at its tip an excellent index of current action through the narrows An incipient spit shows that weak southward moving currents pass through It will be seen from the map that waves of considerable size may be formed from the north The drive of these waves tends to pile up the water on this shore and the only outlet is through this narrowing channel, even though it is tortuous.

The South Arm nowhere reaches a mile in width and the adjoining slopes are consistently steep Consequently, wave action is moderate and shore adjustments are much less striking than along the shores of the main lake. However, the Algonquin and Nipissing terraces, shown in Plate VII, are well developed and encircle this arm of the lake This is to be expected since the lake was larger during these stages and also received some of the swells of the main lake For the most part, the lower beaches are distinct but only locally are they well developed The best development is found on the numerous small headlands, illustrated by point C All four terraces are found here, and, in addition, a small spit is growing to the north at the present level. The only winds effective on this shore are those from northerly or southerly quadrants, and the latter are the more important on account of their long reach. Farther south, point D shows a wide Nipissing terrace into which the waves have cut a low cliff. The lower terraces seem to have been poorly developed here and were quickly obliterated. South of this blunt point the slopes are flatter and all the terraces are present. The effects of ice action are seen in the fragmentary ramparts at the Post-Nipissing and Upper levels, caused probably by expansion here.

With slight variations, the conditions just described continue to East Jordan where the narrow, lower terraces encircle the end of the lake with some extension up the valley of the Jordan river. This stream has deposited large quantities of material and filled in a considerable area at the head of the lake during the lower levels. It enters from the west and has constricted the end of the lake by deposition from this side. The development of the higher terraces is almost identical with that at Boyne City, except that the Algonquin was even more extended.

On the west side of the South Arm the features are so similar to those opposite that a detailed description seems unnecessary. The shore from point E northward to the next prominent projection is worthy of mention on account of the prominence of the Post-Nipissing terrace, which is usually poorly developed. The adjustments at present are mainly due to cutting and this on the north sides of the points. Again, at Holy Island the terraces are well developed. This island first stood above water during the Post-Nipissing stage, and this and succeeding levels are distinctly shown. On the sides, the levels are indicated by notches and low cliffs, and at the ends terraces thirty or more feet in width are present. At the north end a bar has nearly bridged the shallow water between the island and the mainland, and artificial filling with brush has sufficed for a rude roadway to the island.

The west side of the narrows is flanked by narrow terraces which broaden somewhat as the main lake is reached, and on these terraces Sequanota is built. Beyond Sequanota the terraces are again narrow and the lower ones are indistinct in places, as at F, the Upper Level having been entirely removed. The broad embayment west of F is a depression between drumlins and was formerly much more extensive. When the water dropped to the Upper Level, this was reduced to a shallow bay, and during this time a bar and lagoon were formed. The bar stands near the present shore and the lagoon is now a swampy lowland. At Two Mile

Point, a drumlin, the Post-Nipissing and Upper Level terraces are again well developed with a low ice rampart of rock on the shore of the latter This rampart runs around the point into Newman Bay where it changes from coarse material to sand and has the characteristics of a storm beach It is readily recognized by a row of pines growing on its surface Back of it stands the sandy terrace of the Post-Nipissing level, and in front the broad, sandy terrace of the Upper Level extends to the present shore The loose sands on this terrace are being blown into small, irregular dunes Beyond the bay to Charlevoix the upland stands near the shore and the terraces are very distinct.

As may be inferred from the description above, the adjustments of the shores of Pine Lake, although moderate in effects, have been numerous and were made at the higher levels Probably the greatest changes took place at the Upper Level, and the most noticeable of these was the development of bars across the more prominent embayments This level was abandoned less than fifty years ago and only minor adjustments have occurred since that time The main work at present is the cutting by waves and this has seldom advanced to the limits of the Upper Level. Incipient current forms are present in a few localities but are almost negligible when compared with those formed at the previous levels. A well-developed, but narrow, submerged terrace is continuous around the lake and varies in depth at its outer edge from three feet off sheltered shores to ten feet, the latter being more nearly representative for the lake as a whole The interpretation of this terrace in terms of wave lengths developed on the lake is uncertain on account of the small differences in elevation between the Post-Nipissing, Upper and present levels, in all nine feet Nowhere was the undisturbed outer slope of the Post-Nipissing terrace seen, while, as a rule, the Upper Level terrace is continuous with that of the present. Thus, the difficulty arises of determining at which level the present submerged terrace developed The Post-Nipissing adjustments are much inferior to those of the Upper Level and, since we know that the present conditions have existed for an insignificant period of time, it seems safe to conclude that the present submerged terrace is the unexposed portion of that formed during the Upper Level Neglecting the small amount of lowering of the surface of the terrace which may have taken place since that time, the depth was about fourteen feet at the outer edge for most parts of the lake This is probably somewhat less than one-half of the wave length of storm waves on this lake

The lack of adjustment at the present level is due in part to its short period of existence and also to the fact that adjustments were of an advanced stage during the preceding level Thus, the embayments were largely reduced and the submerged terrace was very flat The latter must materially reduce the force of the breakers and will have to be lowered from the outer edge before the waves can strike the shores with normal force The planation of this terrace will be slow because it is covered with a deposit of marl on most shores, which is very compact when wet and also furnishes no tools to aid in the work of the waves. When the waves are finally able to work effectively, the headlands will be rapidly cut away and the broad embayments built out rather than cut off by currents, making a mature shoreline.

The extinction of a large and deep lake such as Pine is an extremely slow process Filling is proceeding at a very slow rate on account of the small and infrequent influents This will increase as the streams enlarge their basins but, up to the present time, has had little effect except at the end of the South Arm. Filling by marl and peat near the shores may have some importance but, as a rule, vegetation finds difficulty in getting started on a wave swept shore It seems probable then that the future of Pine Lake is linked with that of Lake Michigan If the tilting of the Great Lakes basin shall be sufficient to lower the level of Lake Michigan more than one hundred feet, Pine Lake will be drained Otherwise, the slow process of filling will cause extinction.

TORCHLIGHT LAKE

Bordering Grand Traverse Bay on its eastern side are two deep troughs in which Torchlight and Elk Lakes lie. These troughs are depressions in the drumlin area mentioned in the discussion of Pine Lake and run almost north south, conforming very closely to the trend of the drumlins As may be seen from a map of the Traverse region, these basins lie oblique to the eastern side of Grand Traverse Bay, approaching it at the northern ends The narrow strips of land separating the lakes from the bay are at the north ends in both cases a series of bars which developed early in the history of the lakes and have been blown into dunes. Thus, the lakes, from one viewpoint, may be classed as lagoons, but the depressions themselves are similar in formation to that of Pine Lake and have been briefly discussed in Chapter I.

The larger and more easterly basin is occupied by Torchlight Lake which is connected with Elk Lake through Round Lake, Fig 54. Torchlight Lake is one of the larger lakes of the State, its area being 28 5, and is known to be deep, although systematic

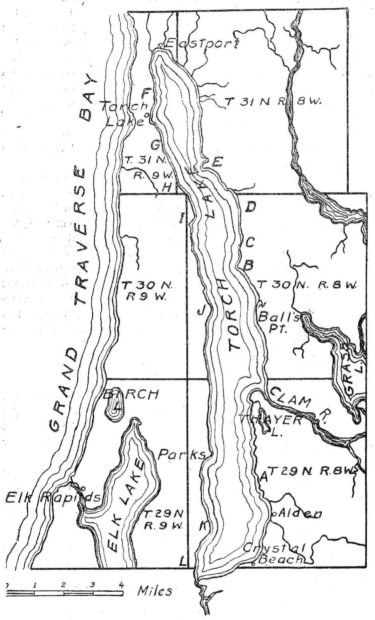

Fig. 54. Map of Torchlight Lake

soundings have not been made. Its length is slightly less than eighteen miles, the longest of the inland lakes of our state, and its width nowhere exceeds two and one half miles, the average being considerably less than this figure. So nearly is the lake oriented north and south that only at the northwestern end does it cross a range line. Furthermore, the outline of the lake is consistently regular. As a consequence of its regular configuration, its size, and orientation, the lake becomes dangerously rough during the "blows" from the north or south. Although this may be disadvantageous for navigation by small boats, it is productive of intense wave and current action, and numerous and important adjustments of the shores may be anticipated.

As may be inferred from the description of Pine Lake basin, the history of Torchlight has much in common. The Algonquin and Nipissing shore lines stand out prominently on the smooth slopes of the drumlins and are counterparts of those on Pine Lake. Also a Post-Nipissing stage is to be found in favorable localities and, where present, is but slightly above the present level. The present stage is artificially maintained by a dam at Elk Rapids which has held the water above its normal level for about seventy years. The head of water at the dam is seven and one-half feet, but the amount of flooding of the lake cannot well be determined, due to lack of both physiographic evidence and human records, although it is believed to be much less than might be inferred from the height of the dam. It is well to keep in mind, however, that an apparently insignificant raising of a lake level may attain considerable importance as the shores develop under the new conditions. As a matter of fact, this lake is an excellent example of the effects produced under such circumstances.

This lake is readily reached by the Pere Marquette R. R. at Alden near the southern end, and is patronized annually by numerous visitors seeking recreation and relief from the summer heat. Its proximity to Grand Traverse Bay mitigates temperatures and its almost parallel trend with the bay makes this condition uniform over the entire lake. Many excellent locations for cottages are to be found, but as yet they are largely limited to the numerous points and the south end. The size of the lake and its flooded condition make storms especially severe, therefore a sheltered location is essential if boating is to be enjoyed. Such locations are found at Clam River and on the south sides of the points. Where shores exposed to wave action have been utilized, it has been necessary to build breakwaters of some kind to prevent the rapid recession of the cliffs.

19

Navigation is possible on the lake and its connecting waters through Elk Lake to Elk Rapids, and when visited by the writer daily service was maintained by boat from Elk Rapids as far as Clam River The surrounding country is a rich agricultural section and the feasibility of connecting this chain of lakes with Grand Traverse Bay is a problem for future development

For the visitor with physiographic bent, Alden is a convenient starting point. See map, Fig 54 Characteristic morainic topography borders the east side of the lake along this shore and extends northward beyond Clam River, a distance of about six miles From this locality to the north end of the lake and along the entire west shore, the smooth and rather steep side slopes of drumlins rise a hundred feet or more above the lake

The view across the lake from Alden is most pleasing, but to the practiced eye the significant observation is the terracing of the slopes An inspection of the immediate surroundings discloses these terraces at hand for closer study Two distinct terraces, separated by a grass-covered slope, are easily discernible, and measurement places their elevations at thirty-eight and fourteen feet above the lake level The higher is the Algonquin beach and the lower indicates the level at which Lake Nipissing stood

Along this shore northerly winds have full sweep of the lake and waves of great power are developed As a result, the intense cutting has formed low cliffs in the Nipissing terrace which, in places, is composed of stratified sand and gravel, see Plate VII, A This represents the outer or built portion of the terrace, but farther inland the boulders which are scattered over the sand covered surface of the terrace are an indication that here the terrace was cut in boulder clay and a veneer of sand was later deposited on its surface. Further evidence of a cut portion of the terrace is found in the numerous springs issuing from the base of the cliff which rises from this terrace to the Algonquin These springs are caused by the surface water seeping down through the built portion of the Algonquin terrace to the impervious underlying till, which was exposed by waves during Nipissing time The ground water which is unable to flow in the compact boulder clay seeps laterally along its upper surface and issues as springs where the clay is exposed The accompanying diagram, Fig 55, illustrates the conditions described

In addition to the exposed terraces, there is a well-defined submerged terrace of varying width and depth that virtually surrounds the lake, and its outer slope is known locally as the "channel bank." The description above holds, in general, for the east shore of the lake south of Clam River Locally, conditions have varied and a

A. STRATIFIED EDGE OF BUILT-TERRACE. TORCHLIGHT LAKE.

B. RAISED BOULDER STRAND, TORCHLIGHT LAKE.

diversity in the development of the shore features is found at the various levels, including the present. Much of the adjustment of the shores has taken place at the higher levels, thus determining to a large extent adjustment at the present level.

At the present shore the cliff, which is receding into the Nipissing terrace, is almost continuous and stands, usually, six to eight feet high. On the longer reaches, this cliff is composed of sand and gravel, which is often stratified, and at its base are smooth sand beaches. At the minor projections the material is resistant boulder clay and the beaches are of coarser material. These points are caused by morainic knobs which were formerly more prominent but have been worn back by wave action. The intervening embayments, however, were never pronounced, and the material derived from intense wave action on the north sides of the salients was deposited in these bays in comparatively wide built terraces rather than in distinct bars. Thus, when the lake level subsided and the terrace was exposed, the shore line was made more regular. In one

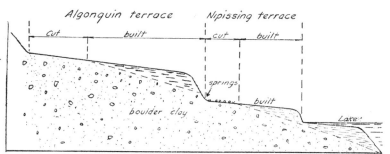

Fig. 55. Diagram showing terraces about the shores of Torchlight Lake. Note the location of springs at the base of the Nipissing cliff which has receded into the built portion of the Algonquin terrace.

locality, point A, the process was aided by the formation of a small delta at the Algonquin level by a stream, now dry. The blunt projection north of locality A shows an excessive amount of cutting on the north side, where the waves have removed the Nipissing shore and are now attacking the Algonquin terrace, forming cliffs of considerable height.

The Algonquin terrace bevels the neck of land between Thayers Lake and Torchlight, which shows that the two basins were connected during Algonquin time. At first, the connection was restricted to the outlet of Thayers Lake but widened as wave action reduced the narrow headland which separated them. During Nipissing time, the lakes were entirely separated, since the Nipissing terrace does not enter Thayers Lake basin.

In the wide embayment one-half mile south of Lone Tree Point,
concentric sand bars are found on the Nipissing terrace At the
north end two such bars are present but they split and double in
number to the south These do not appear to be the typical bars
which are built by currents across the neck of an indentation, since
there is no indication of lagoons and no abrupt change in direction
of the shore to cause the currents to swing out. They are better
interpreted either as storm beaches or a series of submerged sand
bars, sometimes found under similar conditions, which are probably
formed simultaneously by breakers during a storm The close
assortment and fineness of the material makes the latter interpretation the more probable

Lone Tree Point is the most prominent projection in this part
of the lake and was originally due to a morainic knob near the
lake This knob was bevelled by the waves of Lake Algonquin, but
the waters of Nipissing succeeded only in notching its lakeward
side and forming a terrace of considerable width. When the water
level dropped from the Nipissing stage, this projection was sufficient to turn the currents out into the lake, and deposition rather
than cutting became the predominant process Near the present
level, a spit was built at the end of the point, the main portion of
which stands two to three feet above the water and represents a
former level of the lake This we shall call the Upper Level.

Points, such as Lone Tree, which are the result of currents leaving the shore, are interesting and instructive because they serve as
indices to the effectiveness of the forces acting Currents may run
in opposite directions along a shore, depending on the direction of
the winds, and their strength is determined by the force and direction of the waves Not only do the stronger currents transport
proportionally greater amounts of material than the weaker, but
they deposit it in forms which are more nearly in line with the
shore at the point of departure, i. e., have a lesser curvature In
the case under consideration, the curvature of the north side of the
spit is much less than the south, indicating a much stronger current from the northerly direction There is little or no difference
in the resistance of the material upon which the waves are working
along the shores of this lake and the strength attained by the
currents must be determined by the force of the winds Winds
whose directions have no easterly component are effective on this
shore, but there is a preponderance, both as to velocity and frequency, of those from the northwesterly quadrant rather than from
the southwest When we consider the added advantage of a reach
twice as great for northerly winds at this point, the unsymmetrical

form of the spit is readily appreciated. Yet waves and currents of considerable force are active on the south side, as is shown by the even, although sharp, curvature of the shoreline and the presence of storm beaches at the Upper level. The superior strength of the forces at work on the north side is shown at the present time by the decided contrast in the work accomplished under the flooded condition. Current action is still effective on the south side, but on the north the waves are cutting back the point and have necessitated some form of breakwater. In this connection it may be stated that the name Lone Tree is no longer appropriate, for the solitary sentinel has long since succumbed to the force of the waves.

Northward from Lone Tree Point the shore swings to the northeast and is exposed to the full sweep of northwesterly winds. Much cutting by the waves is taking place and the cliffs in the Nipissing terrace are rapidly receding, causing considerable anxiety to the cottage owners in the locality. Breakwaters of brush, placed with twig ends outward, seem to prove temporarily effective. The blunt point presents a decided contrast to Lone Tree Point in that no deposition has taken place here. The Algonquin and Nipissing beaches swing back into the narrow depression in which Clam Lake lies but reappear on the north side. The smooth beach with cliff, above which stand the Nipissing and Algonquin terraces in turn, are present as far as Balls Point. This point is clearly the result of deposition by shore currents of considerable power, as shown by the rather coarse, but assorted, material. It is difficult to assign reasons for the currents leaving the shore at this point, inasmuch as the configuration of the bottom is not known, but, nevertheless, those from both directions do so. The currents from the north, however, are the more powerful and have laid down a much heavier deposit on the north side. In general, a submerged terrace of considerable width is present along the shore, but it widens to nearly one-fourth mile off the point and drops into deep water at eight feet. The great quantity of deposited material shows intensive action at this point, and a widening of Nipissing and present terraces shows also that this has occurred since Algonquin time. Most of the work was done during Nipissing time, with considerable addition at the present level during which the wide submerged terrace has been formed. A small but interesting ice rampart was found at the very tip of the point, off which the lake has a width of nearly two miles. This width is too great for ice expansion and, since ice jams are known to have been effective at one locality on the lake, it is probable that this agent has been effective here.

North of Balls Point the shores offer nothing of additional interest until point B (see map) is reached. This is one of the best
developed points on the lake, having a length of five to six hundred
feet, and is similar to Balls, although much sharper. As it is approached from the south, there first appears along the shore a cliff
rising to the full height of the Nipissing terrace, but as the point
is reached the cliff drops to a height of eight feet and later gives
way to a lower terrace fronted by a storm beach. The explanation
is furnished by the topography of the point which is shown in a
conventional sketch, Fig. 56. From the sketch it will be noted that

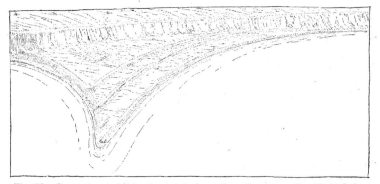

Fig. 56.   Conventional sketch of point designated as B on map, Torchlight Lake.

the highest or Algonquin terrace does not widen at the point but
that below this are three roughly triangular terraces which stand
at successively lower elevations and are separated by low cliffs.
These cliffs diverge somewhat as they cross the point in a northwesterly direction and end abruptly at the cliff on the north side.
The highest of these terraces is the Nipissing and the rise from the
lake level to this is accomplished in three steps. The surface of
the lowest terrace is somewhat irregular, but those above are of
characteristic slope and surface, except for a depression in the
Nipissing terrace which, although slight, is quite noticeable. The
point started to develop during the Nipissing stage and was extended beyond the present limits of this terrace. The depression
in this terrace shows that currents from both directions left the
shore in this vicinity and developed spits which met some distance
off shore and formed a point, a V-bar, see Chapter II. Its position
was slightly north of the present point. Then the water dropped
to the next lower level, called the Post-Nipissing, of which we know
little except that the waves were active on the south side of this
point and cut a well defined cliff in the Nipissing terrace. The

Upper Level is represented by the terrace which stands below the Post-Nipissing and extends to the present shore of the lake The uneven surface of this terrace suggests a somewhat different manner of formation than for the smooth surface of the typical cut-and-built terrace which develops under water. Close examination discloses the presence of indistinct ridges, and the deposit may, therefore, be interpreted as a series of poorly defined storm beaches modified by ice shove.

At present the point is being cut back on the north side, and the material is either being transferred to the south side or carried out into the lake On the south side deposition predominates, although waves of considerable power are active, as shown by a recent storm beach composed of pebbles up to three inches in diameter In general, it may be stated that the point is gradually shifting southward and possibly being diminished in size

North of the point the two lower terraces are absent but the Nipissing and Algonquin are well developed, especially at point C where the waves are now cutting into a hill of boulder clay. The submerged terrace is here scattered with boulders and is therefore, formed by cutting rather than by deposition, a condition infrequently met at present on this lake Beyond C shore action decreases and the Upper terrace reappears on the grass covered slopes

At point D an interesting variation of the general shore conditions is to be found At the present level an ice rampart lines the shore and causes a swampy condition on the gently sloping surface of the Upper Level terrace back of it This terrace rises gradually to the low front slope of the Nipissing terrace, which apparently was not attacked by waves during the Upper Level stage and stands at its original width Similarly, the wide Nipissing terrace is bounded inland by a cliff of such gentle slope that it may be considered the original front slope of the Algonquin terrace

Northward from this locality two small streams flow through a sag in the hills and cross the terraces Singularly, these streams have been able to deepen their channels only in the Algonquin terrace which here has the characteristics of a small delta. if this sudden change in the activity of the streams were due solely to the fact that the older terraces have been exposed to their action for a longer period of time, one might expect a gradational decrease in the amount of cutting in the lower terraces But the change is abrupt and it is probable that a large decrease in the volume of the streams occurred as the water dropped to the Nipissing level, indicating a climatic change

Northward towards point E the shore swings to the northwest

with no unusual variation in the shore. The slopes have not been cleared, and the trees which grow to the water's edge have efficiently protected the shores so that cliffs are rare. The monotony is relieved at point E near which is located the State Y. M. C. A. camp. The bend in the shore line at the point caused the currents to leave the shore and deposit their suspended material in a form which is almost perfectly preserved. The point had its inception during Nipissing time and developed into a perfect hook from the south, see Fig. 57. The curvature of the hook was greater

Fig. 57. Conventional sketch of point near Y. M. C. A. camp, Torchlight Lake.

than that of the main shore and the re-curved portion was growing almost directly toward the mainland. The narrow channel which connected the lagoon, thus formed, with the lake was partially filled by the development of a submerged bar from the north side. This form will be recognized as an unsymmetrical V-bar in process of formation.

Below the Nipissing level is a narrow bench at the Upper Level and at the present shore there is an accumulation of fresh gravel. The Post-Nipissing is absent. During the Upper Level the shores were continuous on both sides of the point and the development was outward into the lake with less tendency towards growth to the north. This is also true at the present time, as shown by the relatively larger accumulation at the end of the point.

The points on this shore previously discussed indicate strong currents from the north but here conditions are reversed. It will be seen from the location of the point near the north end of the lake that the reach of the waves is greater from the south and is the controlling factor rather than the prevalence of storm winds.

As might be expected from the study ot point E, the evidence of wave action is noticeably less along the shore from this point to Eastport, situated at the north end of the lake At the present shore fresh cliffs are much less frequent and the Nipissing terrace is relatively narrow, the intermediate levels being absent About one mile north of point E a line of boulders forced into the base ot a cliff is evidence of strong ice push along this shore.

At Eastport a sand beach curves around the north end of the lake and the hinterland rises very gradually to a well defined bar at the Nipissing level, upon which much of the town is located Back of the bar there is a sandy depression dotted with small sand dunes The narrow neck which here separates Torchlight Lake from Lake Michigan is of sand and stands at the Algonquin level except for a zone of dunes which rise to a maximum of twenty-five feet. Beyond the dunes a series of parallel bars with intervening lagoons extends to the cliff overlooking Lake Michigan. From this description it is evident that the north end of Torchlight lake was connected with Lake Michigan and was cut off during Algonquin time by a series of bars As the water receded to the Nipissing level, the earlier bars were blown into dunes and the somewhat irregular outline of the north end of Torchlight lake was straightened by the development of the bar at Eastport. The lower levels were not productive of adjustments here. This end of the lake is subjected to strong ice jams in the spring, but the sandy beach with its scant vegetation is not favorable for the formation of permanent ramparts However, east of the dock there is a row ot poplars a few feet back from the shore. The roots of the trees have served as binding material for the sand, and a well preserved rampart has been formed in front of the row, but disappears abruptly at each end. Observation of this rampart in process of formation, by inhabitants of the locality, makes it certain that ice jams exerted the shove are, therefore, effective on the shores of this lake.

Along the west side low ground borders the lake and has been converted into a lagoon by the formation of a bar at the present or Upper Level This continues to point F where the divide between this lake and Lake Michigan rises above the Algonquin level and both the Algonquin and Nipissing terraces are present. Off this point the "channel bank" is very decided and drops into deep water from a depth of six feet at a rate of almost one to one, the slope of the bottom being from thirty-five to forty degrees

At Torch Lake the divide narrows and stands at an elevation which is below the Algonquin beach Wells in the vicinity penetrate clay before reaching a water-bearing layer and, since no bar is to be found on the crest of the divide, we must conclude that a connection with Lake Algonquin was open in this locality, although closed at Eastport. This connection was nearly two miles in width, reaching from point F to point G Further evidence of an open connection was found in the vicinity of point G, where a strong spit at the Algonquin level runs in a southeasterly direction into the Torchlight basin from a point of the upland on the south side of the strait

It appears, then, that the north end of the Torchlight basin was connected with that of Grand Traverse Bay by a double connection during Algonquin time The adjustments of the shores of Lake Algonquin were numerous and diverse, and, in general, it may be stated that virtually all indentations, such as those occupied by the border lakes, were isolated by the development of bars In this case, it is exceptional that only the northerly connection was closed, and the most reasonable explanation involves the factors of effective winds and available material The westerly to northerly winds were the most effective and bars developed from the north along the shore of Lake Algonquin The long stretch of shore below Charlevoix furnished sufficient material for the bar across the north channel but the limited amount of land between the two channels, F, was inadequate for a similar development across the south channel In addition, the westerly winds were able to turn the limited deposits on the south side of this channel almost directly into the Torchlight basin, as shown by the bar back of Point G already mentioned, and so kept the channel open

Along the west shore wave action is less intense than on the opposite shore and the terraces are somewhat better preserved, although not so well developed Below the Algonquin level, the Nipissing terrace is always well developed but that of the Post-Nipissing stage is very poorly defined The points were as a rule started during Nipissing time but considerable additions were made during the Upper Level stage This level may also be recognized in some of the bays, for example, that north of point H, either as a terrace or as ice ramparts

Point H started its development in Nipissing time as a V-bar which now stands slightly south of the present point The two bars, enclosing a depression more than ten feet deep, are excellently preserved The greatest deposition occurred during the Upper Level and formed the main portion of the point At present it is being cut away on the north side but is increasing on the south and at the end of the point The deposition is further shown by the broad submerged terrace on the south side Comparing conditions at this

A. ALGONQUIN BAR, TORCHLIGHT LAKE.

B. ALGONQUIN BAR, ELK LAKE.

point with those at E across the lake, we find them reversed, that is,
E has been built mainly by southerly currents and H by northerly
currents

South of point H the slopes are gentle and rise to the Nipissing
level with slight indications of intermediate stages   At point I
a V-bar with characteristics and history almost identical with those
already described breaks the rather even shoreline   The chief interest lies in the amount of deposition that has taken place in recent times   A long spit extends fully one hundred yards beyond the
portion built at the Upper Level in a direction somewhat south of
east but is being cut away on the north side under the present
flooded condition of the lake

South of I the usual shore conditions prevail except where drumlins approach the lake   Here the currents have left the shore and
two such points occur before point J is reached. At J a large
drumlin caused the original projection in the shoreline and became
a locality of intensified wave action. During the Algonquin and
Nipissing stages well defined terraces and cliffs were cut and the
side of the drumlin was steepened considerably. However, late in
Nipissing time conditions changed and two small V-bars developed,
which have been enlarged at the lower levels, making a double
point. It is interesting to note that the more northerly point is
being added to under the present conditions and especially on the
north side, while the southerly one is being worn away   On the
latter numerous large boulders have been lined on the shore by ice
action.

In general, on this lake the adjustments of the shores at levels
below the Algonquin are the more important, due largely to the
fact that cutting by waves predominated almost to the exclusion of
currents on the relatively smooth shores in this embayment of
Lake Algonquin. Thus the rather monotonous description of the
terrace and cliffs of this shore has not been dwelt upon   On the
west side of the lake the topography is less regular, and several
small indentations were encountered at this level within a distance
of six miles south of point J   The result was a straightening of
the shore by the development of completed bars across the mouths
of these bays, Plate IX, A. After the drop to the Nipissing level,
the waves worked back towards the bars and replaced the gentle
front slopes by a steep cliff. In no case was the bar entirely removed and the remnants, with their flat tops and steep side
slopes, now resemble railroad embankments. Ice also was active
during the Nipissing stage but shore conditions were such that the

most noticeable result was the lining of boulders on the beach, illustrated in Plate VIII, B

Immediately south of point J the first of the bars is encountered, but here the Nipissing shore did not advance far inland and the embankment effect is not so pronounced   Between this point and Parks five similar features are to be found   The indentations were all small and at present furnish limited drainage basins, so that the bars are, with one exception, intact and the low ground adjacent to the bars is swampy   In the south part of section 7, T 29 N , R. 8 W, such an indentation of larger size furnished sufficient surface water to cut a drainage channel through the bar. The intervening stretches are marked by relatively narrow terraces of the Algonquin and Nipissing levels which widen at the well developed points indicated on the map as K and L   The higher terraces are complete, except for a short stretch south of Parks where the Nipissing shore has been removed   The waves are working into the front slope of the Algonquin terrace but have not as yet extended the cliff to its full height

The feebleness of the shores of the exposed levels and the presence of a narrow submerged terrace at the present level mark this shore as one subjected to relatively light wave action   Winds from the northeasterly quadrant are the most effective, having an excessive reach which embraces the whole length of the lake   This is clearly shown by the points K and L which are being built to the south   Also the "channel bank" in each case is wide on the north side (the side of stronger wave action) but becomes much narrower on the lee, or south, side   Although this shore has been subjected to light wave action, on the average, it must not be inferred that the waves are of meager development. On the contrary, as study of points K and L shows, the waves during occasional severe storms beat with great power against this shore   Both points started their growth during Lake Nipissing and developed into small V-bars   These bars have since been added to mainly at the present level, and in each case the deposit is in the form of storm beaches. Thus, at K are found two well developed storm beaches on the north side of the point, which merge into a single one on the south side and enclose a triangular cedar swamp   At L the storm beaches are not so pronounced and are confined to a series of southward extending loops at the tip of the point   The activity seems to be less on the more southerly point L, an observation readily confirmed at M, the last point on the lake   The latter is a simple broad point trending southward with no indication of storm beaches

The southward extension of the lake basin is a swampy flat but slightly above the lake level, leading directly to Round Lake. This was formerly a part of the much larger Algonquin and Nipissing lakes, which included Round and Elk in addition to Torchlight Lake Torch River leaves the lake at the extreme southwest corner, a fact readily explained if the south shore is traversed. Starting at the river one soon notices a low sand ridge which gradually increases in strength and elevation and swings with even curvature to the east side of the lake This is unmistakably a bar, although its profile is somewhat obscured by an ice rampart on the front slope, and may be easily traced to the Nipissing shore Thus, during Nipissing time a bar was developing which would have eventually isolated this lake basin, but a drop in the water level accomplished this result before its completion The submerged terrace is very wide at this end, due to the exceptionally strong undertow developed This wide terrace together with the clean sand beach fronting the bar, affords excellent bathing facilities and makes the location, Crystal Beach, a favorite with summer visitors. The presence of two sand bars on the submerged terrace, parallel to each other and the shore, is an interesting development These bars shift during storms and may vary in number and height but, as far as is known, never reach above the water level Since they are formed by breakers, their growth into true barriers is a possibility but it seems more probable that a depression of the water level sufficient to expose a portion of them is necessary for further development Many examples of such forms, composed of a series of parallel bars, are to be found in the Great Lakes and on their former shores now exposed, e g, at the north end of Torchlight Lake, but this is the only inland lake in which more than a single bar was found and is therefore noteworthy.

Having traversed the shores of the lake, we may now attempt a resumé of its history and conditions. During Algonquin time the basin was part of an archipelago which included Elk, Round and Torchlight Lakes and extended into the depression now occupied by Clam, Grass and Intermediate Lakes, which in turn was connected with the South Arm of Pine Lake The connection between the basin of this lake and Grand Traverse Bay was a double one at the north end but was partially closed at this time The development of the shores was largely by waves and the terraces are now continuous on both sides of the lake Currents were effective locally on the west side and succeeded in throwing bars across some minor embayments and in forming a large spit on the south side of the open connection with the main lake at the north end.

With the recession of the water to the Nipissing level the basin was definitely separated from the main lake at the north end and, later, partially so at the south by the growth of a bar which was largely submerged The Nipissing Level was such that wave action during this time encroached on the Algonquin Terrace, forming a steep cliff and terrace somewhat inferior in development to that of the Algonquin stage However, currents assumed a more important role and started the development of the present points With one or two exceptions, the deposits were V-bars which varied in symmetry according to their position on the lake shore Also in some of the broader embayments they aided in increasing the width of the submerged terrace, thus straightening the shore line when the water receded from this level. The most pronounced adjustment of the shores was accomplished at this time by the development of bars at both the north and south ends of the lake

The Post-Nipissing level was of short duration and the forms were of inferior development In fact, were it not for the distinct terrace at point B, its recognition would be difficult.

The Upper Level was of considerable duration and is recognizable largely by the depositional forms existing Nearly all of the points show considerable growth at this level and these forms gradually merge into those being formed at present. In addition to the growth of the points, considerable low ground was cut off by the development of a bar at the northeast end

As has already been stated, the lake is now in a flooded condition Wave action is very active on all parts of the shore exposed to strong winds, and cliffs are common These cliffs are receding rapidly and in a few places have removed the Nipissing terrace The points also show the effect of the increased activity and are being eroded on one side at least Erosion will continue until equilibrium is established and will result in continued cliff recession and in a reduction or shifting of the positions of the points Also the abundant wave-worked material will add greatly to the submerged terrace. As the activity of the waves decreases somewhat, currents may be more effective, causing a greater growth of the points

The final limit of point expansion would divide the lake into several smaller bodies but wave action can hardly be expected to furnish enough material on such a deep lake Tributary streams are few and short and the only large one, Clam River, drains a nearby lake Therefore little sediment can be supplied in this way Little reduction in size by the formation of bars is to be expected since this was accomplished at the higher levels in the few localities where conditions were favorable.

Vegetation has hardly made a beginning and cannot take hold as long as the waves continue to actively erode. This lake shows a revival of activity and presents problems of shore development rather than of extinction

ELK LAKE

Elk Lake is another member of the series of lakes which occupy similar basins east of Grand Traverse Bay These basins were briefly discussed in Chapter I and need no further discussion here. Elk Lake is slightly over nine miles in length and averages less than one and one-half miles in width, the maximum width nowhere exceeding two miles See Fig 58 Its surface covers thirteen square miles and is, thus, less than half the size of its neighbor, Torchlight. We compare it with Torchlight Lake purposely because of the very striking similarity between these two bodies of water. They occupy similar narrow, regular basins which follow the trend of the flanking drumlins, are oriented nearly north-south, are deep, have many features in common in the adjustment of their shores, and have passed through the same succession of events in their past. In fact, it would be difficult to find two lakes in such close proximity so nearly alike The same winds and storms have whipped the waters into waves and developed the currents which have adjusted the shores during the same period of time. The variable factor is, then, the size Differences in shore adjustments, both as to kind and amount. are attributable to this cause

Elk Lake is reached by a spur of the Pere Marquette Railroad, which terminated at Elk Rapids, situated on Grand Traverse Bay at the outlet of the lake. As the name indicates the drop in level from Elk Lake to Michigan occurs rather suddenly near the latter lake, causing a rapids in the outlet Advantage has been taken of the steeper gradient and the river has been dammed at this point. The history of these operations could not be traced back by the writer, but it is known that a dam on the present site was built prior to 1856 and has been maintained since that time with a fall of seven or seven and one-half feet

Beginning our study at Elk Rapids, we find the flooding of the outlet above the dam very noticeable. The current is very slack and tree trunks stand in the water As the lake is approached, the outlet widens and some wave action is evident in the low cliffs. Above the cliffs at an elevation of fiften feet stands the Nipissing terrace which terminates landward in a cliff reaching up to the Algonquin terrace

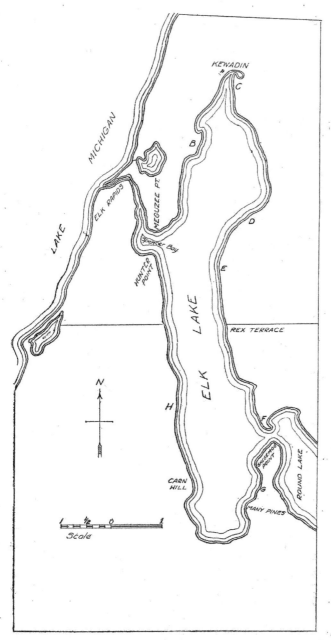

Fig. 58.   Outline map of Elk Lake, Grand Traverse and Antrim Counties.

forty feet above the water   Meguzee Point is caused by a low drumlin which is placed slightly oblique to the lake and runs to the shore
about a mile to the north   On the west side of the point a low
terrace skirts the shore, marking a former level which probably is
the equivalent of the Upper Level on Torchlight and may be so designated.   The end of this blunt point is bounded by cliffs, showing
strong wave action, and is fronted by a well-defined submerged terrace which "drops off" at seven feet about one-hundred yards from
the shore.

The southeast side of the point slopes gently to the shore where
it is being cut into low cliffs. Ice jams have formed a boulder strand,
but only patches of ramparts of feeble development are present,
although conditions for their formation are favorable.   The small
amount of cutting on this unprotected shore seems out of proportion
to that found on other parts of the lake, and a plausible explanation,
but one which cannot be proven, is that a rampart was formed here
under normal conditions of level   Under the present flooded condition, the waves have expended their energy in its removal and are
just beginning the process of cliff formation

At A, see map, conditions change and the waves have cut a more
decided cliff in stratified sand and gravel. This is the built portion
of the Nipissing terrace which is not well developed on the point
below.   The submerged terrace is very definite off A and drops into
deep water from a depth of eight feet   The soundings show a decrease in depth just before the "drop off," indicating the presence of
a low sand bar. This is probably formed by the violent agitation of
the water where the waves first break during severe storms

The hill which forms Meguzee Point gradually lowers north of A
and gives way to a swamp opposite Bass Lake   During Nipissing
time Elk Lake connected with Grand Traverse Bay through this depression, but at present the connection stands slightly above the lake
level and is further separated by a low ice rampart along the shore
of Elk Lake

To the north the upland again appears and forms the broad double
point B. This projection, in reality, consists of two headlands separated by a sag. On the headlands the waves have cut cliffs in sand,
which are uniformly ten to twelve feet in height, while along the
intervening bay the smooth shore is an indication of some current
action   However, the most prominent feature is a low ice rampart
and boulder strand   At the north end of the point currents leave
the shore and are building a small spit which may eventually enclose
the rather deep bay to the north. In this protected bay the weak
Upper Level terrace is again found. Soundings off the north part of
point B disclose a double submerged terrace   The bottom slopes

21

gradually outward to a depth of about four feet where it drops suddenly two feet or more to a second terrace which continues outward until a depth of eight feet is reached before it drops into deep water. This double terrace is probably due to the abrupt change in conditions coincident with the damming of the outlet. The deeper offshore portion was formed at the lower level previous to the flooding of the lake and upon it has been built the shallow part adjacent to the shore under the conditions existing at present. We may designate the parts as the younger and older but, in reality, they are two distinct terraces. Neither is proportional in development at the present time to the waves which were instrumental in its formation. The depth of eight feet over the outer edge of the older part is too great inasmuch as we know that the lake has been lifted an undetermined but appreciable amount, and the younger part has begun its development only in the sixty or more years since the present conditions were inaugurated

The highland encircles the north end some distance from the lake, and the lakeward slopes are interrupted by the Nipissing terrace and cliff. The wet, grass-covered terrace of the Upper Level appears near Kewadin and fringes the shore around the narrow arm of the lake at this end. This terrace is so low that the waves have little to work on. In fact this has not been a locality of intense wave action at any time since the isolation of the lake basin. This statement is based on the presence of a strong bar at the Nipissing level which starts in the locality of Kewadin and runs to the uplands on the east side of the lake in a broad, swinging curve, enclosing a crescent-shaped lagoon. The submerged terrace at this end is exceptionally wide and nearly meets from the opposite sides of the lake off point C. Here again it has the double character as described for B, the inner part dropping from a depth of three feet and the outer at seven. The water is shallower over the terrace than at B and this is due to moderate wave action from the southerly winds, although they are of great reach

Continuing southward along the east shore, conditions at locality C first attract attention. A narrow knoll not over eight feet in height caused the broad projection of the shore line. Back of this knoll, i e , east, a strip of swamp runs from the northeastern extremity of the lake south to the eastward bend of the shore and separates the knoll from the upland. During the Upper Level this knoll at first stood as a low island but later was connected to the mainland by a bar which developed at the south end.

Along this shore the Algonquin and Nipissing shores are much more distinct than on the west side and are well developed in the broad embayment south of C. The Nipissing consists of a cliff and narrow terrace which does not reach the present shore. The front slope of this terrace is somewhat confusing but should not be interpreted as the cliff of a former level of the lake. At D the Nipissing shore is poorly defined but the Algonquin is very strong. A climb up the forty foot rise to the Algonquin level is well worth the effort, for in this vicinity two excellent examples of the straightening of the shoreline by the development of bars across the mouth of an indentation may be seen. The first to be encountered is shown in Plate IX, B. From the slight sag of the top of the bar it may be inferred that spits developed from both sides of the embayment and that the bar was not quite completed before the subsidence of the lake to the Nipissing level. A similar bar is located about one half mile to the south.

Along the present shore to locality E the waves are cutting actively and low cliffs are being formed. The material is largely boulder clay, and the line of boulders on the shore shows that a moderate ice-shove occurs. The "drop off" is very distinct at eight to nine feet, and the submerged terrace has a width of more than one hundred yards in places. Similar conditions extend to the inlet from Round Lake, except that the Nipissing terrace is being cut away by the waves, and cliffs which reach a maximum height of twelve feet are prevalent along the shore. At F the south side of a drumlin forms the point, upon which the Upper Level is shown by a terrace. Most of the re-curved portion of the point was probably formed by current action but is now being worn away, due to the revived activity of the waves.

Round Lake is well protected by highland on all but the west side and the Torchlight depression on the northeast, and shows relatively little shore activity. It supports a heavy growth of water-loving vegetation which is, without doubt, rapidly filling this basin. Skegemog point, on the south side of the inlet, shows very clearly the contrast in the activity along the shores of the two lakes. On the Round Lake side the shores are low and the Upper Level terrace is well preserved. In addition, the beginning of a spit runs into Round Lake from the end of the point. The material for this spit is derived from the low cliffs along the Elk Lake shore, where no evidence of the Upper Level is to be found.

Below G the high ground recedes, this recession forming an indentation during the Upper Level. The curvature of the shore was sufficient to cause the currents to leave the shore, and a submerged bar was formed across the embayment about one hundred feet back from the present shore. At Many Pines Point a hill causes the projection and the Algonquin and Nipissing terraces again appear. The south side ot the point is protected from the strong winds and the Upper Level terrace has been preserved locally

The submerged terrace reaches its maximum development at the south end of the lake where its width exceeds one-half mile This shore is exposed to the strongest storm winds which often blow the full length of the lake, and under this condition the undertow attains its strongest development. Similar conditions may confidently be assumed during the former lake levels, and a wide compound terrace was formed in this locality, which is now the wide swamp extending from the south end of the lake to the hills a half mile away. This should consist ot a series of three steps but it is difficult to determine on account of the mask of vegetation. At the present shore the low sand bar which skirts the entire swamp is being thrown back by the renewed wave activity and is somewhat irregular in outline The writer is inclined to consider this a storm beach which developed under the conditions previous to the present flooded stage but realizes that it may well be a bar built at the Upper Level Conclusive evidence, however, is lacking since the form is being rapidly remodeled

The west shore south of the outlet rises with much gentler slopes on the average than the east side but has similar forms In general, however, wave action is weaker on this shore. The Algonquin and Nipissing terraces are present but are less decided This is due largely to the protection of this shore from the storm winds which usually blow from a westerly quarter The Upper Level terrace is found only in embayments and usually on the north side A submerged terrace is present but is relatively narrow and drops into deep water at seven to eight feet on the average The exposed terraces are poorly drained in many places and support a growth of swamp trees Such a condition is found near the mouth of the stream which enters the lake on the west side near the south end. During the Upper Level this stream built a small delta which is now being removed The low swamp bordering this stream extends northward and around a narrow hill which must have been an island at the Nipissing stage, if not at the Upper Level.

Northward, Carn's Hill causes a projection in the lake which is accentuated by a depression on the south side, forming a muddy bay Currents from the north left the shore at this point during the Upper Level stage but were too weak to carry across the indentation and a hook was formed At present this is being forced back into the bay by the waves, leaving tree trunks standing in the water. North of this hook, cliffs are working back into the Nipissing terrace which developed here at the expense of the Algonquin In fact, the latter was entirely removed and a steep cliff rises from the Nipissing shore to the top of the hill, a height of sixty to eighty feet. North of Carn's Hill no current deposits were found in a number of embayments either at the present or former levels, with the exception of two small indentations at the Algonquin above locality H. The forms found here are duplicates of those found at D on a smaller scale and need no further description.

Northward to the outlet the shores need no special consideration. The Algonquin and Nipissing terraces are universally present and the Upper Level is preserved wherever the tree growth has not been removed, except at the headlands. Ice ramparts are found locally and are more noticeable than on the east side of the lake. This may seem strange, since the ice-shove has been attributed to jams which are usually more powerful on the east side, but is due to the gentler slope of shores which offers more favorable conditions for ramparts. It may also be considered that the ramparts are in the process of destruction by waves on this side of the lake, but this has already been accomplished to a large extent on the east side.

The south bend of the outlet is accounted for by the topography. Another drumlin in line with that forming Meguzee Point causes the low, heavily wooded point on the opposite side of the outlet, Hunter's Point. Spencer Bay is due to a sag between the hills. Another line of drumlins lies to the west and has forced the outlet to the north before it crosses to Lake Michigan. The final bend to the southwest is due in part to the encroachment of dunes, formed from the sands deposited in a great bar which cut off this lake from Michigan during Nipissing times. An excellent example of the movement of dunes may be seen at the tenement of the blast furnace, where a large dune is slowly advancing on the building from the west and will soon cause its complete abandonment. Fig. 59.

Fig. 59.   Tenement house in process of burial by a moving dune, Elk Rapids. (Sketch from photograph.)

Comparison of this lake with Torchlight reveals almost identical conditions, history and characteristics Both basins are similar in shape and manner of formation They were connected during the Algonquin and Nipissing stages at least and show similar development of the shores at these levels There seems to be little variation in the development of the two basins during Algonquin time, except in the strength of the shore features, the stronger being on Torchlight on account of the larger size Neither lake was entirely separated from Lake Michigan at this time but the connections were greatly restricted on Torchlight As on Torchlight, much of the shore adjustment was accomplished on Elk Lake during this stage and consisted both in reducing the headlands and the closing of indentations In both of these particulars Elk Lake shows less shore action

The Nipissing shore is much less prominent on Elk Lake but is generally present. Current action was not important and none of the interesting V-bars found on Torchlight were discovered. The decrease in activity may be ascribed to the restriction of the basin by the development of bars tending to separate it from Lake Michigan

No evidence was found on Elk Lake of the Post-Nipissing Level of Torchlight This stage is considered of very short duration and must have been present on Elk Lake, but the shore features, weaker even than on Torchlight, have been completely destroyed.

The Upper Level is present in favorable locations but is much more evident on the west side, especially in the embayments The flooding of the lake raises the present level very close to that of the Upper and is causing its rapid destruction wherever the shores are exposed to strong wave action The demolition of ice ramparts and the building of a double terrace in places is interesting in this connection.

The development of the shores by wave action is the predominant factor at present and is causing a general recession both of cliffs and of current deposits. The lake is in a youthful stage at present, although complicated by former levels. The causes of extinction are, therefore, not important The only case of filling by sediment of any importance was found in the southwest corner and at the Nipissing level Most of the water is derived from Round and Torchlight Lakes, which are efficient settling basins Vegetation has not taken hold as yet and no marl deposits were found Complete draining is impossible unless the level of Lake Michigan lowers The presence of the dam prevents the deepening of the outlet but with this removed the result would be merely a lowering of the level of about fifteen feet As in the case of Torchlight, the problems are of shore adjustment rather than extinction

CRYSTAL LAKE

Crystal Lake, the last of this group to be described, is situated in the central-western part of Benzie County and at its west end lies within half a mile of Lake Michigan The Toledo & Ann Arbor R R skirts its southeastern shore and has a station stop at Beulah See map, Fig 60 The lake is more than eight miles in length and has an average width of two miles, making the area 16 square miles Its width nowhere exceeds two and one-quarter miles and in no place is it much less than one and one-half miles Thus the lake is very uniform in width The major irregularities of the present shore occur mainly on the south side and consist in a broad projection near Robinsons and a narrowing of the lake from Outlet Bay eastward Another embayment, now closed, occurs on the north shore and is occupied by Round Lake

The topography of the bottom of this lake is not known but it is stated that its depth is as great as two hundred feet A well-developed submerged terrace is uniformly present about all shores, and the drop into deep water is clearly marked by a sudden change in color from the light yellow of the shallow water to a deep blue where the depths are greater This change in color is due in part to the clearness of the water, and the name of the lake has appropriately been changed from Cap, as found on the old maps, to Crystal.

As regards the basin, it may be stated that it is relatively old In fact, it is certain that it was in existence before the ice made its final advance, for it was filled with a small lobe, an offshoot from the Michigan lobe, which pushed through the opening at the west end, now closed with sand This lobe deposited a strong morainic loop around this basin, which is continuous except at the outlet and a depression on the north side which runs northward into the Platte Lake depression, in the vicinity of Round Lake At present the lake shores do not reach the moraine hills but are separated from them by a rather broad zone of sandy terrace This widens greatly at the east end and extends nearly two miles before it is interrupted by the moraine

The striking physiographic characters are the predominating high cliffs from whose base the sandy terrace mentioned above extends to the water's edge The first surmise is that this lake has stood at a higher level and further observations prove this to be correct

The most convenient starting place for a study of the shores is at Beulah The town is built on a flat terrace somewhat more than ten feet above the level of the lake and we might almost say nestles at the foot of the cliffs carved in the moraine slopes which

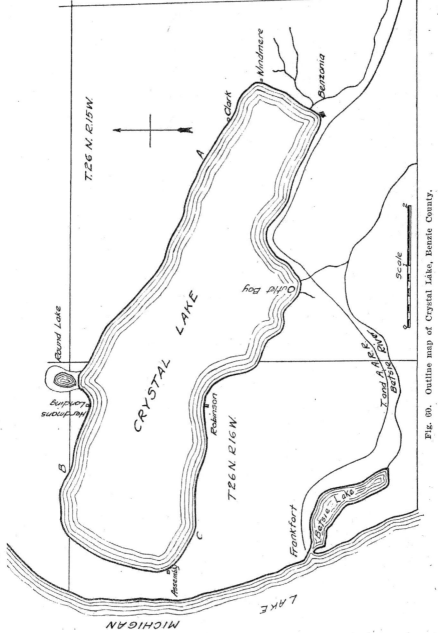

Fig. 60. Outline map of Crystal Lake, Benzie County.

rise rapidly to the south. Proceeding northward along the shore, one may note the cliffs continuing to the east, but with swampland instead of the lake at their base. A short walk allows an uninterrupted view and the physiographic significance of this end of the lake becomes evident. One cannot fail to note the sandy character of the soil, the distinct ridges, three in number, stretching in a broad curve to the limiting cliffs on either side of the lake, and the shallow depression to the east. These bars stand from fifty to one hundred feet from the present shore and about ten feet above the lake level. Curiously, the middle bar is not so well developed as those on either side and stands two feet lower in elevation. The bars are clearly shore features of the same high level of the lake which formed the cliffs and which corresponds in level to Lake Algonquin. During this time wave action was intense wherever the water reached the morainic hills and cut strong cliffs. The quarried material was carried outward by the undertow to a large extent and contributed to a wide submerged terrace. Discussion of the conditions at this end of the lake is reserved until later.

Near Windermere was found a small spit which indicates a level between four and five feet above the present. Although so small as to be easily overlooked, it is, nevertheless, of interest since it is almost the only indication of what may be termed the natural level of the lake. Crystal Lake stands only a few feet above Lake Michigan, the Ann Arbor tracks at Beulah are fourteen feet higher, and a project to make a waterway from Frankfort through the Betsie River to Crystal Lake and thence through Round to Long and Platte lakes was attempted in the early seventies. Operations began and ended with the making of a cut at the present outlet which lowered the lake level considerably. After the project was abandoned a dam was constructed at the outlet but not of sufficient height to raise the lake to its former level, the natural level of the lake. Conditions are now relatively stable and the previous level may be conveniently termed the Upper Level.

Along the north shore as far as the Round Lake depression steep cliffs and a broad terrace, partly exposed, are the predominant shore features. The terrace, largely formed during Algonquin time and exposed by the subsidence of the water to the Upper Level, was further widened by the artificial lowering and in places is swampy and foul near the present shore. The wet condition of the terrace is due to the seepage of ground water from the cliffs and the presence at the shore of ice ramparts which have been worked over by the waves. The submerged portion of the terrace has a rather uniform width in excess of one hundred yards and drops into deep water from a depth of seven feet. The sharpness of the edge of the terrace may be best observed from the top of the cliffs which rise from the Algonquin shore, attaining heights of eighty feet or more.

Even though the exposed terrace is not suitable here for summer cottages on account of its wet condition, this shore abounds in picturesque locations at the frequent sags in the cliffs, caused by the morainic basins which appear from the lake as rounded valleys abruptly truncated by the cliffs. Their resemblance to the famous hanging valleys of Switzerland has been appreciated in one case, at least, where a cottage built in chalet style hangs on the edge of the cliff in one of these depressions. In a few cases the sags are deeper and reach to the lake level or below. Thus, at Clark's cottage, at A, and just east of Round Lake small lagoons were cut off by bars in Algonquin time. Nearer Round Lake the exposed terrace is dry and covered with sand which has been heaped into small dunes.

Ice action is plainly evident here. During Algonquin time ice jams swept the terrace free from boulders which were lined on the shore and at the present level a low, but sharp, sand rampart, Fig. 61, bound together by dune grasses, was found by the writer. The

Fig. 61. Small ice rampart of sand. Crystal Lake. (Drawn from photograph.)

ice-push is asserted with considerable confidence to have been caused by jams since the lake is somewhat large for expansion and is subject to frequent jams during the spring thaws. Copies of photographs of an ice jam which occurred on this lake a few years ago were obtained, one of which is shown in Plate X, A.

The depression in which the miniature Round Lake lies is well below the Algonquin level and extends northward into the large depression in which Platte and several other smaller lakes lie. The Platte Lake depression was open in the early stages of Lake Al-

Michigan Geological and
Biological Survey

Publication 30, Geological Series 25,
Plate X.

A. ICE-JAM, CRYSTAL LAKE.

Photograph by Donald Gibbs

B. "DROP-OFF," COREY LAKE.

gonquin on the west, as were Crystal Lake and the Betsie River depressions to the south, making a rather irregular coast line with an inside passage. Across the Crystal Lake side of the Round Lake depression there now stands a strong bar more than twenty feet above the lake and in alignment with the cliffs on the north side. The height of the bar which is somewhat above the Algonquin level indicates that the bar was well above the water level and, therefore, nearly if not quite complete throughout its extent. However, as the level dropped the water from the depression was able to channel the bar and maintain an outlet to Crystal Lake. The position of the channel nearer the eastern attachment of the bar and the presence of sand dunes at the western end, indicating greater age, show that the prevailing currents came from the west. The maintenance of this channel seems almost prodigious considering the small amount of water in the depression at present and the strength of the bar through which it was cut. It is probable, however, that current action became much less powerful with the dropping of the water level and most of its energies were consumed in building a broad spit-like extension of the submerged terrace eastward from the point at Herdman's landing.

The terrace narrows considerably in front of the Round Lake bar and this, together with the presence of Round Lake on the opposite side, makes it certain that the depression is a portion of the Crystal Lake basin which was isolated by a bar. However, it was not completely separated from the Platte Lake depression until the water dropped to the Upper Level.

The prominent boulder wall at the Algonquin level on the west side of the depression near Crystal Lake is indicative of strong ice action which probably was caused by ice jams from the main lake before the development of the bar, although the possibility of expansion cannot be excluded. In the same locality but at a level corresponding to the Upper Level of Crystal Lake, a well developed bar follows the outline of the west side of Round Lake and joins the back slope of the Algonquin bar near its west end. This bar extends more than one-fourth the circumference of the lake and appears much too large to be accounted for by shore action on a circular lake of less than a half mile in diameter. The possibilities suggest themselves that the bar may have been subaqueous during the late Algonquin stage or developed subsequently to the formation of the Algonquin bar but while the depression was still connected with the Platte Lake area to the north.

From the Round Lake depression to point B on map, cliffs line the Algonquin shore below which a sandy terrace heaped into low dunes extends to the present lake level At the shore these dunes have been eroded by the waves, forming the only cliffs on the north side of the present shore of the lake Since the change in level has been recent and the dunes are but sparsely covered with vegetation, they must be in process of formation

A study of the west end of the lake discloses the fact that Crystal Lake is a lagoon. The material of the land forms is nothing but sand Adjacent to the Crystal Lake shore the subsidence in level exposed a portion of the terrace three to four hundred feet in width which, in general, slopes gently towards the lake but is modified to some extent by low dunes of recent formation. Beyond are the steep lee slopes of the great dunes between which, near their eastern limit, may be distinguished portions of a double bar at the Algonquin level. The dunes, heaped in confusion to heights of one hundred feet or more, extend to the Lake Michigan shore, three fourths of a mile to the west, and the zone stretches in a nearly north-south direction between the two morainic boundaries of the Crystal Lake depression, a distance of about two miles Most of the dunes are fixed in position, due to a vegetal covering, except near the Michigan shore where they are moving landward. In several locations the vegetation has been removed either by cutting or fire, and extensive "blow outs" in the dunes are evidence of renewed movement. This great zone of sand is clearly a bar formed during Algonquin times, since the Nipissing beach has been located in places on its front slope, but the usual concave outline is reversed along the Michigan shore The explanation is that the limiting morainic ridges formerly extended farther into Lake Michigan as headlands and a normal bar of concave outline developed between them However, subsequent erosion has caused a general recession of this shore, as shown by the extensive cliffs, but greater in amount at the northern headland, causing a convex curvature and somewhat irregular outline of the bar

Accompanying the development of the Algonquin bar on the Michigan shore was an adjustment by currents along its inner margin, the Crystal Lake side The result was the formation of long twin bars which extend from the southern morainic ridge in a broad curve north and northwestward to the vicinity of point C (see map) and account for the regularity of the shore along this end of the lake. A narrow lagoon, somewhat irregular in outline on its western shore, was thus formed which was inclosed by bars on either side along the west shore but stood between a bar and the Algonquin cliffs along the northwest shore of Crystal Lake. Along the west side the eastward migration of the dunes has filled the lagoon and partially covered the bar. Fortunately, however, the unburied portions are sufficient for its recognition. To the northwest the dunes have not encroached on the lagoon to so great an extent, and the bar stands out prominently above the dry lagoon on the one side and the exposed terrace on the other.

As far as may be determined the bars consist of two parallel ridges along the west shore but these coalesce and again divide into separate ridges before their attachment to the cliffs at A is reached. In development, elevation, and characteristics they are practically identical and are clearly the result of current action. Why then the two bars?

The key to the explanation is to be found at the attachment of bars to the mainland, that is, the extremities. On a lake of the size and orientation of Crystal, the effective work in the formation of bars at the west end is accomplished by currents driven by northeasterly or southeasterly winds, affecting the south and north shores respectively. The fact that the paths of the larger part of the great storm centers cross or lie above this locality causes a preponderance of storm winds from the southeast over those from the northeast. Consequently, the northern attachment of the bars, B on map, is the critical locality. The shore conditions at B are shown in the accompanying sketch, Fig. 62.

Fig. 62. Diagram showing the attachment of the bars at the west end of Crystal Lake to the north shore cliffs.

Attention is called to the recession of the cliffs in progressive steps or jogs, each jog serving as a place of attachment of a bar. Inasmuch as the cliff continues westward beyond the attachment of the bars, wave action played the important role in this locality during the early stages of the lake. Below the water level this resulted in the formation of a terrace which developed much more rapidly in the loose sand along the west side than in the morainic material of the north shore. As the terrace widened the waves became progressively reduced in size as they crossed the terrace and reached the beach with less and less force, diminishing the force of the shore currents in the same ratio. Currents moving westward along the north shore east of A were relatively strong, since the submerged terrace was narrow, but upon reaching A they were obliged to accommodate themselves both to bends in the shoreline and to a reduction in velocity. This combination of factors caused the currents to leave the shore first at the more westerly bend in the shore, and formed the outer bar The development of this bar hastened the construction of the built terrace which shifted the point of departure of the currents from the shore eastward to the eastern bend in the shore (Fig 62), from which the inner bar developed. The coalescence of the bars west of A may be accounted for by a slight obstruction which modified the curvature of the outer bar locally.

In this connection the triple bars of the east end of the lake demand consideration The question naturally arises concerning the variation in number at the opposite ends of the lake. Several ways of accounting for the three bars at the east end suggest themselves but, in order to deduce the most plausible, it is necessary to consider their characteristics somewhat more carefully In general, they stand at a lower elevation than those at the west end, and below the Algonquin level The curvature of these bars may be seen from the outline of the east shore (see map), and the rather abrupt angle at which they leave the cliffs is not characteristic of current deposits Finally, the lagoon extends nearly two miles to the east Now, if the same conditions are assumed for the development of these bars as were found for those on the west shore, the irregular curvature of the bars and the development of a built-terrace of nearly two miles in width must be accounted for The latter alone is sufficient to force us to seek a different explanation

It seems more likely that the eastern end of the basin was originally shallow and that its bed was remodelled or built up into a terrace in the early stages of the lake The outer edge of this exceptionally flat terrace stood near the east shore of the present lake and determined the outer breaker line of the incoming waves. As frequently happens in shallow bays, a series of submerged bars, three in number, progressively lower in elevation towards the lake, was formed by the breakers These bars were exposed by a lowering of the water level and the inner bar, now forming the beach, was subjected to storm waves on this exposed shore and was built up above the level of the intermediate bar

Along the south shore cutting has been the predominant factor and the Algonquin cliffs are almost continuous to Outlet Bay. One sag in the hills at C, see map, extended below lake level and was cut off by a bar which developed from the west, showing the prevalence of winds from the westerly quarter over those from the east The submerged terrace is very well defined along this shore and drops into deep water quite uniformly at seven feet

East of Robinsons the cliffs are exceptionally high, and the exposed terrace is heaped with low dunes which extend to the present shore of the lake and are cut into low cliffs by the waves Along the west side of Outlet Bay the most distinct development of the submerged terrace on the lake is seen but this may be due to the shallowness of the water which drops at three feet instead of seven, making the effect more pronounced The depression which caused the bay was one of the channels of the inside passage after Crystal Lake basin was cut off from the main lake Currents were active here and not only cut off small indentations on the west side but built a great bar in the vicinity of the outlet which connected with the cliffs on the east side From its elevation it is apparent that the bar was not exposed for its entire length but was sufficient to hold back the water after the subsidence to the Upper Level From the bay to Beulah the Algonquin cliffs are again the prominent feature and are interrupted only by two minor embayments which were cut off by bars at the Algonquin level.

In conclusion we may summarize as follows Crystal Lake existed as a fjord-like bay of early Lake Algonquin This depression was crossed by a much smaller one which connected the bay with the depressions to the north and south, which in turn were open to the main lake The development of bars isolated all three of these basins but left the inside passages free. Wave and current action were excessive in the Crystal Lake depression, after its separation from the main lake, and resulted in the carving of prominent cliffs in the morainic borders, the formation of a broad terrace, and the development of strong bars in front of the depressions and at the west end. At this time the passage to the north was closed and that to the south partially so The formation of triple barrier ridges at the east end caused a great reduction in size by cutting off a large lagoon when the level was lowered In fact, it may be stated that virtually all of the adjustments took place and the outline of the lake was fixed at this time. The waters receded from the Algonquin level to the Upper, a drop of twelve to fifteen feet, and left a broad exposed terrace, the sands of which have been heaped into low dunes. This level persisted until about forty-five years ago when the lake was lowered artificially At present the shore action consists mainly in removing portions of sand dunes and the formation of low ice ramparts of sand which are remodeled and obliterated by waves

CHAPTER V

INTERIOR LAKES OF THE SOUTHERN PENINSULA
WESTERN INTERLOBATE AREA

The lakes discussed so far in this report lie near the borders of
Lakes Michigan and Huron, and the majority have been connected
with them at some time during the past Furthermore, a rather
simple grouping of these lakes suggested itself The interior lakes
are much more numerous and are smaller in size, therefore a relatively smaller number was selected for detailed study Undoutedly
a more extensive study of our lakes would bring to light relations
which would serve as a basis for grouping but for the present this
is not at hand Fortunately we are able to determine more or less
accurately the relative time of formation of these lakes and may use
this as a natural order for discussion, even though other relation-
ships may be very remote

The fact that the glacier receded from the Southern Peninsula
in a general northeasterly direction and that great interlobate
areas were first uncovered between the Michigan-Huron-Saginaw
lobes and the Saginaw-Erie lobes has been mentioned previously.
For convenience we may term the interlobate areas as the eastern
and western, although they merge in the southern part of the Peninsula In general, for each of these areas the relative age of the
lakes is determined by their position, the more southerly being the
older. However, within the moraines which border the interlobate
areas the older lakes necessarily lie nearer the interlobate and it is
only by a consideration of both of these factors that the chronological order may be determined Uncertainties exist as to the correla-
tion of the glacial deposits and, therefore, the order here presented
is tentative and open to revision

LAKES OF ST JOSEPH COUNTY

Probably the first part of the Southern Peninsula to be uncovered
by the ice is a small triangular area included largely in St. Joseph
County Within this county the glacial formations consist of two
morainic tracts, one in the eastern part and the other crossing the
northern part of the western boundary, and a large area of outwash

23

which stands between and around the northern borders of the morainic areas. A number of small lakes occupy pits in the outwash and basins in the moraine in this region. The more numerous, however, lie in the morainic basins and several of these were examined by the writer, namely,, Corey, Clear and Long lakes in the western morainic area and Klinger in the southeastern district. No careful attempt was made to determine the relative age of these lakes and the order of their discussion is of no significance.

KLINGER LAKE. Klinger Lake is the largest of a group of small lakes which are aligned in a northeast-southwesterly direction in the south-central part of St. Joseph County. These basins are morainic in character but that of Klinger Lake is much larger than is usual for this type of basin. It appears to be a depression that is almost surrounded by a narrow zone of moraine, which extends as a spur in a southwesterly direction from the main moraine, and is probably more closely related to lakes situated in basins of till plains than to

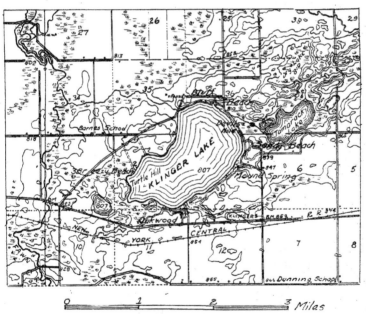

Fig. 63.   Topographic map of Klinger Lake and surroundings.   (From U. S. G. S. Three Rivers Quadrangle.)

those found in simple morainic basins. The morainic topography about its shores is the cause of varied shore conditions and the sandy nature of the glacial deposits has been conducive to shore adjustments to a degree unusual on a lake of less than two square miles in area The many bluffs and clean sand beaches have been instrumental, to some extent at least, in making this lake one of the most popular in this section of the ·State

From the map, Fig 63, it will be noted that the shores of the present lake are relatively free from prominent irregularities The elongate form is rather noticeable, and the direction of the longer axis is such that some of the strongest winds, notably those from the southwest, have full sweep of the lake The adjustments, although stronger along the east and northeast shores, are, nevertheless, distributed about the shores rather consistently

The lake is easily reached by the Toledo, Adrian, Hillsdale and Elkhart branch of the New York Central Lines which runs within a half mile of the south shore of the lake Arriving by train one approaches the lake at Oakwood This thriving summer resort is beautifully located on high ground that commands a view of the entire lake Fresh cliffs rise from the excellent sand beach which lines the shore. Westward, cliffs face the shore for about one-half mile with the single exception of a marshy lowland just west of Oakwood This lowland stands less than three feet above the present lake level and is very suggestive of a higher level If such were the case, one might expect to find this depression bridged by a bar but none can be definitely recognized Yet the presence of a road along the natural course of such a bar is at least significant This lowland proves to be a narrow neck connecting with the flat marsh which borders the southwestern end of the lake and extends westward to the Fawn River A single depression drops below the level of the marsh, forming a small, unnamed pond west of Klinger Lake, and several island-like hills stand above its surface Such a hill causes the broad projection of the shore west of Oakwood In the amphitheater-shaped northwestern side of this hill an exposed terrace of a former level is easily recognized and, in addition, a bar extends westward from the western point of the hill Thus, it seems clear that the lake has stood at a higher level Also since the bar and the terrace stand above the marsh, it is evident that the lake flooded this lowland, including the unnamed pond and possibly extending to the Fawn River. Another hill stands near the present shore at the head of the bay A small spit runs eastward from this "island" but does not connect with that extending towards it from the hill to the east, so that the shore line was not completely straightened in this locality However, on the west side a complete bar extends to Turtle Hill which was also an island during the higher level The greater development of the bars towards the west is readily accounted for by the great reach of the waves and currents from the east

Turtle Hill comes to the lake with gentle slopes which have been cut into low cliffs The material derived from these cliffs was shifted in both directions along the shore, but the greater part seems to have been carried northward and deposited in a well-defined spit which extends from Turtle Hill towards Breezy Beach The development of the spit was interrupted by the lowering of the water level before the opening was completely closed, and the form changed somewhat by recent ice action Much of the west end of the lake is shallow and the bottom covered with marl near the shore In places the submerged terrace of the present level is clearly definable and drops into deep water at about five feet

At Breezy Beach the land rises slightly above the level of the former lake bottom and is dry The shore line was somewhat more irregular during the former stage but currents do not appear to have been effective along this shore Northeast of Breezy Beach low hills slope gently to the shore and a low cliff and narrow exposed terrace of the higher level are present The cliffs vary in height and where highest show fresh cutting Around the broad point the submerged terrace is very decided and drops at thirty inches within one hundred feet of the shore, indicating much less powerful wave action here than on the south shore west of Oakwood A well-developed, but local, ice rampart was noted near the end of the point.

To the north, wave activity seems to be greater and the exposed terrace has been completely removed, the cliffs rising directly from the beach Also the submerged terrace widens gradually towards the outlet where it reaches a width of more than one hundred yards The lowland through which the outlet flows was nearly closed by a bar which developed from the south and forced the stream to the slopes of the hills at the north end of the lake This bar is obscured by the road but the smooth curvature, the tree growth rather than swamp vegetation, and the dry ground make its presence certain

From the outlet to Bluff Beach continuous cliffs are evidence of strong wave activity Between Bluff Beach and Sandy Beach a swamp borders the lake This swamp was clearly a part of the lake during the former level, and from the elevations we may deduce that both Tamarack and Thompson lakes were also included It was stated earlier that the form of the lake was conducive to strong activity at the northeastern end of the lake The almost continuous cliffs and well-defined submerged terrace along the shore southwest of Sandy Beach are evidence of powerful wave action due to westerly winds, even though their reach is less than those from the southwest, and in this locality the shore adjustments are of the greatest magnitude on the lake The most noteworthy change took place during the former stage across the lowland between Sandy and Bluff beaches and was brought about by the development of a great bar of more than a half mile in length, which practically separated the northeastern portion of the lake (Thompson and Tamarack basins) from the present Klinger Lake basin The position of the inlet from Tamarack Lake near Bluff Beach shows clearly that the bar developed from the cliffs near Sandy Beach towards the northwest and that the material must have been derived almost exclusively from the cliffs below Sandy Beach Ice action exerts a strong push along this bar but the ramparts are of moderate strength on account of the sandy character of the material

East of Oakwood the bluffs drop to a low marsh above which rises a small hill near the present shore A bar at the level of the former stage extends from this hill to the bluffs to the west but no such form was noted on the east side From this it is clear that the marsh was formerly an arm of the lake and that the hill was a land-tied island Also westerly winds were the more effective in this locality since the material for the bar must have been derived from the bluffs at Oakwood

From the physiographic viewpoint Klinger Lake is most interesting in its past Clearly it has stood at a level approximately three feet above the present and at that time was part of a lake of much greater area, although shallow for much of its extent. No attempt was made to trace the old shore lines where they deviate greatly from the shore of Klinger Lake, but from the topographic map some conception of the former extent of the lake may be deduced The elevation of Klinger Lake is given as 807 feet above sea level At the former level, then, it must have stood at about 810 feet At this level, marked extensions of the basin existed at the southwestern end, at the northeastern end, including Tamarack (808 elevation) and Thompson (809 elevation) lakes, and possibly at the outlet The latter is most interesting, since there is a possibility that the lake spread over an area of more than five square miles to the north, and is well worth the effort necessary to trace this out

The adjustments of the Klinger Lake basin were accomplished largely during the former stage and, although not completed in many cases, they determined to a large extent the present outline of the lake The activity of all the forces acting on shores excepting that of ice, is excellently shown Ramparts are present but are not exceptional in development. This is due to the prevalence of sandy material which is unfavorable to the development of strong ramparts

This lake is within the limits necessary for ice expansion but the testimony of observers is that the push is exerted by ice jams. They are especially effective on the east and northeast sides, because of the presence of an open zone of water which is maintained throughout the winter by the many springs near the shore.

As regards extinction, the greatest effect has been produced by the lowering of the water level. Little has been accomplished within the present lake basin either by vegetation or sedimentation.

At the present time the adjustment of the shores of the lake is not marked. There is little work for currents except the distribution of material derived in small amount from the cliffs which show fresh cutting in a few localities only. Probably the principal adjustment taking place is the remodeling of the submerged terrace to conform to present conditions.

COREY LAKE. Within the morainic tract in the southwestern part of St. Joseph County are a number of lakes occupying morainic basins of which Corey, Clear, Long, Kaiser, and Mud Lakes were

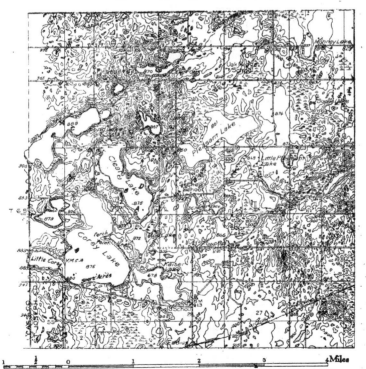

Fig. 64.   Topographic map of Corey, Clear and Long Lakes and surroundings.
(From proofsheet of Three Rivers quadrangle U. S. G. S.)

examined. The latter two were dry at the time of the writer's
visit and are too small to show decided shore features

Corey Lake, Fig. 64, is the largest of those examined and lies at
the edge of the moraine. Its shores are bounded by morainic material
with the exception of about one half mile on the south side   It is
the only one of those mentioned which is at all popular as a summer
resort and may be reached by a short drive from Three Rivers   On
first impression one might expect insignificant shore adjustments
on this small lake of hardly more than one square mile in area,
but a study of its shores quickly dispels the notion. The lake lies
in several connected basins and the shores are not only irregular
in contour but varied in relief as well   Furthermore, the material
is sandy and easily worked, so that the shore features are exceptional for a lake of this size

At present, the lake flows into Kaiser Lake which has no outlet.
Formerly when the lake stood at a higher level the water escaped
southward through an extended swamp, eventually reaching Mill
Creek   An exposed terrace of the higher level stands below the
cliffs at the southeastern shore of the lake but is somewhat obscured
by the numerous cottages   Further west, a flat caused by the recession of the high ground furnishes the key to the former condition
of the lake   The most noticeable feature is a sand bar of smooth
curvature, which stands nearly four feet above and about thirty
feet back of the present shore   This bar at present incloses a lagoon
of approximately three hundred feet in greatest width   Closer examination reveals the presence of a spit attached to the east side
of this indentation farther inland and at a level still higher than
that of the bar   From evidence found on other parts of the shore
the highest level stood seven feet above the present and the spit
just mentioned was in an early stage of development

West of the lagoon cliffs again line the shore and the terraces of
both of the former levels are readily distinguished   The terrace of
the four foot level reaches a width of twenty feet and supports ice
ramparts locally   An especially well-developed rampart has been
formed under present conditions on this terrace just west of the
lagoon. Similar conditions persist to the entrance of Little Corey
with the exception of a sag at Shore Acres   This sag dropped nearly
to the level of the four foot stage and was artificially deepened some
sixty or seventy years ago to allow the water to flow southward
The writer's information concerning this channel is none too reliable
but it seems certain that the lake stood at the four foot level at that
time, and it is presumed that the channel was dug to accommodate
the water under flood conditions   Since that time the ground water

table has sunk, Corey Lake has dropped to its present level, and Kaiser and Mud lakes have dried up

The point on the south side of the entrance to Little Corey is composed of sand and swings northward from the cliffs in an even curve It is clearly a current deposit which developed largely during the highest level, and the lagoon on the west side is therefore dry at present Indications point towards a continuation of its growth but at a very slow rate

In addition to the forms described, a well-defined submerged terrace follows the south shore As a rule it drops into deep water within one hundred and fifty feet of the shore but swings outward to double this width in front of the lagoon The change in color at the "drop off" was very marked near the entrance to Little Corey and the writer had the good fortune to succeed in registering this on a photographic plate, a reproduction of which is shown in Plate X, B

A narrow morainic depression extends westward from the southwestern part of the main lake and is composed of two basins, both of which are filled with water The more westerly, not shown on the map, forms a small pond which drains into Little Corey, situated in the easterly basin The two basins are separated by a swamp which rises scarcely above the present lake level Both exposed terraces are continuous below the cliffs around the depression, showing that the entire depression was connected with Corey Lake, as represented on the earlier maps A sharply defined submerged terrace follows the present shore of Little Corey and supports a heavy growth of vegetation and a deposit of marl as well. Within the depression the waves have been the most active agent and have accomplished the most work on the south side, due to the greater strength of winds having a northerly component Some deposition by currents may have taken place at the west end of Little Corey but the presence of a road across the flat makes this uncertain

However, an easterly drift along the north shore of Little Corey cooperated with a southerly drift along the west shore of the main lake to form a V-bar with characteristic central depression at the north side of the entrance to Little Corey, the point occupied by the Y M. C A camp This V-bar stands fully eight feet above the present level and is considered to have been a fully developed form during the highest stage of the lake, that is, stood slightly above the water level At present, the currents on the main lake predominate and the V-bar is extending southeastward as a spit. This extension is not in line with the spit on the south side of the entrance but there is, nevertheless, a likelihood that the channel will be closed, as indicated by the very shallow water between the two spits, which, in addition, receives each year the deposits from a heavy growth of rushes.

North of the Y. M. C. A. camp the terraces of both of the former levels are present on the cliff-lined shore either side of the point opposite the island. This was the scene of strong wave action which accomplished most during the highest stage, since that terrace is the better developed. Part of the material derived from the cliffs was distributed on the terrace but a considerable portion was carried along the shore in both directions. Thus, at the point opposite the island, currents from both the north and the south left the shore but, instead of forming a simple spit or V-bar, tied a small island to the mainland by spits which developed in accordance with the shores on both sides. See Fig. 65. The currents were unable to

Fig 65   Sketch of small island tied to the mainland by two bars or tombolos.

continue to the island or else were entirely depleted of their load, for the shallow water between the island and the mainland is due to the natural configuration of the bottom, as shown by the clay bottom upon which rest many large boulders.

The island is an oblong "sugar loaf" with steep cliffs on all sides but the north. The shores show the effects of the activity of waves rather than currents, and the exposed terraces of the former level are the predominant features. Slight activity is manifested on the north side but the well-developed terrace, formed at the highest level on the remainder of the shore, has been largely cut away on the exposed south and east sides.

Cliffs line the greater part of the shores of the bay north of the island and usually are notched by the terraces of the higher levels Near the head of the bay and on the north shore are indentations which were completely cut off by bars at the highest level. At the sharp headland on the west side of the entrance to the north arm of the lake, the effects of strong current action are again evident This headland is caused by the projection of the hills into the lake but is so sharp that the currents were unable to follow the shore. The current-borne material was deposited in the form of a spit which runs to the northeast and has a length in excess of three hundred feet The spit began its growth during the highest level and has continued to develop during the succeeding stages, including the present, but at less rapid rate Clearly the southerly winds are the most effective here on account of their long reach and the deep water over which they pass

The west shore of the north arm is lined by a continuous low cliff below which stands the four foot terrace. The bay is shallow and vegetation is encroaching along the shore This is especially notice- able at the north end where rushes extend from two hundred to three hundred yards off shore On the east shore wave action pro- ceeded to an advanced stage of adjustment, as shown by the current deposits about midway between the head of the bay and Perch Point In this locality a slight bend in the shore line of the highest level was sufficient to throw the currents off shore, forming a com- plete bar across a narrow lagoon. Likewise at the four foot level the currents swung away from the shore and built a hook from the east in front of the bar of the highest level. The lagoon in the latter case does not exceed two hundred feet in width The lower bar shows clearly that the effective currents drift northward along this shore and that reach of the wind is again the determining factor

Between the bars just described and Perch Point the cliffs are less prominent and the exposed terraces are better developed Perch Point is almost a duplicate on a larger scale of the point opposite the island The bars which connect the low island to the main- land were built at the highest level The bar on the south side con- nects with a well-defined terrace at the seven foot level, which soon merges into high cliffs The absence of the highest terrace along these cliffs, which are continuous to the outlet, is due to its removal during the four foot stage This shore is exposed to the strongest winds of maximum reach, and the obliteration of the shore features of former levels is to be expected here if anywhere on the lake The material quarried from these cliffs has drifted in large part towards the south and was deposited across the low ground at the outlet which was formerly flooded The bar developed during the highest stage and nearly separated Corey Lake from Kaiser.

It remains to point out briefly some of the more important episodes in the history of this lake At its inception the lake stood at a level approximately seven feet above the present. At this time it flooded all of the depression at the southwestern end of the lake and connected with Kaiser, Mud, and possibly Clear Lake. The adjustments of the shores during this level were carried to an advanced stage and in some cases the currents completed their work before the level dropped The four foot level was in existence a relatively short time ago and the adjustments followed along lines determined during the previous stage. In general, however, they were less extensive. Within recent years the levels of all the lakes mentioned have dropped several feet, which has caused the extinction of Mud and Kaiser Lakes. The adjustments at present are slight, the one of greatest consequence being at the entrance to Little Corey which may become closed.

CLEAR LAKE Clear Lake lies within a half mile of the north end of Corey Lake, see Fig 64, and runs parallel to the northeastern shore As in the case of Corey Lake, this small body of water, which has a length of somewhat more than a mile and a width of less than one-third of its length, is surprising in the number and extent of the adjustments of its shores. The surrounding land rises well above the level of the lake except at the south end. Inasmuch as the Mud Lake basin, now dry, lies but a few hundred feet to the south, this low divide is a favorable locality for beginning our study At this locality it is evident that Clear Lake has stood at a higher level than the present, and from the elevation of the divide it seems probable that the two lakes were connected with each other and with Corey Lake through Kaiser Lake. Conditions are favorable here for the formation of a bar along the south shore of Clear Lake but the presence of a road along the logical position of such a bar makes its identity uncertain. Very often, however advantage has been taken of the higher ground along the course of a bar in the building of roads and such an occurrence may serve as indirect evidence of the existence of the bar

Northward along the west side of the lake, the slopes are gentle and little adjustment of the shore has taken place Proceeding along the shore one notices evidence of an increase in the activity of the shore forces. The first definite feature to be found is a small spit which stands three feet above the present level and points southward from the point designated A on the map, Fig. 64. This spit protects a narrow lagoon which is merely a continuation of the shallow, mud-covered lake bed adjacent to this shore   Vegetation has established itself off shore but is especially abundant in the lagoon which is rapidly being filled   North of the spit the slopes increase in steepness and the activity of the waves becomes evident The wave cut cliffs increase in height to a maximum just south of point B and, where well developed, rise from an exposed terrace rather than from the present beach   This terrace corresponds in elevation with the spit at A and is further evidence of a former level of the lake   The cliffs and hills are wooded but the terrace supports only a limited growth of bushes and young trees, consequently one may conclude that the drop in the water level has been of recent occurrence   The material derived from the cliffs between points A and B drifted in both directions, inasmuch as a current deposit was formed at B as well as at A

The deposit at B is a typical V-bar with characteristic central depression   Its greatest development was from the northwest, due to the greater power and reach of the winds from that direction and to the abundant material quarried from the cliffs which are more prominent on this side of the point   During the former stage of the lake, the north side of the V-bar attained the greater development, and, in addition, a considerable part of the current-borne material was distributed off shore, forming a submerged terrace of greater width and gentler slope than on the south side   At the present time, a small hook pointing northward indicates that conditions are reversed and that the greater growth is from the south side   This reversal was brought about by the general reduction of the activity of waves and currents, caused by the lowering of the water level   Under the present condition of reduced activity, the submerged terraces are more effective than formerly in reducing the size, and therefore the power of the waves passing over them, and the wider the terrace the greater its effect.   In this case the broader terrace on the north side so reduces the power of the incoming waves, and therefore the currents, as to render them less effective than those passing over its narrower counterpart on the south side

North of point B the cliffs which face the shore indicate the source of material forming the north side of the V-bar just described The presence of an alluvial fan and a fossil delta along this shore are of interest although not formed by the agents active on the lake shores   The delta was built by a small stream which entered the lake at the time of the higher level, but the waves and currents were able to distribute the material as fast as supplied, so that the shore line was not affected   The exposed terrace of the former level is a consistent shore feature as far as the north end of the lake   Its elevation with reference to the present level was measured in several places and found to be within a few inches of four feet. This means that many of the deposits formed during this stage did not extend above the water level. Near the north end of the lake the side slopes are gentle and the exposed terrace is wide. An interesting change has been produced at this end of the lake by the lowering of the water level. Areas formerly covered by open water are now swamps filled with rank growth of vegetation. One such was a bay just south of the end of the lake. Currents from the south made some headway in cutting off this indentation but succeeded in building only a submerged bar, now clearly outlined by a row of willows.

The muddy north shores of the lake show little adjustment aside from the exposed terrace. The absence of any indication of a bar between the small island, not shown on the map, and the mainland is evidence of the feebleness of the currents.

The east shore is lined with cliffs which are continuous along the northern half of the lake. Below the cliffs stands the exposed terrace of the higher level, and so uniform are the shore features that any deviation is very noticeable. Thus, the current deposits at either end of the cliffs are readily detected. At the sharp bend near the north end of the lake a small hook is indicative of currents driven by southwesterly winds, and at C a spit shows the effectiveness of the winds from the northwesterly quarter. The reach from both quarters is approximately the same, so that the size of the deposit is an index of the strength and frequency of the winds. The greater development of the spit at C shows conclusively that the northwesterly winds are the more effective. In each case the deposits were built during the former level and are not growing at present.

The turning of the currents from the shore at C has prevented the formation of a spit on the west side of the nearby point to the southeast but some such activity might be expected on the east side. This, however, is not the case and it is due to the topographic features of the southern half of the east shore of the lake. Instead of the continuous cliffs of the shore north of C, which furnished a maximum of material, there is an alternation of cliffs and lowlands. In addition to the smaller amount of material furnished by the cliffs, many of the lowlands extended below the water level during the former stage of the lake and were areas of deposition. Thus, the material, relatively small in amount to start with, was further depleted by deposition at the mouths of indentations. The absence of any deposit at the end of the point indicates that the currents not only were weak but practically without load by the time they reached this locality.

The first indication of the work of currents along the southeastern shore was found in the bay east of the point just discussed   The head of this bay consists of a hooked spit which came within thirty feet of completely cutting off a narrow lagoon. This spit developed from the south and at the former level of the lake   A hundred yards or more to the southwest the cliffs are again interrupted by a small triangular indentation which was completely isolated by a bar   Beyond this bar cliffs again line the shore as far as the depression at D.   The mouth of this indentation was broad but, nevertheless, was completely bridged by a bar, forming a lagoon of several acres in extent, which is still wet.   To the south, the cliffs are less prominent and gradually give way to gentle slopes.   Yet currents, probably from the north, were active and succeeded in cutting off two small indentations between D and the south end of the lake.

From the discussion above it should be evident that Clear Lake has stood at a level some four feet higher than that found by the writer in the summer of 1914.   The presence of only very young vegetation on the exposed terrace is evidence that the lowering of the level was of recent occurrence   This was fully corroborated by information obtained from residents of the locality   Practically all of the adjustments of the shore have taken place at the higher level and the indications are few indeed that they are continuing at the present time

The adjustments are very pronounced for a lake of this size and include those due both to wave and to current action   In general, the eastern shore was most affected, and this is shown by a less abundant growth of vegetation along the shores as well as by more prominent shore features than on the opposite side of the lake

At present the lake has no surface outlet and no inlets of importance   Since there is little adjustment of the shores, extinction is the active physiographic process and this is being accomplished by vegetal accumulation   Little has been said of the submerged terrace in the description above.   The reason for this is that it is impossible to determine its limits on account of the heavy growth of vegetation, not only on the surface of the terrace but on the lake bottom as well   Over much of the bottom a complete carpet of vegetation may be seen through the transparent water which gives the lake its name

Long Lake   Long Lake lies less than a half mile northwest of the north end of Clear Lake and resembles the latter closely in size and form   This lake is also surrounded by moraine and is without

Michigan Geological and
Biological Survey

Publication 30, Geological Series 25,
Plate XI.

BAR, LONG LAKE, ST. JOSEPH COUNTY.

outlet or inlets of consequence The greatest difference is in the di
rection of the longer axis which runs at right angles to that of Clear
Lake. Inasmuch as the contour of the bottom is not known, it is
not possible to determine whether this basin is a simple elongated
depression or a series of connected morainic basins The morainic
material in this locality contains a large percentage of sand and the
shore adjustments are of the same order as those found on the other
lakes of the group.

In Plate XI is shown the adjustment of the northeastern end of
the lake, which is not only the most pronounced on this lake but is
one of the most perfect of its kind found on the inland lakes of the
State As may be seen from the plate, the north end of the lake
has been cut off by a complete sand bar, perfect in development and
preservation This bar stretches from the cliffs on either side of
the lake in a beautiful curve and stands slightly more than five
feet above the present level Inasmuch as there is no sag in its
crest, this bar was fully developed and extended above the water
level which prevailed at the time of its formation This bar, then,
establishes a former level of the lake which probably stood somewhat less than five feet above the present stage The lagoon of
about ten acres in extent is still wet and in late summer is literally crowded with lily pads which are rapidly converting it into
a peat bog

The continuous cliffs which face the shores of the southeastern
side of the lake rise from a well-defined exposed terrace which
varies in width from forty to sixty feet The lake level indicated
by this terrace stood more than four feet above the present level and,
thus, is in agreement with the level deduced from the bar at the end
of the lake The presence of coarse material on the terrace is an
indication that it was formed largely by wave cutting, furnishing
the material for the bar above Along the northwest shore the
cliffs are less prominent west of the blunt projection and become
insignificant to the south, where the slopes are gentle A wide
exposed terrace is the predominant shore feature, although currents were effective in closing two small indentations in the vicinity
of A, see map, Fig 64, and another near the southwestern end of
the lake.

West of the broad point on the south shore, the side slopes are
gentle and the effects of wave action are not prominent However,
currents from the north were effective and built bars across the
mouths of two small indentations which existed during the higher
level. The more westerly embayment was cut off by as perfect a
bar as that described at the northeastern end of the lake but is

less prominent on account of its smaller dimensions Apparently the current-borne material was limited in amount and the greater part was deposited on this bar, since the deposit at the mouth of the embayment nearer the point is a spit attached to the west side

The broad projection on the south shore is caused by a low morainic knoll whose lakeward slopes were carved into the characteristic cliff and terrace profile during the former stage of the lake The material from the cliffs drifted westward and was deposited on the east side of the knoll, forming a small spit This spit would have cut off a large part of the swamp which borders the shore to the east had its growth not been interrupted by the sinking of the water level

The west side of the prominent projection on the southeastern shore of the lake is exposed to the action of strong waves due to westerly winds, and the cliff and terrace of the higher level are continuous to the vicinity of point B Here the velocity of the along-shore currents was reduced at a small indentation south of B, which was completely cut off At B an unsymmetrical V-bar elongated on the south side, indicates that the currents from both directions left the shore but the more effective currents were from the south This bar whose longer side has a length of nearly one hundred yards is an exceptionally strong shore feature for a lake of this size

Between B and C cliffs are again prominent but at C another V-bar, which is a duplicate of that at B on a smaller scale, indicates similar conditions Wave action predominated along the shore from C to the northeastern end of the lake as shown by the well-developed cliff and terrace An interesting break in the cliffs was found in the bay east of C in the form of a dry gully, at the foot of which stands an excellent example of an alluvial fan.

Long Lake also is interesting chiefly on account of its past The water level formerly stood between four and five feet above the present and at this time prominent adjustments of the shore took place Strong wave activity carved steep cliffs where conditions were favorable Currents were also active in like degree, so that there are few localities where adjustments are not readily detected Not only did the currents cut off indentations but also swung away from the lake shores, forming the interesting V-bars commonly found on the long and narrow lakes Little activity is manifested at the present level and the important physiographic process of the future is that of extinction Vegetation has become firmly established in the lagoons but the process is not so active on the main lake as was found to be the case on Clear Lake Since there is no outlet the lake could not have been lowered by downcutting and the drop in level, therefore, must be referred to some other cause.

The lowering in level is shared by all of the lakes in this group, and the idea that it is connected with the pumping of water for the city of Three Rivers from the outwash plain six miles east of the lakes seems to exist. Therefore some pains have been taken to obtain information concerning the lake levels and the pumping operations since the installation of the plant. In particular the writer is indebted to Mr Eugene A. Schall, City Clerk of Three Rivers, Mich, for collecting this information

The levels of these lakes and also all other water-ways in the vicinity have fluctuated somewhat periodically during the last forty years at least, conditions previous to that time being unknown to the writer. Previous low water periods occurred in 1882-83 and 1895-96, and during intervening years the water came back to normal The levels of the lakes during the low periods are not known to the writer and, therefore, cannot be compared with the present low stage.

The city of Three Rivers has been obtaining its water supply from nearby wells since 1876, the amount used increasing to 70,000 cubic feet (approximately 500,000 gallons) daily at the present time Previous to 1896 a few small, flowing wells were utilized but since that time twelve six-inch wells have been installed, five in 1896 and seven in 1910. In 1915 six of these wells were reset about one hundred yards away and, although drilled to the same depth, tapped an entirely different source of supply. In some respects the lowering of the lake levels and the pumping operations are related, but it must be kept in mind that our record of lake levels does not antedate the installation of the water system. Also during the first known period of low water, which occurred soon after the installation of the water works, the wells were not pumped and the amount of water used was insignificant. The low period of 1895-96 occurred slightly previous to the driving of additional wells and could not have been caused thereby. The present low water stage follows the change in position of some of the wells, which tapped a new water-bearing layer, and shows a closer relationship than the previous stages. In addition to the discrepancies which appear in the statements above, the pumping operations have steadily increased and there should have been a gradual lowering of the levels rather than a periodic fluctuation. Also it is probable that the water pumped from the wells comes from a large surrounding catchment area rather than the local area occupied by the lakes, since all other water ways in the vicinity have been similarly affect-

25

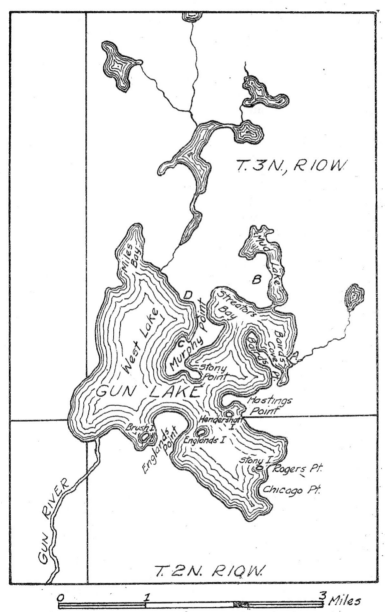

Fig. 66. Outline map of Gun Lake, Barry County.

ed. Thus, it appears from the data at hand that the wells have had little or no effect on the fluctuation of the levels of the lakes.

The cause is probably a natural one and may be related to periodic changes in climate which are none too well established as yet Whatever may be the cause, the effects are very pronounced and a careful study of the problem promises interesting results

GUN LAKE. Of the lakes included in this group Gun was the next uncovered by the retreating glacier. This lake is one of the largest of the numerous small, interior lakes which lie in the southwestern part of the State It lies directly in the center of the western border of Barry County and crosses into Allegan County at the extreme western end of the lake. The lake is not readily accessible but may be reached either from Middleville or Hastings, both of which are on the Grand Rapids branch of the Michigan Central R. R Nevertheless, the lake is a popular resort and draws a large number of summer visitors from both nearby and distant points.

This lake is almost rectangular in shape, see Fig 66, but is nearly cut into two basins by Englands and Murphy points, which are attached to the south and north shores respectively. Numerous other points and bays make the lake most irregular in outline. This is better appreciated when it is known that, although the area is but slightly over four square miles, the shoreline measures more than seventeen miles. If Mud Lake is included, the area is 4 4 square miles and the shoreline nineteen miles (a perfectly rectangular lake of the same area would have a shoreline of eight miles in length). The reason for the complicated shoreline is apparent when the origin of the basin is understood This basin lies on the western border of a strong morainic ridge, trending north-south. To the west is a triangular outwash plain which developed from the north and west and is very thin and incomplete near the border of the moraine. In the vicinity of the lake fragments only of the surface of the outwash are present due to the fact that large ice blocks of irregular shape were present at the time of its formation and prevented deposition of the outwash material. It is doubtful if these blocks were entirely covered by the outwash material since till plain borders parts of the shore of the lake, even though its surface stands below the general level of the fragments of the outwash plain (see Chapter II on the formation of pit lakes). Thus, the lake may be classified as a pit of shallow depth but very complicated in outline. The basins represent the locations of the ice blocks and the points are spurs of the moraine, fragments of the outwash plain, or swells of the undulating surface of the till plain not covered by outwash. The varied conditions along the shore, both as to contour and material, are favorable to adjustments but, on the other hand, the shallowness of the lake and its partition into partially enclosed basins greatly interfere with normal wave development.

The outlet of this lake, the Gun River, flows from the southwestern end and takes a southwesterly course to the Kalamazoo The gradient of Gun River is very flat, and the stream has cut a very shallow trench in the sand flat Shore features are now exposed along certain parts of the lake which indicate a former level in accordance with the down-cutting of the outlet There also exists a probability that at the higher level Gun Lake formed a part of a glacial lake known as Lake Dowagiac, a matter readily determined when the exact level of Gun Lake is known. Furthermore, the outlet gives us a clew to the small amount of variation in the level of this lake during the year The writer was surprised to see the outlet almost filled with a heavy growth of lilies and rushes and realized at once that they must offer considerable resistance to the flow of water which might hold the lake at a higher level An obstruction, natural or otherwise, in the course of the stream would cause a ponding of the water and the encroachment of vegetation in its channel would follow as a result, but the writer knows of no obstruction in Gun River, although a positive statement to this effect cannot be made. Assuming the absence of an obstruction. one might well conceive the encroachment of vegetation in a stream channel such as Gun River which has a very flat gradient and carries little sediment as it leaves the lake. In addition, it flows in an old river channel which is merely a veneer of alluvium over till and, after cutting through the sand, would pick up very little solid material from its bed Thus, with few tools to work with, the abrasive power would be reduced and vegetation could take hold It is also interesting to note that such interference with the outflow would take place mainly during the growing season and would tend to hold the lake level higher during the summer months, normally a time of low water At other times, the dead parts of the plants would offer much less resistance and might be removed during the spring floods Another possibility is that the dead parts may accumulate in the channel and gradually raise the lake level until a new outlet is found or the old one cut off during exceptional floods. The latter is known to have happened on at least one lake in our State

Near the outlet the shores are bordered by a low, grass-covered swamp and have no definite beaches. This condition persists eastward until the low swells of the ground moraine which causes

Englands Point are encountered. One of the smaller swells forms Brush Island, which rises barely above the surface of Pickerel Cove, and possibly is the cause of the blunt projection of the main shore at the head of the cove. The absence of wave action along this shore is probably due to the shallowness of West Lake which, although the reach is large, prevents the formation of large waves and also reduces materially the power of those formed as they approach the shore. Englands Point, however, runs out into the deeper water and has been carved into low cliffs on the north and northwest sides Elsewhere the shores are low and the slopes are in places carved into a low terrace hardly two feet above the present level. Locally the shores have been pushed into low ice ramparts by the expansion of the ice during the winter East of Englands Point another low swell projects above the surface of the lake and is known as Englands Island Some planation of its surface by waves may have taken place in the past, but at present it is covered with a black muck, an indication of vegetal accumulation

The south shore of the large embayment, formed by Englands and Hastings points, is lined by a definite sand beach, and the shore features consist of alternating low cliffs and swales. The cliffs increase in height as the moraine is approached at the extreme southern end of the bay At the swales a narrow but definite terrace of the upper level is present, fronted very commonly by low ice ramparts Considerable adjustment of this shore has taken place, but the low areas were not cut off by definite bars. A single exception to the last statement was found in the embayment below Chicago Point where a sand bar developed across a triangular depression. The lagoon has been filled by vegetation so that the features are none too evident.

The broad projection which includes Chicago and Rogers points is due to moraine hills, and the shore features are those due to cutting. The boulder-lined strand is an indication of strong shove by the ice Off Rogers Point another small island is appropriately named Stony, inasmuch as the finer material of the till has been removed by waves, leaving a mass of rocks standing slightly above the water level. It will be noted that this island is exposed to much stronger winds from the west and northwest than is Englands Island on the opposite side of the bay, therefore the greater amount of wave action

At the head of the embayment north of Rogers Point, a sand beach of even curvature lines the shore and has been pushed up into a low rampart. The terrace of the upper level is distinct on this lowland but no evidence of a lagoon was found. Deposition has taken place, however, but has succeeded in building out a terrace rather than forming a definite bar. On the north shore of this bay wave action is slight, and the swamp vegetation of the swale grows to the water's edge - Northward, the shores are high but drop to a low swamp just south of Hastings Point. The swamp runs across the neck of this peninsula and may have been open water during the higher stage, thus making Hastings Point an island at that time   The point is a swell of the ground moraine rising ten to fifteen feet above the lake level   It is exposed to wave action from the west especially and considerable cutting has been accomplished   Thus the shores are faced by cliffs, and a rocky cut-terrace runs off the end of the point. The rocks on the terrace are an accumulation resulting from the removal of the finer material and many have been transported to the beach by ice action. The ice shove is strong on this point, for boulders up to five feet in diameter are now lined along the shore

The division of the lake into east and west arms by Englands and Murphy points has already been mentioned. The east arm is similarly divided by Stony and Hastings points and the northern basin of this arm is likewise constricted by Bairds Point and a projection on the east side of Murphy Point   The bays on either side of Bairds Point are both shallow and the point itself is low with the exception of two knolls, one forming the end of the point and the other the expansion near the middle   The terrace of the higher level is distinct on all but the west side and, inasmuch as it extends between the two knolls and between the central knoll and the main shore, it is evident that Bairds Point was originally two distinct islands   Considerable adjustment took place along the island shores and also on the north shore of Hastings Point   Not only was the terrace well developed on the low slopes but, in addition, a bar developed across the head of the bay between Hastings and Bairds Points which connected the more southerly of the islands with the mainland   The material of this bar was derived mainly from the north side of Hastings Point, although some may have been added from the Bairds Point islands which are bounded by cliffs on the west side   The higher level terrace is well exposed on the east side of the point and in places reaches a width of one hundred feet   The development of the terrace on this side was due to favorable conditions of shore topography and material rather than to excessive wave action   The latter is much more effective on the west side because the winds from this direction have the advantage of greater velocity and reach and blow across deeper water. When the water level dropped wave activity was decreased in greater proportion on the east side, and sufficiently so that the terrace was preserved on this side but was cut away on the west In fact, the south end of Bairds Cove is effectively protected from wave action and is being rapidly filled with vegetation It is an excellent example of the encroachment of vegetation from the shore in the form of a floating bog, and the present area of open water is but a small remnant of its former extent

The slight projection, A, on the east side of Bairds Cove is a small spit pointing southwestward and is the southerly limit of sand beach which lines the shore to the entrance into Mud Lake At the northern end of this beach there is also a spit which is responsible for the isolation of Mud Lake. It is probable that the spit was complete, but conditions are somewhat obscured by the roadway built upon it The entire east shore, including Mud Lake, is lined by moraine whose slopes were washed by the waves at the former level Considerable adjustment took place at this time and, in addition to the spits mentioned, a terrace was formed which varied in width according to the slopes encountered. In general, the terrace was wider in the embayments and has effected a straightening of the shore line with the subsidence of the lake to its present level. At present, the morainic slopes come to the shore in one locality only, the attachment of the Mud Lake spit, and little material is being quarried from the cliffs at this point It seems reasonable. then, that the active period of adjustment of this shore was limited, to a large extent, to the former level

Mud Lake is well named and is a most uninviting place Shore adjustments on this small lake were much less extensive than on the main lake, and the exposed terrace is not clearly defined In its place are found bogs and muck shores, in fact, there is scarcely a foot of firm beach on the lake The lake is not over five feet in depth and the bottom is composed of soft muck As may have been already inferred, the lake is in an advanced stage of filling by vegetation and this is being accomplished both by plants encroaching from the shores and by floating forms On the west side the peculiarly shaped cove is caused by a narrow strip of boggy lowland which continues southwestward to the north shore of the east arm of Gun Lake In the early stages of these lakes an open but shallow connection existed at this lowland as well as at the present outlet, forming an island of the present large point designated B on the map. This connection was not cut off by current action but was filled with vegetation and abandoned when the water level sank to its present position

The shores of Gun Lake west of the outlet of Mud Lake are lined with low sand cliffs, alternating with patches of the terrace of the higher level. The cliffs are being washed to some extent under the present conditions, but the more prominent shore features are the ice ramparts which form in front of the fragmentary terrace   This condition holds until the former connection with Mud Lake is reached.   Across this lowland the shores are mucky and have no definite beach.   Beyond the lowlands the shores lie on the slopes of ground moraine whose southward extension forms Murphy Point. The swells of this moraine rise barely above the surface of the water and have been carved into low cliffs by the waves, while the sags form swampy shores   On the low shores the terrace of the former level is generally present, and in such localities ice ramparts are usually found.   One of the most conspicuous of the morainic sags extends across the neck of the point near its attachment to the mainland.   It stands slightly below the level of the higher stage of the lake and, therefore, was an open water channel separating the main portion of Murphy Point from the mainland at that time This island was later tied to the mainland by a bar which developed on the east side and may now be readily traced across the swampy lowland

The adjustments of the east shore of Murphy Point are the result of wave activity and consist of alternating low cliffs and flats which are characteristic of the shores in morainic material   Stony Point is a swell of the ground moraine that juts out into the lake and in this exposed position has suffered considerable dissection by waves   On the north shore the terrace of the former level is well developed but on the south this has been removed by the present activity of the waves.   Also the waves have reduced the low neck which connected this point with Murphy Point, and it now stands as an island save for an ice rampart nearly three feet in height which was built during the former stage by material shoved up from both the north and south sides   The push from the south was the more powerful and the stronger rampart follows the south shore Nearer the end of the point many of the boulders which line the shore have been forced into the base of the low cliffs by the expansion of the ice.

The south end and west side of Murphy Point are exposed to the strongest winds, and the shore features are at first due to wave cutting   The material quarried from the low cliffs has been moved largely in a northerly direction along the west shore and deposited in a small spit at C, which has efficiently protected the partially enclosed lagoon to the rear so that it is now filled with vegetation. North of C the smooth shore is largely the result of adjustments at the former level, but no bar was noted crossing the swamp which forms the neck of the point. The absence of a bar in this locality is puzzling in view of the fact that a small indentation at D was completely cut off, evidently from the south.

The shores are low along the north side of West Lake, and the shore features are due to wave action of very moderate intensity on account of the shallowness of this arm of the lake. However, the sandy material was very easily worked, and a terrace was formed at the upper level which is distinct in places. It is best developed in Miles Bay which is a pit of considerably greater depth than West Lake. If currents were active we should expect results at the entrance to this bay, but there seems to be little or no indication of bars The entrance is very shallow and is becoming more so, but this is due to filling by vegetation rather than by currents This end of the lake supports a heavy growth of rushes and other water plants and much filling in the future may be expected in this way.

Farther south along the west shore the sand plain gives way to ground moraine and the land slopes gently to the shore. Where not removed the woods grow to the shore and have aided in the formation of the excellent ramparts which are the most conspicuous shore features in this locality.

From this description it should be clear that in the early stages of its existence Gun Lake stood at a higher level and covered a larger area than at present, including some of the nearby lakes. The shores of the upper level are well preserved and show adjustments which are less pronounced than might be expected from the size of the lake This is due probably to the shallowness of a large part of the basin and to the irregular shoreline Much of the work was accomplished by waves which succeeded in straightening some of the minor irregularities and forming a terrace of flat slope. Current activity played a subsidiary part but succeeded, nevertheless, in producing some important changes, such as the blocking of the channels to Mud Lake and the tying of some of the islands to the mainland. Ice was also very effective and the shove exerted produced many well-defined ramparts and boulder strands The sinking of the level left some of these features within reach of the waves which have since removed them at exposed places. The activity at present, however, is very much less than at the higher level

Vegetation has filled, or is in process of filling, the indentations and is now taking hold in the shallower parts of the lake. The outlet of the lake is especially interesting in this regard, since the growth of vegetation appears to hold the level of the lake more nearly constant throughout the season This, in itself, has to some extent the same effect as though the level were raised and may

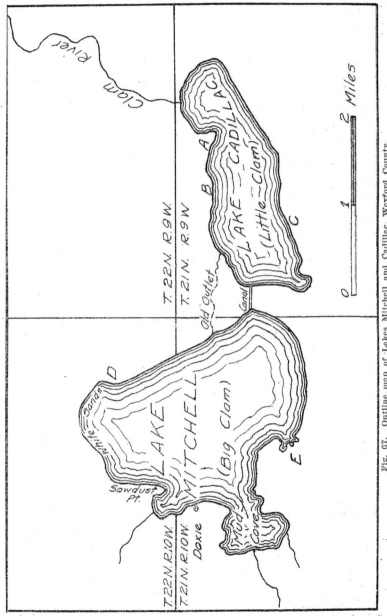

Fig. 67. Outline map of Lakes Mitchell and Cadillac, Wexford County.

account for the slight recession of some of the shores. A continuation of this process will accentuate present conditions and may even raise the level of the lake.

LAKES CADILLAC AND MITCHELL

Lakes Cadillac and Mitchell followed Gun in order of appearance and lie in a region which is most interesting from a physiographic viewpoint. The location of the city of Cadillac is especially fortunate. It is built at the junction of a large moraine tract on the east and an extended outwash plain on the west. The surface of the outwash plain is extensively pitted, but few of the pits hold water. However, two large ones are located just west of Cadillac and form the basins of Little and Big Clam lakes, or Cadillac and Mitchell lakes, as they are now called. These lakes, although not large, are well adapted to physiographic study on account of the adjustments in the easily worked material and, furthermore, are readily accessible, Cadillac being the junction of the Grand Rapids and Indiana, and Ann Arbor Railroads. It is but a few steps from the railroad station to the shore of Cadillac Lake which extends for nearly three miles in a direction south of west. In width it is rather uniform and nowhere reaches one mile. Its area is 1.9 square miles, making the average width very close to three-fourths of a mile. Compared with its neighbor, Mitchell, it is very regular in outline, the main exceptions being the large projection on the north shore and a small bay at the southwestern end.

The outlet, Clam River, leaves the lake at the northeastern end and flows through a depression in the outwash in a broad curve convex northward to the Muskegon River in northwestern Clare County. It flows in a channel which has been cut a few feet below the level of the plain but has been obstructed by a dam of low head built by one of the numerous manufacturing plants in the city of Cadillac. The obstruction of the outlet leads at once to the expectation of flooded shores, which is fulfilled.

The shore facing the city is obscured by buildings and lumber docks and shore conditions are not well represented. Around the north shore, point A, see map, Fig. 67, projects into the lake and continues under water as a shoal of less than four feet in depth for a distance of three hundred yards or more. Little evidence of a distinct submerged terrace is present, and this point is considered as one of the less deep portions of the pit which has been exposed by a sinking of the water level. The swampy condition of the point furnishes early evidence of the flooded condition of the lake. The swamp continues along the shore westward to the vicinity of locality B on

map, wheie the edge of the outwash comes to the lake and stands
in a steep cliff. Between the foot of the cliff and the beach a narrow
terrace stands about one foot above the present level. This terrace
merges into the swamp just described and with its surmounting
cliff may be traced to the northeast

West of B the terrace widens and has been pushed into an ice
rampart near the present shore, forming a foul lagoon which is rapidly being filled with vegetation The rampart persists to the west
end of the lake but the lagoon widens and extends through to Mitchell Lake along the course of the natural outlet of this lake. A canal,
navigable for boats of light draught, was dug about 1870 through
the narrow neck of land which separates the two lakes and has
caused the abandonment of the outlet. This neck of land stands
below the general level of the outwash plain with the exception of
a small flat-topped mound, probably a remnant of the outwash, on
the south side of the canal midway between the two lakes. On the
Cadillac Lake side the neck has been carved into the persistent low
terrace which widens south of the canal and runs to the embayment
at the southwestern end of the lake On this low flat the footpath
follows a well-defined bar of the higher level from the low cliffs
just south of the canal to the bridge which crosses the bay at the
southwest end. Across the bridge the outwash and narrow terrace
soon appear, and the latter is made use of for the roadway as far
as locality C East of this point the land is low and the terrace is
not distinct for a short distance East of the broad bend of the
shore line the outwash again comes to the lake with the usual narrow terrace and continues thus until the shores are obscured by
buildings or docks Along this shore the effects of the artificial
raising of the lake level are very evident The terrace, which practically surrounds this lake, has been utilized for a boulevard but is
quite generally being attacked by the waves, so that some protection
is necessary. The pine stumps, so abundant in this region, have
been used for a breakwater but have proved none too satisfactory,
so that in addition to an unsightly shore, much repair work must be
done

From the above, it is evident that Cadillac Lake has stood at a
somewhat higher level than at present and that the cause of the
lowering of the former level was the deepening of the outlet During
the higher level the main adjustment of the shores was the formation
of a narrow terrace which is well preserved where natural conditions have not been disturbed. Current action accomplished little
during this stage, the only characteristic form recognized being at
the west end south of the canal The condition of affairs previous

to the artificial elevation of the water level has been obscured by the recent increased activity of the waves which are rapidly removing the former terrace, except where protected. During stages of high water this terrace is covered, and it may be considered that it merely represents the activity of the shore agents during such times. This argument would have more force were not the lake held abnormally high. Also the rounded, grass-covered slopes above the wide portions of the exposed bottom are an indication of a definite water level, long since abandoned.

Ice action is very effective wherever shore conditions permit and some well-defined ramparts are to be found. The process of extinction is making slow progress at present and little has been done in the past. At the abandoned outlet and in the bay at the southwest end, considerable filling has been accomplished by vegetation but the main body is still relatively clear Filling by sedimentation is insignificant for the water comes either from seepage or flows from Lake Mitchell, which acts as a perfect settling basin Undoubtedly an unobstructed outlet would continue to deepen but, since the depths of the lake were not taken, the final effect cannot be ventured.

LAKE MITCHELL

North of the canal on Lake Mitchell, the shore, as shown on the map, is particularly regular, but inferences as to the probable shore conditions based on this would be greatly misleading. As a matter of fact, the outwash plain is excessively pitted and the shore consists of a succession of flats interrupted by island-like mounds of outwash. Proceeding northward from the canal, evidence of a higher level for this lake is soon at hand. A low sand bar rises above the flat at a distance varying from twenty to fifty feet back from the shore and encloses a poorly drained lagoon behind it. On the gentle slope in front, faint beaches may be discerned which in places enclose small narrow depressions, now dry. These bars were probably formed as storm beaches during the gradual lowering of the level Farther north, the waves at the higher level succeeded in cutting back the "islands" of outwash, while the currents distributed the material in a series of connecting bars which have been pushed up into ramparts in many places. These bars stand at a somewhat lower elevation than those found on other parts of the lake and it is probable that they did not extend above the water level But, with the dropping of the water level, the bars were exposed and the shore line assumed its present regular contour.

Northward the lowland areas decrease in size and at the north end disappear, leaving a continuous cliff in the outwash This, how-

ever, stands some distance back from the shore and the exposed
flat below is a portion of the former shallow bottom. In order to
get the full view of the flat it is necessary to stand on the embankment of the Ann Arbor Railroad which crosses in this locality.
The beach of the present level, called the White Sands, swings
around the north end in a perfect curve, see Plate XII, A, and is an
exceptionally fine example of an adjusted sand beach   The flat
adjacent to this shore swings far to the west and forms the so-called
"Thousand Acre Swamp," above which rise outwash remnants similar to those on the opposite side of the lake   The perfection of the
adjustments along this shore is again detected in the excellent bar
which stands a short distance inland between the lake and the
swamp   Ice has been particularly active along this shore and has
piled up two distinct ramparts in front of the bar   At the present
level a low rampart is in process of formation, making three in all,
a rare occurrence   The continuation of the bar to the south forms
Saw Dust Point which shows the direction of the prevailing currents at the time of formation. Thus, the material must have been
derived from the cliffs at the north end of the lake

Ice action on this lake is most interesting, not only on account
of its effects but also because of the manner of its occurrence Information from reliable sources makes it certain that both ice jams
and expansion take place   At Doxsie's ice jams have shoved twenty
feet on the shore and have piled up ten feet in height, a statement
well within reason as may be seen from Plate XII, B, which is reproduced from a photograph of an ice jam on the north shore of this
lake taken by Mr W F Sours of Cadillac. Also at Doxsie's, the
ice advances by expansion between four and five feet a season   The
width of the lake at this locality is one and five-eighths miles and
approaches the maximum limit for ice shove of this type.

Below the shallow bay back of Saw Dust Point the outwash, with
cliff and terrace of the higher level, again appears and extends to
the entrance of Mud Cove   From this shore the depths of the lake
are readily distinguished when light conditions are favorable. The
northern part is very shallow with the exception of a narrow channel in the middle running nearly north-south and appears as though
it were almost possible to wade across   The southern lobe lies in a
much deeper portion of the pit and is sharply contrasted in color
with that on the north.

Mud Cove is a partially detached portion of the pit which continues to the west as an extended swamp   Currents have accomplished little or nothing at the entrance and there is little likelihood
of its being isolated in this manner   Nevertheless, its existence as

Michigan Geological and
Biological Survey

Publication 30, Geological Series 25;
Plate XII.

A. WHITE SANDS, LAKE MITCHELL.

B. ICE-JAM, LAKE MITCHELL.

(Photography by W. H. Saurs.)

STREAM DIVERTED BY CURRENTS, LAKE MITCHELL.

a body of open water is very limited on account of the rapid filling by vegetation. On the south side of the Cove, a case of complete extinction of a shallow part of this irregular pit is found. In this case the indentation was separated from the lake by a narrow strip of outwash which, at first sight, appears to be a bar. The extinct part has an uninterrupted, flat surface composed of a black, peaty soil upon which a few shrubs are growing. An attempt was made to drain this for agricultural use but evidently was not an unqualified success.

East of Mud Cove the outwash, with cliff and terrace, lines the shore but soon drops to a small swamp which was cut off by an ice rampart about twenty feet inland from the present shore. The outwash again appears at the shore but finally gives way to a lowland which extends to the double bay at E. This bay is caused by two small pits which drop below the level of the swamp. It is set off from the main lake by very shallow water at the entrance. Currents undoubtedly flow across the entrance of the more southerly lobe but no bar is present, although the water is scarcely deep enough for rowboats to cross. This bay will eventually be isolated, however, by the deposits from the heavy growth of vegetation in the shallow water across the mouth.

From this locality eastward, the outwash cliffs face the shore but the terrace of the higher level is fragmentary. The northwest winds strike this shore with full force, and the waves and currents have accomplished much in the adjustment of the shore. This is shown by the regularity of the beach, see Plate XIII, the well-defined submerged terrace, and the presence of cusps at low water. (See Douglas Lake on cusps.) Near the east side of the lake the outwash cliffs continue to the south shore of Cadillac Lake, and the shore of the higher level is well shown by a bar which follows the curvature of the southeastern shore towards the canal. The land separation between the two lakes stood somewhat above the water level of the higher stage and the connection was restricted to a narrow strait in the vicinity of the abandoned outlet.

Thus, in times past, a large lake of very irregular outline stood in this locality. The greatest variation from the present condition occurred in the Lake Mitchell basin which then included a great part of the swamp areas to the west. In the early stages, the shores were much more irregular than at present, due to the numerous shallow pits above which stood "islands" of the original outwash plain. At the higher level, important adjustments of the shores took place which resulted in the formation of a definite submerged terrace and the straightening of the shore line in many places, due

both to cliff recession and to the development of connecting bars
It is probable that many of the bars were not built to the water
level but it seems clear that the "Thousand Acre Swamp" was partially cut off. The downcutting of the Clam River in the loose
sands of the outwash lowered the level of this lake and formed two
definite basins connected by an outlet, now abandoned   After the
separation of the basins the further deepening of Clam River was
felt directly by Cadillac Lake which stood at a lower level, while
Mitchell was held up by its outlet   At this stage the adjustment
of the shores of Lake Mitchell, accomplished during the upper level,
became fully effective and are the cause of the long stretches of
regular shore line.

Ice exerts a powerful shove on the shores of these lakes and is
especially active on Lake Mitchell.   Wherever vegetation served to
bind the sand, ramparts have been formed and the multiple ramparts
on the front slope of the bar at "Thousand Acre Swamp" are of
exceptional development   The manner of the ice push may be
studied to advantage on Lake Mitchell since both expansion and
jams are active   We are very fortunate in having a photograph
of the latter in action

The cutting of the canal between the two lakes has caused but
little lowering of the level of Lake Mitchell, and its shores remain
practically in their natural condition   However, on Cadillac Lake
the interference of man has obscured a large part of the shore
topography and initiated far reaching changes   Aside from the
buildings and lumber docks along the east shore, the raising of the
level by a dam should be mentioned.   The natural level of the
lake has been covered and obliterated by subsequent wave action.
Also a new cycle of shore activity has been brought about which is
working havoc and has necessitated the novel but unsightly breakwaters

The lakes are fed to a large extent by ground water and the few
entering streams flow from swamps, so that filling by sediment is
not of importance   Vegetation has made little headway except in
the protected bays, and this may be due to some extent to the
sweeping effect of the ice jams near the shore from which the plants
usually encroach   This type of filling, however, may be expected
to increase in the future and eventually will fill the basins   Little
may be expected from deepening of the outlet as long as the dam
is maintained, a condition likely to prevail

CHAPTER VI

INTERIOR LAKES OF THE SOUTHERN PENINSULA, CON'T

LAKES OF THE WESTERN INTERLOBATE AREA AND OF ALPENA COUNTY

HOUGHTON LAKE

Of the interior counties of the Southern Peninsula, Roscommon is perhaps the most fortunate as regards lakes. Others there are which surpass it in number but none in respect to size. Houghton and Higgins lakes, the most important, are both of large dimensions as our inland lakes go, the former with an area of 30.8 square miles taking first rank in the State. They lie in the western and northwestern part of the county and, although not so readily accessible as many, are nevertheless very popular during the summer and fall months. Roscommon on the Michigan Central Railroad is the most convenient point of departure for these lakes, although Houghton Lake is frequently reached from the west.

A physiographic study of these lakes is most interesting and, in fact, surprising. Obviously, for such a study all the advance information possible proves of great service and much information is always obtainable. In this case, one may find that the glacial geology has been thoroughly worked out and described * This region is a great interlobate area between the lobes of ice which filled simultaneously the Michigan and Huron basins. The outline of the Michigan lobe was relatively smooth at this stage and ran northeast-southwest in the northwestern part of the State. The Huron lobe, however, was noticeably irregular and extended far to the southwest into the Saginaw Lowland, forming a large subsidiary lobe, the Saginaw lobe. Thus, between the northeast side of the Saginaw lobe and the Michigan lobe is a broad interlobate area which extends northeast-southwest, see Fig 3. The recession of the ice in this area was to the northeast, and somewhat fragmentary cross-morainic ridges were deposited at intervals in the region extending northeast from Cadillac to Roscommon. Three such ridges cross Roscommon County and in the troughs between them are located Houghton and

_____

*Monograph 53, U S Geol Survey

27

Higgins lakes, see Fig. 68. This accounts for their northwest-southeast trend and similarity in size. With such information at hand one naturally visits the lakes prepared to find other points of similarity but herein is the surprise, which may well be deferred until the lakes have been described.

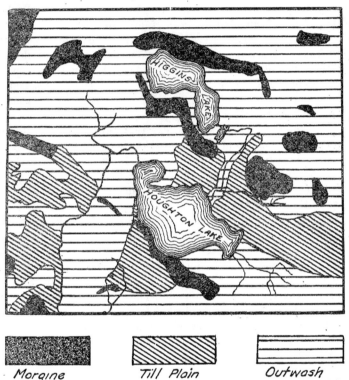

Moraine　　　　　Till Plain　　　　　Outwash

Fig. 68. Map showing the distribution of the glacial formations in the vicinity of Houghton and Higgins Lakes. (After Leverett)

Houghton Lake is not a summer resort, strictly speaking. Its popularity is due to the excellent fishing and hunting and for this there is a geographic reason. This lake, although more than eight miles long and over four wide, does not anywhere exceed twenty-five feet in depth and is filled with an almost continuous weed bed, except in a zone about the shore. This is the lair of countless fish of many kinds and accounts in part for the attraction of this lake to sportsmen. Interesting and instructive though a study of the plants and animals of these waters might be to one capable of undertaking it, the writer must dismiss it with the mere mention of wild rice. This furnishes food supply to migrating birds which flock here in great numbers to feed and rest in the fall of the year, thus the attraction to the hunters

As already mentioned, Houghton Lake lies in a trough between two roughly parallel moraine belts trending northwest-southeast but does not completely fill the depression. In reaching this lake from Roscommon, one crosses the northerly moraine just south of Higgins Lake, see Fig. 68, and drops down to a wooded lowland which becomes swamp within a half mile of the lake. This till plain borders the northeastern shore of the lake. Outwash plains swing around the ends and border the southwest shore of the lake along the constricted portions at either end, with the exception of a small area of till plain near the northwest end. The main body of the lake, however, is retained on the west by moraine. From the shallowness of the basin and the presence of broad shoals in the main body of the lake, it seems clear that this body of water lies mainly on till plain, and is retained at the ends by outwash and on the southwestern side by a moraine. Such basins were classed as inter-moraine in Chapter I.

The first impressions of this lake depend very largely on the point of view. From the heights of the moraine on the southwest side, the broad expanse of water, fringed with forest on the opposite shore and with highland in the background, presents a pleasing landscape. From the east shore, however, conditions are very different. After a trip of a half hour across a low swamp, the first glimpse is caught through an opening in the trees near the water level and, while not so fortunate perhaps, gives the more accurate impression. The horizontal dimension is exaggerated at the expense of the vertical and things appear flat. The familiar fishing boats, which dot the surface during favorable weather, are enlarged by optical illusion and suggest at once the favorite recreation on this lake.

The road from the north reaches the lake at the inlet, or Cut, as it is called, see Fig. 69, and the initial observations here lead to the conclusion that shore action due to waves and currents is feeble, due obviously to the shallowness of the lake. The inlet, a rather sluggish stream in this part of its course, has, nevertheless, brought down considerable silt which has been carried out and deposited in parallel submerged bars on either side of the current, extending from the shore directly out into the lake for a distance of about one hundred yards. A considerable portion of the water of the Cut comes from Higgins Lake which serves as a settling basin, and the stream is not normally heavily laden with sediment. Since this material is not distributed along the shore, it is evident that the waves and currents are not only relatively, but actually, of little power.

The presence of a third bar, similar in form but located more to the south and in front of a recently abandoned stream channel on the flat adjacent to the inlet, shows that a northward shifting of the channel of the stream has taken place. Those qualified to know state that this was caused by a large, temporary increase in volume of the Cut, due to the removal of a dam at the outlet of Higgins Lake a few years ago, and that the more northerly of the two bars which formerly existed in front of the abandoned channel was re-

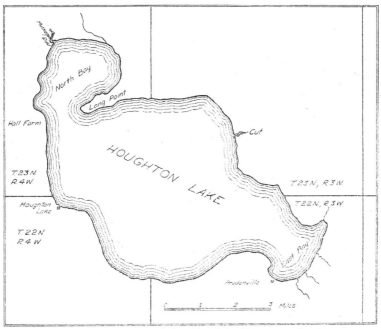

Fig. 69.   Outline map of Houghton Lake, Roscommon County.

moved as the channel shifted. Other evidence of the weakness of the waves and currents is the absence of a well-defined submerged terrace and the broad sinuosities of the shore line.

Some action has, of course, taken place and has formed a rather broad zone of sand off-shore in lieu of a terrace, which does not support the heavy growth of vegetation found farther out in the lake. Also there is an uneven beach of clear sand, which is receding at the present time and laying bare the roots of the trees growing at the high water mark. The recession of the shores is due to the obstruction of the outlet. In the lumbering days a dam of about four feet in height was constructed three-fourths of a mile below the lake and was used to retain the water in the spring. It is probable that the level of the lake was raised only a small amount, if at all, but it was held at the high water mark for a longer period than normally at least and the waves became relatively more powerful. The dam is no longer maintained but the same effect is sometimes produced by log jams.

Quite in contrast to the work of waves and currents is the effect of the ice on these shores. Ice jams, which reached a height of fifteen to eighteen feet at the Cut in the spring of 1913, are of frequent occurrence on this shore. The gentle slope and the sandy character of the shore are not favorable to the formation of ramparts, and the chief effect is exerted on the trees which often stand in water along the shore at this time of the year. Driftwood is piled high on the beach, live trees snapped off and overturned, and the bark is scrubbed from the trunks of trees still standing.

Shore conditions are so uniform on the northeast side of the lake from East Bay to Long Point that no detailed description seems necessary. Cusps, which are low water forms, are found on other parts of the lake and might well occur on this shore where not littered with driftwood. They are, however, very transitory and their occurrence in definite localities would be of little significance.

Long Point, although it extends more than half way across the lake, is, nevertheless, an extension of the outwash and not a current deposit. However, shore action is somewhat more in evidence on the north side of this point than along the shore just mentioned. When this lake was visited by the writer some exceptionally well-developed cusps were present near the tip of the point and a definite sand bar free from vegetation extended a short distance into the lake in line with the shore. Also, a very definite zone of sand off the entire north side of the point indicates an ineffectual attempt at terrace formation.

The land surface bordering the east side of North Bay has very low relief but portions of outwash, standing approximately three feet above a swamp which is at lake level, may be detected. In front of the swamp areas, bars have developed but at a level slightly higher than the present. These bars are probably a single discontinuous bar which becomes less distinct at the northeastern end of the bay but reappears along the swamp at the north end of the lake, the flat of the Muskegon River. It follows the present shore and swings in a gentle curve to the outlet. Across the outlet it continues to the low swells of the ground moraine nearly a mile to the south but stands a hundred yards back from the shore for most of its length. Along the present beach is a similar bar which ends abruptly at the outlet and stands at a slightly lower elevation than the bar farther inland. In general, the bars on the west and north shores are better developed than those in the vicinity of Long Point The short stretch of low shore along the north side of Long Point furnished a very limited amount of material for the currents flowing eastward with the winds from the northwesterly quadrant. On the west side, however, a relatively large amount of material was quarried by the waves from the cliffs to the south and was deposited by currents first in the bar which stands farthest inland This bar swung around the north end of the lake (the outlet was farther to the west at this time) and turned a small inlet to the east before merging into the undertow

The altitude of the bar shows that the lake must have stood at an elevation at least two feet higher than the present high water mark and possibly more, since the bar may have been submerged This higher level must have covered the flat adjacent to the outlet and extended some distance down stream. Also the low swamp bordering the northeast side of the lake was flooded at this time. The drop in level was due to the deepening of the outlet and was gradual. As the level lowered a passage was maintained by the outflowing water through the bar which terminates farther to the east Eventually the currents were unable to continue along the bar, on account of the decreasing depth of the water, and took a course in the deeper water near the present shore In this way the second bar was started but, with continued lowering of the water level, its length became fixed by the establishment of a definite channel by the outlet Its subsequent growth was small but sufficient to force the outlet slightly to the north at its debouchure

South of the grass-covered outwash lie the gentle swells and sags of the till plain which rises to the moraine near Houghton Lake village The moraine borders the shore, as shown in Fig 68, and then drops to the outwash plain which nearly surrounds the southwestern end of the lake The prominent features along this shore are the wave-cut cliffs which rise from the high water mark and show no evidence of the higher level found near the outlet Where the till plain and the moraine come to the shore, the cliffs are composed of boulder clay and are steep The outwash is composed of unconsolidated sand but is covered with a close mat of grass so that the cliffs are somewhat steeper than is usual for this material. The different formations are also expressed in the character of the beach material which contains cobbles and boulders in front of the moraine but is of clear sand along the outwash plain

In conclusion, it may be stated that shore agencies on Houghton Lake have been productive of meager results Waves and currents, although rejuvenated to some extent at the present time, are of little power and this inactivity is due to the shallowness of the lake and the heavy growth of vegetation which effectively interfere with wave and current development. Shore adjustments have been of somewhat greater importance in the past when the lake stood at a higher level. At this time, currents showed their greatest activity in North Bay and succeeded in decreasing the size of this arm to a considerable extent The greatest activity of the waves has taken place along the southwestern shore, as shown by the prominent cliffs An index to the combined activity of waves and currents is the development of the submerged terrace and this is nowhere well-defined Ice jams are of frequent occurrence and great intensity, especially on the northeast side of the lake, but shore conditions are not favorable for decided effects.

The lake is, however, an interesting example of one physiographic process,—that of extinction. Little sediment is brought in by streams and the outlet is deepening at a very slow rate Yet the lake is filling very rapidly due to vegetation Geologic processes are, as a rule, acting very slowly according to human standards of time but one may look forward to the extinction of this lake in the course of a few generations

HIGGINS LAKE

Higgins Lake is reached conveniently from Roscommon on the Michigan Central R R by stage and is well worth a visit With an area of nearly fifteen and one-half square miles and a length of seven miles, this lake ranks among the larger of our inland lakes Also it is one of the most beautiful As seen from the summit of the moraine to the south, the lake consists of two broad arms which stretch west and south from a central constriction The interesting island, the green slopes and the clear blue water blend into a most attractive landscape From most points on the shore, however, the view is restricted but is sufficiently inviting to induce one to explore further The clarity of the water is remarkable and might well have inspired a less prosaic name than Higgins It is so clear that it looks cold and such is the case, for the lake is deep and is fed by springs. The change from the light color of the shallow water to the blue of the depths is sudden So sudden, in fact, that to float across this zone on a peaceful day gives one the indescribable sensations of sailing into space

Likewise from a physiographic viewpoint Higgins Lake is most interesting. The general features of the region are quite simple as regards geology, see Fig. 68 Moraines border the north shore of the west arm and parallel the southwest shore of the entire lake. The morainic slopes on the southwest side do not reach the lake but are separated by a narrow zone of sand which widens into broad outwash plains at both ends of the lake. The outwash was formed when the ice border stood at the northern moraine, and covered the till plain between the two moraines, with the possible exception of the lake basin itself. Nearer the moraines the outwash merges into a terrace, and till is exposed beneath the sands on the southwest side of the lake.

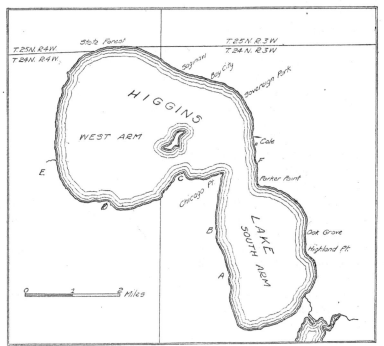

Fig. 70.   Outline map of Higgins Lake, Roscommon County.

Ideas are prevalent concerning remarkable depths of the water in this lake but the greatest depth reported from reliable sources is one hundred twenty-five feet. This depth makes it certain that the lake does not cover a till plain, as does its neighbor Houghton, or else the outwash is excessively thick. From the shape of the lake it seems probable that the basin is a large, irregular pit in the outwash formed by buried blocks of ice, as explained in Chapter I.

In addition, the history of the lake is as complicated as that of some of the lakes which were connected with the Great Lakes and is in itself an interesting story which could not be fully deciphered at the time this study was made The former strands are very distinct and show a lake of much greater size at its maximum height A careful mapping of these shores and the adjustments which took place at the various levels promises a most interesting and profitable study

At the outlet of the lake natural conditions are somewhat disturbed by the activity of man. In the lumbering days a dam was constructed to retain the water for the log runs in the spring The level was raised about forty inches but lowered rapidly during the runs, remaining low during the greater part of the year With the passing of the forests the dam lost its usefulness and the lake assumed its normal level The outlet was again obstructed in 1911 for the purpose of permanently raising the level of the lake This caused a renewal of the activity of the waves, and the effects were sufficient in one year to convince those concerned of the inadvisability of such a condition, so that the dam was blown out. Such disturbances make the interpretation of conditions at the outlet somewhat uncertain but the significant facts may be ascertained

The outlet, see Fig 70, flows in a channel which has been cut approximately eight feet below the level of the sand plain. It flows in a southeasterly direction to the nearby Marl Lake and thence eastward for more than two miles before turning south through a low sag in the moraine which stands between Higgins and Houghton lakes. In the bed of the outlet and along the shore to the southwest a large number of boulders of considerable size are found These boulders lie at the base of the sand plain which is relatively thin here and are washed free from the finer material by the movement of the water. Considering the outlet, it is obvious that down-cutting has taken place rapidly while the stream was running over the sands but was accomplished much more slowly as the boulders were encountered Thus, from this limited locality one may hypothecate higher levels for the lake and be prepared to find conclusive evidence on the slopes adjacent to the present shores.

At the south end of the lake, the outwash soon gives way to a narrow flat which borders the shore to the west side The even curvature of the shore and the clear sand beach are suggestive of current action and further evidence is found in two sand bars a short distance inland. These bars stand about two feet above the present lake level and parallel the shore from one side of the lake to the other. The lagoon, thus formed, was very shallow and is now dry. If these bars were formed by currents, their growth must have been from the west because shore drift on the east side of the lake could not well have passed the outlet. Undoubtedly currents brought much material to this shore from the cliffs along the west side of the South Arm, where an uninterrupted shore of nearly three miles in length is exposed to the northeasterly winds In the early stages of this level, the currents did not leave the shore in this locality but, as the submerged terrace developed and widened, both the waves and the currents were retarded by its influence Finally, the retardation was sufficient to exert a back pressure on the strong currents moving southward along the west side and they were forced from the shore Thus the first bar (farther inland) was formed and a slight lowering of the level as the outlet deepened may have caused the second bar somewhat farther out in the lake (See Crystal Lake for a similar occurrence)

At the present level the submerged terrace is wide but not sharply defined. Soundings showed an exceptionally wide terrace near the west side which extends into water nearly twenty-five feet in depth before dropping into deep water. The zone of sand, however, stopped at depths of ten to twelve feet, and this probably represents the greatest depth of the terrace, since the finer material is usually swept from the terraces in lakes of this size and may possibly be carried from one end of the lake to the other

The west shore of the South Arm is bounded by low cliffs for most of its extent In two localities only were the effects of current action detected At locality A, see map, a small point breaks the regularity of the shore line, and currents have formed a small spit pointing southward, a fact in harmony with the view that the bars at the south end were formed by currents from this shore Again at ·Chicago Point currents are active but this will be reserved for discussion later The cliffs along this shore do not rise above six to eight feet and have been carved in the sands of the adjacent plain which is a terrace of a higher level The material is homogeneous and unconsolidated and has been very uniformly worn by the waves, forming an exceptionally smooth shore line A distinct submerged terrace drops at eight to ten feet but is of relatively narrow width. Off locality B a rock shoal comes to within six or eight feet of the surface It is thus within the zone of action of the waves which have removed the finer material from the north end and deposited it in a bar at the opposite end Clearly the northerly winds are the most effective in this locality

Chicago Point has much of interest for the physiographer. In this locality, evidence of levels higher than the present is at hand and. in addition, changes are now taking place which are of great significance Back from the shore stands a broad sand terrace which slopes very gently upward to the morainic hills in the dis-

tance. Its height was not measured in this locality but a similar
terrace at the State Forest marks a level of the lake sixteen feet
above the present. This terrace, which borders the shore of the
south arm, drops to a lower one standing at an elevation of eight
feet above lake level, formed probably at the time when the outlet
flowed over the surface of the sand flat. The spit began its development at this time but, inasmuch as the outlet cut down through
the loose sand rapidly, the growth was small. The outlet soon cut
through the sand and encountered the boulders at its base which
held the lake at a level two feet above the present for a considerable
time. During this stage the spit increased in length more than two
hundred feet. At the present level the spit is continuing its growth
and, including the submerged portion, extends fully a quarter of a
mile out into the lake. On the opposite side of the lake the sub-
merge terrace is fully as wide as the length of the spit, so that the
narrows is in reality much more restricted than appears from the
map. An ice rampart borders the south side of the spit at the
present level but its counterpart is not present on the opposite
side. This decrepancy may be due to the destruction of the rampart
on the north side. The material of the spit is not suitable for the
formation of a permanent rampart and, if formed, it would be
subjected to strong wave action, due to northerly winds of considerable reach.

West of Chicago Point the eight-foot terrace becomes faint and
drops to the two-foot level in the vicinity of point C, see map. Off
this shore the lake is shallow to the Island, due probably to the
nature of the basin. The condition of the Island during the stages
above the two-foot level cannot be determined but it is probable
that its top was bevelled to some extent at the eight-foot level.
During the two-foot level a much smaller area than the present
stood above the water and was subjected to considerable adjustment by waves and by ice. Terraces and strong beaches were
formed all around the island but were better developed on the northwest side throughout. In addition, the bouldery material was
pushed up into ice ramparts which are very pronounced on the
northwest shore. The expanse from the Island to the west shore,
a distance of more than two miles, is generally considered excessive
for the formation of ramparts by expansion, so that ice jams appear to be effective here. However, the maximum size of lake upon
which expansion is effective is as yet uncertain and it is unfortunate that little could be learned concerning the manner of the
ice push on this shore. At the present level the waves are active
on the northwest side and much of the material quarried is trans-

ported to the point at the northeastern end of the island, where it
is being deposited in a spit extending almost due east   Another
spit was found at the sharp projection on the southeast side, which
was partially removed at the time of the writer's visit, due probably
to the temporary rise in level a year previous

Along the south shore of the West Arm the moraine lies nearer
the present shore and the terrace of the sixteen-foot level is relatively narrow   The small terrace of the two-foot level is quite
generally present but that of the eight foot stage occurs infrequently.   At the two-foot and present levels, the waves have removed the gravel of the higher terraces, and many of the boulders
of the underlying till are concentrated on the beach at the projections   Ice action is of little importance on this shore   At point D,
which is caused by an outlying moranic knob, the eight-foot terrace is well preserved but that of the two-foot level has been removed   The submerged terrace is well developed along this shore.
The line of the "drop off" swings in a southward bending loop from
the Island to point D where it narrows to a width of one to two
hundred yards and continues thus around the west end of the lake
with minor variations only.

About one-half mile west of point D, an indentation not manifest
in the contour of the present beach is to be found   This was an embayment of considerable extent during the eight foot level but was
cut off by a low bar during the two-foot stage   The lagoon was a
shallow portion of the submerged terrace and was readily drained
by seepage through the sand of the bar when the lake level lowered.
At E the waves have demolished both the two and eight-foot levels
and are working on the sixteen-foot terrace, having formed a cliff
twelve to fifteen feet in height

North of point E the moraine drops to the sand plains and there
is a possibility that the lake extended considerably farther to
the west when it stood at the level sixteen feet above the present.
The two-foot terrace is well developd and in places reaches a width
of over two hundred feet   This shore was badly cut during the
temporary high water due to the recent dam at the outlet   Most of
the beach has been worn away to the tree roots and the effects of a
strong ice push are evident in places   The latter is said to have been
caused by ice jams in the spring of 1913

At the State Forest the moraine which borders the northern end
of the lake approaches the shore and the levels are poorly defined
with the exception of that at the two-foot stage   However, the
sixteen-foot terrace is definable and has been accurately determined
at sixteen and one-half feet above the present level of the lake

At the Saginaw Grounds the highest terrace is reached by a continuous cliff of about fifteen feet in height   Farther to the east at the Bay City Grounds morainic hills are being carved by the waves, forming cliffs up to heights of thirty-five feet   These two locations are well suited for resort purposes and afford an excellent view of the entire length of the lake   The only disadvantage is the excessive width of the present submerged terrace, the greatest on the lake   Inasmuch as it drops at six feet, the water is very shallow for a long distance off shore.

Sand plains again border the lake in the vicinity of Sovereign Park and continue along the eastern side of the lake to the outlet   The clump of pines at the Park gives some idea of the wonderful forests that formerly covered this region and adds to the attractiveness of the location   At the two-foot level the shore stood considerably farther back than at present   So much so, that the currents left the shore and deposited a bar nearly a mile in length in front of a very narrow lagoon   As is frequently the case on Higgins Lake, the lagoons of this level stood on the sandy terrace and were quickly drained when the water level lowered. Along the shore in the vicinity of Cole low hills come to the shore and have been carved into cliffs which step down to the two-foot terrace. This higher ground leaves the shore about one-half mile north of Parker Point, F on map, and swings back from the lake in a broad curve, reaching the lake again at Oak Grove   The lowland between this and the lake was flooded at the higher levels and was thus a shallow embayment whose bed was worked into a submerged terrace of gentle slope   The change in direction of the shore line at the sides of this embayment was abrupt and especially so at the northern end, F, where the angle was approximately ninety degrees   Currents must have left the shore at each side, but, strange as it may seem, accomplished little at the north side   However, on the south side a series of bars converging on the low cliffs above Oak Grove, stand at progressively higher elevations inland, or in other words, are arranged in steps. They sweep around the bay in broad, swinging curves and are truncated by the somewhat irregular shore north of Parker Point.

Apparently the bars did not begin to develop until the eight-foot stage, during which the outlet was being cut down rather rapidly   As the water level lowered at least four bars were formed, which may be readily distinguished along the road running east from the head of the bay   The individual bars were not traced through the swamp back of Parkers Hotel and there is the possibility that the number is increased in this locality by splitting   As the water subsided to the two-foot level, the embayment was drained with the exception of a narrow strip adjacent to the present shore, which was isolated by a low bar during this stage The submerged terrace is very well defined along this shore but gradually decreases to a depth of about four feet and a width of less than fifty on the south side of Parker Point Beyond the end of the point it makes a broad loop to the southward and also widens in conformity with the terrace fronting the east shore above the point.

In the development of the shore features in this locality several factors have been of importance Obviously, winds with a westerly component are the only ones effective on these shores and those from the northwest are probably the more important both as to strength and frequency That the currents caused by these winds have been powerful is shown by the development of the shore between Parker Point and the bluffs at F in accordance with that to the north, and by the southward extension of the submerged terrace off the east side of the point. Nevertheless, the deposits in the embayment have been made almost exclusively by northward moving currents in the South Arm and something other than the force and prevalence of the wind has been the determining factor

From either direction the material is derived from sources which are practically equivalent but the waves have a slight advantage at Oak Grove on account of the narrower submerged terrace. This, however, is not sufficient to account for the great preponderance of the work of the currents in the South Arm and the explanation must be found in the form of the lake basin The lake lies for the most part in a deep pit, but during the higher levels overflowed on the adjacent slopes, forming shallow embayments Such an embayment is the one under discussion but off the point lies the deep water of the main basin. The currents from the West Arm left the shore at the abrupt turn, F, and ran directly into deep water, causing a rapid reduction in velocity and therefore deposition of the suspended load This material was utilized in filling the deep basin and consequently was not localized in characteristic shore forms However, on the south side of the embayment the currents flowed over shallow water after leaving the shore at Oak Grove and deposited their load in bars which crossed the bay and terminated at the shore north of Parker Point where the stronger cross currents of the West Arm were encountered

The protuberance of the shore in the vicinity of Oak Grove is of higher ground and was the source of the materials of the bars in the embayment just discussed. Here the sixteen-foot level is well defined and the terrace is utilized as a building site for several summer cottages. The eight-foot level is not well defined, much of it having been removed at the lower levels. Recent cutting due to the temporary raising of the lake level is much in evidence along the low cliffs which line the shore. At Highland Point the land drops in elevation and the two-foot level is prominent as a wide terrace. Ice action has built a low rampart at the present shore but is of moderate intensity. Between Highland Point and the outlet a low sand flat extends several miles to the eastward. This flat was covered by all of the higher levels but the borders of the sixteen and eight foot stages were not traced. During the two foot level a low bar, conforming to the present contour of the shore, developed and definitely cut off this lowland from the lake basin.

In conclusion, it seems fair to state that Higgins Lake is one of our most interesting and instructive lakes. The history of this interior lake is exceptional and is merely sketched in this account. This phase of the work is left with reluctance for it is felt that a detailed study of the various levels would be productive of most interesting results. We may be certain of a much larger lake during the highest or sixteen-foot level. At this time, the ends were extended in broad, shallow embayments and the southwestern border reached to the moraine slopes. Much work was done by the waves, and broad terraces were formed which now appear as a veneer of sand on till adjacent to the shores. With the lowering to the eight-foot level, accomplished probably by deepening of the outlet, a new cycle was inaugurated. At this time the waves were working on the unconsolidated sands of the sixteen foot terrace and quarried great quantities of material which was distributed by currents on the submerged terrace and in the embayments. The rapid deepening of the outlet through the sand caused a gradual depression of the level to two feet above the present stage. The adjustments at this level were mainly by currents which cut off numerous minor embayments, notably at the south and west ends. The slight drop to the present level served mainly to reduce the activity of the shore agents, a condition emphasized by contrast when the lake was held temporarily at a high level. A re-adjustment to present conditions is undoubtedly taking place but the results are not striking. However, a continuation of the development of the spit at Chicago Point will have far-reaching results, since it is growing across the narrowest part of the lake. Eventually, the lake must be divided in this locality, but much filling is necessary on account of the deep water and the progress will be slow.

The process of extinction has hardly started. Filling by vegeta-

tion and sediment is of slight importance at the present time on
account of the great depth of the lake and the absence of entering
streams The deepening of the outlet will eventually drain the
lake, but this process is making slow progress now that the stream
is flowing over boulders   It seems reasonable, then, that the
shores may become adjusted to a late stage of development before
the cycle is interrupted   Ice push is not of great importance on
this lake as regards effects but observational work on this phase of
our study should produce interesting results, especially in the West
Arm which is near the maximum limit for expansion.

Before leaving these lakes the writer wishes to point out the
unexpected (to him at least) contrast between the two lakes in
this region   Higgins Lake is deep, its limpid, blue water is derived from underground sources; the adjustments of its shores
are numerous and varied, and its history is punctuated with
interesting episodes. A few miles to the southwest Houghton
Lake occupies a similar position with reference to the glacial
formations, but is almost diametrically opposite in characteristics.
Thus, it is shallow, its turbid waters, derived from surface drainage,
are agitated throughout by every storm, it is choked with vegetation; the adjustments of its shores are infrequent and of little
significance; and conditions have varied little in the past from those
existent today

PORTAGE LAKE, CRAWFORD COUNTY

Portage is a rather popular name for lakes and it seems necessary to state that the one under consideration is situated in the central-western part of Crawford County. It lies about eight miles
almost due north of Higgins Lake, and, thus, came into existence
at a later time   It is reached from Grayling on the Michigan Central Railroad by a short drive

The best idea of the outline of this lake may be gained from
the accompanying map, Fig 71, drawn from the U. S Land Survey
map of the region It is approximately three miles long, less than
a mile in width except across the broad embayment at the north
end, and has an area of slightly less than three square miles, 2 96.
It lies in one of the deeper pits of an outwash plain but at the
border of a moraine which stands not far back from the south and
west shores Although within three miles of the Au Sable River it,
nevertheless, is the source of one of the tributaries of the Manistee
which leaves the lake at the northwestern end   The lake is best
known on account of the location of the state camp of the National
Guard on the west side

The entire east side of the lake presents little of physiographic interest. Shallow depressions which sink below the level of the outwash plain but stand above the lake level cause swampy shores for the greater part of the distance. The swamp condition is further accentuated by low ice ramparts of sand through which occasional small streams break. Along the north shore the adjustments are better defined and the broad salient, Eagle Point, is the index of this work. A well-defined bar extends out into the lake from

Fig. 71.   Outline map of Portage Lake, Crawford County.

the end of the point and connects with the beaches on either side in unbroken curves. The low cliffs in the vicinity of McIntyres' west of the point have furnished a considerable portion of the material for this spit. On the opposite side some material drifts in from the northeast, as shown by the turning of the stream courses towards the point before they cross the beach. The west side of the point is exposed to the strong westerly winds and the adjustments of this shore should, therefore, be more pronounced. This, however, is not striking and may be due to the formation of return currents

29

on the east side during "blows" from the southwest in addition to
the direct effect of the easterly winds

At the northwestern end of the lake the land drops to a low
swamp through which the outlet runs A strong ice rampart follows
the shore, but fails at the outlet and near the southern edge of the
swamp This rampart totally obscures any possible current deposits but, nevertheless, the fact that it plays out to the south suggests the possibility of its being a remodeled bar which developed
from the north

South of the swamp low, outlying knobs of the moraine relieve
the swamp conditions. These knobs determined the position of
currents along this shore and are connected in some cases by bars
In one locality a definite bar with a well-developed rampart on its
front slope stands above the present water level. These forms,
which show a higher level of the lake, are made more prominent
by the presence of a second rampart at the present water level
Northwest of Bear Point the moraine comes to the lake shores and
the slopes are cut into steep cliffs which rise from the exposed terrace of the higher level At Bear Point the currents left the hills
during the former level and built a strong bar in a southeasterly
direction which now ends abruptly at the present shore on the south
side of the point The lagoon behind this bar is filled with vegetation A rampart has been pushed up on the front slope of the bar
but is being removed by waves under the present conditions This
material is being carried outward and deposited on a submerged
bar in line with the northeast shore of the point, one of the few
adjustments in process

South of Bear Point the morainic topography has given rise to
an alternation of cliffs and small swamps The activity of the waves
is unmistakably evident but the currents seem to have carried little
of the material along the shore, for the swamps are not cut off
except at the small indentation near the rifle range and this by an
ice rampart Near the south end the land drops to an extensive
swamp which is separated from the lake by ice ramparts rather
than by typical bars Beginning at the western side two ramparts
fringe the shore, the inner rampart reaching a maximum height of
five feet They decrease in strength towards the east and die out
before reaching the higher ground of the moraine at the south end
of the lake In this locality the slopes are gentle and an exposed
terrace of the former level is present locally. Wave action seems
to have been very slight for the cliffs are very low or are entirely
lacking

The shores of Portage Lake show a relatively small amount of
adjustment and this was accomplished at a level somewhat higher

than the present   The lack of well-defined shore features makes an
accurate determination of the elevation of this former level somewhat difficult but it probably stood between two and three feet
above the level of the lake at the time of the writer's study.   The
original lake was much more irregular in outline than the present
and the opportunities for adjustments were numerous   Nevertheless, the greatest change was brought about by the draining of many
of the shallow indentations when the level lowered. At the present
level the adjustments in process are few in number and progressing
very slowly

It is interesting to compare the development of the shores of
this lake with that of such lakes as Corey, Clear and Long in St
Joseph County. These lakes are much smaller than Portage and
are surrounded by material which, although sandy, is probably
more consolidated than the outwash sands along the east and north
shores of Portage Lake   Nevertheless, the shore features are much
more decided than those of Portage Lake and have been carried to
a more advanced stage of development   In the absence of complete
data one is inclined to infer that the greater age of the more southerly located lakes is the determining factor.   .

OTSEGO LAKE

Further retreat of the ice in the western interlobate area uncovered the region centering about Otsego County, in the southwestern
part of which Otsego Lake is situated   This lake is nearly five miles
in length but is scarcely a mile in greatest width. Its area is three
and one-quarter square miles, so that the average width is approximately three-fifths of a mile. This lake is hemmed in on both sides
by moraines for most of its extent, but the material at the shores is
outwash sands, so that the lake may be classed as a pit   It is,
however, somewhat exceptional in form and topographic location,
and, therefore, some discussion of its manner of formation may not
be out of place

The glacial deposits of this region lie south of a well-defined
moraine which was formed by the ice of the Michigan lobe on the
northwest and by that of the Huron lobe on the northeast, thus
the right-angled bend   See Fig 72. An extensive outwash plain
stands south of this moraine and surrounds a number of morainic
tracts which rise above the plain as island-like forms   The morainic
tracts have a general north south trend and are separated by narrow, sand-filled troughs, three of which, designated I, II, and III

on map, are well defined. The central trough, II, branches north-
ward and Otsego Lake lies at the north end of the eastern branch.
Attention is called in particular to the eastern troughs, I and the
Otsego Lake branch of II, which lie in the drainage system of the
Au Sable River.

The drainage of these troughs divides near the north end, the
major part flowing southward. The upper parts, however, flow
southeastward around the morainic tracts and contain lake basins
which are pits in the outwash. Thus, in accounting for these
basins, and in particular that of Otsego Lake, the elongated form

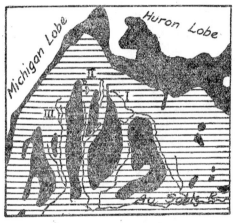

Fig. 72. Map of the glacial formations in the vicinity of Otsego Lake. Solid black
indicates moraine. Lined areas are outwash. (After Leverett.)

and the presence of divides in the sand-filled troughs must be considered.

The recession of the ice border in this locality was to the northwest within the Michigan lobe and to the northeast within the
Huron. Thus, it is very probable that at one stage the ice front
stood near the northern border of the morainic tracts and extended
in narrow tongues into the inter-morainic valleys to approximately
the position of the present divides. During this time, the drainage
flowed southward and the valleys were partially filled with outwash
material. As the ice melted the higher elevations were completely
uncovered, but parts of the tongues of ice in the depressions became
detached and were buried by outwash from the ice front which was
receding northward. At the same time a lower channel, parallel to
the ice border, was opened to the southeastward which in the case
of Otsego Lake crossed the northern tip of the moraine on the east
side. Finally the melting of the buried ice block formed the depression in which Otsego Lake stands.

The loose surface material, the irregularity of the shoreline, and the elongated form of the lake, presenting a broad expanse of water

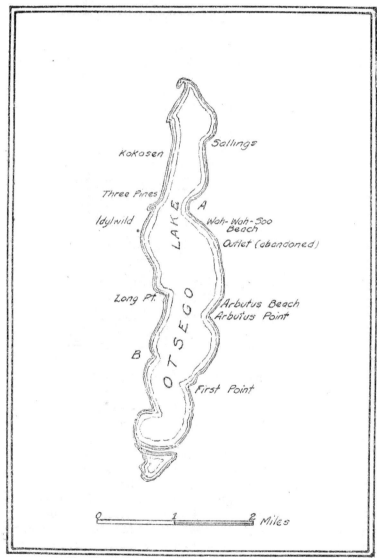

Fig. 73. Outline map of Otsego Lake, Otsego County.

to winds from certain directions, have caused numerous adjustments of the shores which are exceptional for a lake of this size. Many excellent beaches and cottage sites are, therefore, available

but are most appreciated on the east side in proximity to the
railroad

On a map one looks in vain for an outlet of Otsego Lake (Fig 73)
but may notice that the North Branch of the Au Sable River heads
straight for the east side of the lake somewhat north of the center
It does not extend to the lake, however, and one interested in drainage problems naturally wonders what the conditions at the head
of this stream may be   In this case a trip is worth while, so we may
advantageously begin our study at this place

Back from the lake a dry channel, with even floor and gentle
slope away from the lake, runs through a break in the hills and
connects directly with the North Branch of the Au Sable. Nearer
the lake the channel broadens to a low marsh in the sands of the
trough and splits before reaching the lake shore, having formed
an island in past times   At present the water stands four to five
feet below the level of the outlet, long since abandoned.

The shores along the head of the broad embayment from which
the outlet leads are bounded by cliffs of stratified sand which reach
to the surface of the outwash about ten feet above the lake   This
unconsolidated material was easily quarried and was distributed
in both directions by shore currents and offshore by the undertow.
The relative importance of these agents is dependent very largely
on the reach of the winds which may be rated in the following order ·
Southwest, northwest and west   Thus, shore currents developed at
the expense of the undertow and the submerged terrace is poorly
defined   In most places it is merely a zone of sand which shows a
sharp line of demarcation from the muddy bottom of the deeper
part of the lake   Of the shore currents those which develop under
southwest winds have the advantage and the northward drift along
this shore is the more powerful   Therefore, much of the material
has been deposited along the south side of the broad point north of
the outlet   The current action is first apparent at the outlet where
a bar started to develop at a level four feet above the present and
partially enclosed the small marsh bordering the outlet, which must
have been a shallow arm of the lake at that time. At the present
level ice-shove, probably of the expansion type, has formed a poorly
defined rampart, although shore conditions are unfavorable   North
of the outlet this upper beach extends to the broad point and is
known as Wah-Wah-Soo Beach   The point is caused by an original
irregularity of the basin and was almost obliterated by wave action
during the early stages of the lake. Thus, in the background stands
a cliff in the outwash and from the foot of this stretches the now
exposed submerged terrace of that time   But with the subsidence

of the water, caused by the downcutting of the outlet, the activity of the shore agencies was reversed and currents from the north deposited a bar almost in line with that shore, enclosing a very narrow lagoon just in front of the cliffs. Either during or following this period the currents from the south became effective and carried the Wah-Wah-Soo Beach beyond the bar from the north and are at the present time flowing to the end of the point. This condition is expressed by a well-defined submerged terrace which drops into deeper water from a depth of two feet. This very shallow terrace in a locality favorable for its development indicates a poorly developed undertow.

From this point to the north end of the lake the land slopes gently to the shore and the only discernible adjustment of the shore has been the carving of low cliffs by waves of very moderate force. Some of the material which was removed from the cliffs has been transported to the north and deposited in a bar which stands slightly above the swampy lowland bounding the north end. This bar leaves the higher ground some distance inland but borders the lake at the north end. On the west side similar currents have built a strong bar at right angles to the one from the opposite shore which has partially cut off an extensive swamp and caused a peculiar gourd-like outline of the shore. These deposits were both formed at the higher level but probably were not above water for much of their extent.

The northward drift of the currents along the west shore is again evident at the narrow hook which has developed in front of a low exposed terrace a short distance south. In the early stages of the lake waves have been energetic along this shore, and the terrace of the higher level is well exposed, in places reaching a width of nearly one-fourth mile. At the higher stage this smooth shore was broken by bays north of Kokosen and in the vicinity of Three Pines. In both cases complete bars were formed across the mouths of these embayments, forming lagoons which are still swampy. Between Three Pines and Idylwild the same process is being repeated at the present level by the formation of a spit across the neck of the small bay. Below this bay the moraine recedes from the lake and the outwash is considerably wider. In places the waves have removed the higher terrace and are sapping the sands of the outwash. Ice-shove is effective in this locality at the present level and has formed ramparts at the edge of the exposed terrace which is, therefore, poorly drained. The greater part of the eroded material is carried by shore currents rather than by undertow, and the submerged terrace is poorly developed. Most of it drifts to the south and is dropped at Long Point where the currents are forced from the shore. The activity at this point began during the higher level and shows features similar to those found on the point north of the outlet. The main part of the point is an exposed terrace of this level upon which was built a strong bar from the north, indicating a reversal from wave to current action The bar stands about twenty feet back from the present beach and is sharply truncated by the south shore The revival of wave action, as shown by the removal of the tip of the bar, was due to the inauguration of a new cycle by the sinking of the water level and is still in progress at periods of excessively high water such as occurred in 1913 On the north side of the point, however, the currents are still active, the point having been extended approximately two hundred feet offshore below the water level As is the case at many of the points, the submerged terrace is well developed on the side affected by currents, here the north, and drops into deep water at four feet at distances offshore which increase towards the ends of the points

The shore from Long Point to the south end of the lake shows features very similar to those just described. The long stretches are generally regions of wave action which in many places has removed the terrace of the former level and is working in the sands of the outwash Two strikingly similar points, B on map and point to the south, break the shore line Both are V-bars which began their development at the higher stage and were interrupted by the drop in level In each case the currents from the north were the more active and built strong bars which probably stood above water level Likewise, on the south side bars developed which met those from the north, forming a more or less symmetrical triangular embankment with enclosed lagoon, but were not completed at the time of the sinking of the water level However, at the present stage the triangular form is well shown and the lagoons are filled with water or are swampy

The south shore of the lake is bounded by the so-called "beaver dam" which, local tradition to the contrary, is one of the best examples of a bar seen by the writer. This form, shown in Plate XIV, is composed entirely of sand and joins the east shore in an unbroken curve. Its crest stands slightly above the level of the higher stage, except for the last hundred feet at the west end, and supports a fringe of trees which accentuates the linear character of this bar In the photograph, Plate XIV, a similar bar may be seen stretching across the triangular lagoon isolated by the "beaver dam." This bar, however, stands at a lower elevation and is poorly defined. Both of these bars were formed during the higher stage and obviously

A. "BEAVER DAM," OTSEGO LAKE.

B. ICE-FORMED V-BAR, LONG LAKE, ALPENA COUNTY.

the outer bar developed first For some reason the point of departure of the currents from the shore was shifted to the north before the outer bar reached the water level and remained in the position now occupied by the inner bar, the "beaver dam" The currents instrumental in their formation were those driven by northwest winds along the shore south of First Point At flood stages of the present level waves have been active and have steepened considerably the front slope of the bar, which normally should be gentle

Along the east shore cliffs in the outwash reveal the source of the material of these bars In places the cliffs show fresh cutting which may be laid directly to the excessively high water in 1913 Near First Point the cutting is less active and the terrace of the higher stage appears and widens towards the point In the early stage of the lake this point was merely a blunt projection of the outwash which was carved into a cliff and terrace Then followed a period of reversed activity, ascribed to the downcutting of the outlet, during which currents predominated The drift from both directions left the shore at this point but that from the south was the stronger. The material from this side was deposited in a strong bar which splits twice before meeting the single bar on the north side. Thus, on the south side of the apex there are three distinct bars separated by marshy lagoons In front of the bars a triangular terrace of considerable extent developed, which was exposed by the sinking of the water to the present level Since that time, the point has been extended under water for nearly three hundred feet and drops at a depth of four feet The stretch of shore on either side of the point along which currents may develop is slightly longer on the north side while the northwesterly winds have quite an advantage in reach over those from the southwest The greater effectiveness of the currents from the south is, therefore, somewhat unexpected. The determining factor seems to be a blunt projection just north of the point, which causes considerable deflection of the currents from this direction, as is shown by the distinct submerged terrace

In the broad embayment north of First Point waves are again the active agent and sand cliffs are the conspicuous shore features The terrace of the higher level has been removed except in proximity to the points Arbutus Point is very similar to First Point and requires no special discussion except for slight modifications. The main episodes in its development are identical but the predominating currents came from the north. Instead of the split bars found on the south side of First Point there developed here a compound hook with several spurs recurving to the shore. In front of the hook on the north side is a series of parallel beaches which may mean a gradual lowering of the water level This point is not growing at present and some cutting may take place at flood stages. However, a very well defined submerged terrace has developed in conformity with the north side of the point

As regards origin and general features, Otsego Lake presents many interesting features The major shore adjustments have taken place when the water stood higher than at present and show many variations The sandy material of the surrounding outwash has been easily eroded and each change of conditions is clearly registered Although the full extent of the lake in the early stages was not determined, cutting by waves prevailed generally along the shores. The reversal of activity, making currents effective at the numerous points, is remarkably consistent and is ascribed to the downcutting of the outlet Then followed a period of stability during which the points were increased by the development of bars The drop in level to the present stage was probably accomplished slowly and allowed the growth of a series of minor bars on some of the points Since the drop has caused the abandonment of the outlet, it must be ascribed to a decrease in the amount of ground water which is the main source of supply The depressed level of the surface of the ground water is a subject full of complications, but one important factor may have been a general drying-out following the disappearance of the glacier which supplied immense quantities of surface water in melting

At the present level the adjustments are not striking and occur for the most part during stages of high water. No important changes are to be expected but minor adjustments may be accomplished by currents in a few localities With wave action limited to exceptional conditions of infrequent occurrence, there is little probability of any extended growth of the points Considering the amount of current action, the submerged terrace is of very inferior development A more distinct terrace may have been formed at the higher level and is now being slowly adjusted to the present conditions.

Little sediment is being brought into the lake and filling in this way is a negligible factor. Vegetation is taking hold on the muddy bottom but has as yet made little growth on the off-shore sands Fishing is the favorite recreation on the lake and this, with many sand beaches and excellent locations for summer colonies, has made Otsego one of the more popular of the interior lakes of the State

HUBBARD LAKE

Hubbard lake lies in the drainage of the Nenelon River which flows almost directly north from the lake to the Thunder Bay River. It lies just south of the northern boundary of Alcona County in the central part and, thus, is not readily accessible from the railroad. Yet a lake of nearly thirteen and a half square miles in area ranks as one of our larger inland lakes and is well worth a visit, even though a ride of sixteen miles from Alpena is necessary. The ride, however, need not be monotonous for a variety of glacial formations are crossed and serve to hold the attention.

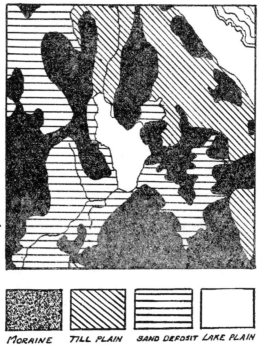

MORAINE   TILL PLAIN   SAND DEPOSIT   LAKE PLAIN

Fig. 74. Map of the glacial formations in the vicinity of Hubbard Lake. Note: Hubbard Lake is the white area in center of map.

The first part of the trip is across the sandy lake bottoms of the forerunners of the Great Lakes but in the distance may be seen the strong relief of the moraines to the west and south. The moraines stand well above the lake beds and afford many opportunities for distance views of the neighboring region. It is impossible, of course, to get a comprehensive idea of all the glacial formations in a single trip across the region, but careful mapping of this locality has shown that the moraines are fragmentary rather than arranged in continuous belts The fragments often cover large areas and are in a very general way aligned in a nearly north-south direction. Between the moraines are till plains or sandy deposits similar in topography but standing at a considerably lower elevation The distribution of the various deposits is shown in Fig 74 and from this it will be seen that Hubbard Lake is hemmed in by four patches of moraine. These come to the shores in two places on the east side but on the south and west stand back a short distance The intervening lowlands determine the position of the larger drainage channels, including most of the inlets and the outlet at the extreme north end.

In a region of such complicated glacial deposits it is difficult to imagine the behavior of the ice The irregular morainic tracts in themselves nearly enclose basins and show that during the melting the distribution of the ice was very complex and even fragmentary. Thus, it is probable that large masses of ice stood in the depressions after the moraines were free from ice In the case of Hubbard Lake, it may be supposed that an exceptionally thick mass of ice covered a distinct basin which was uncovered by subsequent melting. The origin of the basin is, however, still a question, due to the lack of knowledge as to the form of the submerged portion of the basin and to the uncertainty as to the interpretation of conditions during the waning of the glacier

The outlet, see Fig. 75, furnishes a good starting place for a physiographic study of this lake At the time of the writer's visit a dam of nearly five feet head was holding the lake above its natural level. The present dam has been in for a few years only but the waters for some time previously were periodically held up by logging operations The submergence and subsequent obliteration of the former shore makes the determination of the amount of flooding difficult, but it is quite evident that this has been sufficient to cause a decided renewal of the activity of the waves and currents, as will be seen from the description that follows.

The outlet flows northward through a narrow channel which has been cut from three to four feet below the level of the swampy lowland at this end of the lake. The outstanding feature in this locality is a strong bar composed of sand and gravel which separates the swamp from the lake It stands well above the present level even under the flooded condition and indicates a higher level of the lake, which is amply confirmed at other points on the shores. This former stage must have been the original level of the lake, during which considerable adjustment of the shores took place, and was interrupted by the deepening of the outlet. The bar at the outlet developed from the east side and partially cut off the swampy lowland which now lies adjacent to the stream. The material for this bar was derived from the almost continuous cliffs which rise from five to ten feet above the straight shore to point B, see map,

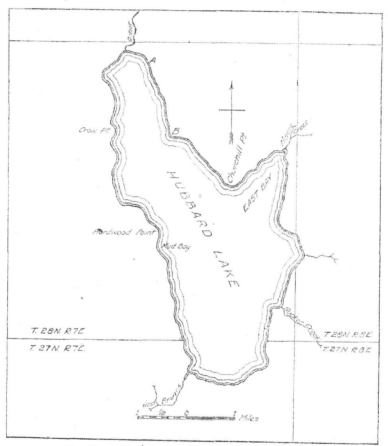

Fig. 75. Outline map of Hubbard Lake, Alcona County.

Fig. 75. In one locality only, A, have the shore currents persistently deposited material. The deposit is in the form of a spit which swings outward with very gentle curvature for a distance and then continues parallel to the shore as a sharp spit. The partially enclosed lagoon is open at the north end showing unmistakably that the effective currents flow northward along this shore. The cause

is the greater reach of the waves from the south The presence of
good-sized tree trunks standing in water along the bar may be
taken as an indication that this bar developed during the former
level and also that the lake has been flooded The reason for the
currents leaving the shore in this locality is obscure and must
remain so until the configuration of the bottom of the lake is known

Again at point B the currents have been active and the cause of
their departure from the shore is obviously the abrupt bend in the
shore line In this case currents from both directions were involved
and a V-bar which enclosed a triangular swamp was built at the
former level The currents from the southeast were the more effective and the bar is unsymmetrical, the sharper curvature occurring on the north side From the map it will be seen that the shores
from which the material of this bar may have been derived are
about equal in length on each side This balance is an apparent
one, for the moraine which causes Churchill Point comes to the
lake shores just east of the point and has furnished the greater
amount of material, as shown by the height of the cliffs which exceed twenty feet in places In addition, the reach of the southerly
winds is much greater than that of those from the northwest, the
only ones which could be effective in the formation of the north
side of this bar

Along the shore from B to Churchill Point considerable cutting
has been accomplished by the waves and a distinct submerged terrace is present The outside edge is found usually at about two
hundred yards out and drops to deep water from a depth of from
fifteen to sixteen feet This seems rather excessive as compared
with the depths found on other lakes of like size, but it must be
remembered that this lake stands considerably above its normal
level. The recent renewal of wave action is here attested by the
fresh cliffs which frequently slump, carrying trees and soil to the
beach

Around Churchill Point the moraine drops to a till plain into
which East Bay heads This bay is exposed to waves of long reach
from the southwest which are intensified by the convergence of the
shores, and the shore adjustments were, consequently, exceptionally
well defined The submerged terrace is wide and drops at a depth
of twelve feet to the channel of deeper water. Also bars were formed
at the higher level on each shore by currents running towards the
head of the bay As in the case of the outlet, these bars cut off
the swampy lowland adjacent to Misery Creek, and the lagoon,
as well as the exposed portion of the terrace, grew up to forest
after the sinking of the level Under the present flooded condition,

the trees stand in water most of the time and are rapidly dying. The bar on the west side of the bay extends to the mouth of Misery Creek, which has some difficulty in keeping an open channel. But wave action is the predominant agent on this side and the bar is retreating landward in a very irregular fashion, due to the presence of the drowned trees. On the east side of the bay the bar is better preserved and terminates in a graceful hook at the entrance of the small embayment into which Misery Creek flows.

To the south cliffs prevail as far as Sucker Creek and reach a maximum height at the projection opposite Churchill Point, which is caused by a morainic fragment. The broad swells and sags cause an alternation of freshly carved cliffs and sandy beaches, which may be definitely described as bars only in the vicinity of the mouth of Sucker Creek. The shore-drift is here to the south as shown by the turning of the stream in this direction. This small stream has brought much material into the lake and has deposited it in a broad shoal, best described as a flooded delta. Ice-action has been powerful along this shore but the only locality where its effects may be observed is at the attachment of the bar to the cliffs north of Sucker Creek. It is likely that much more extensive ramparts or boulder-lined strands were formed but have been submerged or destroyed since the flooding. The formation of strong pressure ridges on this lake in winter, one of which occurs regularly in this vicinity, makes it almost certain that the ice-push is exerted by jams rather than by expansion. Where the pressure ridge occurs, the lake is two miles in width as nearly as can be measured on the map, an observation of value to the physiographer interested in differentiating between the two types of ice-shove.

Below Sucker Creek cliffs again predominate to the south end of the lake, which is bordered by the undulating lowland through which the West Branch flows. The raising of the water level has flooded this lowland and caused wholesale destruction of the trees, except on low knolls which stand as islands above the swamp and are sharply set off by the green foliage. During the higher level, the flooding was even more pronounced than at the present time and a shallow embayment extended inland along the course of the West Branch. The development of a bar from the east forced the West Branch to the west side of the valley and cut off the embayment, except for the channel maintained by the stream. The bar is in process of destruction at present, due both to the wash of the waves and the spring freshets during which the West Branch frequently inundates the lowland, including the bar. The current of the stream is especially strong near its channel and consequently the destruction of the bar has been carried farthest at the east end. In fact, this process in conjunction with the flooding of the lake has so far obliterated the end of the bar that the only surface indication is a row of dead trees standing in water.

Along the west side of the lake the lowland runs northward in a narrow strip as far as Mud Bay, where it is interrupted by a spur of the moraine which usually stands from one-fourth to one-half mile back from the lake shore. The lowland strip is somewhat higher than at the south end and, although swampy, has no marked shore features below Mud Bay. This broad bay is caused by a sag at the northern extremity of the lowland strip and was formerly more extensive than at present. The reduction in size was caused by the development of a complete bar which now forms the shore at the head of the bay. This bar is exceptionally well developed, due largely to its enlargement by subsequent ice-action.

Hardwood Point is being attacked by the waves to some extent and has furnished the material for the bar at Mud Bay. However, to the north ground moraine again borders the shore. This stands considerably higher than the lowland below Hardwood Point and low cliffs are the predominating shore features. In one locality only have the sags extended below the lake level and this was completely isolated from the main lake by a bar. As at Mud Bay, ice has succeeded in intensifying the bar and has remodelled it into an ice rampart which rises nearly five feet above the lake. Crow Point is another interesting locality because a considerable portion of the terrace of the former level is exposed here. The sandy material of the ground moraine in this locality was very easily eroded, and the low knob which extended well out into the lake at the former level was planed into a terrace of greater width than usual, so wide that it is not entirely flooded under present conditions. Ice-action is again evident in the series of parallel ridges which rise above this terrace.

From the above description it should be clear that but two stages stand out in the history of this lake basin. Of these, the latter is now submerged by an artificial flooding of the lake and we know practically nothing concerning the adjustments which took place at that time. Of those described all, except possibly some of the effects of ice-shove, have occurred at the higher level. However, the adjustments were carried to an advanced stage of devlopment which determined to a large extent the outline and the general character of the adjustments during the later stage. It is true that the shores were not completely adjusted to wave action and much material was therefore being distributed by currents.

Nevertheless, much was accomplished and, in addition to the submerged terrace, the embayments were reduced by bars. In most cases the bars were completely developed and in numerous instances strengthened by ice-action Among the notable changes accomplished in this way may be mentioned the embayments at the outlet, West Branch, Sucker Creek, and Misery Creek

The lowering of the level was due to the downcutting of the outlet which was sufficient to account for a drop of about five feet. Judging from lakes whose main adjustments have occurred at higher levels, we may be reasonably certain that changes of a minor character only were in process previous to the flooding of the lake When a considerable depression of the level of a lake has taken place, it frequently happens that the activity along a, given shore may be reversed from cutting to deposition (see Otsego Lake) Such reversals are likely to take place where the terrace is locally wide and probably occurred on this lake at Crow Point and the delta of Sucker Creek This, however, is conjectural and cannot well be substantiated under the present conditions

The most striking thing of physiographic import is the renewed activity on the shores of Hubbard Lake, due to the artificial raising of the water level to within about one foot of its former position. The flooding of the adjacent lagoons, previously dry as shown by the forest growth, and the freshly cut cliffs are the more evident effects of this rejuvenation In places, however, unexpected effects such as the degradation of the bars of the higher level are found, even though the water level stands lower than formerly. The sapping of cliffs and destruction of depositional forms of a higher level is due to the fact that the ponding of the lake by a dam holds the water at the flood stage for a longer period than normal each year and thus causes effects that are greater than would be the case if the lake were allowed its normal seasonal fluctuation

Ice action exerts a powerful shove on the shores of the lake and mainly by jams, although some expansion may take place in the narrower parts In general, the effects are more frequently encountered and are better developed on the west side and consist almost exclusively of ramparts formed on the bars which cross the mouths of identations. Boulder-lined strands are not present, although conditions both as to material and topography are favorable for their formation. Ice jams are active on all shores of a lake but have a tendency to exert a greater push on the east side. Likewise wave action is more intense on the east side due to the prevalence of storm winds from the west, and it is possible that

31

many of the features due to ice shove have been destroyed on this side while on the opposite side they are still preserved

During the higher stage of the lake, its area was considerably reduced by the cutting off of indentations but the lagoons had not been filled when the level lowered   At present they are again flooded and are rapidly being filled with vegetation   As regards the main lake, little filling of any kind is taking place and, since the outlet is dammed, we may have little concern about the further extinction of the lake. Shore adjustments are far more important at the present and will continue to be so as long as the high level is maintained

LONG LAKE, ALPENA COUNTY

This lake should not be grouped with the interlobate lakes nor was it ever isolated by current action from one of the former stages of the Great Lakes but is appended here for want of a better place. In the naming of lakes descriptive terms are very often employed and those most frequently used are "round" and "long"   This is especially true of the inland lakes of Michigan and since these names are duplicated many times, it is necessary to add a statement as to their location   The lake under discussion crosses the boundary between Presque Isle and Alpena counties near its eastern extremity and is divided into two almost equal parts thereby. It extends seven and a half miles in a northwest-southeasterly direction and nowhere exceeds one and a half miles in width   The area is slightly greater than eight square miles, making the average width in excess of a mile   The basin lies on the exposed terrace of Lake Algonquin whose shore stood just west of the lake   The terrace in this locality consists of a series of troughs and ridges which run parallel to the glacial striations found on the bed rock. It is probable that the ridge-and-trough topography existed previous to glacial times and was modified, but not obliterated, by the passage of the ice over it   As regards the troughs the modification where the ice moved parallel to the trend of the topography consisted mainly in a widening and deepening process, and the effects produced varied locally due to variations in hardness of the rock, fracture systems, and other factors. Where the erosion was greater the trough was deeper and this, in conjunction with the damming of the trough by glacial deposits may account for the Long Lake basin. Yet the irregularities of the shoreline and in the depth of the lake and the occurrence of numerous limestone blocks, both on the shores and the bed of the lake as well, lead one to believe that some other factors have been instrumental in the formation of this basin. Although positive evidence is not at hand, one cannot overlook the possibility of the effect of underground drainage and the resulting sink holes. It is certain that a considerable amount of the rainfall sinks below the surface in this region and flows to Lake Huron in subterranean channels. Sink holes and disappearing streams are numerous in the area from Thunder Bay to Black Lake in Cheboygan County, and the former are found

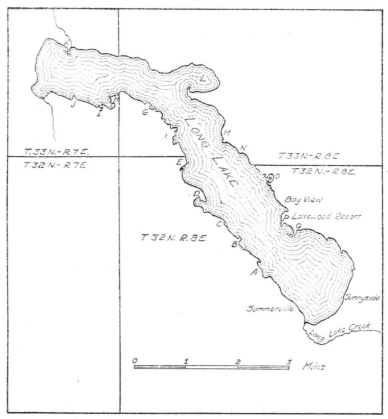

Fig. 76. Outline map of Long Lake, Alpena County.

within a few rods of Long Lake. Many of the smaller irregularities of the shore are due to the removal of blocks along the frequent joint planes but it appears difficult to account for the larger embayments unless the possibility of sinks is admitted.

The surrounding region is very thinly drift covered and in several places the bed rock outcrops on or near the lake shore. These outcrops, however, are not numerous and have little effect on the

general outline of the lake   The numerous large boulders are largely of local derivation, that is, are of limestone, and many have been
pushed on the shores from the lake bottom by ice

The lake is reached by a six mile drive from Alpena which brings
one to the southwestern shore   The south end of the lake is held
by a low sand plain which stands but slightly higher than the lake
and is swampy during high water   The sand beach which forms
the lower end of the lake is the best example of shore adjustment
to be found on this body of water   Not only is the material well
assorted and the curvature even but a well-defined submerged
terrace is present which has a maximum width of one-fourth mile
and drops at five to six feet   A low ice rampart skirts the present
shore but evidence of a definite current deposit was not found. The
rampart may possibly be a remodelled bar but this is not certain.
Yet the position of the outlet at the southwestern side and its turn
to the east after leaving the lake indicate a drift from the east side
of the lake   The adjustment of this shore is due to some extent
to the topography and material but largely to the great reach of the
prevailing storm winds from the west and northwest   The outlet
has cut a shallow trench through the sand flat; a matter of importance in explaining the presence of shore features above the
present level found elsewhere on the lake

About a mile inland from the southwestern side of the lake the
bluff of Lake Algonquin runs approximately parallel to the lake
The exposed terrace of this lake has a very thin surface cover near
the southwestern end of Long Lake and in places the rock beds are
exposed   At all outcrops the rock has been planed off and is
marked with striations which run parallel to the lake basin. Such
evidence shows the part played by the glacier in the formation of
this basin

The shoreline north of the outlet on the west side has few irregularities for about one mile and shows little adjustment   A broad
bay at locality A, see map, Fig 76, marks the beginning of a very
irregular shore which persists nearly to the north end of the lake.
At A the waves and currents have accomplished little, but a small
indentation on the north side of the bay has been isolated by an ice
rampart and is now well on the way to extinction by vegetation.
In fact, ice has been the most powerful agent on this shore and
waves and currents have been effective only in the most favorable
locations   Thus, ramparts are the common shore feature and in
many places are strong ridges of coarse material   At B currents
have turned from the shore and a well defined, but small, hook

pointing up the lake has been formed Again at C the currents have deposited detritus but in this case the spit is turned to the southeast, showing a reversal in the direction of the effective currents

Along the south shore of the bay below point D an excellent ice rampart of at least five feet in height and containing boulders of several tons in weight was found The rampart diminishes towards the head of the bay and disappears at the low flat which continues to the northwestward more than one hundred yards This lowland was formerly a part of the lake but has been partially drained and filled with vegetation The bay is shallow and the muddy bottom contains a heavy growth of reeds In places the shore and bottom are lined with a white sand which is found to be composed almost entirely of shells, indicating the active formation of shell marl On the north side of the bay current action is well shown by the spit which has grown an appreciable distance across the bay The material averages nearly three inches in size and indicates the presence of a powerful drift into the bay from this side The presence of a rampart on the spit and the coarseness of the material leads one to conclude that ice has been of considerable importance in the building of this form The spit is not increasing under the present conditions and its period of most rapid development must antedate the cedars of more than two feet in diameter growing on its crest

On the end of point D, where one might expect current deposits, a submerged terrace, composed of rocks except for a sandy zone near its outer edge, is present This terrace, therefore, has been swept free of finer material by the waves and undertow and has a comparatively narrow built portion On the side of the point facing the lake a narrow, but distinct, exposed terrace upon which boulders are scattered is evidence of a former level of the lake between two and three feet higher than that at the present time and shows that the terrace was cut, wave activity having been the predominant factor in the adjustment of this point in the past The tendency for the boulders to stand near the former shore shows, furthermore, that ice has been active during the higher level

The broad embayment north of D is caused by an extensive sag in the Algonquin terrace The present shores are composed of rubble and show little adjustment. For the most part the irregularities of this shore are due directly to variations in the Algonquin terrace and adjustments, if present, are found at the projections One of the most interesting was found at F. The projection itself does not differ materially from those occurring so frequently along

this shore, but the small point which runs to the northwestward
from its extremity is of considerable interest   In all but one respect
this minor feature resembles an unsymmetrical V-bar, see Plate
XIV, B   Two bars meet in a blunt point and enclose a shallow
depression.   That on the east, or lake, side is the better developed
and is fronted by a submerged terrace while that on the opposite
side drops steeply below the water level   On the east side the
bar has been remodelled in part into an ice rampart.   The most
interesting feature in connection with this point is the coarseness
of the material of which it is composed   The smallest size of
particles was not less than one inch but the maximum was as great
as two feet in largest diameter   Also the rubble is for the most
part angular in form rather than rounded, the form characteristic
of water-worn material   Clearly this material has not been transported by waves and currents unaided and yet is not the typical ice
rampart   It seems possible that stray blocks of ice in whose bases
rocks have been frozen may have been blown against the point
and upon partial melting dropped some of their load.   The material was then worked over to some extent by the pounding of the
ice blocks as they drifted with the waves, causing a spit-like form
of very coarse material   The exposure of this point to the southeasterly winds which sweep up from the lower end of the lake accounts for the greater development on that side   ,

Beyond F the irregular shore shows little adjustment until the
small bay designated as G on the map is reached.   On the east side
of this bay the terrace of the former level is present and is emphasized by ice ramparts at the shorelines of both the present and
higher levels.   On the opposite side of the bay, which has the advantage of a relatively smooth shore to the west, the currents, aided
by ice, have succeeded in building a hook of coarse material similar
to the form found at F   That the currents along this shore are reversed with the shifting of the winds is shown by the hook which is
developing westward from the end of point H   The material of
this hook is sand and extends under water as a shoal of considerable extent   The point has been abruptly turned by the westerly
winds, giving the effect produced by tidal races in the ocean, as at
the tip of Cape Cod   In the small reentrant at I an interesting
series of five parallel cusps pointing towards the middle of the
bay was noted at the time this study was made   These low water
forms are similar to those found on Douglass Lake, under which
their manner of formation was discussed   Just west of the indentation, a small projection of the shore is caused by an outcrop of

thinly bedded limestone which shows some undercutting by the waves at the higher level At present, however, the waves have not been able to keep the foot of the low cliff free from talus and the point is, therefore, receding at a very slow rate.

Westward to the end of the lake, the shore is relatively smooth and little adjustment has taken place One rather prominent exception is the point at J which breaks the continuity of the currents along this shore A spit of rubble up to six inches in diameter is growing in a southerly direction from the west side and may cut off a small bay in time The contrast between the coarse material of the spit and the sandy bottom of the bay in process of inclosure emphasizes the importance of drifting ice as an aid to currents in the formation of such features It is interesting to note that the northeasterly winds play the more prominent part in the shove exerted by ice on this shore.

Beyond J there is little of interest until the shore turns to the southwest to form the small bay at the end of the lake. Here two incipient spits are developing and the material is again coarse rubble indicative of ice-shove The probability of these spits developing across the mouth of the bay is remote, for vegetation is well started in the bay and literally carpets the bottom Lilies and rushes have also taken hold and extinction by vegetation before the spits are completed may be expected. Within the bay the noticeable shore adjustment is a well-developed ice rampart which stands just above the high-water strand. The west end of the lake is very shallow and is lined for most of the distance with a good sand beach.

In general, the northeastern shore of the lake is more regular in outline than the opposite shore and especially so from the west end to the large bay at L Adjustments by waves and currents are very slight and are, therefore very noticeable when present. Thus, the spit which has developed from the end of the narrow point at K stands out prominently and is an indication of the strength of the easterly winds which have a much greater reach than those from the west But the relatively smooth stretch of shore to L is not without interesting features, for here are found some of the best examples of the effects of ice shove on the shores of the lakes of our State Ramparts are the striking features of the shore and they are found in two almost continuous belts, representing the former and the present levels As a rule the rampart of the former level is the stronger and stands from five to ten feet back of the one formed under the present conditions. The stronger rampart is a distinct ridge which frequently reaches five feet or more in height and contains boulders of several tons in weight. The off-shore slope was not swept free of boulders before the water level receded and a quantity of material has been piled up since that time in the present rampart. Nor is the process complete at the

Fig. 77. Boulder pushed on shore by an ice jam, Long Lake, Alpena County. This boulder will travel up the beach in stages and eventually become a part of the rampart. (Sketch from photograph.)

Fig. 78. Boulder pushed on shore by an ice jam. This boulder has nearly completed the journey to the strong ice rampart which stands a few feet to the right and is hidden by the trees in the sketch. Long Lake, Alpena County. (Sketch from photograph.)

present time for boulders are seen in the process of transportation across the terrace towards the rampart. Two such boulders are shown in Figs. 77 and 78 from which may be seen the trench along which the rock has moved and the rubble piled in front like the

A. ICE-FORMED SPIT, LONG LAKE, ALPENA COUNTY.

B. ICE RAMPART, APPLE ISLAND, ORCHARD LAKE.

"bone in the teeth" of an ocean liner Several of these boulders were seen on this shore and the paths of all were found to be practically in the same direction This direction, moreover, was not at right angles to the shore but from southwest to northeast These rocks were undoubtedly moved by the ice but the manner of shove has not been observed by the writer However, the fact that large ice-jams occur on this shore of the lake and that the direction of the movement of the boulders over the terrace is diagonal leads one to believe that ice jams have been more effective than expansion, although the width of the lake is well within the limit for the latter

The lake is very shallow off this shore and the bottom is composed of large angular boulders except for a zone of sand near the shore No "drop off" could be detected but the sand zone is considered its equivalent, its outside edge marking the outer limit of the effects of the undertow

The bay at L is shallow but, nevertheless, waves of considerable power have removed the thin drift cover and exposed the limestone on the west side. Vegetation is gradually taking hold and will aid in the extinction of this arm Another factor of importance in this connection is the action of currents and ice off the point at the east side of the entrance The greater portion of the point which separates this bay from the main lake was original with the lake basin, but the end has developed into a hook, typical in all respects except the size of the material, which is frequently as much as six inches in diameter Thus, the beach is evenly curved, a depression stands to the rear, and the bottom slopes gradually off shore into the lake but drops steeply on the bay side Currents have clearly been the important factor in its formation but the large size of the material leads to the conclusion that ice has been instrumental to some extent However, near the end of the hook a peculiar offshoot, see Plate XV, A, has developed at right angles to the general trend of the shore This spit, which is composed of large, angular material, is, furthermore, serpentine in form and could hardly have been formed by currents alone One is compelled to account for its formation in a manner similar to that of the point at F on the opposite side of the lake Currents are effective on the south side of the point also and have built a blunt spit of rather coarse material Currents from both directions are contributing to this point but are making slow progress, due to the deeper water in this part of the lake. Ice push is very effective on the end of this spit and has piled up a rampart fully six feet in height

To the southeastward the beach, although composed of rather coarse material, is of even curvature until the bluffs of the higher ground at M are reached Considerable adjustment has taken place along this shore, as is shown at the small indentation just north of the bluffs which has been separated from the main lake by an ice rampart It is probable that currents were instrumental in the isolation of this indentation in the early stages and that the bar thus formed has been remodelled by ice. The currents in this case came from the west and, after the completion of the bar, swung around the apex of point M and were turned from the shore a little farther on Currents from the opposite direction also left the shore in this same locality and as a consequence a blunt spit has developed which is similar to the V-bars already described The material is large for such a form, the usual diameter being about one-inch with a maximum of four inches Here also the ice has been effective and has formed a rampart comparable in size to that found on the point below bay L When seen by the writer the currents from the southeast had the advantage and were building out on the north side, but this condition may have been temporary In general, the symmetry of such a form is a safe indication of the strength of the forces which are active in its development. Shoals run out into the lake from two hundred to three hundred feet in front of the points along this shore and are sufficient to turn the currents out into the lake. In most cases the shoals are of rock, but at N a definite built terrace of sand which drops into deeper water at five feet is present.

To the southeast, the shore is broken by a number of small points and the shallow bay at O A small spit on the north side of the bay indicates some current from the northwest but this is necessarily feeble due to the irregularities of the shore along which the currents develop On the south, however, the currents from the opposite direction are much more powerful and have built a hook which, with its submerged continuation, extends two-thirds of the distance across the mouth of the bay. The shore to which the hook is attached has a very low slope and a broad flat is exposed during periods of low water Much of the material on this flat is coarse and several boulders were noted which had halted in their journey towards the shore These have undoubtedly been pushed by ice and, inasmuch as the direction of the paths agrees with that found on this shore near the upper end of the lake, ice jams are believed to have been the propelling force.

The shore to point P is more regular and shows little adjustment save for the assortment of the beach material which is relatively coarse for a lake of this size At P currents, developed on both sides of the projection, have left the shore and built a blunt V-bars This bar is, in reality, composed of two V-bars, one built outside the other The one nearer the land is the older and the enclosed lagoon is now filled with vegetation, whereas the outer has developed subsequently and the wet lagoon supports a growth of rushes It is probable that the older lagoon was formed at the higher level but not until a strong ice rampart had been piled up at the old shore The outer lagoon is the result of the activity of currents under the present conditions and is developing most rapidly during high-water Obviously, the currents from up the lake are the more powerful on account of the greater reach of the winds, the longer stretch of shore, and the protection afforded by point Q to the short strip of shore to the south

Point Q is a peculiarly shaped projection which originally was a narrow strip jutting out into the lake Strong currents evidently swing around this point from the southeast, and as a result the end is a well-developed hook whose point of departure from the original point may be readily detected by the ice rampart at the former shore At present the hook is growing directly towards point P and may in the course of time enclose the narrow strip of water between the two points The turning of Q to the northwest is interesting in view of the fact that the two points between this and the southeastern end of the lake are both spits pointing in the opposite direction. It appears, then, that the turning of Q is due to the protection of the shore to the northwest by P rather than to exceptionally strong currents from the opposite direction

The first of the spits below Q was caused by a bend in the original shoreline sufficiently abrupt to throw the currents from the shore. The material is coarse and has been pushed into a rampart on the lake side The main shore protected by this spit is a smooth sand beach but gives way to coarser material beyond the end of the spit. Nearer the lower end of the lake a narrow strip of the lowland borders the lake and forms a fringe of swamp The second point developed across a depression in the swamp during the higher level and enclosed a narrow lagoon which is now grown up to marsh grass and may be flooded during very high water.

The basin of Long Lake, then, may be assigned to glacial scour with the possibility of solution by ground water as an added factor The irregularities of the shoreline furnished opportunities for numerous adjustments of the shores by waves and currents, and the abundance of coarse material as well as the topography of the shores is favorable to development of forms due to ice push   The adjustments by waves and currents have seldom passed beyond the early stages but those due to ice have produced some very marked results   In fact, ice ramparts are by far the most pronounced of all the shore features on this lake and there is hardly a locality where they may not be observed.   Both types of ice shove are effective but the writer is inclined to lay the greater stress on ice jams.   Furthermore, floating cakes of ice seem to have played at least a subordinate role in the shaping of some of the depositional features

The lack of adjustments by waves and currents may be assigned to several factors   Undoubtedly waves of considerable size run lengthwise of the lake but lose much of their force before reaching the shore on account of the uneven surface and the flatness of the off shore slopes   The greater part of the work done by the waves has been the assortment of the beach material, accomplished by the removal of the finer particles   The paucity of current deposits is due in part to the very irregular shore which prevents the formation of currents of sufficient continuity for large effects.   In addition, the material upon which these forces are acting may be of some importance   In general lake clays, boulder clay, and limestone are the materials encountered   The disintegration of both the lake clays and the till furnishes little sand but rather a slimy mud which is carried out onto the lake bottom.   This mud is very calcareous and may account for the lime deposits which accumulate on the pebbles near shore, although it is recognized that such deposits are formed by the action of lower plant forms.

The two stages in the history of the lake conform to the general conditions found on our inland lakes   The drop in level is due to the downcutting of the outlet and has occurred rather rapidly.   If this is continuing at the present time, the process is a slow one and the probability of the lake being drained is remote.   Vegetation has taken hold in a few localities and some marl is being deposited but it seems best to consider the lake in a youthful stage of development.

CHAPTER VII

INTERIOR LAKES OF THE SOUTHERN PENINSULA, CON'T

LAKES OF THE EASTERN INTERLOBATE AREA

ORCHARD LAKE

In a glaciated region the largest and most diversified deposits are found in the interlobate areas. As has been stated heretofore, in the reentrants between any two lobes of ice the rock debris is supplied from two ice fronts, and the accumulation is, therefore, not only much greater than that of a single front but also the forms are very irregularly distributed. In such regions the continuity and arrangement of the deposits are greatly disturbed, or wanting entirely and the topography consists of an intricate patchwork of the various glacial forms. Undrained depressions are, therefore, especially numerous but are usually small on account of the lack of continuity of the deposits. In the interlobate area which stretches southwestward from the Thumb, the surface is literally dotted with lakes and from certain eminences as many as ten to fifteen may be seen. Oakland County is especially favored in this respect; more than one hundred named lakes appear on the Pontiac topographic map which represents about one-fourth of the area. The lakes are all small, ranging from a maximum of about two square miles down to insignificant ponds, and lie for the most part in morainic basins or pits in the outwash. Two of the larger of these lakes, Orchard and Cass, were selected for study on account of their size, popularity, and accessibility, but the writer realizes fully that the work should be extended to include groups of lakes, possibly on the basis of drainage systems.

These two lakes are part of a group which lies southwest of Pontiac and drains into the Clinton River. They may be reached via the Jackson Branch of the Grand Trunk R. R., the Detroit and Orchard Lake interurban cars, or by automobile over excellent roads. They both lie in rather large morainic basins and are, therefore, rather simple as to origin. The shores, bounded by moraine, are varied as to relief but uniform as to material. The stiff boulder clay is not readily eroded by shore agents, and on small lakes, such as Orchard and Cass, the adjustments of the shores are not on a large scale. Nevertheless, sufficient work has been done both at the present level and a higher level to make the study interesting.

The nearly circular form of Orchard Lake is emphasized by Apple Island which stands slightly north of the center of the lake. See

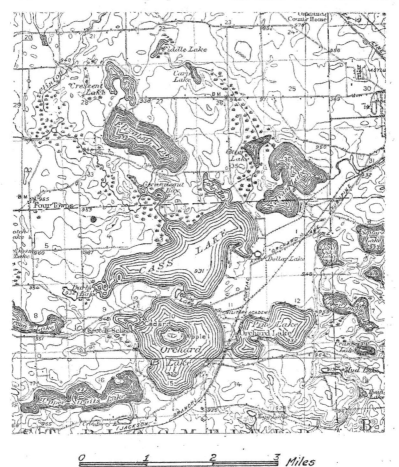

Fig. 79. Topographic map of Cass and Orchard lakes and vicinity, Oakland County. (From U. S. G. S. Pontiac quadrangle.)

Fig. 79. The lake is entirely surrounded by moraine which rises well above the water, dipping only occasionally to small undrained swales. The shores are well drained for the most part and advantage has been taken of the many excellent locations for summer homes. The lake is deep (reputed to be one hundred and seventy-five feet) but systematic soundings have not been made, so that the exact depths are not at hand   For our purpose it is sufficient to know that the waves may develop free from interference by the bottom except in the vicinity of the shores   The lake receives the water of Pine Lake, which stands to the west, through a small channel of very sluggish current as the lakes stand at about the same level   Orchard in turn empties into Cass Lake, which stands one foot lower through a similar channel across the narrow neck of land on the north side   From Cass Lake the drainage passes through Otter and Sylvan Lakes to the Clinton River which is dammed a short distance below Sylvan Lake   The total fall from Pine to Otter Lake is about two feet, a fact which may be accounted for in part by the damming of the Clinton River   Yet, it is doubtful if the drainage above Cass Lake is affected by the dam, and the slight difference in the levels of Pine and Orchard Lakes is due to the flat gradient and short course of the outlet.

The outlet of Pine Lake enters Orchard at the narrowest part of the land strip which separates them   This insignificant stream flows through a swamp which extends to the shores of Pine Lake. No indication of bars or ramparts was noted along the Orchard Lake shore but a well-developed bar crosses the flat on the Pine Lake side at a level slightly above the present   Thus, the two lakes were originally connected, forming part of a larger and very irregular lake which included Pine, Orchard, Cass, Otter, Sylvan and possibly Elizabeth lakes   Also during this early stage Pine and Orchard were separated by the development of the bar just mentioned

South of the outlet of Pine Lake the shores of Orchard are exposed to the powerful west winds and the waves have the full sweep of the lake   The land stands well above the lake level except for two small sags, so that the adjustment of the shore has been accomplished mainly by waves.   They have formed a steep cliff in the compact till and a well-defined submerged terrace which reaches a width of one hundred to one hundred and fifty feet and drops into deep water from depths of five to six feet.   The recession of this cliff straightened the shoreline to some extent but currents were also instrumental, as shown at the sags.   In both cases the re-entrants were cut off by bars which have since been remodelled into ice ramparts   The first sag, A on map, Fig. 79, is a small morainic depression which, since its separation from the lake, is filling rapidly with vegetation.

Around the south side the lakeward slopes are very gentle and the adjustments much less pronounced than on the east side.   The submerged terrace swings in close to the shore and the cliffs are very low   The adjustment of this shore consists mainly in the transportation and distribution of material from the east side by currents, forming a sand beach and built terrace   Between Orchard and Upper Straits lakes a flat saddle interrupts the uniform conditions of the south side, and the adjustments of the shores are negligible.   The lowest part of this saddle stands about five feet above the present level of Orchard Lake and served as a very narrow divide between the two lakes during the higher level   The blunt point, B on map, is a part of the saddle and shows no current activity.   North of this point the land rises to a rolling moraine and low cliffs of variable height face the shore   The absence of current deposits at B leads to the conclusion that the material from these cliffs has been transported northward   This material was deposited in two spits near the entrance to the embayment at the northwestern part of the lake   The first spit lies directly south of Cedar Island and is too small to be shown on the map   It is slightly recurved near the tip, almost enclosing a narrow lagoon, and has been converted into an ice rampart near its attachment to the shore   The second spit lies west of Cedar Island and is much the larger   The currents along the west shore continued beyond the first spit but were forced directly out into the lake at the second. Thus they dropped practically all their load and have built the larger spit in this locality   It is doubtful if any material was supplied from the west for the bay is small and the shores are mucky   In fact, the bay is being filled with vegetation at a rapid rate and the heaviest growth occurs on the south side

The hills which form the west and north sides of the bay are separated by a low sag which extends through to the west end of Cass Lake   This channel is a swamp from Cass Lake to the road and stands less than three feet above Orchard Lake at its highest point,—the road crossing   If allowance is made for some filling along the highway, it seems probable that a shallow connection formerly existed between the two lakes in this locality.

North of Cedar Island a small knoll forms a point on the main shore which was sufficient to turn the currents from the shore   The material transported along the north shore to this point is apparently very small in amount, since the spit has made little headway. However, it is pointing directly towards Cedar Island and its continuation would tie the island to the mainland   A contributing factor in this connection is the spit growing landward from the north end of the island but much is yet to be accomplished   Cedar Island is a low knoll which may serve as an excellent index to the activity of the shore agents in this part of the lake. The north shore shows no adjustment and the waves have not prevented a thriving growth of vegetation. On the south side the waves have carved the slopes into low cliffs, and the material has been transported in both directions by reversing currents, as shown by a spit at the west end as well as at the north. In addition to the waves and currents, ice has been effective and has pushed boulders into the cliffs and the landward portions of the spits into well-defined ramparts. The possibility of the island attaching itself to the mainland by the growth of the spits at either end suggests itself, but this is improbable on account of the limited amount of material in this small island.

The north shore is a succession of cliffs which drop to lake level in two places only. In both cases the low areas are channels which connected with Cass Lake during the early stages of the higher level. Bars developed from the west across both channels on the Orchard Lake side and were later pushed up into ice ramparts. The westerly connection was completely obstructed in this way and Beebe Lake was formed midway between the two lakes. The easterly channel was never completely closed and is now occupied by the outlet of the lake. In the vicinity of the Military Academy the adjustments are obscured by "improvements." One might expect at least the beginning of a spit where the land drops to the flat separating Pine and Orchard lakes but, if so, it has been covered by the highway.

Apple Island is a somewhat elongated cluster of morainic knobs that stand well above the level of the lake. Its location near the center of the lake exposes all of its shores to agents of approximately equal intensity, and differences in topography are, therefore, more important in determining the adjustment of the shores than the wind direction. Waves are very active and have carved steep cliffs along the entire southern and the greater part of the northern shores. At the blunt projections, however, the slopes were originally flatter and the effects were more pronounced in some respects. Not only were the waves able to cut a wider terrace but also currents were able to add to this, although no definite bars were formed. In such localities the sinking of the water level exposed relatively broad terraces which are excellently preserved and furnish the clearest evidence of the former level of the lake. The points on the west, north, and northeast shores are well worth inspection. The expansion of the ice during the winter is also effective on the shores of the island and especially so on the south and

33

east sides, due to the greater expanse of the lake. On the east side
the outer edge of the exposed terrace has been pushed into a rampart, see Plate XV, B, which obstructs the drainage and causes
swamp conditions in places

CASS LAKE

A convenient starting point for the study of Cass Lake is Dollar
Lake This little pond lies in a pit in a fragment of outwash that
borders a part of the east shore of Cass Lake and is now a muck
basin, rapidly decreasing in size on account of the encroachment
of vegetation Dollar Lake was formerly in direct connection with
Cass Lake but the channel became so crowded with plants that it
was necessary to open it by dredging

With the exception noted, Cass Lake is surrounded by moraine,
composed of broad swells and sags rather than sharp knobs and
basins Consequently the shores are either dry or are swampy for
long stretches The south shore stands consistently well above the
lake and the shore features are so uniform that the few exceptions
are greatly emphasized Leaving Dollar Lake, one's attention is at
once attracted to the point across the bay The major portion of
the point is due to a knoll which juts well out into the lake but
the narrow eastward projection is clearly a spit. The spit stands
more than two feet above the present level of the lake and is covered
with grass and trees See Plate XVI, A Near its attachment it
has the characteristics of an ice rampart which continues along the
edge of an exposed terrace surmounted by a cliff The effects of
waves, currents and ice may be seen within a short distance and
indicate a higher level for this lake which corresponds exactly with
the former level of Orchard Lake The disturbing feature is the
present activity of the waves which is removing the rampart and
spit, laying bare the roots of trees See Plate XVI, B This is unquestionably a renewal of activity and is due to an elevation of the
water level, probably a result of the obstruction in the Clinton
River

South of the spit the exposed terrace soon plays out and the
shore is faced by a cliff which is continuous to the outlet of Orchard Lake, with the exception of a narrow gully about midway
This cliff, pounded by waves driven in from the west, has furnished
the material for the spit above The renewed activity of the waves
is clearly seen in the fresh cliffs, landslides, and undermined trees
and may result in further extension of the spit after it has adjusted
its position to the new conditions

Michigan Geological and
Biological Survey

Publication 30 Geological Series 25,
Plate XVI

A SPIT CASS LAKE

B DISSECTION OF ICE RAMPART CASS LAKE

The outlet of Orchard Lake and the Beebe Lake channel interrupt an almost continuous cliff to the west end of the lake Wave action is less intense along this part of the shore on account of the restricted reach of the waves and fresh scars are not abundant on the face of the cliff. Also a boulder-lined strand is still intact Farther west wave activity is still less and two neighboring gullies are able to maintain a small delta in the lake Strong currents are undoubtedly set up along this shore but conditions are unfavorable for deposition at present During the former stage, the depressions at the Orchard Lake outlet and the Beebe Lake depressions were crossed by currents, but the latter only was obstructed by a bar. The position of the outlet of Beebe Lake near the east side of the depression shows that the bar developed from the west

Near the west arm the exposed terrace of the upper level appears and widens towards the bay It reaches its greatest width on the south side of the bay and then diminishes Outside the bay on the west shore the cliffs rise directly from the beach The presence of the exposed terrace in the more protected places leads to the conclusion that it was formerly continuous and has been removed subsequently to a very large extent The cliffs extend to the neighborhood of Gerundegut Bay, which was formerly an extended but shallow arm of the lake The dropping of the water level exposed more than one-half of its bed and the shores are consequently low and swampy at the present time The entrance to this bay is restricted to a channel which does not exceed forty feet in width, the remainder, as shown on the map, being blocked by very shallow water grown up to rushes The shallow water appears to be due to submerged terraces which were extended from either side by current action The greater extension of the terrace on the west shows that the currents from this direction are the stronger. This may be due to more favorable shore conditions combined with the greater effectiveness of the southwest winds Within the bay the adjustments are uncertain, for the shores are lined by swamp, and filling by vegetation is the dominant physiographic process Between Gerundegut and Coles bays, the shores consist of the swampy terrace for the first half of the distance but beyond rise to cliffs which extend to the west side of Coles Bay In contrast with Gerundegut Bay, Coles Bay is deep and has a relatively narrow entrance A minor indentation just west of the entrance to the bay was cut off by currents but much more important adjustments are found at the bay and along the shore to the east. The small spit at the west side of the entrance to Coles Bay seems rather insignificant on

first sight but closer examination discloses that its continuation
under water nearly blocks the channel, the water above it nowhere
exceeding three feet in depth   Furthermore, this bar rises to the
higher level of the lake east of the bay and runs as far as the outlet, causing it to turn to the southeast.   Near the east side of Coles
Bay the bar stands at the present shore but is fragmentary and
irregular in form, due to the renewed activity of the waves which
is causing a recession of the shore.   East of the outlet the old
lake bed extends towards Sylvan Lake but is dotted with small
hills which stood as islands above the lake at its higher stage.
In building the shore road advantage has been taken of a well-
defined bar which extends southeastward from the outlet and connects directly with one of the "island" hills whose slopes were
carved into a cliff and terrace during the higher stage.   Farther
south the old lake bottom connects with the Dollar Lake depression without definite shore features

A study of the shores in the vicinity of the outlet shows that
currents were the active agency in their development   The work
was practically all accomplished when the lake stood at the higher
level, but some deposition may now be taking place on the submerged portion of the Coles Bay bar   The most conspicuous adjustment was the building of bars across the flat now occupied
by the outlet.   They developed from both directions and would
have met, if the currents east of the outlet had run a little farther
to the south   As it is they dove-tail and Cass Lake was never completely isolated during the higher stage

Briefly stated, the outstanding fact in the history of the lakes
under discussion is the existence formerly of a large, irregular
body of water which not only included the basins of Orchard and
Cass lakes but of some of the neighboring lakes as well   During
this stage considerable adjustment of the shores took place and, as
a result, the present lake basins were at least outlined, if not isolated.   It it may be assumed that the bars stood above the water
level, Orchard and Pine lakes became definite basins and Cass
nearly so   Many of the changes, however, were interrupted by the
lowering of the level and little seems to have been accomplished
during the lower stage. A renewal of activity, however, is clearly
indicated at the present time, due probably to the interference
with the flow of the Clinton River, and adjustments are beginning
anew   It may not seem possible that the effects of an obstruction
of the drainage would be so far-reaching but it must be kept in
mind that an actual rise in the water level is not necessary to
produce an increase in the adjustment of the shores   Small lakes

vary considerably in level during the season and any cause which will prevent a fall during the dry season is equivalent to a higher level on the average. As has already been stated, this study was not complete but it is hoped that from what has been done the work may be extended by the reader to the other lakes of this group

LONG LAKE, GENESEE COUNTY

In the discussion of Orchard and Cass Lakes the confused arrangement of the glacial formations of the interlobate area in the southeastern part of the State was mentioned. Outside this area on the Saginaw Bay side the deposits are distributed with a regularity which, by way of contrast, is very pronounced Moraine ridges, separated by till plains and occasional outwash aprons, form a series of wide, roughly parallel loops about the Saginaw Lowland, extending from Genesee County westward to Ionia County and thence northward to the southeastern part of Roscommon County In many localities the streams follow the moraines for long distances but in others they flow directly across the trend of the ridges Numerous small lakes occur in this region, the majority filling depressions in the till plains or moraine basins. A group of such lakes is located in southern Genesee County, north and west of Fenton, some members of which were examined by the writer The most common type are the shallow basins in the till plain which often contain great quantities of marl, utilized in the manufacture of Portland cement, for example, Mud Lake The larger lakes show the more interesting physiographic development and Long Lake, see Fig 80, was chosen as more or less representative

The glacial formations in this region have a general east-west trend but are less regular in their distribution than farther to the west. A high, strong moraine follows the southern border of Fenton Township, marking a decided halt of the ice front at this locality The next halt of the ice is shown by a fragmentary moraine which crosses the region near the south end of the lake and was of short duration Another moraine crosses the north arm of Long Lake but turns abruptly to the south just east of the lake, merging with the fragmentary moraine mentioned above From this it appears that the ice front held its position east of the offset but receded to the westward and uncovered the southern part of the Long Lake basin. During the halt of the ice border which followed a local outwash apron developed, fragments of which surround the south arm of the lake North of the outwash the shores are bordered by till plain, which may be interpreted as a fosse, followed by moraine along the northarm and till plain at the north end.

The orientation of the Long Lake basin transverse to the trend

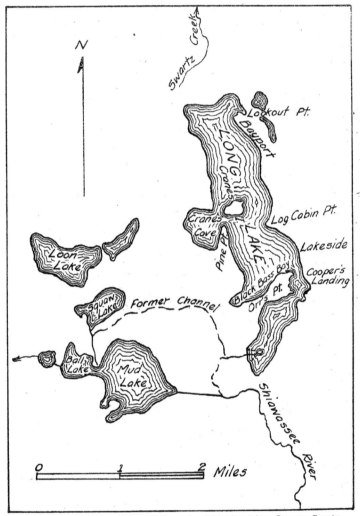

Fig 80. Outline map of Long Lake and neighboring lakes, Genesee County.

of the moraines suggests that a depression existed prior to the
advance of the ice. Some scour by the advancing ice probably took
place, deepening the depression somewhat to form the Long Lake

basin, in which case Orrs Point and Cranes Island were deposited later when the ice retreated During the retreat of the glacier the ice persisted in the basin and upon melting formed the outwash about the south end of the lake.

Long Lake lies in the drainage of the Shiawassee River which now flows directly into the east end of Mud Lake through an artificial channel From Mud Lake it follows the south side of a moraine westward for more than fifteen miles before crossing On all maps which the writer has seen the outlet of Long Lake is placed at the north end connecting with a branch of Swartz Creek This outlet undoubtedly functioned but was artificial Discussion concerning the former natural outlet will be found below

An excellent distance view of Long Lake may be had from the high kame south of Fenton and from this eminence the irregular outline of the lake is very apparent From this view and a study of the map it is seen that the lake consists of three basins set off by Orrs Point, and Log Cabin Point and Cranes Island It also appears that the west shore is much more irregular in outline than the east, but this is less pronounced when the adjustments of the east shore are taken into consideration, as will be seen later

At the south end of the lake the low remnants of outwash slope gently to the lake and have been carved into a well defined terrace which stands between two and three feet above the present level Wave activity in this small arm of the lake is moderate and the shores are grown over with vegetation, consequently the beach is poor Towards the outlet the land is higher and well-defined cliffs were formed at the higher level In the neighborhood of the outlet a low flat which stands below the former level of the lake extends westward and connects with the former channel of the Shiawassee River The south arm of Long Lake now shows an interesting anomaly in that the outlet now leaves the lake across what appears to be a delta which extends to and includes the small island in this part of the basin

If this formation is correctly interpreted, it is evident that the Shiawassee entered the lake at this point during the former level At this time two outlets were possible, one just north of Orrs Point leading back into the present Shiawassee valley, and another at the north end of the lake Of the three channels leading from the lake, the one now occupied by the outlet was the lowest and naturally accommodated the outflow when the lake level dropped permanently Yet it is possible that it may have served as an inlet during the former level under flood conditions of the Shiawassee, at which time great quantities of material were brought into the lake and deposited, forming the delta On the other hand, when the waters lowered during the dry season this channel may have served as the outlet which had a sluggist current so that the delta was left intact.

The south arm of the lake is relatively deep and a well defined off-shore terrace drops into deep water from a depth of four feet This terrace has been remodelled under the present conditions to an uncertain extent and inferences from it as to the strength and work of the waves are of little value. As a rule the surface of the terrace is covered with heavy deposits of marl which is of commercial value on some of the nearby lakes.

North of the outlet the shores are low and in places the terrace of the upper level is exposed. Similar conditions prevail on the south side of Orrs Point, a moraine ridge which runs nearly to the east shore, forming a narrows of less than one hundred feet in width During the former level considerable material was carried outward along the south side of the point and deposited in a spit which threatened to close the channel Under present conditions little work is being done on this shore and the spit is not growing appreciably A like condition exists on the north side but the spit, although possibly of greater extent than that on the south side, had accomplished relatively less in the filling of the channel The north shore spit is attached to a narrow terrace of the upper level which stood thirty inches above the water level at the time of measurement Ice shove is here evident in the line of boulders along the shore and a partly demolished rampart at the outer edge of the terrace Westward into Black Bass Bay cliffs rise from the present shore, showing that the waves not only have removed the upper level terrace but are still furnishing material some of which is being added to the spit at the end of the point Thus, there is still a possibility of the isolation of the south arm.

Black Bass Bay stands on a till plain and is very shallow with the exception of a small hole near the west end. This probably was the location of an isolated ice block Within the bay a slight swell near the north shore forms Duck Island. The low relief, as indicated by the shallowness of the bay, extends westward from the lake to the old channel of the Shiawassee. This flat stands slightly below the level of the former stage and, if not an outlet, was a broad arm which connected this basin with the lake basins which lie to the west.

The west shore north of Black Bass Bay is lined with a gravel beach above which stands an almost continuous terrace of the upper level Currents as well as waves are active along this shore and those from the south leave the shore at the end of Pine Point. Southeasterly winds are the only ones which cause northward drift-'ing currents on this shore and, since these winds are not of long duration nor great intensity, the amount of material transported is relatively small Nevertheless, a well developed spit was formed at the point during the upper level and is continuing its growth under the present conditions Ice action is also effective near the attachment of the spit and has formed ramparts at both the upper and present levels

Within Cranes Cove wave action is slight and the exposed terrace is well preserved. Near Crane's cottage ice has formed a rampart at the present shore which obstructs the drainage of the exposed terrace locally, forming a lagoon-like swale At the head of the cove the terrace widens to a swamp which extends westward to the road and was a shallow arm of the lake during the upper level.

The shallow water between Cranes Island, or Cases Island, and the west shore establishes a close relationship between the two The shallow water, however, is not due to current action, and any direct connection of the island with the mainland will be accomplished by filling by vegetation which has already established itself The island is a low knoll of nearly twenty-five acres in extent. The greatest activity along its shores at present occurs on the south side and is due to waves They have removed the terrace of the former level and are cutting back cliffs of from twelve to fifteen feet in height On all other shores the exposed terrace is well preserved. The preservation of this terrace on the north side seems singular in view of the exposure of this shore to strong winds of considerable reach It is due to the flatness of the off-shore slope, which has been intensified by the sinking of the water level and greatly reduces the effectiveness of the incoming waves The adjustment of the shores during the higher level was accomplished mainly by the waves, as shown by the exposed terrace on all sides but the south However, westward moving currents developed on the north shore and succeeded in building a small spit at the northwest corner of the island.

North of Cranes Island on the main shore, the terrace of the higher level makes a slight notch in the gentle slopes and is continuous to the swampy depression which may have functioned as the outlet of the lake. This channel is partially closed by a strong ice rampart, the best example of this feature found on the lake. It is possible that this channel served as an outlet during the higher stage but, if so, was secondary to the Shiawassee River.

In case both outlets functioned, the northern channel was abandoned by the deepening of the channel of the Shiawassee River.

Moraine borders the north shore and the slopes have been cut into almost continuous bluffs ranging from fifteen to twenty feet in height. The northeastern shore is low and the exposed terrace appears along the shores of the bay at the northeast end of the lake. High bluffs again come to the shore at Lookout Point but drop to a low sag near the end of the point. This sag stands slightly below the former level and the tip of the point was, therefore, a small island during that time. South of the point the bluffs recede and below Bayport a small crescent-shaped lagoon was cut off by current action during the higher level.

Between Bayport and Log Cabin Point the shores are faced for most of the distance by bold cliffs. A well defined "drop off" follows this shore and extends outward as much as two hundred yards in places, dropping at a depth of six feet. The depth of the "drop off", it will be noted, is greater than on the west side of the lake, and this is due to the greater power and size of the waves developed by winds from the westerly quadrant. Weves are active under the present conditions on this shore and breakwaters are necessary in places to prevent the recession of the cliffs. Sags in the cliffs are infrequent but where present show both current and ice action at the bars that developed during the former level.

Log Cabin Point is an extension of the moraine into the lake but originally had a gentle slope. Consequently it now shows a wide terrace. The original slopes were much flatter on the south side of the point and the submerged portion of the terrace is, therefore, much wider on this side. A small embayment on the south side of the point was completely cut off by a bar at the higher level and this has since been remodelled into an ice rampart. Bluffs line the shore to the vicinity of the narrows with the exception of another indentation south of Lakeside which was cut off by the usual combination of bar and ice rampart at the higher level. This indentation runs back of the bluffs and appears again at the lake shore north of the narrows where it is similarly cut off.

The two small points on the east shore opposite Orrs Point are due to current and ice action during the former stage and were built of material brought in from the cliffs to the north. In this vicinity the shore consists of an alternation of cliffs and swamps, the latter being as a rule cut off. An excellent rampart-bar isolates a small swamp just south of Coopers Landing. In the same way a nearby swamp, which extends a considerable distance to the east, was cut off, definitely separating a small pond from the Long

Lake basin. The point below the narrows consists of several small knolls surrounded by swamp on the east. This swamp was undoubtedly open water at the former stage but has since been filled to some extent by vegetation •

The east shore to the south end of the lake is lined by low cliffs and vegetation grows to the shore. The exposed terrace is not well developed and in many places is wanting entirely. Also the submerged terrace is but moderately developed and drops usually within one hundred feet of the shore. Vegetation is much more abundant along this shore than in other parts of the lake. In general, wave action is moderate in this part of the basin, due probably to the restricted reach of the waves

There appears to be sufficient evidence to show that Long Lake has stood for a considerable period of time at a level about thirty inches higher than at present, an almost universal occurrence on the inland lakes of Michigan. When first formed the basin was connected with those of Squaw and Mud Lakes and also included a number of small and large indentations which were either isolated by current action or drained by the sinking of the water level. That the former stage was of long duration is shown by the fact that practically all of the shore adjustments took place at that time. Thus, strong cliffs and an almost continuous terrace were cut by the waves. Currents succeeded in throwing bars across many of the indentations and added to the terrace formed by the waves. In addition, spits were started from some of the points, which show little growth under the present conditions. The greatest change has been the reversal of the Shiawassee drainage with the cessation of delta building. In general, the adjustments were carried to such an advanced stage that the present outline of Long Lake was determined at that time. At present, the waves are doing most of the work on the shores and in places are cutting back the cliffs, the exposed terrace having been removed. The change of greatest moment that one may foresee is the possibility of the growth of the spit at the north end of Orrs Point which will eventually isolate the south arm. Vegetation has taken a firm hold on the submerged terrace, following a more or less abundant accumulation of marl. Some of the shallower parts of the basin are in process of filling in this way, but a large part of the lake is too deep for such method of extinction. The absence of entering streams precludes filling by sedimentation.

CHAPTER VIII

LAKES OF THE NORTHERN PENINSULA

BREVORT LAKE

Brevort Lake is one of the largest lakes of the Northern Peninsula and lies approximately twelve miles northwest of St Ignace and within one mile of Lake Michigan. Allenville on the Duluth, South Shore and Atlantic R R is the nearest stop and a short drive brings one to the east end of the lake

The lake is five and one half miles long and nearly two and one-half miles in greatest width See Fig 81 The south shore runs nearly parallel to that of Lake Michigan, that is, northwest-southeast, but the north shore takes a nearly east-west direction so that the lake tapers towards the west in general outline. It covers an area of 6 7 square miles and its average width is about one and one-fourth miles

The lake lies in a shallow basin surrounded by low ground for the most part. Near the southeastern end two low knolls rise above the sandy plain. These knolls are of hard rock thinly covered with glacial material. They are surrounded by a sand plain which formed a portion of the bed of Lake Nipissing and now borders the east end of the lake On the north side a flat swamp extends from the lake shore northward to the Carp River This swamp closely resembles outwash in that its surface is flat and the material is sand, but stands somewhat lower in elevation than the outwash plain at the west end of the lake. The south shore from Luepnitz Bay to the west end is bounded by a belt of sand dunes which rise nearly one hundred feet above the lake and are the highest land in the vicinity. These dunes form the inner border of a narrow sand strip that separates this lake from Lake Michigan. Beyond the dunes is a series of bars, parallel to each other and the Lake Michigan shore, which are separated by shallow troughs grown up to swamp grass. Near Lake Michigan another belt of dunes is found From the elevation of the bars it is clear that Brevort Lake was a part of Lake Nipissing in its early stages but was cut off by a bar which stood near the location of the inner belt of dunes This stage was of relatively long duration and the constant

addition of sand to the shore by currents furnished the material
for the dunes. Then followed a recession of the shore accompanied
by rapid encroachment of vegetation on the exposed bars and

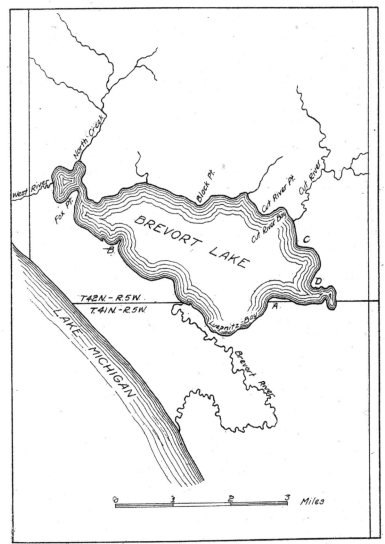

Fig. 81. Outline map of Brevort Lake, Mackinac County.

dunes, which fixed their position. The final belt of dunes probably represents another halt in the recession of Lake Nipissing
but may belong to the present stage. Just what may have been

the cause of the depression in which Brevoit Lake lies is not clear at present but it is certain that the lake has been isolated by current action and thus may be classed as a lagoon

The relatively smooth east-west shore on the south side of the east end is caused by one of the low rock knolls covered with a veneer of drift. Along the shore the waves have removed the finer drift and exposed blocks of limestone which have been forced into the low cliff by ice. Some expansion of the ice takes place in winter but ice jams are the more powerful, according to the statements of the inhabitants of the region. Along this shore as far west as the point, A on map, which is caused by the southward turn of the shore into Luepnitz Bay, is a wide submerged terrace which drops into deep water at six feet. The west edge of this terrace is in line with the extension of the shore of Luepnitz Bay. On the west side of the point a distinct boulder-lined strand stands above the sand beach of the present level. This strand probably represents a natural level of the lake, which is low at the present time, due to the blowing out of a log jam at the outlet. The blowing out of the dam accomplished more than its purpose and deepened the outlet.

Along the east shore of Luepnitz Bay two small swamps drop below the general level. No current action was noted at the swamp nearer point A but the more westerly swamp is completely cut off by two parallel bars. The bar farther inland is the stronger and indicates a stage during which the lake stood nearly six feet above the present level. This stage will be referred to as the Higher Level. The second bar was formed during the Upper Level which preceded the deepening of the outlet. West of this swamp a smooth sand beach runs to the southwest shore of the lake. The shore of Luepnitz Bay is exposed to strong westerly and northerly winds which have caused a well-defined submerged terrace extending approximately one hundred yards off shore. Also much material is carried eastward along this shore and deposited on the terrace off point A, forming a broad, submerged hook

The entire south shore is lined with sand dunes whose back slopes rise steeply from the lake. At present, the dunes are fixed but formerly they encroached on the lake from the west, causing a projection of the shore at each dune. Such projections were more exposed to wave action than the intervening shore and were cut back rapidly on account of the easily eroded sand. In this way a relatively smooth shoreline developed, but below the water level a triangular terrace extended off shore from each dune. The recession of the cliffs and the formation of the triangular terraces probably took place during the Higher Level of the lake With the recession of the water to the Upper Level, conditions were reversed and currents began to deposit along the edges of the triangular terraces Thus, at the present time these terraces are deeper in the center and resemble V-bars From the vicinity of the outlet to the west end of the lake, westward moving currents are the more powerful and the triangular terraces have been remodelled in form as well as surface. They, therefore, are extended in a northwesterly direction The best example of this is point B which extends northwest two hundred yards beneath the water

The outlet bends abruptly to the southeast soon after leaving the lake and flows in a direction parallel to the southwest shore of Brevort Lake for nearly three miles before turning towards Lake Michigan It then doubles back on its course for more than a mile and finally enters Lake Michigan on a reverse curve, that is, swings back to the southeast The turning of the upper part of its course is due in part to the growth in a southeasterly direction of the original bar which separated Brevort from Lake Michigan and also to the general trend of the topography where not covered by dunes The outlet was not followed by the writer to Lake Michigan but the final turn to the southeast is probably due to the drift along the shore in this direction

The sags between the dunes vary in elevation above Brevort Lake and in many places are low enough to cause swamp conditions along the shore. At such places the exposed terraces of the higher levels are wider than usual and have no distinct line of separation, giving the effect of a single terrace of exceptional width No definite bars cross the mouths of these indentations which were relatively broad, but occasionally an ice rampart is found, for example, west of point B These ramparts may be remodeled bars but this is uncertain

A well-defined submerged terrace fringes this shore and drops consistently at six feet, except off the projecting dunes As has been intimated, the outline of its outer edge is much more irregular than the present lake shore Fox Point is a blunt sand spit which developed mainly at the Upper Level and nearly closed the channel into the west arm of the lake At present the growth is very slow but, nevertheless, may complete the spit. The west arm is shallow and very muddy, and there is a possibility that the rapidly encroaching vegetation may fill the basin before it is isolated by the spit at Fox Point.

The entire north shore of the lake is bordered by a broad exposed terrace which terminates at a low cliff approximately one

mile north of the lake. This terrace correlates with the great bar
along the south shore which isolated Brevort Lake and was formed
during the late Nipissing stage of the Great Lakes. For the greater
part of its extent the terrace drops to the shore of Brevort Lake
in a low cliff at the foot of which rests a line of boulders, indicative of ice action. The points are caused by excessive accumulations of boulders which, obviously, retard the action of the waves.
On the other hand, minor indentations were present along this
shore but were virtually all cut off by bars during the Higher
Level. In front of the bars the beach is of clear sand and has been
pushed into a rampart in many places. Just east of Black Point
a small terrace, standing below the elevation of the bars, is evidence of the Upper Level. The evidence of the latter, although
sufficient to establish this stage, is meager and the obvious conclusion is that it was of short duration.

A submerged terrace of variable width and slope follows this
shore. In general, the depth at the drop off increases from two
feet near the west end to six feet at the east end. This variation
cannot be entirely accounted for but may be ascribed in part to the
increased effectiveness of the storm winds from the west as the reach
becomes greater. It was noted that the lesser depths at the drop-
off were in many cases due to a low ridge near the edge
of the terrace and may be accounted for to some extent by
ice action. Powerful ice jams occur on the north shore and reach
heights of ten to twelve feet at times. The interesting fact is that
they not only drive on the shore but are also piled on the edge of
the terrace where the low ridges are located. The effects are more
pronounced in the shallower water, that is, nearer the west end,
and the stronger ridge is formed at the edge of the terrace in this
part of the lake. It seems reasonable, then, that the large variation in depth at the drop off is due in part to ice action. The
effect of these jams on the shore is best seen west of Black Point
where an excellent rampart has been formed.

In the vicinity of Cut River Point currents have produced some
decided effects. The point itself is a V-bar which is better developed on the west side, indicating stronger current action from
this direction. It stands well above the present lake and was
formed during the Higher Level. But the most striking effect is
the formation of the Cut River reef which is a submerged bar extending far out into the lake in accordance with the curvature of
the west side of the point. It has been somewhat modified on the
east side, but the abrupt drop into deep water indicates that the
activity of waves and currents is slight on this side. Cut River

35

Bay has a sand beach of even curvature back of which is a low ice rampart The possibility of a bar, remodelled by ice action, naturally suggests itself but is difficult of proof. The river is forced to the east before entering the lake, showing the prevalence of currents from the opposite direction A large quantity of silt has been deposited by the stream and has been distributed on the east side of the bay, forming a broad, submerged terrace

At C currents of about equal intensity left the shore from both directions and built a symmetrical V-bar of greater dimensions than that noted at Cut River Point This also was formed at the Higher Level but the enclosed lagoon is still a good sized pond. In addition to the exposed V-bar, a submerged bar similar to the Cut River Reef extends well out into the lake The balance of the currents on either side of this point is due to the protection afforded the shore north of the point by the Cut River reef Thus, only local currents are set up on the north side and by winds of short reach, but on the south side the currents are formed along a greater stretch of shore and by winds of longer reach, although of less power However, part of the material derived from the shore between C and D was carried southward and deposited at D in a spit The greater part of this deposit is submerged and, together with the submerged terrace on the opposite side of the lake, leaves only a narrow channel of deeper water leading into the east bay. The north and east shores of this bay are low and the only shore feature of importance is a well-defined ice rampart The effect of vegetation as an aid in the formation of ramparts where the material is sand is here well shown, for the rampart is not present across the clearings. During the higher levels a distinct submerged terrace was formed which now supports a heavy growth of rushes The edge of the terrace is the off-shore limit of rushes and may thus be readily traced during the growing season

Brevort Lake was originally an arm of Lake Michigan but was completely shut off from the main body of water by a bar of large dimensions which has since been heaped into dunes. During the Nipissing stage the broad, exposed terrace bordering the north side of the lake was formed Later the water subsided and halted for a relatively long time at a level six feet above the present stage. At this level the greatest adjustment of the shores took place but the permanent effects were accomplished by currents. Undoubtedly waves were active and aided materially in the formation of a submerged terrace, but this has been subsequently remodelled. Numerous spits began their development at this time and in some cases became bars, but no very striking changes in outline resulted.

The strongest action took place on the north side, as shown by the cut off indentations and the V-bars at Cut River Point and locality C. It is possible that the reef at Cut River Point and the projections to the east were at least started during this stage

A second subsidence halted at an intermediate level whose features are poorly preserved and was probably of short duration Nevertheless, many of the forms of the preceding stage were remodelled and in some cases added to The spits were either planed down to the water level or greatly extended The terrace of the Higher Level was generally cut down to conform to the lower water level, and, on the south shore, parts of the remodelled terrace have become areas of deposition The present stage was initiated by human interference and minor shore adjustments are progressing slowly The work to be done consists in remodelling the forms of the previous levels by waves and the extension of the previous deposits by currents The most prominent change will result from a continuation of Fox Point across the entrance to the west arm

Ice jams have been and still are very active on the lake with marked results where conditions are at all favorable Some headway has been made towards the extinction of the lake but this is of local importance Vegetation is well established at the ends of the lake and considerable filling has been accomplished. This is especially true of the west arm where the process is aided by the silt of North Creek. Another locality where sedimentation is important is at the mouth of Cut River, but, in general, it may be stated that the process of extinction is in an incipient stage

THE MANISTIQUE LAKES

The moraine which extends across southern Luce and western Mackinac counties has already been mentioned in the discussion of the Lowlands of the Northern Peninsula in Chapter I. Within this belt the local relief is low, and the topography consists of irregularly placed knobs of gentle slope and shallow basins which are larger than is usual in moraines of strong relief. Subsequent to its formation, the moraine was covered by Lake Algonquin and, inasmuch as the depth was moderate in this locality, received a veneer of sand over its surface Numerous lakes stand in the basins, and attention is called in particular to the Manistique lakes which are situated near the western borders of Luce and Mackinac counties These three lakes are named North Monistique, Monistique, and South Monistique on the Land Survey maps but are now called Round, Manistique, and Whitefish respectively, the o in Monistique having been changed to a.

These lakes lie in the peculiar drainage system of the Manistique River, a brief description of which follows. The main stream has

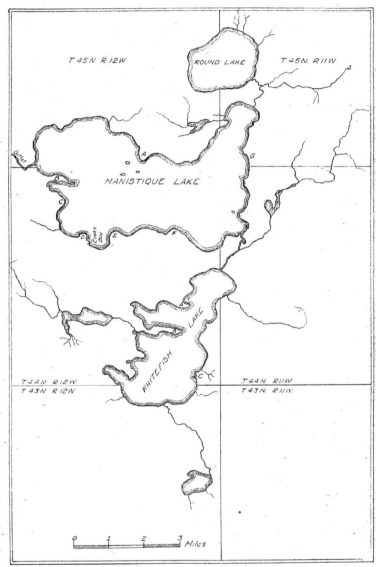

Fig. 82. Outline map of the Manistique Lakes, Luce and Mackinac Counties.

a general southwesterly direction and, in its upper course, seems to follow the border between the moraine on the east and the swampy plain on the west which rises very gradually in elevation to the northwestward and extends to within a few miles of Lake Superior in the vicinity of Munising. The greater part of the water of this drainage system flows southeastward in numerous parallel tributaries which join the trunk stream at approximately right angles. On the other hand, the tributaries from the east are not only smaller but less numerous and, moreover, have the hap-hazard pattern typical of the drainage of a morainic country. Round and Whitefish lakes drain into Manistique Lake and thence to the Manistique River, forming the largest tributary entering the main stream from the east

The two larger lakes, Manistique and Whitefish, were examined by the writer. They may be reached by conveyance either from Gould on the Soo Line or from McMillan on the Duluth, South Shore and Atlantic R. R. A railroad spur runs from Seney to Curtis which is located between the two lakes, but the train schedule was uncertain at the time when this study was made.

MANISTIQUE LAKE

Manistique is the larger of the two lakes, its area being 15 8 square miles as compared with 6 4 square miles for Whitefish. It probably floods several contiguous morainic basins and has, therefore, a very irregular shore-line. A few knobs rise above the surface of the lake, forming small islands. The lake is very shallow, the reported maximum depth being twenty-five feet. Random soundings were made in the course of this work, but no depths greater than twelve feet. were obtained. But, assuming the larger value to be correct, it is to be expected that the larger waves agitate the water to the bottom of the lake and their development, therefore, is greatly impeded. That this is actually the case is shown by the excessive turbidity of the water after storms. In general, then, adjustments of the shores are on a small scale, even though the topography is favorable to the development of forms by both waves and currents.

Along the entire north shore the most consistent adjustment is the submerged terrace which, however, is not sharply defined. It is merely a zone of sand whose outer edge is marked by a change in material rather than by a steeper slope. In many places the position of the outer edge may be approximated from the reeds of circular cross-section which seldom grow beyond the terrace and often form a fringe at the edge. On account of the gentle off-shore slope, a small amount of material has sufficed to form this terrace, and

the effects of waves and currents at the shore are not pronounced
At the higher land clay bluffs line the shore, as at A and along the
south shore, see map, Fig 82, but along the flatter slopes the activity of the waves and currents seems to have been limited to the
formation of beaches, the material of which is well assorted

On the west shore in the vicinity of the outlet, the off-shore slope
is so flat that it is doubtful if even the largest waves strike the
beach with any considerable force. The key to the activity in this
locality is the long, narrow point, B on map, at the end of which
currents from either direction must run directly out into the lake.
A small bar has been built outward from the end but is submerged
for most of its extent. Thus, some current action is indicated, but
wave action is not sufficient to pound the material above the water
level The greater width of the submerged terrace on the north
side of the point is evidence that the currents on this side (possibly
return currents from the northwest shore) are the better developed
This is due not only to the greater reach of the waves affecting the
north side of the point but also to the smoother shoreline which allows stronger currents to develop, other conditions being equal

The blunt projection C stands well above lake level, rising like
an island above the lake on the east and the swamp on the west
This elevation is composed of till which furnishes coarse beach material, consisting of gravel and boulders The presence of a faint
terrace ten to twelve feet above the present level on the lakeward
slopes of this point is an indication of a higher stage of the lake
This in itself is not sufficient to establish this stage but, inasmuch
as another fragmentary terrace at the same elevation was found
at the opposite end of the lake, it seems reasonably certain that
the lake formerly stood at this level. This point, therefore, must
have been a low island at that time. South of this former island
the vegetation of the swampy lowland is encroaching on the lake
and there is no definite beach

The land bordering the south shore of the lake stands higher in
general than that along the shores already described, and cliffs of
moderate height are more frequent. Thus, from the low shore
south of C to F an almost continuous bluff faces the lake at varying
distances from the present shore The bluff does not follow point D
but extends directly across to the head of Cooks Bay where it
rises twenty feet above the lake This point is a low swamp and
is apparently the terrace of a level of the lake which was intermediate between the highest and present stages From the head
of Cooks Bay the bluffs make a large loop eastward and return to
the shore about one-half mile east of point E A small spit on

the west side of this point is the only definite current deposit noted on this shore of the lake. The adjustments have been slight, and the fact that the spit is composed of cobbles, ranging in size from three to six inches in diameter, suggests ice as an aid at least in the formation of this feature

Beyond E the topography is undulating and causes a series of broad headlands and wide embayments. Invariably the beaches at the headlands are of coarse material and in the embayments they are of sand. At the apex of the broad outward curve between E and F the ice has pushed up a distinct ridge of boulders off shore This was probably formed by ice jams, since the lake is somewhat large for expansion At F a bluff and beach of the intermediate level, mentioned in connection with point D, are readily detected The alternation of headland and embayment continues along the east shore and offers little of additional interest except at G Here a patch of the terrace of the highest level was found

In conclusion, it seems unnecessary to add to the statement concerning the shore adjustments made in the introductory part of this description. Yet from the study it seems probable that the lake has stood at two higher stages in the past, one at ten to twelve feet above the present level and another at three to four feet Obviously, the highest level must have covered a much greater area than the present lake and possibly included Round and Whitefish. As regards extinction, vegetation appears to be the most important factor. A heavy growth of rushes forms an almost complete fringe about the lake, but the accumulation of their dead parts is not important as yet. The entering streams apparently bring in little sediment for, if such were the case, deltas would be formed at their mouths

WHITEFISH LAKE

Whitefish Lake lies within a half mile of Manistique and extends four and one-half miles to the southwest The east shore winds about in broad curves, but the opposite side is very irregular, consisting of long points and narrow intervening bays The longest of the points almost crosses the lake near the middle, point B in Fig. 82. The lake is deeper than Manistique and, although less than one-half the size (6.4 sq. mi.), shows considerably greater adjustments of the shores Yet, as compared with those found on the shores of many of the lakes of the Southern Peninsula, the adjustments are on a small scale.

At the narrows between this lake and Manistique, the low shore is lined by a sand beach which soon gives way to the westward to

bluffs which rise to a maximum height of thirty feet. Along the
west side the shores are poorly adjusted and little of interest was
found north of locality A. The sand spit at this point has been
built by currents moving eastward along the south side with but
slight additions from the north   The total amount of material deposited here is relatively small, a fact confirmed by the lack of adjustment of the shore to the west. In fact, the shore of the entire
bay to the south has suffered little change and is being encroached
upon by vegetation. The lack of adjustment must be due to the
shallow water, which interferes with the development of the waves,
and to the short reach of the strongest winds. Point B is the index
to the activity of the shore agents in this part of the lake and
the essential feature is a small sand bar which extends northeastward from the end of the point. Unquestionably here, as at A,
the currents along the south side of the point have accomplished
most but apparently are not powerful No great amount of cutting has taken place but much of the finer material has been removed, leaving a beach of coarse material interspersed with numerous boulders

No adjustments worthy of description were noted between point
B and the south end of the lake, although the irregular shore offers
many opportunities for adjustment. Minor indentations at the
heads of the first two bays south of the point would surely have
been cut off if currents had been active along these shores Obviously, with no currents developed in the bays, spits would not be
formed at the headlands

At the south end, the beach becomes sandy and has a more even
curvature, which is suggestive of better adjustment. Weak currents are driven eastward along this shore and swing out into the
lake at C on the east side A small spit is growing here but has not
reached the islands which stand off shore Inasmuch as the spit is
located south of the main bend in the shore line, currents from the
north have not contributed to its formation. Aside from this spit
the shore features on the east side of the lake are of little interest.
The alternation of sand and boulder beaches at the embayments and
headlands respectively persists to the outlet. As mentioned previously, the boulder clay is covered with a veneer of sand. At the
embayments the sand is not removed but merely adjusted along the
beach. At the headlands wave action is sufficient to remove the
sand and enough of the finer material of the till to concentrate
the boulders on the beach.

In general, wave action is the predominant force in the adjustment of the shores of this lake. In the more exposed locations

rather prominent cliffs have been cut The quarried material, however, was very largely distributed on the off-shore slopes, forming a
zone of sand which corresponds to a distinct submerged terrace
Rushes have established themselves on the terrace quite generally
but are frequently limited to a thin fringe at the outer edge, giving
a ready means of determining its location. No evidence of the
higher levels noted on Manistique Lake was found, although the
highest level of Manistique must surely have flooded this lake.

INDIAN LAKE

Indian Lake lies in the drainage of the Manistique river, forming
a catch basin for the Indian River, whose head waters lie more
than twenty-five miles to the northwest It empties into the Manistique about two miles above the mouth through a short outlet
which is navigable for small craft in its upper part. Thus the lake
may be reached by boat from the outskirts of the city of Manistique

Indian Lake is five and three-fourths miles in length and has an
area of thirteen square miles Thus, the average width is two and
one-fourth miles but the maximum width, measured from the outlet
to the head of Big Spring Bay, see Fig 83, reaches nearly double
this figure From one viewpoint this lake may be considered a lagoon, for it was isolated from the Lake Michigan basin by a short
sand bar which bridged the rather narrow connecting channel. On
the other hand, the lake basin lies directly transverse to a pre-
glacial ridge of rock which is thinly covered with glacial material
Limestone outcrops in Manistique, at Millers Point on the east
side of the lake, and on the west side between Silver Creek and
the south end. From this it seems probable that the Nipissing bar,
which cut off this lake, extended between rock buttresses

The rocks in this region are stratified and dip towards the center
of the Southern Peninsula, that is, slope down to Lake Michigan
The trend of the layers at the surface is, therefore, approximately
parallel to the Lake Michigan shore Previous to glacial times,
harder rock layers came to the surface in this vicinity and formed a
somewhat elevated ridge, or cuesta (see Chapter I), while on either
side broad troughs were formed by the more rapid erosion of the
weaker layers. In the vicinity of Indian Lake a stream flowing in
a southeastward direction crossed the cuesta through a narrow
gap. It so happened that the movement of the glacier was also
towards the southeast, that is, along the course of the stream which
flowed through the gap, and the valley may have been enlarged in
this way. The enlargement of the valley by the glacier was more
pronounced in the softer rocks north of the gap than at the gap,

and a broad basin with a relatively narrow outlet to the south was formed. After the melting of the glacier, the basin was partially filled by the sand plain which lies north of the lake and the southern end was closed by a bar.

In the journey up the outlet which flows over bare rock in places, it is interesting to note that the channel has been deepened

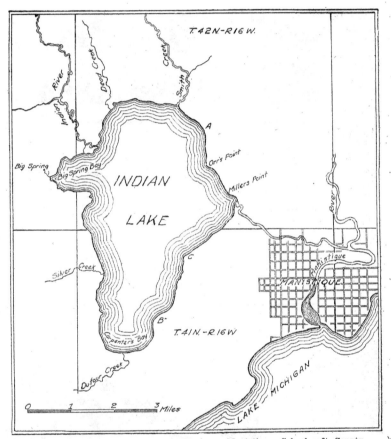

Fig. 83. Outline map of Indian Lake near Manistique, Schoolcraft County.

approximately three feet. This arouses expectations of a higher level of the lake which is not apparent along the shore from the outlet to Millers Point. This stretch of shore is faced by a low cliff of limestone rubble. The rock is a thinly bedded, highly fractured limestone and has been greatly disturbed by the push of ice on the face of the cliff. Around Millers Point, however, the cliff recedes and between it and the shore stands a well-defined terrace which

A. ICE RAMPART, INDIAN LAKE.

B. VEGETATION, LAGOON AND BAR, NEAR INDIAN LAKE, SCHOOLCRAFT COUNTY.

corresponds in elevation with the outlet before it was deepened
At the point of departure of the cliffs from the present shore a
strong rampart of five to six feet in height has been pushed up by
ice. Northward the rampart splits into two distinct ridges, one of
which follows the present shore The other swings back from
the shore and extends to Orrs Point as a ridge on the terrace Near
the northern end the material of this ridge becomes clear sand
and the front slope flattens, or in other words, the rampart merges
into a bar.

Back of the cliffs of the higher level mentioned above, the land
slopes so gently towards the lake that it appears flat A few higher
spots rise above this flat and in each case the foot of the normally
gentle slope has been carved into a low cliff. This is interpreted
as a terrace and shore of a still higher level of the lake, which stood
higher than the Nipissing stage of the Great Lakes, but below the
Algonquin. Thus, evidence is at hand to establish two higher stages
of the lake, the Upper and the Intermediate. The activity during the
Upper stage was largely that of waves in this vicinity and resulted
in the formation of low cliffs and a well-defined terrace. During the
early stages of the Intermediate Level, wave action likewise predominated and similar forms developed. Later, however, conditions
changed, due possibly to a slight lowering of the level, and currents, aided by ice, built a rampart-bar along the terrace, which
served as a breakwater for the cliffs to the rear. At the present
level, waves and currents are engaged in removing the finer material from the beach, leaving the coarser to be pushed into a rampart by the ice

At Orrs Point rock again outcrops and the shore is lined with
angular fragments of limestone. North of this point this coarse
material is piled into one of the best ramparts found on our lakes
See Plate XVII, A The rampart rises fully six feet above the
lake and is a sharp ridge with steep front and rear slopes.

At the point of deflection of the shore to the northwest, A on map,
the cliffs turn to the northeast and the high land drops to a wet,
grass-covered plain which rises barely above the present lake level
This swamp borders the entire north end of the lake as far as the
south shore of Big Spring Bay and extends for miles to the north,
rising with imperceptible slope. Obviously, the lake covered a considerable part of this lowland during the higher levels but no attempt was made to determine its limits Sand ridges, which may
be either spits or off-shore bars, were noted crossing the lowland,
but the only one traced was the spit which extends from the cliffs

at A to Smith Creek. The present shore is mucky and has no definite beach.

Indian River enters the lake just north of Big Spring Bay and, in fact, has been instrumental in forming the north shore of this bay. Great quantities of silt have been brought to the lake by this stream and deposited in a typical delta across which runs a number of distributaries. The shore line has been built out in this way and the delta is encroaching on Big Spring Bay from the north. In addition to the exposed part of the delta, a broad submerged platform extends fully a mile off shore. Little sediment is brought in at low water stage under present conditions but there is a possibility of large additions to the submerged portion of the delta at least during times of flood.

Big Spring Bay takes its name from a large spring nearby. This spring has no effect on the lake shore but as the "wonder point" of the vicinity deserves mention. It is a large pool about 200 feet by 100 feet in surface extent and nearly fifty feet deep. The water issues with considerable force through a fracture in the bottom and is so transparent that the cloudlike effects of the sand fountain at the bottom may be clearly seen.

The west side of the lake from Big Spring Bay to the south end is bordered by high ground, and the prominent shore features are the cliff and terrace of the Intermediate Level. The limestone outcrop, mentioned in the introductory remarks on this lake, occurs at the small point about one mile north of the south end of the lake.

Carpenters Bay is lined with an adjusted sand beach which has been thrown up into a storm beach in places. A lagoon of about fifty feet in width stands to the rear and in turn gives way to the beach of the Intermediate Level. These beaches run to the dunes on the east side of the bay. The dunes are composed of the sands of the Upper Level bar which cut off the Indian Lake basin and are situated farther inland than the original bar. From this locality south to Lake Michigan, the material is all beach sand and is distributed in a succession of topographic forms similar to those found on the Nipissing bar at Brevort Lake. Thus the gentle slope between the dunes at the east side of Carpenters Bay and Lake Michigan consists of a series of nearly parallel bars and narrow lagoons. The swamp condition of the lagoons is interrupted by the bars, and the two forms may be readily differentiated by the vegetation which consists of lanes of swamp grass between lines of evergreen trees, the latter marking the bars and the former the lagoon. The contrast between the two types of vegetation may be appreciated from Plate XVII, B. The number of these bars was not determined but, judging from the plate, must be large   It is probable that those nearer Lake Michigan run approximately parallel to the Michigan shore, but in the vicinity of Indian Lake there is a tendency for them to swing to the shore south of C from both directions, that is, to come together and form a V. Those from the northeast are the stronger and are truncated in some instances at the present shore, forming slight projections of the shore line and increasing the height of the cliffs   From the vicinity of C to the outlet, the bars follow the direction of the present shore   The growth of these bars in a northeasterly direction has forced the outlet to the north side of the depression through which it flows and accounts for the southward bend of the stream after leaving the lake   Obviously, these bars were formed after the isolation of the Indian Lake basin. The tendency of the exposed bars along this part of the lake to come to the shore south of C is puzzling   The shore is exposed to winds having a westerly component and, on the average, the stronger currents flowed to the northeast   The material carried by the currents must have been derived from the south, inasmuch as the outlet would have prevented acquisitions from the opposite direction. Some source of supply of material near point C seems essential and the large off-shore shoal in this locality is at least suggestive.

Summing up, it may be stated that two higher levels may be recognized from a study of the shores of Indian lake   Also the outlet is dammed at present and the water is somewhat higher than formerly. The flooded condition, however, is not serious and has resulted in but a slight increase in the activity of the shore agents. During the highest level, the lake was much larger than at present, the principal extension being to the north and northeast. During this stage, the lake was separated from the main lake, and its northern border very probably adjusted by the development of bars across the sand plains   The latter was not determined by the writer, but the presence of sand bars in proximity to the present shore substantiates the inference   The subsidence to the Intermediate stage caused a large reduction in size and brought the shores near their present position, except at the north end. However, in this locality important adjustments were made by current action, so that there was little change in the outline of the lake after the final subsidence   The activity of ice on the shores of the Intermediate and present levels at least is clearly shown and the ramparts thus formed are among the best found by the writer. This lake, especially on the northeast shore, is well beyond the maximum limit of size for ice expansion, and ice jams, there-

fore, have exerted the shove It is evident that sedimentation by
streams from the north has greatly reduced the extent of this lake
in the past but is of less importance at the present time The lake
is of sufficient size to act as an efficient settling basin, so that
there is little probability of rapid deepening of the outlet, ignoring
the presence of the dams A slight revival of activity has resulted
from the obstruction of the outlet and modification due to this may
be anticipated in the future

HURON MOUNTAIN LAKES

In general, the surface of Michigan stands at a relatively low
elevation In the Northern Peninsula the western part, or Highlands, rises considerably above the eastern Lowlands and includes
the highest elevations in the State Two areas only, the Porcu-
pines and Hurons, rise above 1800 feet and have been dignified by
the term mountains The appropriateness of this appellation depends largely on the viewpoint Speaking more particularly of the
Huron Mountains, the summits certainly do not tower above the
land to the south, but from the north they rise sharply a thousand
feet and more above the level of Lake Superior. Such elevations
may seem insignificant to one accustomed to the lofty, snow-capped
peaks of our western mountains but to the plains-dweller or navi-
gator might appear formidable The writer is unaware of the
history of the naming of the Huron Mountains but suggests that,
perhaps to the explorer whose paths are guided largely by the water
ways, the name mountains may not have seemed inappropriate,
much less ridiculous

The so-called Huron Mountains consist of a number of hard rock
knobs, bare or sparsely covered with vegetation, which form the
western terminus of a narrow belt of ancient crystalline rocks extending from the vicinity of Marquette to the Huron River This
belt outcrops along the shore of Lake Superior for about ten miles
above Marquette and then extends slightly more to the west than
the lake shore, leaving a narrow coastal strip which is underlain
by the brown Lake Superior sandstone. The mountains rise above
the coastal strip, which is considered a part of the Lowlands of
the eastern half of the Peninsula, and were never reduced to the
level of the ancient peneplain which was formed in this region. The
last great episode in the geological history of this region was its
erosion by glaciers. The entire surface of the land was covered by
the ice and the most important work in the Huron Mountain area
was degradational By this the soil was removed and the
rock surfaces were smoothed and rounded Thus, the elevations

were fashioned into knobs and the valleys into broad depressions with gently undulating floors. Deposition by the ice occurred largely south of the mountains and was slight within the mountains and on the lowland belt   On the coastal belt thin deposits of till and sands of Lakes Algonquin and Nipissing are present, but in the mountains the veneer of disintegrated material, where present, seems barely sufficient to support the heavy forest growth

The region has suffered from forest fires and but little virgin forest still remains. The country is as much a wilderness as may be found in the State and furnishes ideal conditions for the get-back-to nature recreationists who desire a complete change   Quite naturally, this locality has been selected by the Huron Mountain Shooting and Fishing Club for its private grounds. The fascination of this region need not be analyzed but it may be ventured that not the least important factor is the numerous small lakes. Ten of these are named on the map issued by the club and none exceeds two square miles in area. They may be divided into two groups. Those lying in basins within the mountains and those on the piedmont, or on the lowland belt. Mountain and Ives lakes are described here as illustrations of the former type, and Conway, Pine, and Rush of the latter group.

Mountain and Ives lakes, see Fig 84, stand more than a hundred feet above those lying on the lowland, and their outlets cascade steeply to the lower level, exposing the underlying rock for part of their courses. They appear to stand in rock basins which were gouged out by the ice and later partially covered with drift or lake deposits of Algonquin age   The elongated form of Mountain Lake is due to the fact that it rests in a valley which crosses the range and extends into the thick glacial deposits to the south   The character of this valley will be better understood when the geology of the broad embayment between Huron River and Pine River points is known   Cliffs of brown sandstone face the Lake Superior shore along these points and for some distance within the bay   They then recede from the shore and converge towards Pine Lake and the mouth of the valley in which Mountain Lake lies   Along the Superior shore the cliffs give way to a great sand deposit which forms the head of the bay   This sand formation holds back Pine Lake and is, in reality, a great sand bar, the north slope of which consists of no less than twenty-five small bars, conforming in direction with the Lake Superior shore   From this it seems clear that this embayment formerly extended back to the Mountain Lake valley and was cut off by current action during a higher stage of Lake Superior, probably the Nipissing. Moreover, the elongated.

form and alignment of Howe, Rush and Pine lakes approximately parallel to the border of the crystalline rocks is suggestive of a cross-channel at or near the contact of the crystalline rocks and

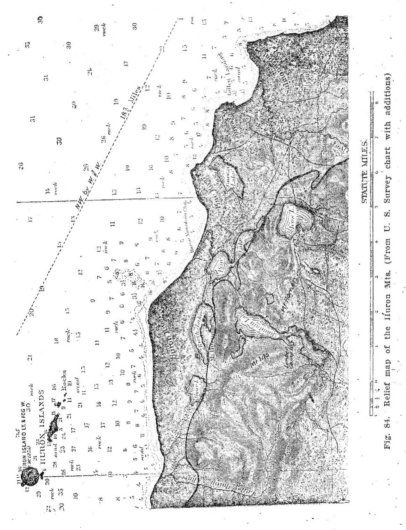

Fig. 84. Relief map of the Huron Mts. (From U. S. Survey chart with additions)

the sandstone. This is further strengthened by the fact that the sandstone north of Howe and Rush lakes rises well above the level of these lakes. It seems probable, then, that in pre-glacial times a stream flowed northward to the Lake Superior basin, cross-

Michigan Geological and
Biological Survey

Publication 30, Geological Series 25,
Plate XVIII.

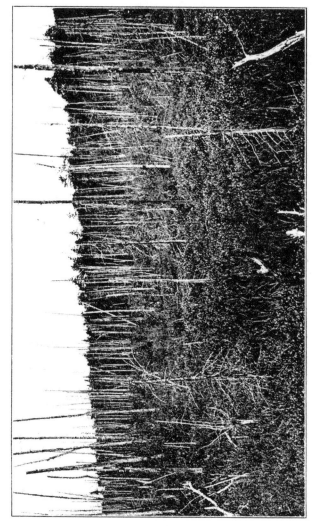

EXTINCTION BY VEGETATION, ARM OF PINE LAKE, HURON MOUNTAINS.

ing the crystaline rocks of the Huron Mountain range and the brown sandstone. The latter was much more easily eroded and not only a wider but deeper valley was cut, causing the steep slope between Mountain and Pine lakes. Also tributaries developed near the contact of the different formations and entered the main stream from both sides in the vicinity of the western expansion of Pine Lake.

Conway Lake lies in a separate depression which was likewise cut off from Superior during Nipissing time by a bar which developed between Pine River and Conway Points.

PINE LAKE

The Club House and Cabins of the Huron Mountain Club are located on the Superior shore in the vicinity of Pine River A short walk from the Club House across the sand beaches brings one to Pine Lake near the outlet The presence of a dam prepares one for the fringe of dead timber and large quantity of driftwood West of the outlet the waves are moderately effective and a beach of even contour extends to the west end of the lake. Near the outlet the beach material is rubble and is taken as an indication of the sorting action of the waves. Farther west, the waves wash the clear sands of the retaining bar and have formed a beach of even curvature, faced by a sand cliff of varying height up to ten feet The variation in height of the cliff is due to the fact that the shore does not run parallel to the bar There is also a well defined submerged terrace in this vicinity The projection at the west end of the lake is caused by a knoll of till. This material is in itself more resistant than the unconsolidated sand but, in addition, contains numerous boulders which accumulate on the beach, due to the selective action of the waves and possibly to ice push, and effectually hold up wave action. South of this projection the trough which connects Pine Lake with Rush is encountered. Near the inlet a low flat, scarcely above the lake level, extends for a short distance northeastward The flat surface, black soil, swamp shrubs, and dead tamaracks are adequate evidence that this was formerly an arm of the lake but has been entirely filled by vegetation. See Plate XVIII

South of the inlet till borders the shore and little adjustment has taken place. The beach is uneven and of coarse material, and no submerged terrace is present. To the southeast the slopes are flatter and the material is sandy. Currents have carried considerable material to the southeast and deposited it in a spit which runs out on the lowland surrounding the inlet from Mountain Lake.

37

On this bar are two ridges which are probably storm beaches The projection at the mouth of the inlet appears to be a delta but is badly flooded on account of the dam. Continued growth of this delta would surely close the entrance to the middle arm of the lake, Second Pine This, however, is not probable because the waters of Mountain Lake carry little sediment and the course of the outlet is too short for much to be acquired after leaving the lake The present delta probably consists of the material eroded from the channel of the outlet in the early stages of the existence of this stream

Within Second Pine the till soon gives way to the smooth, side slopes of a prominent rock knob upon which the waves have made no impression The abrupt projection beyond the rock shore is caused by a till knoll The shore has the usual breakwater of boulders and is but slightly affected by the waves Nearer the entrance to Third Pine abundant snags form a still more effective breakwater and the shore shows still less adjustment. Third Pine is a narrow embayment upon which small waves only are possible and, consequently, little adjustment is to be expected. In addition, the hard crystalline rock is exposed on most of the south shore and shows no effects of wave action Along the north shores of Third and Second Pine the material is sandy drift, and the beach is of sand or fine rubble Nevertheless, there has been little adjustment, otherwise bars would have been thrown across the restricted entrance to these basins

As regards shore adjustments, then, this lake has little to offer. This is due largely to its small size, but other factors are hard rock exposures and, at present, the large quantity of driftwood. The extinct embayment at the northwestern end, however, is a perfect example of complete extinction by vegetation

CONWAY LAKE

Conway Lake lies about a mile northeast of the upper end of Pine Lake and is easily reached by trail. This lake is also a lagoon of Lake Nipissing, which was not drained by the sinking of the water level The narrow retaining bar may readily be recognized This lake, although of good size, has no outlet and is probably drained by seepage through the bar to Lake Superior or across the swamp which extends from the northeast end of the lake to the Salmon Trout River The lake is evidently very shallow because small waves disturb the lake to the bottom, making the water very turbid, and this is to be expected from the swampy lowland upon which the lake stands The only evidence of shore adjustment by waves and currents found was at the southwest end where a small indentation has been completely isolated by a sand bar. The interesting thing here is that the lagoon is dry, although its bed is apparently below the level of the lake. The absence of effective waves and currents, however, has proved favorable to the preservation of the ramparts formed by the expansion of the ice, even though the sandy material is not especially conducive to their formation. An almost continuous rampart surrounds the lake but never exceeds two feet in height. In places it is so small that even a slight cutting by the waves would destroy it. Vegetation in the form of rushes and lily pads has taken hold and one may predict a relatively rapid extinction of the lake from this cause.

RUSH LAKE

The adjustment of the shores of Rush Lake seems all out of proportion to the size of the lake, after a visit to Pine and Conway. The lake is irregular in shape and not greatly different in size from the foregoing. It, nevertheless, exhibits shore features which are indicative of intense activity in spite of the fact that the eroded material is to a large extent the Lake Superior sandstone.

In the vicinity of the depression through which the outlet flows the beach is of sand and of even curvature. To the south the beach curves around a blunt projection, the cause of which is not apparent at the shore. A short distance back, however, stands a well-defined cliff cut in brown sandstone, which was formed at a level approximately four feet higher than the present. Inasmuch as Rush Lake stands more than sixty feet above Lake Superior, this must have been a transitional stage between Algonquin and Nipissing. The projection, therefore, was more prominent during the early stage of this higher level and was cut back by wave action. Below this point along the south shore is a beach, smooth except for one small point, caused by an accumulation of boulders. The beach material increases in size from sand to rubble and where coarse has been pushed up into a low ice rampart which extends practically uninterruptedly beyond the boat house. Fringing the entire south shore of this bay is a well-defined submerged terrace of varying width up to fifty feet, which drops into deep water at about four feet. This terrace is evidence of strong wave action along this shore which, furthermore, may be corroborated on the slope to the south. Proceeding back from the shore, one encounters first the cliff of the four-foot level which in places is undercut in the brown sandstone. Still higher, thirty feet above the lake, may be found fragments of a shore line formed during another of the transi

tional stages between Lakes Algonquin and Nipissing An especially good example of an undercut cliff may be seen at this level above
the south side of the narrows of the bay. Above the thirty-foot
level there appears to be a broad terrace with cliff which may be
the Algonquin shore This, however, is not distinct and the interpretation is uncertain.

The trough in which this bay lies rises gently to the west and
extends through to the south shore of the lake During the four-
foot level the shore stood about one hundred paces to the west
and at the thirty-foot stage completely flooded the narrow channel,
making an island of the present peninsula which forms the north
shore of the bay The peninsula is composed of brown sandstone
which has been carved into an almost continuous cliff at the four-
foot level along the south side, being undercut in places as much
as fifteen feet The amount of recession of the shore during this
period is shown by the width of the exposed terrace which reaches
a maximum of twenty feet For a body of water so small as this
lake must have been, the wave activity appears excessive, especially
so since its effects are negligible at the present level Since there
was little difference in the size of the lake during the four-foot level
and at present, the excessive cutting of the former stage must be
attributed largely to a longer period of time during which the waves
were acting

Wave cutting is also the predominant factor in the development
of the north shore of the peninsula. The greatest effects are found
at the four-foot level and in the brown sandstone, as on the south
side An eastward drifting current along the south shore of the
main part of this lake is formed during northwest "blows" but is
dissipated in the bay near the end of the peninsula Thus, no deposit is found at the tip and none will be formed until the bay
is closed A small sand deposit on the west side of the entrance to
the bay is taking the form of a spit but its growth is apparently
very slow. Farther west the activity of the waves is especially
noticeable, inasmuch as the shore of the thirty-foot level was entirely removed by the recession of the cliff of the four-foot stage, which
is exceptionally high

Near the west end of the lake the heavily timbered slopes rise
steeply to Mount Huron, in places making a 40° angle with the
horizontal, and show little erosion by the shore agents at the higher
levels, although hard rock was not encountered The shore of the
thirty-foot level is not distinguishable and that of the four-foot is
relatively faint The lack of strong shore features along this part
of the lake is due, to some extent, to the short reach of the effective

winds, but the possibility of their partial obliteration by the slump-
ing of material down the steep slopes is suggested by the peculiar
submerged projections along this shore, which may be material
brought down in landslides.

At the west end of the lake a sand beach skirts the trough which
continues westward towards Howe Lake. This trough rises
above the thirty-foot level, so that the Rush and Howe lake basins
were not connected during that stage. Along the north shore near
the west end, the material is a sandy till but soon gives way to
the brown sandstone The four-foot level is marked by a continuous
cliff as far as point B on map, but the thirty-foot shore is fragmentary, appearing infrequently as a notch in the cliffs. Along
this stretch of the shore the submerged terrace is narrow, varying
from five to twenty feet in width, but east of point B it widens to
more than one hundred feet, the depth at the outer edge remaining
at four to five feet. North of this shore stands a flat topped ridge
of sandstone thinly covered with glacial material, beyond which is
a dry trough extending parallel to that in which Rush Lake lies.
The ridge continues to the boat house at the northeast corner of the
lake, rising well above the lake level Along this naturally smooth
shore there was little opportunity for current deposits so that the
features consist almost solely of cliffs, notched at the four and
thirty-foot levels. However, some activity by currents from the
west is shown by the gradation of the material on the present
beach, the size diminishing toward the east end where the beach
is of fine sand The coarser material has been pushed into local
ramparts by ice, but the action is evidently of but moderate intensity.

Concluding, it may be emphasized that wave cutting has been the
most important factor in the adjustment of the shores of Rush lake
at the various levels. Furthermore, it may be stated that the results accomplished by the waves on this small lake, which probably
never exceeded one half mile in average width and two and one-
half miles in length, were exceptionally great and surprisingly
so after a study of the nearby lakes of like size.

IVES AND MOUNTAIN LAKES

Of the two lakes within the Huron Mountains, Ives is by far the
simpler. This nearly circular basin was covered by the waters of
Lake Algonquin, but this fact is disclosed by the elevation rather
than by distinctive shore features. At this time its shores were open
to the buffeting of the waves of the main lake and, if these shore
features are indistinct, the adjustment at the present level must be

slight indeed. As a matter of fact, where the hard rock is exposed the waves have made no impression. The best defined shore feature on the lake occurs on the northeast shore south of the outlet where the sandy material has been washed into a shallow submerged terrace of approximately thirty feet in width.

Mountain Lake, on the other hand, is long and irregular in outline, and presents numerous opportunities for adjustments by all of the shore agents. The shore materials are the hard rocks of the Huron Mountain mass and glacial material, including both till and sand. Obviously, the adjustments are more pronounced in the glacial material.

In the vicinity of the outlet the material is sandy, and an excellent beach and submerged terrace are present. The latter is more than one hundred feet in width and drops into deeper water from a depth of thirty inches. At the north end the sand has been cut into low cliffs but towards the outlet these drop to a sand beach upon which stands a low ice rampart. The outlet cuts through these forms and, within one-quarter mile of the lake, begins to cascade over the granite rock.

South of the outlet the material changes to till and the beach contains many boulders. The shore as far as Mt. Homer is irregular due to a succession of minor projections and small bays. The shores consist uniformly of boulder strands at the projections and sand beaches in the bays. This would indicate wave action on the points and a gradual filling process by currents in the bays. In addition to the effects of waves and currents may be seen some excellent ramparts, formed by the expansion of the ice during the winter. In fact, the rampart is almost continuous but is much better developed at the projections because of the coarser material. At such locations these ridges contain boulders up to three feet in diameter and rise steeply to heights of several feet, the largest standing seven feet above the lake.

At the foot of Mt. Homer the crystalline rock comes to the shore and very little adjustment is noticeable. Where the rock slopes gently to the lake, the surfaces appear as smooth as when uncovered by the glacier, but on the steeper slopes a slight roughening of the rock at the water level was noted. This roughening is due to the breaking off of small angular blocks of the rock along fissures. It seems probable that frost action has been more effective than the waves in this process, inasmuch as the water deepens rapidly at such locations and the fragments sink below the reach of the waves, thus depriving them of the tools which are necessary for abrasion.

South of the narrows the east shore is more irregular than to the north and, in addition to the projections of till, has two rock promontories off which lie small rock islands The glacial material is till and the beaches along such stretches of shore are lined with boulders. On the rock promontories the rock exposed on the north side is roughened as described above but that on the southern exposure shows little change. The greater effectiveness of the northerly winds is clearly shown here and this may be attributed to their long reach as well as their high velocities The small islands off the rock points are likewise of solid rock but are not outliers which have become detached from the points by wave action They are formed by ice scour and their smooth convex surfaces appear so like the backs of sheep that such forms are known as *roches moutonnees* (sheep backs).

At the south end a forked bay extends to the southeastward. The depression which causes the north fork leads to the small but interesting Canyon Lake which was discussed in Chapter I under lake basins due to faulting The Cliff River enters through a depression at the southwestern end of the lake, and this sluggish stream is depositing its sediment in a delta which, as yet, has caused no great projection of the shore This is not necessarily an indication that the delta is small for the valley of the lower course of the stream is a low swamp and possibly was an arm of the lake which has been filled by the deposits of the stream. A similar form lies at the mouth of a small stream entering the lake one fourth mile north. In both cases the front slope of the deltas drops steeply into deep water from depths of not more than fifteen inches, indicating active growth of the delta and moderate wave activity.

The west shore is very similar to that on the east side but, in general, the slopes are flatter Thus, the shores of the bays are inclined to be swampy and are fringed with alders. The beaches are bouldery except in the bay which lies south of Lumber Camp Bay and is connected with it by a swampy trough The trough is sand-filled and the beach of the bay in the south arm is due to the working over of this material rather than to current action Northward the shores are cut in till as far as Lumber Camp Bay and the beach contains many boulders. Within this bay, the beach material gradually reduces in size to sand at the head. This is due largely to a variation in the glacial material but may result in part from transportation of the finer material southward along the beach by waves and currents.

Northward along the west side, conditions are similar to those on the opposite side but the outline of the shore is more regular. At the foot of Mt. Ida the rock outcrops on the shore but does not form a projection The rock shore gives way to a boulder beach and this in turn is interrupted by the only current deposit on the lake which can be recognized with certainty Currents from both directions, but particularly from the south, have turned from the shore and built an embankment nearly two hundred feet out into the lake The exposed part is similar to a V-bar but lacks the central depression. The submerged portion drops steeply into deep water from a depth of thirty inches

Within the bay at the northern end the boulder beach presents little of interest This bay is a part of the same depression in which Portage Lake lies. At the north end of the lake the hard rock of Mt. Huron comes to the shore and shows a very slight amount of abrasion This gives way to the sand cliff described at the beginning of this discussion

In general, it may be stated that the lake is too small to show the effects of intense wave action. The presence of a submerged terrace which drops at about thirty inches is an indication of waves which may reach a length of eight feet and a height of less than one foot. Such waves have had no effect on this hard rock in the many years they have been active. The glacial deposits, however, show wear consistent with the size of the lake. The greater effectiveness of the winds having northerly and westerly components is a natural consequence of the form of the lake and the prevalence of storm winds from these directions. This is seen in the tendency towards stronger wave action on the east shore and current action on the west. The effects are also greater in the northern arm than in the southern, due to its greater size and regularity in outline The lake is in a youthful stage and a discussion of the possibilities of extinction seems futile

LAKE MICHIGAMME

On the extreme western border of Marquette County lies the "Big Lake," Michigamme. With an area of seven square miles, it seems insignificant compared to the Great Lakes, which were well known to the Indians who frequented this country, but locally, its importance probably justified its Indian name. For miles about it is the largest inland lake, but its claim to our interest is not based on size alone. Unique in form, picturesque in location, studded with numerous islands and broken by bays, this lake possesses a charm equalled by few, if any, of the lakes of the State, and in addition offers abundant material for physiographic study

In shape, it resembles a large Y, spreading its arms to the west and southwest a distance of about six miles from its eastern end, see Fig. 85. The first view of the lake is usually obtained from the railroad whose tracks follow the north shore. The part seen is the island-studded north arm set among the bald hills of the Marquette Range, which project above the tree tops.

Although the glacier covered this region and the rounded and smooth rock knobs present striking evidence of its action, it is necessary to go to the rock formations and structures in order to understand the origin of this peculiar basin. The ridge-and-valley topography of this section is due to the varying resistance of the

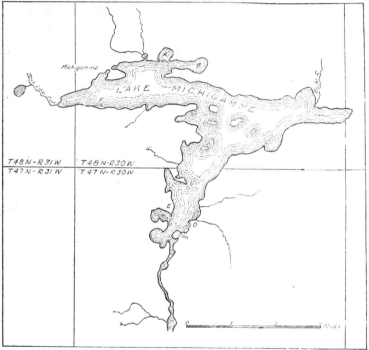

Fig. 85. Outline map of Lake Michigamme, Marquette County.

rock formations of the Marquette Range which have a general east-west trend. In this region the range is a great trough or syncline which is deformed by a minor fold on the north side just east of the lake, as shown in Fig. 86.

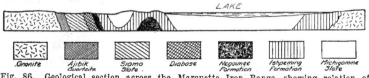

Fig. 86. Geological section across the Marquette Iron Range, showing relation of Lake Michigamme to the formations. (After Van Hise and Bayley)

The upturned edges run along the north side of the lake in a narrow belt, but the range spreads out to the southwest, and from this expansion two small troughs extend to the south and southeast, the latter reaching to Republic The different rock formations vary greatly in their resistance to erosion and of these the Michigamme, which underlies the greater part of the lake, is the least resistant. However, this formation is variable in hardness and is very resistant where changed by metamorphic processes. This is illustrated on the islands and along the southwest side of the lake, where the rocks stand in bold hills. These rocks were greatly eroded by running water previous to the invasion of the ice, and a general system of east-west valleys and ridges was formed. This trend is consistent along the north side of the lake, but on the opposite side swings towards Republic in a broad curve to the south and southeast. The valleys followed the least resistant rocks and, in particular, the Michigamme formation which in itself appears to be softer in proximity to adjacent formations. Thus, in addition to the east-west valley in which the northern part of the lake lies, a branch extended towards Republic and is now occupied by the south arm and the outlet of the lake

Such probably was the topography in its main aspects when the ice advanced from the northeast The presence of islands indicates that the scouring action of the ice was able only to modify the existing surface by rounding off the hills and deepening the basin. The passage of the ice was across the main trend of the ridges and, while its general movement was independent of the topography, that of the ice border must have been greatly influenced by the relief features over which it passed Thus, it is probable that the ice poured through the gaps in the ridges on the north side of the lake and spread laterally into the valley, deepening it locally into a basin As the glacier was disappearing a remnant of ice filled this basin and deposited great quantities of sand at the east and west ends and along the outlet. In this way the Michigamme basin, due largely to pre-glacial conditions, was modified and isolated by glacial action

In a lake as irregular as Michigamme frequent adjustments to wave and current action are to be expected, and the observer is not disappointed in this case Hard rock outcrops in places on the shores but the greater part of the material within reach of the shore agents is of glacial origin. The drift is sandy as a rule and is, therefore, easily attacked Along the sides it is thin or absent but reaches considerable thickness at the ends, especially the west. The adjustments may best be described in the order of a traverse around the lake, beginning at the west end, a trip easily made by boat but offering difficulties on foot.

. At the west end, the Three Lakes River enters the constricted arm of the lake from a narrow sand-plain which extends to the northwest beyond Nestoria About a mile to the west the land rises to elevations of a hundred feet above the lake and has a rolling surface composed of heavy sand interspersed with large boulders A well record in this locality gave twenty feet of heavy sand underlain by ninety feet of quicksand which, therefore, extends below the level of the lake. This sand plain, although not typical outwash, is broken by several pits in which small lakes and swamps lie Bass Lake in T. 48 N., R 31 W is an excellent example and is rapidly being filled with vegetation which completely encircles the lake and is in the floating bog stage. Just before entering the lake the Three Lakes River has deposited the sands brought from its upper stretches and nearly filled a former bay of the lake through which it now flows in a broad serpentine course. In addition to the sedimentation, vegetation is now rapidly completing the filling of the bay The bay was caused by a projection of till from the north shore along which the road runs to a bridge across the narrows. The lakeward side of the projection has been straightened by shore action under the influence of easterly winds, which here have a long sweep, and a short but complete bar cuts off a narrow swamp now grown up to vegetation Along the north side as far as the town of Michigamme, the strand is of large boulders swept clear of smaller material. Wave action is slight at present, but soundings indicate a terrace of about one hundred feet in width which drops into deeper water from a depth of seventeen feet A rock bottom was encountered out to depths of eight feet; but beyond this firm gravel was encountered to the south side of the lake A terrace extending to a depth of seventeen feet indicates an intensity of wave action far too great for a lake of this size. The writer is, therefore, inclined to believe that there is present here only a cut-terrace, represented by the rock-paved bottom, and that the gravels are due to a strong return current at this end of the lake rather than to local undertow.

The boulder beach continues around the peninsula east of the town of Michigamme where it is interrupted by a railroad fill North of the railroad tracks in this vicinity precipitous rock cliffs form the south side of a ridge running parallel to the lake shore The base is generally of uniform elevation several feet above the present level of the lake but is obscured by a talus of large rocks Below the cliffs is a flat upon which the South Shore tracks are built. The formation bears a striking resemblance to a wave-cut cliff and terrace but the writer was unable to find further evidence of a former level of the lake at this height.

Beyond the cliffs the tracks leave the shore and turn northeast across a bay that is half filled with floating bog. Between this bay and the indentation, designated as A on the map, the shore is of sandy drift which has been cut back recently into low cliffs. The recent cutting is due to a renewal of activity caused by the artificially raised water level. The material of this shore has been carried in both directions and deposited in bars at the turnings of the shore. The bar at the eastern extremity of this beach is submerged but its presence is indicated by the breaking of waves over it during storms, see Plate XIX, A. On the west side, however, the bar stands above water but is being cut away rather than added to at the present time, and has been bisected as shown in sketch, Fig. 87.

Fig. 87. Sketch showing plan of the spits on the north shore of Lake Michigamme.

The eastern side of the entrance shows much less action, indicating less powerful waves from the east winds of restricted reach. The north shore of the arm to the east, B on map, is likewise composed of sandy drift and is cut into fresh cliffs ten to fifteen feet high. In this case the material is transported to the east end of the bay where, augmented by the sediment of an entering stream, it is deposited in a sand bar which cuts off the swamp to the rear. The undertow has been active in carrying the sand out at the head of this bay and an excellent submerged terrace has developed, the surface of which was covered with well developed ripple marks when seen by the writer. The point forming the south side of the bay is caused by a ridge of hard rock veneered with drift and shows little wave action on the bay side. The main shore of the lake along this point shows active cutting, the beach varying from fine sand to boulders, depending on the character of the drift. This material is broken up by the waves and transported eastward by the prevailing westerly winds. Otherwise we should expect some deposition at the tip of the point. Along this shore, especially well shown at point C, was found a wave-cut notch in solid rock about two feet above the present level. The cliffs vary from two to ten feet in height and are bordered by a terrace ten to fifteen feet wide at its foot. At the present level the strand is lined with boulders accumu-

A. WAVES BREAKING OVER SUBMERGED BAR, LAKE MICHIGAMME.

B. STORM BEACH, EAST END OF LAKE MICHIGAMME.

lated from the drift which covers the hard rock on its lower slopes. This upper level, as indicated by the notch, does not correspond in elevation with the base of the high cliffs farther to the west and probably marks the higher water level of the lake.

About a mile from the east end of the lake the Bijiki River brings down, for the most part in the spring, great quantities of sand which is carried out into the lake in a great bar extending almost to the south shore. This bar has a pronounced effect on the waves, in that they are suddenly shortened in length and increased in height, making a rather treacherous bit of water during storms. The river is able to keep its channel open on the average but during a strong west wind at the time the writer visited this locality a sand bar was being formed across the channel. East of the Bijiki River rock hills again stand near the shore. An interesting bar was noted just to the east of a rock projection where the railroad embankment begins. The bar which resembles a cuspate foreland, extends onward in line with the shore to the west for some distance and then turns abruptly back to the shore, as shown in the accompanying sketch, Fig. 88. The enclosed lagoon is compound,

Fig. 88. Cuspate foreland on the north shore of Lake Michigamme. (Sketch from photograph)

the different parts being separated by sand bars, and shows a development in steps similar to the formation of a hook. This is further emphasized by the heavy growth of vegetation in the older part to the west. During the writer's visit a storm beach was being piled up on the front of the bar and enclosed a narrow lagoon. This probably was not permanent but illustrates the importance of storms in the building of such features. One exceptionally heavy storm may do more work than a long period of moderate

winds As may be inferred from its shape, the bar has been built
mainly under the influence of westerly winds but it is probable
that easterly and southerly winds have played some part in forming the portion which extends from the point to the shore on the
east side

Beyond the bar a railroad embankment of stone borders the lake
nearly to the eastern end. At this end of the lake the beach receives
the full force of the waves thrown up by the westerly winds, which
regain their form after crossing the sand bar of the Bijiki River,
and is a perfect curve except where littered with drift wood. The
slope is flat and a broad beach of fine sand is exposed. The force
with which the waves strike this shore is indicated by the presence
of two storm beaches which are too low to appear in the photograph, Plate XIX, B, but are denoted by the lines of drift wood
resting in the shallow trenches to the landward of each beach The
upper or landward storm beach was formed during higher water,
probably in the spring, while that next the shore was in process of
formation when the picture was taken The broad submerged
terrace which extends off this shore indicates an exceptionally
strong undertow

Along the southeast shore, bouldery drift is abundant and the
shore is lined with large rocks which hold up wave action. This
continues to the point north of the dam, D on map, where deposition has increased the length of the point In addition to the exposed part, this point extends for some distance under water, as
shown by the growth of rushes. At present, however, it is being
cut away rather than added to In the bays on the west side of the
south arm little wave action takes place, but the promontories are
being attacked At point E the material is sandy and the cutting
has been rapid However, the currents lose their force in crossing
the mouth of the bay and a spit runs south from this point, continuing under water nearly to the opposite shore North of this
point the headlands are due to hard rock which outcrops on the
shore in places. The cutting by the waves in such places is a
matter of a few inches only at the present level, due in part to the
resistance of the rocks but chiefly to the fact that they extend
steeply below the surface and the fragments quarried by the waves
drop into deep water and do not serve as tools In many places a
higher water level which agrees with that found on the north shore
was noted

Along the south shore of the west arm hard rock comes to the
shores locally but much of the beach is of boulders. Opposite the
town of Michigamme and lying close to the shore is Sundstrom's

Island, F on map, a small island of till which is slowly being tied to the mainland at the southwestern corner The bar runs to the southeast and is submerged at the present time but may have been dry during low water before the dam was put in From this point to the west end of the lake the shore is composed of large, in some cases huge, boulders

The islands of the lake form one of its most picturesque features With the exception of some of the smaller off-shore islands, they are composed of the more resistant rock The larger ones in the main lake are surrounded by low rock cliffs or a boulder strand but show little off-shore deposition They have been rounded off by the glacier and, in the south arm, are elongated in the direction of the ice movement The latter may be considered as roches moutonnees (sheep backs) partly submerged.

PORTAGE AND TORCH LAKES

The Portage and Torch Lakes under discussion are situated in Houghton County and together form a very irregular shaped basin which is most interesting with regard to its origin. In a general way, it may be considered as consisting of two troughs which intersect at an angle of about 50°. See Fig 89. The broader, or main trough, runs approximately parallel to the west shore of Keweenaw Bay and also to the trend of the rocks which form the Keweenaw Peninsula. The narrower trough winds across the peninsula in a general northwest-southeast course but has been closed at the north end by current activity during an earlier stage of Lake Superior Dredging operations readily converted this trough into a ship canal which affords this important copper region direct shipping facilities both to the east and west The expansion at the intersection of the trough is occupied by the main body of Portage Lake Closer examination, however, shows that the main trough is consistant only from Dollar Bay on Portage Lake northeastward, and is occupied by Torch Lake and the Trap Rock River; also that the continuation of this trough across Torch Lake is followed by the Pilgrim River and is a much less conspicuous topographic feature The depression in which the main body of Portage Lake lies runs slightly west of south, joining the Torch Lake trough at an angle of about 35°. It is followed by the Sturgeon River which in its lower course meanders across a valley flat formed by the deposition of its heavy load of silt. Briefly stated, then, the depressions in which these lakes lie consist of three troughs: One running parallel to the Copper Range, a second which crosses the range, and a third extending almost due south from the intersection of these two.

In order to make clear the manner of formation of these troughs, the more important episodes in the physiographic history of this

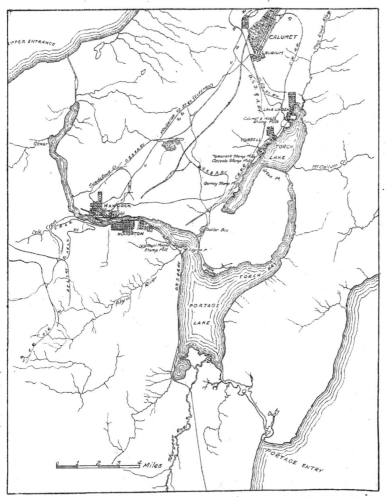

Fig. 89. Outline map of Portage and Torch Lakes and vicinity, Houghton County. (From U. S. Lake Survey chart.)

region will be briefly sketched. The first great event of interest in this connection was the complex folding of the ancient rocks of the Lake Superior region. The axes of the folds are parallel to Lake Superior, and, as a result of this, the rock layers dip beneath the lake and extend in an approximately east-west direction. A notable exception to the latter is the copper-bearing rocks of the Keweenaw Peninsula which have a northeast-southwest trend After the folding, these rocks were subjected to prolonged erosion during which the surface was peneplaned However, considerable relief existed on the peneplaned surface, due to the differences in the resistance of the rocks, also the complexities of the folding caused varied topographic features among which the ridge-and-valley type was prominent The period of erosion was followed by a sinking of the land below the level of the sea, during which sediments of great thickness were deposited These filled the valleys and covered the ridges in the vicinity of Lake Superior so that, when an uplift occurred, the streams flowed directly to the Lake Superior depression over the surface of these nearly flat lying rocks Then followed the removal of the greater part of the sediments by erosion, exposing the former topographic features. The ridges were encountered first but the trunk streams were able to maintain their courses across them The tributaries, however, developed along the former valleys in many cases In this way a system of transverse drainage was imposed upon the former topography Finally, the region was invested by glaciers which modified its surface both by abrasion and deposition.

Applying this sequence of events to the region under consideration, the resistent rocks of the Copper Range were folded and, at the close of the first period of erosion, formed a prominent ridge This ridge was buried later by sediments which also filled the depression between it and the Huron Mountains When the land was again lifted above the sea, the drainage flowed in a northwesterly direction from the Huron Mountains across the buried Copper Range. During the period of erosion which followed, the range was uncovered but the trunk streams succeeded in maintaining their courses across it for a time, forming numerous gaps. In addition, tributaries developed along the southeastern edge of the ridge. Later, streams developed from the northeastward in the less resistant sediments of the Keweenaw Bay depression and diverted the head waters of the trunk streams, forcing them to abandon their courses across the range Within the Keweenaw Peninsula proper but one of the gaps has been worn down to the level of Lake Superior and this is occupied by Portage Lake. The reason for the persistence of this particular gap is uncertain but it seems probable that it follows a fault plane along which erosion was more easily accomplished.

If the existence in former times of a trunk stream flowing northeastward through this gap is conceded, the troughs occupied on the

39

one hand by Torch Lake and the Trap Rock River, and on the other by the Pilgrim River may be easily accounted for as tributary valleys on the upper side of the ridge In addition, it is known that the rocks on the east side of the entire range have dropped along a great fault and it is believed that this has had some influence in the location of the courses of these tributary streams

The meager information at hand does not warrant a definite conclusion as to the origin of the Sturgeon River depression The occurrence of hard rock outcrops between it and Keweenaw Bay seems to be an argument for a pre-glacial valley If such is the case, it must have been a tributary to the trunk stream which crossed the peninsula through the Portage Lake gap, and its size seems disproportionately large. Enlargement of this valley by glacial scour is not probable for the movement of the ice which affected the east side of the peninsula was almost directly across this valley. On the other hand, the lobe of ice which ran into the Keweenaw Bay lowland deposited moraines in a festoon which conforms more or less closely to the outline of the bay, and the possibility that the valley stands between morainic ridges cannot be dismissed without further study

As in the case of a number of the inland lakes of Michigan, the Portage and Torch Lake basins were flooded by the predecessors of Lake Superior—Lakes Algonquin and Nipissing. The beaches of Lake Algonquin stand more than four hundred feet above Lake Superior and take one far afield During Algonquin time the greater part of the peninsula was submerged and only the tops of the higher hills stood above the water, forming a chain of islands which were aligned in conformity to the trend of the peninsula and, for the most, elongated in the same direction. The Nipissing shore, however, stands but thirty-four feet above the present lakes, and may be easily recognized a short distance back from the shore for most of its extent It is, however, usually beyond the reach of the waves of the present level and is well preserved The greatest departure from the present outline of the lakes during this stage occurred along the course of the Sturgeon River, whose lower course was flooded for a distance of twelve miles The present connections with the main lake existed but were necessarily somewhat greater in width The Upper Entrance (north) was closed by a sand bar in Nipissing time, but the Portage Entry remained open. The closure of the Upper Entrance was due not only to its lesser width and more favorable shore conditions, but also to its position on the west shore of the peninsula which is exposed to the full force of waves driven by the strongest winds.

The narrow north arm of Portage Lake, see Fig 89, nowhere reaches a half mile in width and, furthermore, is protected from strong winds by the high flanking hills, so that the shore features are not noteworthy. The most pronounced features are the delta-like accumulations of sand   In some cases these occur at the mouths of streams and appear to be natural, but others are the stamp sands from the copper mills. The accumulation of the latter was rapidly obstructing the channel and it became necessary to establish harbor limits for this part of the lake   At Pilgrim Point the deposit is a delta of the Pilgrim River which has shifted its course on the flat at least once   The submerged part of this delta shows clearly a northerly drifting current along the shore south of the point   The broad submerged terrace which extends eastward from the point may be, in part, the deposits of such currents previous to the present extension of the delta of the Pilgrim, but the deposition of a large quantity of stamp sand from the Isle Royal mill makes this interpretation uncertain

The records of the weather bureau station at Houghton show that the prevailing storm winds in this locality are from the west, northwest and north   Thus, the entire west shores of both Portage and Torch Lakes lie in protected positions and should, therefore, show less pronounced effects of the shore agencies   This is well shown along the shore which extends almost due south from Pilgrim Point to Pike Bay at the south end of the lake   Not only the features of the Nipissing shore but those of the present level as well are meagerly developed. Cutting has been the predominant process but, as a rule, has been slight in amount, as shown by the low cliffs and narrow submerged terrace   A number of minor projections, which need not be specifically mentioned, occur along this shore and are due to one of several causes, among which may be mentioned deltas of streams entering Lake Nipissing, similar forms at the present level, old docks, and vegetation. The latter protects the shores and, where removed, allows a recession of the shore line by wave cutting, see Fig 40, Mullet Lake   Obviously, the projections occur where the vegetation is intact   The abundant growth of rushes and, in places, lily pads is an indication that this shore is nearing complete adjustment to the present conditions

The extension of the lake far to the southward during Nipissing time has already been mentioned and also a hint as to the activity of the Sturgeon River been given   A better appreciation of the work of Sturgeon River may be gained from a study of its lower course. At its mouth stands a large delta which causes the irregular projection of the south shore of the lake. The stream does not split into distributaries but has shifted its course a number of times in the past, causing the ragged growth of the delta. An abandoned channel at the northwestern point indicates the position of the stream when the growth of the delta threatened the complete isolation of Pike Bay. Other abandoned channels exist southeast of the present mouth of the Sturgeon. Deposition at the mouth of the Sturgeon in its present position will in time tend to obstruct the outlet which has a feeble current. The small channel leading into Pike Bay is artificial, having been cut for logging purposes. In the vicinity of this cut a sudden rise in the surface of the delta occurs on both sides of the Sturgeon River. This rise, although slight, is interesting because it indicates two stages in the growth of the delta. The higher, or up-stream, part developed during the Nipissing stage and is evidence of the great quantity of silt carried by the Sturgeon during that time. Some idea of the amount of material deposited may be gained from the submerged portion of this delta alone, which fills a valley twelve miles long and more than two miles in width to a depth of at least twenty feet and possibly double this figure, a volume estimated at twenty million cubic yards. In addition, the exposed part of the delta, the extent of which is undetermined, must be considered. The lower stage of the delta has grown since the drop to the present level and is relatively insignificant compared with the Nipissing delta. Including both the exposed and submerged parts in the estimate, it probably has an extent less than one-tenth the submerged part of that of the Nipissing stage.

The channel through which the Portage River flows is of considerable width and carries on its side slopes the well-defined cliff and terrace of the Nipissing level. The undisturbed frontal slope of the terrace drops to a low swamp across which the stream winds in broad curves which closely resemble meanders. At the Portage Entry the river has been turned to the right before entering the lake by a sand bar which grew from the bluffs to the east and has nearly closed the entrance.

Along the east side of Portage Lake the slopes are uniform and gentle. Consequently, the shores are unbroken by large indentations but still have minor irregularities which indicate a lack of perfect adjustment to waves and currents. Wave cutting predominates, as on the west side, and low cliffs line the shore for most of its extent. The activity on this shore is somewhat greater than on the west side but the effects are hardly more noticeable. At present the accumulation of drift wood affords considerable protection to the shore.

The irregularities of the shore-line are greater in the narrow Torch Bay than on the shores of the main lake and consist of projections rather than of embayments. A number are due to artificial structures but the numerous natural points in this protected arm lead one to suggest that perhaps more emphasis should be placed on the adjustment of the shores of the main lake.

Within Torch Lake the east shore is exceptionally smooth for about one mile, a fact which may be attributed to current action The blunt projection northeast of McCallum Creek is clearly a hook but formed at a level higher than the present From this locality to the north end of the lake, the shore features are similar to those on the main shore of Portage Lake Around the depression at the north end of the lake the contour of the shore has been modified somewhat by the silt of the Trap Rock River, but no definite delta has been formed. As at the south end of Portage Lake, Lake Nipissing flooded the lower part of the depression through which the Trap Rock River now flows but extended hardly more than two miles from the present shore.

The Nipissing terrace is well defined along the west shore of Torch Lake and upon it are located rail and wagon roads, as well as numerous stamp mills and smelters To the sands of the formei, e. g., the Calumet, Hecla, Osceola and Quincy stamp sands, are due the large projections of the shore line. So prominent are the projections that the natural shore agents on this protected shore are of little effect. But on the opposite shore in the narrow part of the lake below Ureux Point, the waves and currents are much more effective. Cliffs line the shore from the point to within a half mile of the southwestern end of the lake, and for a considerable part of the distance are cut in red sandstone The material quarried from these cliffs has been transported southwestward and deposited in a spit at the end of the lake. The Torch Lake depression continues through to Dollar Bay on Portage Lake but nowhere rises above the Nipissing level. It therefore formed a second connection between the two lakes at that time.

Before leaving the discussion of these lakes, the shore of Portage Lake from Dollar Bay to Grossepoint demands consideration. The Nipissing shore features, although distinct, are on a small scale, and the activity is not great at the present level Thus, the small projection opposite Pilgrim Point, a delta of Nipissing time, has neither been reduced nor added to Yet off Grossepoint there exists a submerged hook, the Middle Ground, which in extent far surpasses any similar feature to be found on the lake Clearly this hook is much too large to have been formed by wave and cur-

rent action on the short stretch of shore northward to Dollar Bay
This discrepancy may be readily accounted for by considering that
the hook is an incipient form built during the Nipissing stage,
when the currents had full sweep of the shore northward to Ureux
Point on Torch Lake

GOGEBIC LAKE

For the origin of the euphonious name of Gogebic Lake, we must
go back to the Indians. Its derivation, however, is uncertain, some
authorities suggesting that it is a contracting of *agojebic,* meaning
"rocky" or "rocky shore," and others that it comes from *gogebing,*
"dividing lake" The former seems the more appropriate on account of the rock outcrops in the vicinity of the lake, notably the
Alligator Head which occupies a commanding position about the
southwestern shore of the lake.

Gogebic Lake, see map, Fig 90, has a total length of fourteen
miles, if the eastward extension at the north end is included, and
covers an area of somewhat more than twenty square miles. It is
remarkably consistent in width and is relatively free from prominent projections and deep embayments In fact, where widest
it does not exceed two and one-half miles and nowhere narrows to
less than three-fourths of a mile except at the ends It extends
in a general direction which is somewhat east of south and departs
from this only at each end. The direction of the south end is almost due north-south while at the north end an abrupt bend to
the east occurs. These changes in direction of the lake will be better
understood after a discussion of the origin of this basin

Obviously, much of the surface of a region over which continental
glaciers have passed is covered with a variable thickness of drift
which obscures the underlying rocks and increases the difficulty of
interpreting the preglacial conditions. If, however, the relief of
the land over which the ice passed was great, as was the case in
this region, the depressions were quite consistently covered by the
glacial deposits, while the uplands received a thin veneer of drift
or were left bare Nevertheless, the deposits are usually not of
sufficient thickness to conceal the former topography, and the general features of the pre-glacial landscape may be deciphered.

The prominent topographic features of this region are two rock
ranges which stood well above the surrounding lowlands in pre-
glacial times and still form the commanding elevations The more
northerly is the Copper Range which forms the backbone of the
Keweenaw Peninsula and extends southwestward into Wisconsin,
following the trend of the Lake Superior shore Near the western

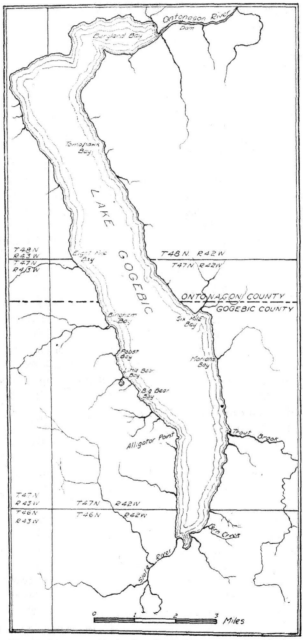

Fig. 90. Outline map of Lake Gogebic, Ontonagon and Gogebic Counties.

boundary of the State it comes in contact on the south with the Gogebic Range which is the eastward extension of the Penokee Range of Wisconsin. This range has a nearly east-west trend in Michigan but ends abruptly at the west shore of the south end of Gogebic Lake. These two ranges thus form a westward-pointing V, the southern limb of which is relatively short. See Fig. 91. The

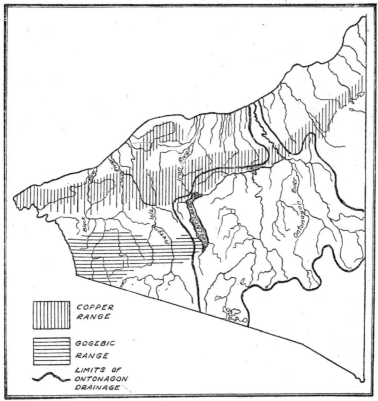

Fig. 91. Map of western part of the Northern Peninsula showing the general distribution of the Copper and Gogebic Ranges and also the basin of the Ontonagon River.

pre-glacial drainage developed in a manner described for the region to the northeast (see Portage and Torch Lakes), and the streams flowed across the ranges into the Lake Superior basin. Thus, numerous gaps were formed, some of which are still occupied by streams. Many, however, have been abandoned and are now wind gaps.

In order to attain our immediate purpose, that is, the origin of the Gogebic Lake basin, it is necessary to consider the Copper

A. LOOKING NORTH ON LAKE GOGEBIC.

B. MOUNTAIN LAKE, HURON MOUNTAINS.

Range only, inasmuch as the basin apparently does not cross the Gogebic Range See Fig. 91. From the map it will be seen that Gogebic Lake occupies a narrow depression which skirts the east end of the Gogebic Range, extends northward to the Copper Range, and then turns abruptly to the east along the edge of the Copper Range. The Ontonagon River which drains the lake likewise follows the south side of the range and extends fully twenty miles to the east before breaking through Directly north of Gogebic Lake is a low wind gap through the range, see Plate XX, A, in which are located the headwaters of the Iron River From the gap this river flows almost due north to Lake Superior Furthermore, Gogebic Lake is relatively shallow, and it therefore seems reasonably certain that the two depressions—the Iron River valley and the basin of Gogebic Lake—were formerly continuous If such were the case, the cause of the abandonment of the gap offers a problem.

The solution of this problem is difficult on account of the glacial deposits, in particular the morainic material in the bottom of the gap, and will remain uncertain until further work has been done In fact, the problem of the drainage of the entire Copper Range is one that the writer desires to study further. As it is, two ways by which the gap may have been abandoned suggest themselves The simpler way is to account for this by glacial action The ice passed over this region in an almost southerly direction, as may be seen from the striations on Pilot Rock at the south end of Gogebic Lake. It seems certain that the ice must have passed directly up the pre-glacial valley whose course is now marked by Iron River and Gogebic Lake Some abrasion was, of course, accomplished but, inasmuch as Gogebic Lake is relatively shallow, it is felt that the basin was not greatly enlarged in this way Soundings taken off Six Mile Bay show a gradual increase in depth to fifteen feet in more than one-third the distance across the lake. These soundings, although very incomplete, seem to indicate a flooded channel rather than a definite basin

During the recession of the ice, the border halted along the heights of the Copper Range At this time the waters to the south were impounded and formed a large lake, Ontonagon, which spread eastward into Houghton County but discharged through an outlet to the west. Further recession of the ice, the details of which we may omit, uncovered the gaps and that of the Ontonagon River proved to be the lowest in the range between the Fire Steel and Presque Isle rivers. This gap then served to drain the ponded waters south of the Copper Range and still continues to drain not only the area occupied by this lake but also a large area to

the south which extends to the Wisconsin line south of Gogebic
Lake During the halt of the ice, however, morainic material was
deposited along the range but in greater amount in the gap
north of Gogebic Lake than in that occupied by the Ontonagon
River Thus, the portion of the stream flowing in the Gogebic
Lake-Iron River valley south of the range was diverted eastward to the Ontonagon The lowest course open to this water lay_
just south of the Copper Range, due probably to preglacial tributaries which followed the south side of the range and flowed into
the Ontonagon on the one hand and to the Gogebic drainage on the
other Obviously, the divide between these two streams originally
stood higher than the gap of the Gogebic drainage Thus, when
the water was forced to flow across this divide by the plugging of
the gap north of Gogebic Lake, the lower portion of the diverted
part of the stream was flooded, forming Gogebic Lake.

Another conception of the origin of the basin of Gogebic Lake is
based on the action of pre-glacial streams As stated previously,
it is believed that this region was once completely covered with
sediments. After an elevation of the land which lifted the region
above the level of the sea, stream courses developed on the surface
of the sediments, flowing northwestward into the Lake Superior
basin. This drainage system was maintained for the most part as
the streams cut through the sediments and encountered the buried
rocks below. In this way there was imposed on the folded rocks
below a system of drainage, the trunk streams of which ran across,
or transverse, to the rock ridges. Less is known of the tributaries
inasmuch as the valleys are masked with drift, but, drawing an
analogy from well known regions where this type of drainage pre-
vails, it may be stated with some confidence that many of them
developed along the upper sides of the ridges. The headward extension of such tributaries of adjacent streams brought about con-
flicts for territory which eventually resulted in the formation of
secondary divides. The trunk streams, however, varied in their
ability to deepen their channels, mainly on account of differences
in volume, and the larger streams cut the deeper gaps. This, in
turn, gave an advantage to the tributaries of such streams which
were able to lengthen their courses at the expense of the weaker
streams on the opposite sides of the divides In this way the divides
shifted from the larger streams towards the smaller and at
the same time became lower in elevation In some cases this
process continued until the upper courses of the weaker streams
were captured by the tributaries of the stronger and the water
gaps abandoned

According to this conception, the Ontonagon River, the largest stream in Michigan which crosses the Copper Range at the present time, was of like magnitude in pre-glacial times. Tributaries developed along the south side of the Copper Range, but that working eastward was much the smaller on account of a conflict with the drainage of the Keweenaw Bay depression. On the west side, moreover, the tributary had a decided advantage over the tributaries of the adjacent streams and steadily worked headward until it captured the upper course of the stream flowing in the Gogebic Lake-Iron River valley. See Fig. 92. Between this depression

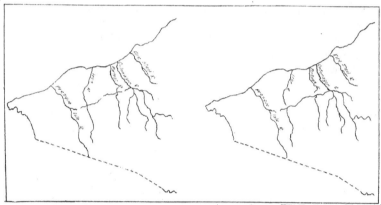

Fig. 92. Map to show the change in drainage which has taken place within the present basin of the Ontonagon River. Map to the left illustrates probable drainage in former times, and map to the right shows the series of stream captures and present drainage system.

and the Ontonagon gap other cases of capture by the same stream are, of course, possible. Following the capture, continued downcutting by the Ontonagon resulted in a deepening of the upper part of the Gogebic Lake-Iron River valley.

The flooding of the valley to form Gogebic Lake is still to be accounted for, and consideration of this phase of the problem brings to our attention the abrupt eastward turn of the north end of the lake. This arm is consistent in size with the remainder of the lake and may be interpreted as a portion of the pre-glacial valley which continued to the eastward, thus corroborating the idea of stream capture. If this be the case, the flooding must be due to glacial deposition in the course of the stream below Gogebic Lake, although some deepening by glacial scour is possible.

. With this discussion of the two ways in which Gogebic Lake may have originated, we leave the subject for future work to settle and

pass on to a description of the shores of the lake   The study of
the lake, aside from the origin of the basin, was less interesting
than was to be expected, for two reasons. The absence of prominent headlands and deep embayments gives little opportunity for
the distribution of wave-cut material in forms that produce striking results In addition, the lake has been dammed for power purposes and at the time of the writer's visit stood nearly three feet
above its normal level, obscuring to a large extent the natural shore
features

The popular Gogebic Resort at the south end of the lake may be
reached by a five mile drive from Gogebic Station on the Chicago
& Northwestern R. R   At the opposite end, however, the Duluth,
South Shore & Atlantic skirts the north shore, stopping both at
Bergland and Lake Gogebic   The latter route is perhaps the most
convenient for a physiographic study because the flooded condition
of the lake and the reason therefor are at once apparent

In general, the slopes rise more steeply from the lake on the east
side than on the west   The relief of the lake, however, is considerably more on the west side than on the opposite side, and this is
due to the existence of the heights of the Gogebic Range at the
south end and of a low swamp which leads westward from the
northwestern shore   The swamp borders the lake from Eight Mile
Bay to the north end, a stretch of more than four miles

In Bergland Bay and, in fact, along most of the north shore, the
flooding of this lake is very apparent   Where the shores are high,
wave action is particularly effective, but along the low shores and
for an undetermined distance inland, the forest trees stood in
water when seen by the writer. The normal shore features were
so obscured that little could be made out except at the sharp point
on the south side of Bergland Bay   This appeared as a submerged
sand bar upon which stood dying trees and is interpreted as a sand-
spit in process of disintegration   It is claimed by the interests who
maintain the dam that the summer of 1913 was the only time since
the dam was built (1906) that the water remained consistently
high   This, however, does not mean that the effects of the revival
of the shore agents will not be felt, for the water stands abnormally
high in the spring which is a time of frequent and powerful storms.
The material along the east shore as exposed by the waves is a
sandy till, and the topography of the land may be described as
gently rolling   Thus, there are minor points and bays but not of
sufficient prominence, as a rule, to turn currents from the shore
Waves, then, are the prevailing agent of erosion and cliffs of variable height the prominent physiographic feature   At the slight

projections, boulders are concentrated on the beach but in the embayments the material is smaller in size. The indications of current action are slight indeed and are, thus, the more noticeable. Those found were opposite Eight Mile Bay a short distance north of the township line and consisted of two short stretches of gravel beach and a small indentation which was cut off by a bar. The material of the bar was coarser towards the north end and shows that the effective currents are driven southward along the shore.

The abrupt turn of the shore into Six Mile Bay appears favorable for current deposition, but none was found. East of the stream which enters this bay, a well defined spit separates the low swamp along the stream course from the lake, but joins the cliffs a short distance south. South of the bay a boulder ridge below the cliff indicates strong ice shove which is not generally evident along this shore. Once discovered, however, the numerous boulders lined on the beach become significant. Cliffs prevail to the south end of the lake but are interrupted at the mouths of the streams. Evidence of ice push is found in places, but the most noticeable feature along this stretch of the shore is the spit on the south side of the mouth of Trout Brook. As was the case at Six Mile Bay, northward moving currents left the shore and built a small spit which has turned the mouth of the stream in the same direction.

A reversal in direction of the effective currents takes place between Trout Brook and the south end of the lake, for the shore east of Ice House Bay is lined by a smooth sand beach which continues into the bay as a spit. Under normal conditions this spit would in time close the entrance to the bay but at present is being removed. The promontory between Ice House Bay and the Slate River is a hard rock knob upon which the glacier recorded the direction of its movement by striations. These show the movement to have been parallel to this part of the basin.

The high banks on the east side are wooded to the beach and show but moderate activity of the waves as compared with the opposite shore. Just south of Alligator Point a most unexpected V-bar was found. This, of course, is a deposit built by currents from both directions, but no reason for the currents leaving the shore is ventured at present. Above Alligator Point a large rock outcrop of suggestive shape peers through the woods and has been descriptively dubbed the "Alligator Head."

North of Alligator Point the shore swings to the northwest and is somewhat more irregular. Nevertheless, wave action predominates and but one current deposit was noted, a V-bar between Pabst and Bingham bays. Along the low shore from Eight Mile Bay

northward, ice ramparts are the striking feature   The singular
number might almost be used in referring to them, for the ridge is
nearly continuous and reaches a height of fully five feet in some
places

In conclusion it may be stated that the most striking fact brought
out by the study of the shores of Gogebic Lake is the revival of the
activity of the shore agents. This is of very recent date and the
most. pronounced effects are those produced by waves. The cliffs
are universally freshened unless protected by vegetation, and shore
currents are ineffectual   Examples of active deposition under the
present conditions are few indeed, and in some cases the forms
built under former conditions are being removed   In general,
greater activity is displayed on the east shore than on the west and
this is to be expected on account of its position on the lee of the
prevailing storm winds

Ice shove is apparently very strong but shore conditions are
usually unfavorable for the formation of ramparts   On the northwestern shore they are very well developed but elsewhere the lining
of boulders on the beach is the usual occurrence   The way in which
the ice works on this lake is not known to the writer but, judging
from the width of the lake, both jams and expansion may be effective.

CHICAGON LAKE

This small lake is situated a short distance north of the Wis-
consin-Michigan boundary line in Iron County   It lies for the
most part in a northeast corner of T 42 N , R 34 W , but small portions spread out into the adjoining townships, from which it flows
northeast to the Paint River. It is most readily reached from Iron
River over the excellent Iron River-Crystal Falls road, which
crosses the outlet about a mile from the lake

Its shape is elongated, as would be expected, for it lies in a valley
between the drumlinoidal hills which are characteristic of this
region. As may be seen from the map, Fig 93, the valley is blocked
by morainic knobs across which the Crystal Falls road runs and
which separate this basin from the one to the north occupied by
Trout Lake   The lake, then, may be assigned to the class formed by
morainic dams to which type Fortune Lakes, situated about two
miles to the west, also belong

The shores along the sides are generally high and dry and afford
many excellent locations for cottages which have as yet not been
taken advantage of to any great extent   Both ends of the lake are
swampy and this is especially true of the north end. The lake at

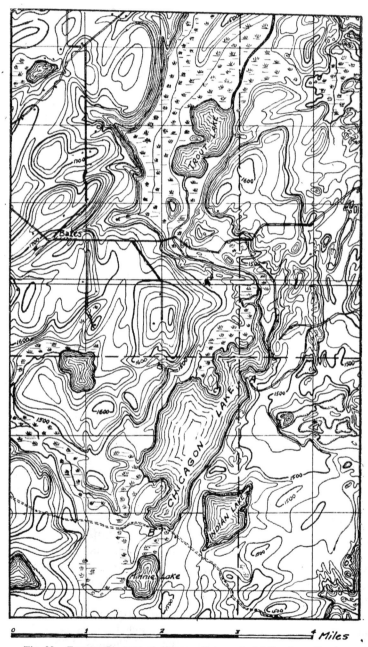

Fig. 93. Topographic map of Chicagon Lake and vicinity, Iron County.

this end is shallow and supports a growth of rushes Shrubs grow to the water's edge and hold up any slight wave action that may occur in this restricted part of the lake The encroachment of vegetation is marked in this locality and has reached the advanced stage of quaking bogs which appear as flat, grass-covered areas

The east shore is comparatively straight with the exception of a projection near the north end and is flanked by smooth, rounded slopes which are steep in places On a lake of this size wave action is not intense and shore forms are not to be expected on a large scale Along the northeast shore as far as Park's farm the shores are lined with a pavement of boulders which extends a short distance above the present water level This gives way in places to a small but definite boulder ridge, elevated about three feet above the lake and a smaller amount above the narrow strip to the landward side The regularity of the boulders on the shore has given rise to stories to the effect that Indians had paved these shores in times past but this may readily be accounted for on physiographic grounds. The material of the banks is a sandy till and the wave action weak, so that only the sand is carried away The boulders, thus concentrated, are then shoved to the shore by ice expansion which is sufficient to form definite ridges locally The elevation of the boulders indicates a higher level for the lake and this is well supported by the frequent occurrence of an elevated shoreline about three feet above the present level

This higher level marks the original position of the shores but may also mark a temporary high level Forty years ago an extensive beaver dam is known to have been maintained on the outlet of the lake and has since been destroyed The water may have stood at the upper level during the existence of the dam but it hardly seems probable that this would have been maintained long enough to allow the cutting off of indentations, as is the case just below Park's farm where a bar completely closed an opening at the higher level The lowering in level seems to be better accounted for by the cutting down of the outlet.

At Point A, see map, an interesting change has taken place This point is incorrectly shown on the map for the tip of the point is in reality a rather elongated knob with a low, flat tract between it and the main shore On the slopes of the knob and also the main shore, the strand of the upper level may be seen above the flat This indicates clearly that the knob once existed as an island, separated from the mainland by shallow water From this point to the south end, the shores are high and are nipped by the beach of the upper level The extreme south end of the lake is bordered by a good sand beach which gives way to an ice rampart along point B, where the land is higher The west shore of the lake presents little of interest until the point C is reached, at which wave action seems to be most effective On the very tip of the point the beginnings of a spit of coarse cobbles pointing to the south was noted. The effective winds, therefore, come from the north and northeast. Beyond this point the shores merge into the swamp at the north end of the lake

From the description, it is clear that wave action is slight on this lake. It seems to be limited to the transportation of sand, except in one case, point C The effects as to cliff formation are almost negligible because of the presence of numerous boulders which rapidly become concentrated on the beach and hold up the wave action The absence of a cut-and built terrace is in keeping with the slight amount of wave action and the lack of adjustment by current deposition. Ice action is relatively prominent and is of the expansion type, for the probability of any extensive ice jams on so small a lake is slight

41

CHAPTER IX

LAKES OF THE KALAMAZOO MORAINIC AND OUTWASH SYSTEM

As stated in the Introduction, the work, the results of which are given in this chapter, was undertaken in order to include a much wider representation of the lakes in the various parts of the State but has been confined to the Southern Peninsula It is possible that the distribution of these lakes would have been emphasized more had a county unit been used as a basis for their grouping. Such a unit, however, is not only artificial but difficult to adhere to and it was decided to group them according to their relation to the various positions of the border of the glacier during its retreat. Following this system the lakes may be referred to the three morainic systems shown in Fig. 3 with a fourth class of lakes bordering the Michigan-Huron shores

The order of discussion is chronological in that the groups are taken up in the order in which they were uncovered by the ice but no attempt has been made to arrange the individual lakes in each group in the succession of their appearance This grouping is used largely as a matter of convenience and emphasis should not be placed on the sequence for which no claim of accuracy is made.

GROUP I

In this group are included the lakes which lie in that portion of the State not covered by the ice at the time of formation of the Kalamazoo morainic system, see 2, Fig 3, and also those within the moraine itself. They occur in Lenawee, Washtenaw, Jackson, Hillsdale, Branch, Cass, Kalamazoo, Calhoun, and Barry Counties, those of St Joseph County having already been described. During this stage the reentrant between the Erie and Saginaw lobes of the glacier was located in northwestern Washtenaw County. The strong relief of the surface at the angle of the V formed by the junction of the two moraines presents a strong contrast to the greatly pitted outwash plain that spreads out like a fan to the southwest into Jackson County. Numerous lakes are found both in the morainic basins and in the pits in the outwash.

The greater number of morainic lakes is found within Washtenaw County and of these Sugar Loaf was selected as typical

SUGAR LOAF LAKE

Sugar Loaf Lake is located somewhat more than five miles north of west of Chelsea and can be reached by conveyance from that city The basin is larger and more irregular than the outline of the lake suggests and consists of several connected basins A more flooded condition formerly existed and there is a probability that a much greater territory was covered by this lake at that time. The former shore line is well shown just east of the inlet at the north side At this higher stage some of the smaller indentations were cut off by bars, a good example of which may be found a short distance east of the inlet mentioned The material for the bars was carved from the bold cliffs which line this shore of the lake, but was limited in amount for bars were not thrown across the larger indentations and the exposed terrace is narrow. At the present level the slight development of the shores is consistent with the small expanse of the lake which is not conducive to strong wave action and vegetation is getting started at the shore This lake is not so popular as some in the vicinity but cottages were in the course of construction at the time of the writer's visit

CAVANAUGH LAKE

This small lake lies four miles west of Chelsea and a mile and one-half north of the Sylvan Road stop on the interurban line. It is one of the most popular lakes in this section of the State The many excellent locations for cottages have been used, especially on the south and east sides, and a number of excellent summer homes have been built. The lake lies in one of the numerous basins formed in this locality Many are morainic basins but that of Cavanaugh is a fosse. Several of the lakes in this vicinity are separated by low sags which served as connections during a former flooded condition of drainage. Thus Doyle Lake to the east was once connected with Cavanaugh but a bar developed across the opening and may have separated the lakes during the later stages of the high water This bar which swings around the southeast part of the lake may serve as a starting point for a study of the shores Other features of the higher level are an exposed terrace at the foot of a cliff which rises locally to considerable height.

CROOKED LAKE

Crooked Lake is located a short distance northwest of Cavanaugh and, although longer, is much narrower and more irregular in outline The east shore of the lake for most of its extent is faced by steep cliffs consisting of the sand of the outwash plain west of Cavanaugh Lake. On the west, however, the land rises with more gentle slope to the moraine on the west. Such a trough-like depression between an outwash plain and a moraine has been termed a fosse and it seems logical, therefore, to call a lake situated in such a depression a fosse lake The lake, however, is more true to type along the northern part than near the south end. The east side of the lake is used to some extent for resort purposes and affords good locations This lake has also stood at a higher level but the shore features are not as pronounced as on Cavanaugh

In the extreme southeastern part of the outwash, and also of Jackson County, are located two interesting lakes, Wamplers and Vineyard

WAMPLERS LAKE

Wamplers Lake lies on the line of Jackson and Lenawee counties. It is not on a railroad but near the Chicago Pike and is reached by automobile over good roads. This pleasing body of water extends nearly two miles in an east-west direction but is less than one mile in width. The lake is much visited during the summer months and has a well appointed hotel in addition to numerous cottages. The greater number of buildings are located on the northeast shore and in particular on a split bar of a former level which stands several feet above the present level. This bar developed westward from the high cliff at the east end of the lake, splitting into two separate bars in the vicinity of The Farm. Soon after leaving the cliff it crosses a swale which formerly served as a connection with a small lake basin to the east. An exposed terrace may also be made out in places but this is rapidly being worn away by a revival of wave cutting due to damming of the outlet A complete study of the drainage and shore conditions of this lake should prove interesting The basin lies at the junction of the moraine to the south and outwash on the north but has the characteristics of a pit rather than those of a fosse.

VINEYARD LAKE

Vineyard Lake lies a mile or more west and north of Wamplers Lake and may be reached most conveniently from Brooklyn about three miles distant on the Ypsilanti, Hillsdale Branch of the New York Central Lines. The lake occupies a large, irregular pit in the outwash which has a length of more than two miles and a width in excess of one half mile The principal irregularities are two long bays which extend to the north and to the northwestward The lake is not as attractive as many in the vicinity because of the shallow water near the shore which is covered with a heavy growth of rushes and weeds This condition is due to the partial exposure of a well-developed terrace, which was formed at a higher level. Steep and prominent cliffs face a large part of the shores, indicating strong wave action at the higher level, but most of the quarried material seems to have been carried out by the undertow to form the terrace, inasmuch as no bars were seen in the course of the rapid study made of this lake.

CLARK LAKE

Clark Lake, situated ten miles south of Jackson on the Cincinnati Northern R R. which maintains a station stop at the west end of the lake, is another popular summer resort in southeastern Jackson County. This narrow basin—the lake measures less than one-half mile in width but more than two miles in length—appears to be part of an east-west drainage line which extends eastward from the lake to the Raisin River north of Brooklyn. In the immediate vicinity of the lake the channel is flanked on both sides by patches of moraine which rise above the till plain but to the east runs through outwash. The writer's information as to the depth of the lake is unsatisfactory but indicates relatively shallow water. It is evident, however, that the basin is not true to any one type. Inasmuch as it clearly is not a pit and also is not characteristic of morainic basins, a process of elimination leads to its classification tentatively as a sag in a till plain

The long stretches of high ground along the sides due to the presence of moraine furnish excellent locations for summer cottages and the lake is well populated during the summer months

The east-west orientation of the lake allows the stronger storm winds full sweep of the lake and consequently considerable adjustment of the shores has taken place. This adjustment occurred during a level between two and three feet above the present and the shore features stand a short distance back from the water. These features include forms resulting from the action of waves, currents and ice, the latter two frequently combining in the formation of a single form In particular, the rampart-bar at Pleasant View may be mentioned Well-developed bars encircle the ends of

the lake, that at the east end proving useful in damming the outlet.
Among the more interesting features are the cuspate foreland and
completely enclosed lagoon in the vicinity of Eagle Point

DEVILS AND ROUND LAKES

The moraine which flanks the outwash just discussed on the east
and south is of exceptionally high relief and includes the well
known Irish Hills which lie south of Wamplers Lake. From one
locality in these hills as many as seven lakes may be seen   These
lakes are for the most part too small to be used extensively as
summer resorts and were not studied   Many of the basins, however, are separated by very low land and, furthermore, show some
alignment, suggesting the problem of former drainage conditions,
the solution of which could not be undertaken at this time.

Among the larger lakes of this district are Devils and Round.
These lakes are very popular with summer visitors as may be sur-
mised from the extensive resort at Manitou Beach at the southwestern end of Devils Lake. Round Lake is less than a mile in
diameter and is well named. Devils Lake is considerably larger
than its neighbor, having a maximum length of more than two
miles, but is much more irregular in shape, the outstanding feature
being a narrow arm which extends nearly a mile and one-half to
the northward. The lakes may be reached via the Cincinnati Northern R. R. but the greater number of visitors come in automobiles.

As regards origin these basins may be classed as morainic. That
of Devils Lake appears large for basins of this type   Soundings
may show, however, that the lake floods several basins   This was
the case formerly with this lake and Round. The merging of the
two lakes occurred when the water level stood about four feet
higher than at present and the important adjustments of the shores
took place at this stage   The most consistent feature is the partially exposed terrace which stands at the foot of the numerous
cliffs. Currents also were active and deposited their loads at the
indentations A striking example of this may be seen at the narrow
neck of land which now separates the two lakes   Currents in both
lakes aided in building a strong bar which extended nearly across
the opening and, with the lowering of the water level, divided the
continuous sheet of water into the present Devils and Round Lakes.
This locality serves as an excellent starting point for a physiographic study of these lakes.

BAWBEESE, COLDWATER AND MARBLE LAKES

The lakes visited in Hillsdale and Branch counties are discussed as a group because of the similarity of the origin of the basins. They all lie in channels through which the waters of the melting ice escaped to the south and southwestward. Within these channels tongues of ice of uneven thickness become stagnant and were covered by the deposits of the streams, forming narrow strips of outwash of even surface below the general elevation of the surrounding country. The subsequent melting of the ice caused a settling or pitting of the surface which took the form of channels at a still lower elevation through which the present drainage flows. Due to uneven thickness of the ice tongues these lower channels are ungraded, the deeper parts being filled by the present lakes

One of these channels runs in a southeasterly direction through Hillsdale and forms the setting for a string of five lakes the largest of which is Bawbeese on the outskirts of the town This lake, named after an Indian chief, is very popular locally, the south shore being lined with cottages For a lake of this size, one and one-half miles in length by less than one-half mile in width, the adjustments of the shore are strong These adjustments all took place at a level five feet above the present level and may be accounted for by the sandy character of the material of the outwash which is easily worked. Cliffs are neither frequent nor prominent but, nevertheless, strong bars were built across indentations along the sides, the most prominent standing a short distance back from the present shore along the south side and that connecting Wolff Point on the north shore to the mainland. The outlet of the lake is now dammed and the rejuvenation may best be observed in the rapid cutting at Wolff Point.

About three miles west of Hillsdale a similar channel almost parallels that just discussed. Within this channel are numerous small lakes whose shores show little development but whose basins were formed in the same manner. A third channel runs nearly north-south about one mile east of the line between Hillsdale and Branch counties. Likewise in this channel are numerous lakes, the largest of which are Hamlin and Long, which are too small to show decided adjustments of the shores. The fourth and last of these channels lies in southeastern Branch County and is much wider and less defined as a channel than those just mentioned. The pits are correspondingly larger and less elongated in form but are arranged along the course of the channel Our interest lies in the larger lakes at either end of the string, Marble and Coldwater, the intermediate ones, Long, Mud, Bartholemew and Middle being too small for special consideration.

COLDWATER LAKE

Coldwater Lake is the southern member and also the largest of the chain, having a length of three and a maximum width of one and one-half miles The lake is triangular in shape and contains a large island in the southeastern part A road skirts the east shore for most of its extent and forms an approach for the large number of cottages which have been built on this part of the lake. It is the only lake of the chain whose extensive marl deposits have not been tapped for the manufacture of cement and is therefore the most popular, although an eight mile drive from Coldwater is necessary to reach the lake. This lake probably stood at a higher level formerly but, if so, the drop in level has been not more than two feet, an amount so small that the present high water stage in the spring might well be confused with a definite higher level The shore features are relatively simple. Waves have been very active in forming the steep cliffs. Most of the material carved from the cliffs seems to have been distributed by the undertow rather than by long-shore currents, inasmuch as a well defined submerged terrace lines most of the shore and little evidence of the closing of indentations by bars was found.

MARBLE LAKE

Marble Lake extends three miles south from the edge of the town of Quincy on the Hillsdale-Adrian branch of the Michigan Central R. R. and is therefore easily accessible by rail. This lake, although of practically the same length as Coldwater Lake covers less area on account of its nearly uniform width of slightly more than one-half mile. It is essentially rectangular in shape except for the large embayments at either end The lake has been of considerable economic importance in that its extensive marl deposits have been utilized in the manufacture of Portland cement at the Quincy mill. These deposits are now virtually exhausted in this lake but are being worked in the lakes to the south. The removal of the marl with steam shovels has caused an abrupt drop into deep water, a condition which makes the lake dangerous from the viewpoint of the resorter and has worked to the detriment of the lake. The workable deposits of marl appear to occur off the west shore mainly and consequently the east side of the lake has not suffered from artificial destruction of the shore. In addition, the east shore from Cedar Point southward is favored with one of the best locations for summer cottages the writer has seen, consisting of a flat well above the water and covered with a grove of beautiful oaks. This location has, of course, been "discovered" and numerous cottages line the shore   Here also is found the key to the shore adjustments of the lake   A well defined submerged terrace extends off-shore and slopes outward so gently that a zone of considerable width is exposed during low water.   Great quantities of small shells which have contributed to the formation of the marl may be found on the beach, thrown there by the waves.   An almost continuous cliff lines the shore but breaks at an elevation of five feet above the present level   This cliff with the occurrence of complete bars at the same elevation crossing the occasional indentations is sufficient to establish a former higher level of the lake   The action of currents is best shown at Cedar Point which extended out into the lake as a spit at the higher level.

GOGUAC LAKE

Goguac Lake is located just outside the southwestern limits of Battle Creek.   The street car system of the city has extended its service to the lake which has become a recreational center.   On this account and also the fact that a considerable part of the shore is utilized for a public amusement resort, Willard Park and a golf course and Country Club, the number of private cottages are not as numerous as might be expected.

This small lake lies in a pit which in outline is roughly like an hour glass and is nearly twenty-five feet below the general level of the outwash   The shore is faced by steep cliffs of sandy material broken occasionally by minor indentations.   The adjustments of the shores, therefore, were largely confined to the attack of waves and the accompanying undertow which formed bold cliffs and a well defined submerged terrace.   In places a part of the terrace is exposed at the foot of the cliff, indicating a former level between two and three feet above the present   This is further shown by the exposed bars and spits at the indentations and at the cuspate foreland at Willard Park   In addition to the shore features of the lake, an interesting example of the extinction of a lake by vegetation may be seen on the Willard farm just east of the road leading to Willard Park.

GULL LAKE

Gull Lake is one of the best in the southern part of Michigan.   It is nearly five miles in length and more than one mile in width for most of its extent. It is located about equidistant from Kalamazoo and Battle Creek but some three miles north of the main road between these cities. The popular means of transportation to the lake is by automobile but interurban service is maintained by the Michigan R. R. Co, connecting Grand Rapids as well as the cities mentioned. However, it must not be inferred that the appeal of this lake is limited to the locality for many of its visitors come from far without the State. Cottages are numerous, especially along the east shore, but, in addition, there are a number of imposing estates The popularity of the lake, however, is not due entirely to its fortunate location and large size. Another reason is the excellence of the shores, due in large part to the physiographic developments that have taken place.

This basin is sunk below the surface of the extensive outwash plain which developed in the wide angle between the Michigan and Saginaw lobes when the ice border stood a few miles from the lake. The lake is large for a typical pit but may be included in this class until more detailed studies are made.

One of the first observations to be made at Yorkville which is situated on the outlet is that the lake has been dammed, causing what appears to be a serious flooding of the lake. The flooding of the outlet is clearly in excess of eight feet and it is, therefore, surprising to find the shores of the lake uniformly dry. The explanation is soon found in unmistakable evidence of an abandoned level more than six feet above the present lake at which stage the major adjustments of the shores took place.

The lake furnishes a wealth of material for physiographic study which could not be attempted at the time this work was done and, therefore a brief description of conditions near Midland Park is given as a key to other adjustments. At this locality the broad flat upon which the cottages are built is the exposed terrace of the higher level. It ends abruptly at the foot of a steep cliff, twenty or more feet in height, which marks the former shore line. On the terrace may be found two distinct sand bars which swing northward towards Bryant Point The bar nearer the lake stands at the lower elevation, indicating a halt in the lowering of the lake level.

At present the adjustments are not important. Ice action is perhaps the most effective but prominent ramparts are not found on account of the sandy character of the material on the shore.

CROOKED LAKE, BARRY COUNTY

Of the numerous small lakes which lie in the outwash that developed in the reentrant angle between the Michigan and Saginaw lobes of the glacier only Crooked and Wall lakes were visited by the writer Crooked Lake is located in southwestern Barry County and is reached most conveniently by automobile, although the Chicago, Kalamazoo and Saginaw R R. passes the resort on the northeastern shore.

The lake lies near the apex of the elbow shaped outwash plain and occupies either a single pit of very irregular outline or a number of connected pits which have a striking northeast-southwest orientation.   It has a length of more than four miles but consists of narrow parallel channels and bays separated by islands and peninsulas so that its area is relatively small. Lower Crooked is, in fact, an oblong channel which surrounds a large island and is not only narrow but shallow Little adjustment of the shores has taken place and they are consequently muddy The chief interest in this part of the lake lies in the heavy growth of vegetation which will eventually convert Lower Crooked into a marsh

At the northeastern end, Upper Crooked, the lake expands to more than a mile in dimensions and some adjustment of the shores may be seen at a level nearly five feet above the present beach One of the best localities to observe this higher level is at Stony Point which is a spur of the nearby moraine covered with a thin veneer of outwash material The end of the point is a steep wave-cut cliff from which the material to form the spits on either side was carved. This locality indicates the adjustments that may be expected on other parts of the shore of Upper Crooked. In addition to the development of the shores considerable filling by vegetation has been accomplished and is especially evident on the numerous shoals or "blind islands".

WALL LAKE

Wall Lake is located two miles northeast of Crooked in the very apex of the outwash plain which developed in the reentrant between the Michigan and Saginaw lobes. The north shore is bounded for the most of its extent by moraine but from the opposite side outwash stretches southward for miles. The basin was caused by the melting of buried ice and is, therefore, classed as a pit

This small lake has a length of less than one and one-half miles and a width of somewhat more than one-half mile but is interesting nevertheless. In contrast to Crooked Lake its shores are broken by a single long peninsula and it is deep, so that the waves have an un-obstructed sweep Many adjustments of the shores, therefore, may be observed and those on the north shore are selected as typical.

The most striking adjustments in this locality are the steep cliffs at the headlands, the perfect bar which rises fully five feet above the present water level and is responsible for the name of the lake, and the decided off-shore terrace. In addition, strong ice ram-parts were noted along the west side. This almost perfect adjust-ment means excellent shore conditions for resort purposes and the lake is deservedly popular during the summer months

AUSTIN GROUP

AUSTIN, LONG, WEST (PIKE) AND GOURD NECK LAKES

This group of lakes lies some seven miles directly south of Kala-mazoo on the Grand Rapids and Indiana R. R. trains of which stop at Austin Lake The lakes are discussed as a group because they all occupy pits in the outwash plain first mentioned in the account of Gull Lake Furthermore they all drain southward through the Portage River into the St. Joseph and were once connected, with the possible exception of Gourd Neck, during a former swollen condi-tion of the drainage which appears to have been general in the State.

Austin Lake is the central member of the group and has a length of two and one-half miles and a maximum width of slightly more than one mile. It is very shallow a fact which evidently has effec-tively hindered wave action for there are few shore adjustments to be found The lake has been artificially lowered and as a result a broad sand flat is exposed along the shore The flat is covered with reeds which with other water plants are encroaching on the shallow lake The lake is popular as a fishing ground but the cot-tages are built on the neighboring lakes which have more attractive shores

West, or Pike Lake, lies a few rods directly west of Austin and is nearly circular in form, the largest diameter being somewhat more than one mile. The sudden darkening in color of the water off shore gives the impression of a deep lake and a decided sub-merged terrace Such is not the case, the effect being produced by the change from sand to mud which marks, nevertheless, the limit of effective wave action. The shallowness of the water has not interfered with the wave action as on Austin and decided ad-justments of the shore are to be found. An excellent and conven-ient starting point for the study of these features is the resort at the east end where the land between this lake and Austin rises but slightly above lake level The most decided feature is the strong sand bar at an elevation of about four feet above the lake which crosses the flat between the lakes and shows that the lakes were connected during a higher stage and that later West Lake became an independent basin This part of the lake is the most popular and the bar, although obscured somewhat by cottages, is, neverthe- less, easily recognized Similar adjustments are to be expected on other parts of the shore but probably are not as well developed inasmuch as the east shore is exposed to the strongest winds

LONG LAKE

Long Lake is situated a short distance to the northeast of Austin into which it drains across a flat so low that it must have been flooded at the earlier stage indicated on West Lake. In this case no bar crossed the flat and the separation of the lakes must have been caused by the lowering of the water level. Elsewhere along the shore no evidence of current action was found but sharp cliffs indicate work by waves. This, however, was not great inasmuch as both bars and submerged terrace are lacking The lack of these features has not proved a deterrent influence on its use as a sum- mer resort as shown by the resorts on the south and southwest shores.

DIAMOND LAKE

The last lake in Group I to be considered is Diamond Lake. It is located just east of the limits of Cassopolis which is the junction point of the Grand Trunk and Air Line Division of the Michigan Central so that no difficulty need be encountered in reaching the lake. The lake is attractive and of good size for this section of the State, its dimensions being two and one-half miles in length and more than a mile in width Many cottages and costly summer homes have been built along the shores near Cassopolis and on the island

From the physiographic viewpoint the lake is of little interest except as to the type of basin which is one of the numerous pits which break the surface of the outwash plain The level of the lake is high due to the obstruction of the outlet by a dam at Browns- ville and, although the shores are not badly flooded, the waves are gradually wearing back the banks and undermining trees

CHAPTER X

LAKES OF THE VALPARAISO-CHARLOTTE MORAINIC AND
· OUTWASH SYSTEM

In Group II are included the lakes which lie in the area between
the Kalamazoo morainic system, 2, Fig 3, and the Valparaiso-
Charlotte morainic system of Southern Michigan, 3, Fig. 3   It will
be noted from the figure that both the eastern and western interlobate areas became greatly accentuated as the ice shrank back to
the position indicated by the Valparaiso-Charlotte moraine during
which stage they existed as narrow valleys with ice walls.   The
western interlobate was much more pronounced, extending from
the vicinity of Grand Rapids northward beyond Cadillac, a distance
of nearly one hundred miles, as compared with less than half that
distance for its eastern counterpart.   Both, however, are made up
of a patch-work of deposits which is characteristic of such locations.
Between the two interlobates the formations are much more regular
and have an east-west trend.

WALLED LAKE, OAKLAND COUNTY

This lake is roughly triangular in shape and has a length of one
and one-half miles and a maximum width of somewhat more than
one mile   Its shores are regular in outline with the exception of
one long point on the northwest shore, thus the sweep of the waves
is unobstructed   The lake lies for the most part in a morainic
depression but at the south end overflows on the till plain which
spreads southward from the lake   A road circles the lake and follows the shore on all but a part of the west side so that the shores
are readily accessible   As to train service, the Jackson Branch of
the Grand Trunk runs within one-half mile of the north end and
the Detroit-Saginaw Line of the Pere Marquette has a stop at
Wixom, three miles west of the lake.

For physiographic study the west shore is the best, although
sharp cliffs and an exposed terrace are present on the east side
The sharp point on the west side is a spit which may be followed
without difficulty southward for nearly a half mile.   Soon after
leaving the point one notes that the bar takes on the characteristics
of an ice rampart or wall which is so distinctive as to give the lake

its name   The absence of bars at other points on the shore where they might be expected leads to the conclusion that ice push has been the dominant force active on the shores   The lake is very popular as a summer resort and nearly all the available frontage on the west, east and southeast has been built upon

WHITMORE LAKE

Whitmore is another of the popular lakes of this group. It is located ten miles north of Ann Arbor on the boundary between Washtenaw and Livingston counties. Trains of the Ann Arbor R. R stop at the south end, but with the improvement of the roads the automobile is the more popular means of reaching the lake.

The lake lies in a region of complicated glacial deposits and many interesting features of this type as well as shore features may be seen   The high hills at the north end are kames. On the east a strip of outwash borders the lake but gives way to ground moraine which extends to the south end of the lake. The south side consists of a flat outwash plain, on the west of which lies a narrow stretch of ground moraine followed by a moraine of low relief along the greater part of the west side   The lake has neither outlet nor inlets and for most of its extent the shore is bounded by banks which are of moderate height but steep for unconsolidated material. The basin appears to be a pit formed by a rather large block of ice of irregular thickness buried by outwash which developed from the southward   The outwash is a broad channel which carried the water escaping from the ice when the front of the glacier stood a short distance northwest of Ann Arbor.

As to the shore features, the chief interest lies in a higher level of the lake during which the water discharged through an outlet at the southeastern part. After leaving the lake the former outlet turns abruptly to the north and extends to the Huron valley. The development of the shores at the higher level was exceptional for a lake of this size and resulted not only from the activity of waves and currents but of ice as well. The best locality for study is along the northwestern shore where excellent examples of cliffs, spits, bars and ice ramparts may be found. At present the encroachment of vegetation is beginning in parts of the basin and is progressing rapidly on the spit-like form extending out from the south shore of the lake

HURON RIVER GROUP

PORTAGE, BASE LINE, STRAWBERRY, ZUKEY, ETC.

The lakes included in this group are located in the valley of the Huron River southwest of Lakeland, situated at the junction of the Ann Arbor R. R and the Jackson Branch of the Grand Trunk R. R They all occupy parts of an elongated pit that extends in a northeast-southwest direction from Lakeland to Portage Lake. This pit was formed by the burial of an ice mass of very irregular outline and thickness in a former drainage channel through which the water from the glacier escaped in a northwesterly direction beyond Pinckney and thence to the southwest towards Jackson The subsequent melting of the ice left a depression below the level of the outwash, which conformed in general outline to the ice mass and also contained a number of deeper basins which contain the present lakes.

The several lakes of the group are not discussed independently because the adjustment of the present shores is insignificant and also because a higher level was found at an elevation sufficient to have merged all into one large lake having numerous bays, peninsulas and islands The principal indication of this stage is the gently sloping flat which extends from the lake shores back to the sharp cliffs and is interpreted as an exposed terrace. In addition, bars which swing out from steep cliffs were found Thus, the study of the former shore will give the best results. Some of the most interesting localities are the sand point on the east side of Portage Lake north of the cottages, the north shore of Base Lake near the outlet, and the great bar which swings southwestward from the cliff on the southeast side of Bass Lake

These lakes are used extensively as summer resorts, the most popular being the pairs, Portage-Base and Zukey-Strawberry, located at the ends of the chain

DUCK LAKE

Duck Lake is located in northeast Calhoun County almost equidistant from Albion, Charlotte and Eaton Rapids, from which cities it draws many summer visitors. The nearest railroad stop is Springport on the Hillsdale-Lansing Branch of the New York Central, but good roads have made the automobile the principal means of reaching the lake. This small lake of one and one-half miles in length and somewhat more than one-half mile in width lies for the

43

most of its extent on a till plain, the land rising to the moraine
at the south end The basin is, in general, shallow and has, furthermore, numerous shoals Thus, it may be considered as one of the
larger sags in the till plain modified by minor sags and swells

The material of the shores is compact till except for the sandy
morainic material on the south end; and consequently the attack
of the waves has been slight. The adjustments have taken place
at a level four feet above the present stage and are found at either
end and the east side At the south end clean sand beaches indicate
an assorting of the material by the waves; and a fairly well defined submerged terrace is the result of the accompanying undertow.

At Charlotte Resort a strong bar crosses the mouth of a former
bay and at the north end there is the possibility of a similar form,
obscured by the road. Waves and currents have had little force on
the west shore as shown by the presence of marl beds. The ramparts on this shore, however, show a powerful shove by ice. A heavy
growth of rushes on the offshore terrace indicates the beginning, at
least, of the extinction process by vegetation.

CHIPPEWA LAKE

A number of small lakes are situated in the large morainic tract
of north-central Mecosta County, and Chippewa Lake, which lies
twelve miles east and north of Big Rapids, was selected as representative of these lakes There are no rail connections but a good
road from Big Rapids insures a comfortable trip by automobile
or other conveyance.

Except for a narrow strip of outwash at the north end, the lake
lies in a very sandy moraine of strong relief The knobs and basins
of the surrounding land have counterparts in the shoals and deep
holes of the lake bottom so that the lake is typical of those which
flood several adjacent morainic basins

The slopes to the lake are a series of cliffs and flats, thus furnishing numerous possibilities for adjustments which were readily carried on in the sandy material but at a level nearly five feet above
the present lake In addition to the steep, wave-cut cliffs, the work
of currents at the entrances to bays is noticeable. Many of the
smaller indentations of the original lake were completely cut off
by bars which have been remodeled into ice ramparts in some
cases However, at the larger bays spits are found An interesting
example of this was noted along the southwest end of the lake
where the road follows the spits which developed from each side
of the large bay, now nearly dry. Along the outwash at the north

end the terrace of the higher level is well exposed and is from two hundred to three hundred feet wide. Another of the many interesting features is the land-tied island of the former level on the east shore   This lake has exceptionally interesting physiographic features which, together with the sinking of the water level, account for the present rather regular outline of the lake   It is becoming a very popular summer resort, the more favored locations being the village of Chippewa Lake, the north shore, and the land-tied island with connecting bar.

HESS LAKE

Hess Lake lies about two miles southwest of Newaygo, located on the Grand Rapids-Petoskey Branch of the Pere Marquette R. R. This lake has a length of nearly one and one-half miles and a rather consistent width of about three-fourths of a mile.   The shores are regular in outline on all but the south side, which is broken by a number of bays and promontories   The lake is shallow —it probably does not exceed thirty-five feet in depth—and is surrounded by outwash except at the southwestern shore   It is, therefore, classed as a pit.

From the study of this lake it is apparent that the northerly and easterly winds have not been effective in the adjustment of the shores   The irregular south shore consists of headlands, which show few effects of wave action, and mucky bays, sparsely grown up to lily pads   The power of the westerly winds, however, is well shown on the north shore. As usual the adjustments were found between three or four feet above the present level and bars first appear near the middle of the north shore. The bars increase in strength towards the east end where former bays have been completely cut off   Ice action is also powerful and ramparts of sand, bound by the roots of trees, were noticed. The north shore of the lake is a popular summer resort and, due to the favorable shore conditions and its accessibility, is almost completely lined with cottages. The south shore is reached by a roundabout route over sand roads, and but one location, a camping ground, was found.

REED LAKE

The location of Reed Lake within the city limits of East Grand Rapids accounts for the great popularity of this small lake of but slightly more than a mile in length and less than a half mile in width   It lies in a morainic basin that is irregular both as to depth and outline   The shore is generally well drained except

about the muddy bay at the east end. As a recreational center
the lake is interesting but as an illustration of physiographic developments little can be said. The shore agents working in hard
till accomplish little on a lake of this size and the adjustments of
the shore are few and simple. Waves have succeeded in steepening
the banks and forming a moderate off-shore terrace, a part of
which is now exposed due to a drop of at least three feet in the
water level Bars are found only at the smaller indentations and
stand back of the present shore. One example of a bar completely
enclosing a small bay was found in the vicinity of Pierce's Landing.
A heavy growth of vegetation both in the lake and on the shore
indicates the initiation of the extinction process.

MINER LAKE

Miner Lake is a small lake one and one-half miles in length and
less than a mile in width but is, nevertheless, one of the larger
lakes of Allegan County. It is located about three miles northeast
of Allegan and lies in an irregular depression of a till plain near
its junction with the moraine As is usually the case for small
lakes whose banks are till, the adjustments of the shore are not
far advanced Inasmuch as there has been a lowering of the level
of the lake, the adjustments are now beyond the reach of the waves
and have virtually ceased to develop.

Furthermore, vegetation has taken hold and extinction appears
to be the next step. Aside from wave cut cliffs and a partially
exposed offshore terrace little of interest was noted. The lake is
not popular as a summer resort but is frequented mainly by fishermen.

PAW PAW LAKE

Paw Paw Lake lies within two miles of the northern border of
Berrien County, within a mile of the towns of Coloma and Water-
vliet and six miles west of Hartford. These towns are all located
on the Chicago-Grand Rapids Branch of the Pere Marquette. The
lake may also be reached directly by interurban from Benton
Harbor In addition, the main roads are excellent.

The total length of the lake is two and one-half miles but its
width is but slightly more than a half mile, the elongation being
nearly east-west The chief irregularities are bays at the southwest
and northeast ends, the latter being set off from the main lake by
two distinct peninsulas. The peninsula on the east side and the
east shore of the lake near the outlet are the favored locations for

summer homes which line the shore even though the shore conditions are not uniformly good.

The lake lies on a till plain but is not typical of such lakes in that it is reported to be one hundred feet deep The banks slope gently to the shore on the north side but on the south rise more abruptly from the lake, due possibly to a general rise in the till plain towards the moraine whose border stands about one mile to the south.

The lack of the adjustments of the shores is very noticeable considering the size of the lake and may be accounted for in part by the fineness and compactness of the till of which the shores are composed. The features found were all at a higher level and consisted mainly of sharp cliffs and an exposed terrace fronting the elevations One small spit was noticed at the west end but none were seen at the other favorable localities, such as the peninsula at the east end which was an island at the higher level.

In recent times wave action has been renewed and is actively cutting back the shores wherever the vegetation has been removed Such a condition suggests an obstruction in the outlet, in this case a dam four miles down the outlet.

This lake is a good example of the service of a lake as a reservoir for during the spring floods the Paw Paw River backs into the lake, causing exceptionally high water and the flooding of some of the low ground upon which cottages unwisely have been built.

CORA LAKE

That part of the surface of the outwash plain extending southwestward through Paw Paw in Van Buren County and drained by Dowagiac Creek which was not covered by glacial Lake Dowagiac is dotted with numerous small pits A number of these pits hold water and are very typical of this kind of basin, having in many cases no outlets and insignificant inlets.

A group of lakes of this type is located some six miles southwest of Paw Paw and of these Cora, Three Mile, Little and Big Reynolds and Eagle lakes were visited. Conditions are so similar in these lakes that the brief description of Lake Cora will serve as a key to the many interesting examples of shore adjustments that may be found on all of them.

This lake may be reached via the Kalamazoo, Lake Shore and Chicago R. R. which stops at the summer resort on the north side, although the automobile is proving a more popular means of reaching Cora Lake on account of the excellent roads. The resort, consisting of a commodious hotel and a number of cottages, is an indication of the popularity this small lake has enjoyed. The basin of the lake consists of a main pit surrounded by numerous smaller connecting pits, making a rather irregular depression. Yet the shores are of exceptionally even contour, the greatest break being Paradise Point, and the disparity may be accounted for by the shore adjustments that have taken place. This lake which has no outlet has varied in level within recent times and now stands low. It has stood between three or four feet higher and at this level the adjustment of the shore occurred. The change in color off-shore indicates a well defined terrace, the upper part of which is now exposed as a sand flat. At the higher ground steep and prom-inent cliffs rise from the terrace, and at the indentations completed bars are found in virtually all cases. Paradise Point is of sufficient interest to warrant special mention for short bars have tied a former island to the mainland. As stated earlier, similar condi-tions hold for the other lakes of this group and their study should prove interesting.

SISTER LAKES

Another group of pit lakes in the outwash drained by Dowagiac Creek, including the Sister Lakes (Round and Crooked), Dewey and Magician lakes, was visited by the writer. They are located five to six miles northwest of Dowagiac on the northern boundary of Cass County and have no direct railroad connections. These lakes, which are classed as pits, stand near the edge of the moraine to the west and are sunk well below the surface of the thin veneer of outwash, so that till is frequently exposed on the shores. Further-more, the pits are so numerous that the outwash in places has a hill and depression topography very similar to the morainic knobs and basins. Since the moraine is very sandy, these two types of topography are best differentiated from the hill tops which rise to approximately the same elevation within the outwash but are of variable height in the moraine.

Considerable variation is found as to shore features on the different lakes of the group. Crooked, Round and Dewey are similar in development but Magician presents a decided contrast.

The latter is very irregular in form, having many bays and points and some islands. Strong wave action is possible only on the headlands and islands, and currents have little chance to de-velop on the irregular shores. Consequently the adjustments are limited to wave cutting in favorable localities and consist of sharp cliffs and an off-shore terrace. The outer edge of the terrace now appears as a flat at the foot of the cliffs, due to a lowering of the water level.

The lake is very attractive from the scenic viewpoint and numerous cottages line the shore

The remaining lakes of the group, Crooked, Round and Dewey, are very similar, except in form, and present a contrast to Magician in that the adjustment of the shores by both waves and currents is very decided   They have all stood at a level tour to five feet higher than at present and are, therefore, fringed by a broad sand flat   Improved roads lead to almost all parts of the lakes and they are, consequently, developing as summer resorts.

Among the more interesting features are the very noticeable cliffs fronting the high ground   Considerable recession of the cliffs has taken place, and a sharp off-shore terrace is of general occurrence. In addition, strong currents built bars across the mouths of indentations and spits at some of the points. Thus, on Crooked Lake a completely enclosed lagoon was found at the east end of the lake. Also the first point on the south side has been increased in length by a spit, and at the west end a bar may be made out, although very much obscured by the road, which indicates a probable connection between Round and Crooked lakes

On Dewey Lake the most interesting developments have occurred at the east end which leads into a marsh nearly as large as the lake. This marsh was formerly a shallow arm of the lake connected by a narrow but deep channel   Spits started at the higher level on each side of the channel and succeeded in closing about one half of the gap. The marsh is a good example of almost complete extinction by vegetation which obtained an early start in this shallow part of the lake

INDIAN LAKE

Indian Lake is located in the northwestern part of Cass County just off the western boundary line   It lies nearly six miles west of Dowagiac and the roads leading to it are improved   From the geological standpoint it is located on an outwash plain within a short distance of a moraine which skirts the west side of the lake. It is, thus, a pit but a large one for the lake is nearly two miles in length by almost a mile in width and is regular in outline   The regularity of the shore is due in large part to the adjustments of the shore which are numerous and interesting   They were accomplished at a level some three feet higher than the present and on the sides of the lake show a close correspondence to the strength and frequency of the winds.

On the east side the waves have formed bold cliffs and sand beaches, and currents have thrown complete bars across the embayments On the opposite side, however, the cliffs are less steep, the beaches muddy and the bars with a single exception conspicuous by their absence This is a spit which developed southward across the entrance to a large huckleberry swamp and probably did not rise above the former level for much of its extent. This contrast, which is emphasized by the encroachment of vegetation at the more protected places on the west side, shows clearly the greater effectiveness of the westerly winds

At the ends of the lake the topography of the shores is very dissimilar, and the more pronounced effects have been produced at the north end under the drive of southerly winds, although the spit noted on the west side indicated stronger northerly winds. Thus, the land at the north end is low with the exception of the island-like hills at Highland from which complete bars swing in either direction around the head of the lake and cut off a broad swamp At the south end, however, the land is higher and cliffs predominate.

With these general considerations the specific features may be left to those interested to work out. As a final consideration attention may be called to the geographic relationship between the physiographic development of the shores and the settlement of all but the west shore of this very popular lake. .

CHAPTER XI

LAKES OF THE PORT HURON MORAINIC AND OUTWASH SYSTEM

The lakes included in this group are located within the Port Huron morainic system, 4, Fig. 3, and in the area between this system and the Valparaiso-Charlotte moraine, 3, Fig 3. In general, the glacial deposits of this area are irregular in distribution with the exception of two areas. The lake plains of the southeastern part of the State and the regular series of formations which mark the retirement of the Saginaw lobe. In the latter of these areas the lakes are few in number and relatively unimportant and in the Erie plains they are almost entirely absent. The one lake of the Erie lowland (Ottawa) seen by the writer is little more than a mud hole, a large part of which dries up during the summer, and is interesting only as an example of a lake located in a sink. There are also no lakes of importance in this section of the eastern interlobate area, which extends well into the "Thumb" region. Therefore, the lakes in this group are located in the north central and western parts of the Southern Peninsula but do not include the lagoons along the west coast which are discussed in the following chapter.

CRYSTAL LAKE, MONTCALM COUNTY

Crystal Lake lies seven miles south of west of Stanton in eastern Montcalm County and may be reached by a drive of about ten miles over roads that were found in excellent condition It is one of the few popular lakes which are located in the regular series of deposits of the Saginaw lobe

The glacial formations have a north-south trend in this locality and the lake lies in an irregular morainic depression that originally consisted of several basins. This depression is situated on the edge of a sandy moraine which gives way to a till plain just east of the lake. The easily eroded material, the irregular outline of the lake, and the succession of hills and swales at the shore made favorable conditions for the numerous adjustments found on all the shores except the north, in which locality the lakeward slopes are uniformly gentle. At the uplands sharp cliffs show cutting by the waves, at the swales bars, usually complete, indicate the activity of currents, and on the gentle slopes ramparts signify shove by the ice.

In addition, the shore adjustments enable one to decipher an interesting series of events in the physiographic history of this lake. The most favorable locality for this study is along the southwest shore where a former bay has been cut off by a series of bars and rampart-bars. The highest is a large sand bar which stands fully six feet above the present level of the lake. Between this bar and the lake are two distinct rampart bars at intermediate elevations which mark halts in the lowering of the lake to its present level. This locality requires careful study but, once solved, will simplify further study of the shores.

The most significant adjustment was the closing of the mouths of embayments by bars which, with the lowering of the water level, reduced the original area of the lake by at least one-half. In this connection the spit which developed along the northeast shore on the flat between Crystal and Mud lakes may be mentioned.

COLDWATER LAKE, ISABELLA COUNTY

Coldwater Lake is ten miles northwest of Mt Pleasant in west central Isabella County, but a drive of fourteen miles from this city is necessary to reach the lake. The lake rests in a pit in a narrow strip of outwash, which fronts a moraine to the eastward and was formed by border drainage, that is drainage running parallel to the ice front. The pit is located so close to the moraine that the southeastern shore is composed of the till of this formation. The relief along this shore, therefore, is great and presents a decided contrast to the surface of the outwash which rises barely more than ten feet above the level of the lake.

The adjustments are slight indeed along the shores bounded by outwash although many lakes similar in size—the length is approximately one mile and the width one-half mile—have decided shore features. The cliffs on the east shore show some wave action, but the southeastern shore, where the uneven morainic topography furnished more favorable conditions for adjustments, is the most interesting. In particular, may be mentioned the large amphitheatre which opens into the lake. Two well developed spits, which stand at elevations of three and five feet above the present level, swing out into the opening in parallel courses from the south shore and show that this indentation would have been cut off eventually, if their development had not been stopped by a lowering of the water level

It is evident from the spits just mentioned that the lake has stood at two higher levels but the presence of an old dam on the outlet a few rods from the lake makes uncertain the relationship between at least one of the spits and a natural level of the lake. The level of the lake when the dam was operative and the length of time that this level was maintained was not learned, and it is possible, then, merely to make the suggestion that the lower and weaker spit was formed at this artificial stage

Aside from the shore features at the southeast end, the lake furnishes an example of the partial filling by marl, formed in part of the minute shells that are abundant on the beach.

MISSAUKEE LAKE

Missaukee Lake is the largest of a group of ten or more lakes which are located in west central Missaukee County. It may be reached via the Lake City Branch of the Grand Rapids and Indiana R. R. which stops at Lake City on the east shore of the lake.

All of these lakes lie in pits in an outwash plain and of these the Missaukee Lake depression is by far the largest; it is nearly circular with a diameter of somewhat less than two and one-half miles The lakes either have no outlets or drain eventually into Missaukee, the southeastern member of this group Inasmuch as the drainage of the region in general is to the southeast, Missaukee Lake occupies the key position and it has no natural outlet, the artificial channel operating only at infrequent periods of exceptionally high water. The Missaukee Lake depression, although it contains the deep holes characteristic of pits, is nevertheless, very shallow The writer's information is that the general depth of water is approximately fifteen feet, and, inasmuch as the surface of the lake stands about ten feet below the surface of the outwash, the total depth is twenty-five feet. The shallowness of the water must hinder the development of the larger waves but, nevertheless adjustments of the shore have taken place, due probably to the ease with which the outwash material is worked.

The adjustments are found above the present surface of the lake and indicate the usual higher level in past time. Along the south and east shores the depression has regular walls, and an almost unbroken, wave-steepened cliff faces the lake. At the foot of the cliffs there is now exposed a broad sand flat which continues beneath the water to a decided "drop-off" wherever the water is deep, as at the east end. The effects of current action are best seen along the very irregular north shore and are too numerous for specific mention in this brief report. Before leaving Lake City a well developed bar may be seen, and along the north shore examples of exposed spits, bars enclosing lagoons, and land-tied islands are numerous The north shore bars are distinct but stand at a lower elevation than that at Lake City which is interpreted as an indication that these forms were in process of formation when the lake level subsided

The extinction of former embayments by draining and vegetal accumulation is another interesting phase of a physiographic study of this lake, the details of which should prove to be well worth while.

The lake has not kept pace with many others as a summer resort but has qualifications which are superior to some of the more popular, including good fishing and favorable shore conditions on the south side.

MANISTEE LAKE

Manistee Lake is in northeastern Kalkaska County and may be reached from the town of Kalkaska on the Grand Rapids and Indiana and the Pere Marquette railroads A drive of ten miles is necessary but the writer found the road good with the exception of the last mile

This lake is located on the southwestern extension of the interlobate area between the Michigan and Huron lobes which joined at approximately right angles in the vicinity of Gaylord The formations involved are a moraine, the Port Huron, and a rather broad strip of outwash lying to the southeast. The lake lies on the outwash at the junction of these two formations. It is the largest lake in the region, having a length of two miles and a width that averages nearly a mile. The basin is regular in contour but varies most on the west side, due possibly to the influence of the moraine whose border runs not far from this shore The basin forms a part of a broad drainage channel which is followed by the Manistee River to the southwest. Either the outwash is excessively pitted near the lake or the basin is not a pit, for the slopes quite generally rise gently from the lake Whatever the origin of the basin may be, a small amount of material was furnished by wave action but this was distributed to such advantage that pronounced changes were effected. Thus, at a higher level the waves cut a broad terrace on the east shore and the material was worked southward into a strong sand bar which crosses the lowland at the south end as far as the outlet On the opposite side of the outlet the material derived from the short stretch of low shore was carried in both directions and deposited in small spits near the outlet and on the south side of the entrance to an embayment to the northwest. Other adjustments were found on the west shore including well defined ice ramparts where conditions are favorable for their formation. The lake is not popular as a summer resort so far, as there are no cottages but it is visited by fishermen and campers who can get boats at the south end.

BIG STAR LAKE

Big Star Lake is located in the southwestern part of Lake County and has an area of about two square miles. Its length is more than two and one-half miles but its outline is so irregular that the width varies from less than one-fourth mile to more than one mile. It is not so popular as similar lakes nearer Lake Michigan but, nevertheless, is an attractive lake which should develop as a summer resort in the future The nearest railroad stop is Baldwin on two lines of the Pere Marquette system, eight miles distant by road. The writer found the road from Baldwin to the lake in good condition and advises this route for those unfamiliar with the winding sand roads of the jack pine and grub oak plains

The nature of the Star Lake depression is very easily recognized for one may almost fall from the edge of a most monotonous sand plain to the lake shore, so sharp are the bluffs which surround the lake. It is clearly a pit but is large and much more irregular than the present crooked outline of the lake. This disparity between the outline of the pit and the lake is due to the adjustments of the shores at a higher level, the greatest changes having been caused by the deposition of bars across the mouths of bays. Such adjustments are best defined on the south side and are well illustrated along the southwest shore where a bar completely closes a narrow lagoon. Similar forms, but not complete at the larger embayments, may be found on the south shore The source of the material of these bars is the numerous sand cliffs which rise nearly twenty feet above the lake. Apparently a small amount of recession of the cliffs was sufficient to supply the material inasmuch as the off-shore terrace, although well defined, is narrow, and the strip exposed by the recession of the water has been removed from the foot of the cliffs.

The north shore consists of broad bays and headlands, and currents have developed along the shores of the bays rather than across the entrances, eventually dissipating in the lake off the ends of the points. Thus the changes in the outline on this shore are less striking than on the south side.

Fremont Lake is situated on the southern edge of Fremont in southwestern Newaygo County, the city limits extending to include a park on the north shore of the lake   The town is located on the Muskegon-Big Rapids Line of the Pere Marquette R R , and the lake is not an unreasonably long walk from the station.

The basin lies at the border between outwash and till plain and is rather difficult to classify as to type   The till plain borders the north and east sides of the lake, the remainder of the shores consisting of the sands of the outwash   Also the eastern part of the basin is shallow, a characteristic of lakes in the sags of till plains, but the western part is deep   Thus, it appears that we have here a pit which is open to the east and that the water is sufficient in amount to fill not only this pit but also flood an adjoining depression of the till plain to the east

The basin is very regular in outline and consequently very few adjustments by shore currents are to be found   The two bars noted stand at an elevation which denotes a former level of the lake about three feet above the present surface   One, a very indistinct spit, runs northwestward on the low flat at the southwestern part of the lake, and the second, also a spit but much better developed, extends from the bluff on the west side of the outlet to the stream channel. A much greater adjustment resulted from the action of waves and undertow and consists of numerous cliffs but more especially a decided submerged terrace. The terrace is uniformly present but varies in width, being greater along the shores bordered by outwash. The outer part of this terrace is exposed by the sinking of the water level, forming a sand flat which has a width of more than one hundred feet in places on the south shore   Ice shove is also effective as shown by the decided ramparts in the vicinity of the outlet. In some places as many as four ramparts were found, giving the impression of an ice-shove terrace although it is probable that such is not the case.

Another interesting feature is the delta which is the site of the park on the north shore   This delta consists of the silt deposited by the stream which enters at this point and was built at the higher level   The stream now carries a different type of load, consisting of the refuse of the canning factory and tannery which makes a very unpleasant condition of the shore.

BIG BLUE LAKE

Big Blue Lake is in the northeast corner of Muskegon County and may be best reached from Whitehall on the Pere Marquette R. R. One may go in from Twin Lakes or Holton, but, in any case, the roads are not good for automobile traffic at the present time. They are sand roads which offer difficulties even to those who are familiar with their peculiarities. A favorite description of such roads is parallel snake tracks through second growth woods, which means constant attention to the steering of the machine in order to avoid getting out of the tracks and striking trees or stumps. Also the sand becomes loose in dry weather and the traction is very heavy making it almost impossible for heavy machines to "plow through." Frequently, the familiar north-south, east-west system of roads is sadly lacking, and numerous branch roads offer opportunities to stray, none too pleasant an experience for most people in such thinly settled areas. The writer suggests the road from Whitehall.

It is obvious from the foregoing statements that Big Blue Lake, although within ten miles of a railroad, is not readily accessible at the present time. Yet it is a very attractive lake and is frequented by those who desire a complete change from the formalities of city life. The visitors come almost entirely from the vicinity of Chicago and have built a number of cottages which are grouped at the east end and at two localities on the north shore.

The lake measures nearly two miles in length by about three quarters of a mile in greatest width and lies in a deep pit in an outwash plain. In addition to the main depression, small pits are so numerous that the lake shores have a rolling topography, and the varied shore conditions made possible numerous adjustments which have been readily accomplished in the loose sand. These changes occurred at a level five feet above the present and are so numerous that mention of each feature would entail a description of almost the entire shore of the lake. The bluffs have been steepened by wave action and drop to a narrow exposed terrace which frequently continues under water to a "drop-off". At the embayments the bars, which rise well above the present level, are so well developed that it is possible to follow the shore around the lake dry shod except at the small brook which drains the lake. In addition to the work of waves and currents evidence of strong ice push may be found. This is the only noticeable adjustment which is taking place under present conditions.

TWIN LAKES .

Under this heading are four small lakes which are located about
ten miles northeast of Muskegon on the Muskegon-Big Rapids Line
of the Pere Marquette R. R. They are now known as East, Middle,
North and West lakes All of these lakes lie in shallow pits in
the same outwash plain as Big Blue Lake, six miles to the north.
None of the lakes has an area of one-half square mile but, inasmuch as they are connected, the group may be considered as one.
The water level now stands about ten feet only below the outwash surface. The lakes have no surface outlet and consequently
the water level varies over periods of years, the highest level as
recorded by the shore features having been three feet above the
present or about seven feet below the plain Thus, at that time
the waves were able to accomplish much without the removal of
an excessive amount of material and as a result there is present
an off-shore terrace that appears out of proportion for a lake of
this size A part of the material quarried by the waves was distributed along the shores also and formed a number of distinct
bars. One of the best localities to observe these is on the north
shore at the connection between East and Middle lakes. The bars
on Middle Lake are stronger than those on East, one in particular
nearly crossing the lowland connecting the two lakes. Also in the
same vicinity an island was tied to the mainland of Middle Lake.
Two spits extend out from the south end of this island and show
clearly the difference in activity of the currents in the two lakes at
this point. The larger spit developed in Middle Lake, due to the
greater power of the westerly winds. Another interesting example
of the development of a spit occurs at the east end of North Lake
where a broad arm of this lake was nearly isolated and has since become a marsh. Other similar features may be found on the shores of
these lakes, and their discovery may be left to those interested.
The lakes are connected with Muskegon by an improved road in
addition to the railroad and are popular summer resorts. A camp
ing ground and boat livery are located at the east end of East Lake
but the majority of the summer inhabitants own cottages many of
which are much more pretentious than the usual summer resort
cottage.

WOLF LAKE

Wolf Lake is six miles east of the city limits of Muskegon and
within one-fourth mile of the main road between Muskegon and
Grand Rapids Auto bus service to the lake is maintained in sum-

mer so that no difficulty need be experienced in reaching it The ride, however, is most monotonous for one travels over a sand plain so flat that even a slight variation in the surface claims the attention, and the variations are few indeed. Once there, the lake comes into view abruptly and is recognized at once as a pit for the sand plain near the lake is outwash and steep bluffs rise consistently from the water to a height of about twenty-five feet on all sides

The regular outline of the lake as shown on the map is misleading as far as the original basin is concerned for there are small embayments on all but the south side This change in outline is due to the natural development of shores which occurred when the lake stood nearly five feet higher than at present The lowering of the water exposed the former shore and, thus, facilitated the study of its features Inasmuch as the lake has no outlet, the drop in level is an indication of a climatic change, the significance of which is not as yet clear.

On a lake the size of Wolf,—less than one square mile in area and with a greatest diameter of less than a mile,—the waves and currents are comparatively feeble, but the high bluffs of loose sand were easily eroded, thus furnishing abundant material without seriously reducing the power of waves or currents Consequently, the bluffs, although steepened, have not receded to any great extent and there is no decided off-shore terrace. The work of the shore currents, however, is much more noticeable in that a relatively small amount of material was deposited in such a way as to cause very decided changes in the outline of the lake. The reference here is to the bars which developed across the necks of embayments. These bars do not completely close the openings in all cases but are consistent in that their development shows a direct relationship to the prevailing winds. Thus, along the east shore which is exposed to the strongest winds one may follow the shore irrespective of cliff or swale because the bars are complete, but on the north and west shores only spits are found.

The lake has insignificant inlets and is fed mainly by springs, which accounts for the exceptionally clear water. This in combination with clean beaches, excellent locations for cottages along the bluffs, and good fishing has made this lake a favorite with the residents of the vicinity.

45

CHAPTER XII

BORDER LAKES AND LAKES OF DIVERSE ORIGIN OUT-SIDE THE PORT HURON MORAINIC SYSTEM

The lakes described in this chapter constitute our fourth group and include those which lie outside the limits of the Port Huron Morainic system, 4, Fig 3, as well as the border lakes which are within the area of the third group The border lakes are so numerous that the fourth group may be conveniently subdivided into border lakes and those of diverse origin

BORDER LAKES

The border lakes are all former coastal embayments which have been cut off by the development of great sand bars across the openings and are, therefore, lagoons. The bars developed during higher stages of Lake Michigan—Algonquin or Nipissing—and were left well above the water level when the waters of these lakes subsided. Then there followed a period of eastward movement of the finely assorted sand of the bars caused by westerly winds and deposition of the sand in great rows of dunes which are unsurpassed, at least as regards size, so far as is known. Later the dunes became covered with vegetation which so effectually stopped their movement, always to the east, that they have remained fixed in position to the present time, except for occasional blow outs.

A blow out is merely the renewal of the movement of a fixed dune but apparently originates in a limited area and works up the front slope in a narrow zone to the very crest This results in a great trough on the front slope, the transformation of the crest into a saddle, and a fresh deposit of sand on the back slope which is very steep Often the blow outs encroach on the lagoon, causing a projection of the shore, and in this way contribute to the filling of the basin It is recognized that the dunes are but indirectly related to the study of lakes, but they are most attractive and furnish such excellent locations for summer homes that this brief sketch of their history seems warranted

Even though the manner in which these embayments were isolated be known, there still remains the problem of the type of embayment, of which there are several Some are easily recognized

but others, for example Pine, Walloon, Torchlight, etc., which are
described in an earlier chapter, present difficulties Among the
types of basins easily recognized are the numerous drowned mouths
of streams The causes of the drowning, or partial submergence, of
the mouths of the streams entering the southern part of Lake
Michigan is due to the uplift of the land in the northeastern part
of North America following the retirement of the glacier. It is
not necessary to go into the details of this complicated subject to
realize that, if the lower part of Lake Michigan were not affected
by the uplift while the northern part was being elevated, the water
would pile up in the southern part of the lake and, thus, rise with
reference to the land Such was the case and in the tributaries
of Lake Michigan as far north as the Betsie River at Frankfort the
water backed into the mouths of the stream valleys

The outline of such lakes is very irregular and, in a typical case,
consists first of a main channel which may, or may not, be winding.
Farther inland the main channel ramifies and each ramification
may in turn divide so that the pattern resembles that of a deciduous tree In all cases in Michigan the lakes branch to the
east and, inasmuch as the strongest winds are from the west, the
force of the waves is so largely dissipated in the diverging channels that the effects are insignificant Conditions were unfavorable
for adjustments by shore currents and the occurrence of features
due to these agents are very exceptional Waves and undertow
were effective in forming cliffs and terraces which are found with
monotonous regularity at levels above the present, in particular
the level of Lake Nipissing which stood about fifteen feet above
the present lake along this part of the shore. One other common
characteristic of these lakes is the tendency for the heads of bays
which have entering streams to be silted up, forming a delta-like
flat which has pushed a singularly even front into the lake.

This degression, which possibly over-emphasizes the characteristics of the drowned-river lagoon, was made purposely in order to
avoid the dull repetition which became very apparent when the
attempt was made to discuss individually each lake of this type.
Nine of these lakes were visited by the writer, as follows· Kalamazoo near Saugatuck, Black near Holland, Spring near Grand Haven,
Muskegon, White near Whitehall, Pentwater, Pere Marquette near
Ludington, Manistee, and Betsie at Frankfort. A number of these
are well known ports which need no discussion here except that
they are thereby made more accessible. Their use as summer resorts, however, is of interest The exposed terrace of the higher
level serves as an excellent site for cottages and their location just

east of Lake Michigan assures at least a tempering of the summer heat. It is not surprising, therefore, to find some of them almost lined with summer homes many of which are costly estates. Of these mentioned Black, Spring and White are the most popular.

The lagoons of diverse origin, obviously, cannot be discussed as a group as were the drowned streams nor can the probability of shore adjustments be postulated in advance. Consequently they are discussed individually, although this method may give undue prominence to some of these lakes.

BASS LAKE

Bass Lake is located about five miles north of Pentwater and twice this distance south of Ludington, both on branches of the Pere Marquette R. R. Ludington is also accessible by boat, but in either case a drive is necessary to reach Bass Lake, which is situated near the excellent West Michigan Pike.

The most distinctive feature of this lake is that it parallels the Michigan shore instead of extending inland. The west shore consists of an exposed sand bar which is not wholly obscured by dunes and on the opposite side the land slopes gently upward to a sharp rise at the same elevation as the bar, this elevation being that of Lake Nipissing. Furthermore, the lake gradually increases in depth towards the west side and at most hardly exceeds twenty-five feet. The basin, therefore, is the deeper part of a shallow embayment which existed during Lake Nipissing and is masked by sand so that the surface indications are of little aid in the determination of its origin. It appears to be part of a narrow crescentic lagoon which was isolated during Nipissing time, the position of the bar having been determined by the then prominent headland a few miles north. This type of lake is rare in Michigan, the only other example seen by the writer being Devil's Lake near Alpena, an unattractive lagoon rapidly filling with vegetation.

The shore features of Bass Lake are very similar to the lagoons already discussed. The Nipissing shores are best developed and stand about fifteen feet above the lake. They consist of a broad terrace and cliff on the east side, and of a sand bar and flat on the west. Below the Nipissing terrace a lower exposed terrace is evident on the east shore but no deposits by shore currents were found. Aside from the terraces the most interesting physiographic development is the large delta formed by a stream entering the east side of the lake. This delta is triangular in shape but is exceptional in that it extends into the lake as an apex rather than one of the sides of the triangle, due to the fact that the stream did not form distributaries

The lake is developing as a summer resort and cottages have been built on both sides The west shore in the dune area is by far the better location and is also the more popular.

PORTAGE LAKE, MANISTEE COUNTY

Portage Lake is located eight miles north of Manistee and may be reached by the boats of the Michigan Transit Co , the Manistee and Northeastern R. R. from Manistee, and by automobile over excellent roads The lake is three and one-fourth miles in length. Two broad points, one each on the north and south shores, break the otherwise regular shores but are offset in position so that they give the effect of a sinuous channel of about one mile in width This is misleading, as may be determined from the very excellent Lake Survey Chart No 777 which shows that the lake consists of two basins separated by a narrow submerged ridge over which the water is but sixteen feet in depth The greatest depth of the basins is sixty feet in each case but the eastern basin is much the larger in extent The lake is separated from Lake Michigan by a narrow row of high dunes which is continuous except for two gaps, one across which the present channel has been dredged and another one mile north which was the natural outlet of the lake.

The basin resembles an elongated amphitheatre, the walls of which are moraine of high relief, the floor is till plain and the stage the dunes Such a distribution of glacial formations is evidence that the depression was in existence at the time of the last advance of the glacier and that a small lobe flowed into the depression, the front of the ice halting for a time sufficient for the formation of the moraine The bar which closed the open end was formed during Nipissing time and the dunes were formed subsequent to the subsidence of that lake

The shore features of Portage Lake are very simple and require little more than brief mention The specific features are all found at the Nipissing level and consist almost exclusively of a cliff, below which a broad terrace slopes to the lake. The only example of a bar seen on other than the west shore was at Onekama where a small stream is turned westward by it. Another physiographic form is the broad flat at the east end of the lake which is interpreted as a delta built during Nipissing time The northern half of the submerged ridge which crosses the lake off North Point, as shown on the Lake Survey Chart, is at least, suggestive. The material is sand, and the form and location are characteristic of the beginnings of a shore current deposit

This lake shares the popularity of the lagoons of the Lake Michigan coast but has not developed as a summer resort to the same extent as some of those farther south. Numerous cottages are scattered along the shores but the favorite location is on the dunes at the west end Here is a large colony which includes a well appointed hotel, a recreation pavilion and a large number of private cottages. A water supply system is maintained so that a very comfortable vacation may be spent on this lake.

PLATTE LAKES

The Platte Lakes, Big and Little, are situated in western Benzie County on a triangular-shaped flat bounded on the east and south by moraine and on the west by Lake Michigan The nearest railroad stop is Honor on the Manistee and Northeastern, but railroad connections from the south are not convenient. A drive of less than three miles brings one to the narrow strip of land which separates the two lakes. Another route is to drive from Frankfort which is the northern terminus of the Ann Arbor R R and also a stop for the boats of the Michigan Transit Co The latter route involves a ten mile drive the last half of which was found to be over heavy sand road The more comfortable trip for automobiles is through Honor.

The writer attempts no explanation of the origin of the lake basins in this flat because the area was covered by one of the predecessors of Lake Michigan and is, therefore, masked by sand Whatever the type of basin, it is known that this area was once flooded, with the exception of a group of high moraine hills on the north shore of Big Platte, and furthermore was connected with Crystal Lake through the Round Lake depression which is followed by the road. The narrow connection between the two lakes was closed by a bar along the Crystal Lake shore and the main depression at least partially separated from the main lake in a similar manner.

The shore of Lake Algonquin in this vicinity washed steep cliffs that stand well back of the present lake shores and furnish the chief source of interest in the study of the Platte Lakes, for the adjustment of the present shores is negligible. A complete study of this former lake involves an area of more than twenty square miles and a similar number of miles of shoreline Time was not available for such a study but a hint of the possibilities was gleaned from the bars noted near the outlet of Big Platte Near the lake the bars follow the outline of the shore and, therefore, are evidence that this lake was isolated from Lake Algonquin and that this level was maintained for some time. A study of these lakes might well begin in this locality and should by all means include the area along the outlet to Lake Michigan. Another locality that should prove interesting is that to the northwest of Little Platte

The Platte Lakes are extensively fished but in other respects are not so well adapted to general summer resort purposes as many of our lakes There are a number of excellent locations for cottages on Big Platte but a large part of the shore is low and, not desirable as a building site

GLEN LAKE

Glen Lake and surroundings form one of the most attractive bits of scenery of its kind the writer has had the pleasure of seeing We may pass over the details of its location in western Leelenau County and the routes to the lake very briefly The trip by the Michigan Transit Company's boat is pleasant but the sailings are infrequent The trip in from Empire, seven miles distant, must be tedious on account of poor railroad connections The trip from Traverse City by automobile is long, although the roads are not bad. The inference that the lake is somewhat difficult to reach is correct, but the effort is well worth while

The Glen Lake depression may be likened to a great oval race track in the center of which is a large island, the present Glen Lake filling the entire eastern and the southwestern part of the oval course. The stands which surround all but the north side of the depression show an evolution, the originals consisting of a loop of high hills on the east and south Later developments erected a west stand, the sands of the great Sleeping Bear. The best seats are located in the south and east stands for from here one may see below the cobalt blue water of the circular main basin of the lake with its fringe of maize, and off to the west is the narrow arm of the lake which bows to the Sleeping Bear.

The depression was very probably in existence previous to the final invasion by the glacier which slightly overran the depression and persisted in its position During this time earthy material was constantly being brought forward and dropped as the ice melted This material was piled higher and higher in huge hummocks so that when the ice finally disappeared a high moraine or wall was left, which constitutes the south and east limits of the basin But this explanation does not account for the high land, (island) in the central part of the basin and, therefore, is qualified.

This high land was once certainly an island for the waters of Lake
Algonquin entered the basin through channels on the north and
on the west sides isolating it   For a time the waves and currents of Algonquin coursed the track but eventually the western
entrance was closed by a sand bar.   Then followed a subsidence
of the lake to the level called Nipissing and the west stand (the
Sleeping Bear Point) was erected, the material being the sand of
the bar and the builder the wind   The great Sleeping Bear is now
a blow out, or better a moving dune   The colors of the lake are
significant   The blue is due to a modification of the sun's rays as
they pass through the water and the depth of color varies with the
thickness, therefore the lake is deep   Similarly, the narrow but
sharply defined fringe is the yellow of the sands seen through a
thin layer of shallow water, signifying a submerged terrace   A
final step was necessary for the complete isolation of the lake,
namely the closing of the north entrance during Nipissing time by
a series of bars which still retain the water at an elevation of
seventeen feet above Lake Michigan.

Our interest in the lagoons lies primarily in deciphering their
geologic history but Glen Lake also furnishes many examples of
shore features so generally lacking on lakes of this type farther
south   These features, formed to a large extent when one or both
of the entrances were open, are naturally on a large scale   Thus,
the cliffs are high and steep, the bars complete and large, and the
off-shore terrace wide and distinct.   A final episode is due to the
interference of man and is unfortunate   Reference is made to the
damming of the outlet which has not seriously flooded the lake
but has renewed the activity of the waves   The consequent recession of the cliffs is serious and will result in the destruction of
portions of the newly graded boulevard, for effective preventive
measures are too costly to be feasible.

This lake is beautiful, its physiography is most interesting, and
the shore conditions are excellent, but, nevertheless, cottages are
not numerous   It appears to lag on account of its isolation but
must develop rapidly as a summer resort once its qualifications
are appreciated   .

GRAND LAKE, PRESQUE ISLE COUNTY

A number of lakes that would naturally be discussed here, Elk,
Torchlight, Pine, etc, have already been described in detail, so
we must pass on to the Huron shore to complete this part of the
group   Grand Lake is situated in western Presque Isle County
within three miles of Lake Huron and a somewhat greater distance

directly north of its neighbor Long Lake, which is described in detail in an earlier chapter A long ride is necessary to reach the lake from Alpena, the most convenient railroad stop, but the road is excellent for most of the drive Reference is made to Long Lake because of the great similarity of the two lakes in form, size, orientation, shore conditions and type of basin With slight variations a single general description could be made to serve for both. Grand Lake varies in two respects· It has numerous islands and is a lagoon or at least an arm of the predecessor of Lake Huron

The basin probably does not exceed thirty feet in depth and on the average is considered shallow Its total length is more than eight miles and the maximum width not greater than two. A conclusion as to the origin of this elongated depression is a matter of considerable difficulty, inasmuch as a number of factors which cannot be accurately determined must be considered.

The lake is located in a region in which the bed rock is thinly covered with glacial deposits and in places outcrops at the surface. A logical inference, therefore, is that the basin is not due primarily to glacial action insofar as deposition is involved. However, the course of the lake is parallel to the movement of the glacier and the possibility of glacial scour suggests itself at once In following this suggestion, the distribution of the underlying rocks is an important aid They are all tilted sediments and, if not covered, would appear at the surface in belts which correspond quite closely with the orientation of the lake and the movement of the ice as well The geological map of the region shows us that the lake stands on a narrow belt of shale on either side of which is limestone and also that the lake shores along the sides coincide fairly well with the boundaries of these formations Inasmuch as shale is much more easily eroded than limestone, it is logical to conclude that a trough was eroded in the shale The presence of the numerous islands, however, is evidence that this was accomplished to a greater extent by running water than by ice for ice would have swept the basin clean The final isolation of the basin was accomplished by shore currents of Lake Nipissing which closed the ends of the trough This conclusion, however, is too definitely drawn. The glacial cover is more complete on the east side than on the west, and the position of the boundaries of geological formations, where not actually exposed, are relative at best. Therefore, the manner of formation of this basin as given should be considered as a basis for future work which will furnish the facts necessary to the solution of the problem

The study of the shore of this lake was a disappointment   The effects of ice shove were noted in several localities but aside from this little was found   The beaches are almost uniformly of coarse material and show little assortment, the one exception being the sand beach near Birch Hill   Such a condition is, however, not surprising if certain features of the lake are kept in mind   The shallow water and numerous islands greatly hinder the normal development of the waves, and the moderate waves that are formed are further reduced in crossing the off-shore shoals   Finally when they strike the beach they encounter a compact till, which is heavily laden with large rock slabs, and can accomplish little. Also the currents are of a like order with the additional deterrent factor of an irregular shoreline which, obviously, does not furnish any extended stretch of shore along which the currents may develop The most conspicuous feature about the lake is the sheer rock cliff which follows the west side   The cliff stands above and back from the lake and is probably the shore of Lake Nipissing the waves of which were capable of a powerful attack

The lake is especially attractive on account of the numerous bays, headlands and islands and is extensively visited during the summer months   Numerous cottages occur in groups at the more favorable locations on the east side and future development is to be looked for

VAN ETTEN LAKE

Van Etten Lake is located within a mile of Lake Huron about two miles north of the village of Oscoda on the Detroit and Mackinaw R R The lake has a length of nearly four miles and a width of less than one   This narrow basin extends from Lake Huron in a northwesterly direction to an extensive swamp and apparently continues as the valley of the Pine River. It drops below the surface of a sand flat in bold cliffs and is exceptionally regular in outline. The sand flat is a long strip which lies between the Algonquin and Nipissing beaches and is, thus, the off-shore terrace of Lake Algonquin. Upon this eastward sloping terrace Nipissing bars developed hemming in several shallow lakes such as Tawas, which is little more than a marsh, and Cedar Van Etten Lake is also located between the two shores, the Algonquin passing just west of the upper end of the lake and a Nipissing bar serving as a retaining wall at the lower end. The basin is much deeper than those of the other lakes on this plain and is clearly of different origin. Just what the origin may be is difficult to determine and one can do little more than conjecture until detailed studies are made. As a working hypothesis the writer suggests that, when the configuration of the basin is known, it may be apparent that the basin is a broad channel cut through the sand flat by the Pine River after the recession of the lake to the Nipissing level

The shore features of Van Etten lake are relatively simple. Cliffs predominate and step down to the shore showing a former level about four feet above that at present, probably the Nipissing. Although the west shore is less regular than the east there are no decided embayments other than the valleys of entering streams, and bars are not found. Nevertheless, currents were active and left the shore at the points, forming poorly developed cuspate forelands, all at the higher level The most decided physiographic feature, however, is the partially isolated basin at the upper end which is an excellent example of filling by vegetation

The excellent East Michigan Pike parallels the west shore a few rods back from the lake and possibly accounts for the growing popularity of this side of the lake This shore is rapidly being built up but the east side is apparently being deserted, although skirted by a good road

LAKES OF DIVERSE ORIGIN

The lakes described in this chapter, Group IV, which are not lagoons are located with one exception between the limits of Lake Algonquin and the Port Huron Moraine, 4, Fig 3. The lakes visited occur in two groups with the exception of Carp Lake near Mackinaw City and Bear Lake on the west side of the State. One group is located along the boundary between Iosco and Ogemaw counties and the other a few miles southwest of Traverse City.

The lakes of the first group lie on a strip of moraine of very irregular shape and of great relief. The sharp slopes and sandy material of the moraine are not conducive to good roads, and a trip through this region by automobile is not an unalloyed pleasure. Ellake at the west end of Long Lake is a station stop on the Rose City Branch of the Detroit and Mackinaw R R but a visit to Sage Lake necessitates a drive

LONG LAKE, IOSCO COUNTY

Long Lake appears more like a channel than a lake for its width barely exceeds one-fourth mile but its length is more than two and one-half miles, if its sinuous course is measured The eastern part of the basin is a very irregular morainic depression which continues westward onto a till plain Many of the irregularities of the basin do not appear on the map because their depths are not sufficient to bring them below the present level of the lake. In the past, however, a higher level was maintained which, although it stood only four feet higher than that at the present time, flooded several large embayments on the north side. From the study of the shores it is apparent that these indentations were abandoned because of the sinking of the water level rather than by their isolation by bars A number of small bays were cut off by bars and some of the points lengthened by spits but, in general, the adjustments were still in an early stage of development when interrupted.

Among the specific localities where adjustments may be seen may be mentioned the sharp point on the southeastern shore The greater part of this point is not a current deposit, but the distal end is clearly a spit which continues as a submerged bar across the narrow channel between it and the north shore. Another interesting locality is at Kokosen Resort Currents were especially active on the west side of the point and, in addition to a straightening of this shore, have built a small hook which curves to the southeast from the tip of the point East of the point several small indentations are completely isolated by bars and, at the large bay that runs north to a small circular lake, a long spit extends eastward part way across the depression These forms are all at the higher level and may be readily observed.

The lake has a large group of excellent buildings at Kokosen Resort which apparently has declined in popularity in recent years

SAGE LAKE, OGEMAW COUNTY

Sage Lake is not easily reached and a long drive is necessary whatever route is taken. The roads were not in good condition at the time of the writer's visit to the lake and the route taken was so roundabout that no directions as to roads are suggested.

The lake is more than two and one-half miles in length and has a maximum width of one mile Perhaps the homely comparison of a meal bag tied near each end will serve to describe the shape of the lake The main part of this lake lies in a depression consisting apparently of a number of moraine sags so placed as to form a large basin which completely trenches a strip of very sandy moraine, and the narrow ends are the extension of the basin onto the till plains which flank the moraine The basin was not studied in sufficient detail, however, to venture a conclusion as to the cause of this peculiar grouping of the sags.

The moraine is one of very strong relief in this locality and the road which skirts the northeast shore is a succession of hills and swales. The swales are large and the shore, therefore, consists of an alternation of broad bays and prominent headlands The southwest shore, however, is much more regular and is fronted by a cliff that is almost continuous The adjustments of the shores of this lake all stand at an elevation between three or four feet above the present level and indicate an even earlier stage of development than those found on the shores of its neighbor, Long Lake The headlands and high banks have been carved into steep cliffs but the off-shore terrace, where present, is poorly developed Conditions are favorable along the northeast shore for deposition by currents but little had been accomplished when the sinking of the water level interrupted the work No case of a complete bar was found but several spits were noted on the northeast shore. In all cases the spits are attached to the east sides of the headlands, indicating prevailing currents from the west The best example is located just west of the Lake View House and is a hook about one hundred feet in length

Sage Lake has not been developed as a summer resort but a beginning has been made The writer is inclined to believe that this is due very largely to the difficulty encountered in reaching it When the roads are improved this lake will be better known and should attract an enthusiastic summer colony.

CARP LAKE

Carp Lake is located on the boundary of Emmet and Cheboygan counties about seven miles south of Mackinaw City. The Dixie Highway and the Grand Rapids and Indiana R R. both pass the west end of the lake The lake is more than three miles in length and one and one-half miles in greatest width but is shallow. The basin lies within the limits of Lake Algonquin which flooded the region with the exception of a small patch of moraine which borders the northwestern shore of Carp Lake. The original characteristics of the basin are, thus, concealed by the sand which was distributed over this area by the waves and currents of Lake Algonquin. However, the presence of a moraine suggests the possibilities that the depression may be a large morainic basin which was partially filled by sand or a sag in a till plain with a small amount of filling

The shores of the lake are rather uniform, and, therefore, no great changes in outline have resulted from the adjustment of the shores. Yet interesting shore features are to be found and among them a series of bars and ramparts along the shore at Carp Lake Village. These bars are spaced on the gentle slope which extends from the lake shore back to a low cliff and mark former levels of the lake Two well defined sand bars skirt this shore but in places as many as four rampart bars were seen Inasmuch as the writer could not determine the elevation of these bars in this work, the relation of the lake levels represented by them to Lake Algonquin cannot be given However, the very strong bar of cobbles which cuts off the marsh along the northeast shore must be an Algonquin beach because currents of sufficient power to move rock fragments of cobble size do not develop on lakes of the dimensions of Carp Lake. Another Algonquin bar swings part way around the east end of the lake and is located about two hundred and fifty paces back from the shore The action on the present shores is limited very largely to ice shove and the main interest in the study of the lake lies in its relation to Lake Algonquin, a more extended study than could be made for this work

The north shore of the lake is well adapted to summer resort purposes and is very easily reached from the main highway. As a result several groups of cottages have been built and future development may be expected.

GRAND TRAVERSE LAKES

DUCK, GREEN, LONG AND SILVER

Another group consisting of more than a dozen lakes, large and small, is located a few miles southwest of Traverse City and of these lakes Long, Silver, Duck and Green were visited. These lakes all occupy pits in an outwash plain and those seen by the writer have a north-south trend Some of the lakes show similarities in other respects, which are well brought out from a study of Green and Duck lakes

GREEN AND DUCK LAKES

These two lakes, which are separated by a strip of outwash of hardly more than one-fourth mile in width, might well have been named Twin Lakes In addition to a like orientation and origin, their area and form are very similar Furthermore each has a projection on the east side, that on Duck being the more prominent. Also the adjustments of the shores are alike in character, in both cases being in a very early stage In fact, very little adjustment

has taken place, although the lakes are approximately three miles
in length and one mile in width, and they are not especially interesting from this viewpoint The most prominent features are
the steep cliffs, but apparently little recession has taken place
Currents have accomplished almost nothing except to remove the
material from the cliffs, and depositional forms are rare. At the
end of the peninsula on Green Lake, for instance, one might expect
a large deposit but finds instead a relatively small submerged bar
Likewise on Duck Lake but one or two bars were found and they
crossed very minor indentations

The problem in connection with the study of these lakes is to
account for the lack of adjustment of the shores We may immediately eliminate the size and time elements in this consideration,
for nearby lakes which are smaller and have been existent for a
similar length of time show a much greater development of the
shores, but farther than that the problem is as yet unsolved

Long stretches of the shores are suitable for resort purposes
and the fishing is considered good, so that the lakes are popular.
Green Lake, however, appears to be the choice for those who build
summer cottages but for the itinerant recreationist with camping
outfit the State Park between the two lakes furnishes an excellent
location on either This park of eighty acres is almost unique for
it is one of the few remaining tracts of Michigan's once famous
pine forests A trip to this region is well worth while and is easily
made from Interlocken, the junction point of the Manistee and
Northeastern and Pere Marquette R R.

LONG LAKE, GRAND TRAVERSE COUNTY

Long Lake which is located some six miles southwest of Traverse
City is one of the most attractive lakes in the vicinity. It is more
than four miles long and nearly two miles in greatest width but
is so irregular that its size is not appreciated on first sight. The
view is also obstructed by several islands which add to the picture.
One must drive to the lake but will surely encounter difficulties with
sand roads to the south if the attempt to circle the lake is made by
motor. Such a trip, however, will emphasize the sandy character of
the outwash in which this lake lies for the basin is a pit, but a most
irregular one This irregularity in addition to the islands, which
interfere with the full development of waves, may give rise to expectations of poorly adjusted shores; however adjustments have
taken place

At the north end one is in doubt as to whether the swamp was cut off from the main lake or not, for the bar, if such it be, is faint, but evidence may be found of a former level of the lake about three feet above the present level, at which stage the swamp was surely connected. Also the off-shore terrace is well developed here, and in places the part exposed by the sinking of the water is still intact. To the southward the bars increase in development and completely close the narrow openings of the embayments. One of these closed embayments on the shore extends some distance inland and is occupied by Mickey Lake.

It is not our purpose to cite all of the individual examples of adjustments. As a working basis, however, it may be assumed that the smaller embayments are cut off. The larger bays are open to the lake as would be expected from the exceptionally tortuous shoreline along which continuous currents could not develop, even though no islands obstructed the reach of the waves. The headlands have furnished the material for the deposits and have retreated somewhat under the attack of the waves. But the progress of the adjustment of the shores was interrupted at an early stage by subsidence of the water and little has been done since that time.

As a summer resort Long Lake has lagged in comparison to many others that are less attractive. This is due in part to its location near the beautiful Grand Traverse Bay but also to some extent to its inaccessability. Roads are being improved and people are using lakes more and more for recreation, so that this lake will surely share in summer resort development.

SILVER LAKE, GRAND TRAVERSE COUNTY

Another lake of the group under consideration is Silver, located about two miles east of Long Lake. It also lies in a pit in the same outwash plain but very near the margin of the moraine, so near in fact that the narrow basin continues northward from the north end of the lake as a stream valley in the moraine. The lake averages less than one-half mile in width but is more than five times this figure in length. It actually appears much narrower on account of the numerous islands which obstruct the view across the lake. Furthermore, the lake is very deep and the black water comes close to the shore. This makes the lake very dangerous and is detrimental to its development as a summer resort.

It is, however, most interesting as a physiographic study. It has no outlet and varies greatly in level over a period of years. At present it stands nearly five feet below the highest water mark

47

which has determined the elevation of the features formed by the adjustment of the shores This higher level may be reached during exceptionally wet periods, but the higher levels which are almost universally found on other lakes make it more probable that this is a permanently abandoned higher level

It is difficult to select a starting point for the discussion of the numerous shore features of Silver Lake unless one describes them all in detail. Waves have been very active but there has been little cliff recession Of the material derived from the cliffs some has undoubtedly been carried out by the undertow but it was not sufficient in quantity to build a wide off-shore terrace, which would require an excessive amount of material in this deep lake. The material which was worked along the shore by currents, however, although possibly not greater in amount, has produced more noticeable effects. All of the indentations except two are small and have been cut off by bars. And of the two larger embayments one only, the large bay on the southeast side, is open The other is at the north end and is completely bridged by a strong bar which separates the small Mud Lake from the main basin In this connection the islands are interesting. The original islands were nine in number most of which are distributed off the east shore opposite Silver Lake Resort, but this number is now reduced by at least three by the development of bars which either tied islands to each other or the mainland The details of these bars were not worked out and should prove an interesting part of the study of the numerous physiographic features on the shore of Silver Lake which offers such a decided contrast to the nearby Duck and Green lakes.

BEAR LAKE

Bear Lake is located in northwestern Manistee County about midway between Manistee and Beulah, eighteen to twenty miles distant Such distances seem rather long but the road in each case is the West Michigan Pike which was found to be in excellent condition An automobile ride of this distance is preferable to the trip of seven miles from Norwalk which has a one-train-a-day service on the Manistee and Northeastern R R

The lake is an open expanse of water of very regular outline and has dimensions of two and one-fourth by one and one-fourth miles, the longer axis having an east-west direction. The western part of the basin hardly exceeds fifteen feet in depth but depths of fifty to sixty feet are reported for the eastern part. The glacial formations may be readily made out as one approaches the lake on the

Pike from the south. At first the route is through a rugged moraine from the crest of which a broad outwash plain may be seen below in the distance, extending northward to another moraine some six miles away. Beyond the crest the moraine slopes sharply to the north and the entire lake appears in view, extending from the foot of the slope onto the outwash The basin is limited on the east side by upland but stretches eastward as a low, heavily-wooded swamp to Bear Creek, several miles away Briefly stated the lake basin is part of a depression in the outwash at its junction with the moraine This depression has some of the characteristics of a fosse but is in part a pit, as shown by the deep basin which forms the eastern part of the lake

The shore features of Bear Lake are very simple because the shore conditions are singularly uniform The shore is lined by wave-cut cliffs except at the east end. Where the depression continues eastward conditions were favorable for deposition by currents, and, in spite of the presence of a road around this shore, a well defined bar may be traced across the flat to the higher ground on the north side. Also a similar form developed eastward in front of the swamp at the northeastern part of the lake but was never completed. These forms stand well above the present level and mark a higher stage of the lake At present the shore agents are rejuvenated and the recession of the cliffs is very evident. The reason for this revival of activity is high water but the cause of the high water is uncertain. The natural conditions of the outlet which flows from the east end have been altered by the building of a road, and, in particular, the position of the outlet has been shifted south of its normal position This may account for the filling of the artificial outlet which functions only at high water and has no definite channel for some distance east of the bar.

The lake has not yet developed as a summer resort, although it is well suited for such use. This seems to be due to the fact that it was formerly isolated, for, since the construction of the West Michigan Pike and the thereby more convenient access to the lake, it is becoming popular.

INDEX

INDEX

A

CPSIA information can be obtained
at www.ICGtesting.com
Printed in the USA
LVHW080213120922
728136LV00003B/40

9 781363 686957